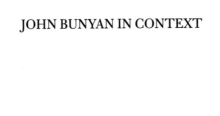

JOHN BUNYAN IN CONTEXT

To Lorna

STUDIES IN PROTESTANT NONCONFORMITY
EDITED BY ALAN P. F. SELL

John Bunyan
in Context

Michael Mullett

KEELEUNIVERSITYPRESS

First published in 1996
by Keele University Press
Keele, Staffordshire

© Michael Mullett

Composed by
Keele University Press
and printed in England by
Hartnolls, Bodmin, England

ISBN 1 85331 162 6

Contents

General Editor's Preface

The volumes in this series will comprise critical evaluations of the Protestant Nonconformist heritage of England and Wales, with special reference to the historical development of the several groups and their contribution to modern Christian thought.

The series will include conference papers of the Association of Denominational Historical Societies and Cognate Libraries, a body established in 1993 to foster co-operative research in the field; and a sub-series entitled Protestant Nonconformist Texts. In the latter, significant texts from the several traditions will be edited and introduced.

The Reverend Professor Alan P. F. Sell

Preface

It may be difficult to justify yet another study of Bunyan, especially within a few years of the appearance of Christopher Hill's outstanding *A Turbulent, Seditious and Factious People* (1988). However, Hill's book marked the Bunyan tercentenary, which in turn released a flood of new work, much of it by younger scholars, some of which I have been able to use for this study.

My own emphases, which may give this book some reason for being, include: Bunyan's links with medieval and popular culture and piety; the quest for balance in his work between a trust in divinely implanted grace and a quest for personal merit; and his comparability with other figures who recur in my pages, including Luther, Calvin, Fox, Baxter, Donne and Herbert. I have investigated Bunyan's ecclesiology and his attitude to the position of women in the church and have also dealt with his political views, discovering him to have been, on the whole, less radical than some other commentators have found. In my selection of Bunyan's works for comment-ary, I have been concerned to give a reasonably wide sampling of his types of production.

I have been extremely fortunate to work standing on the shoulders of great Bunyan scholars, including Christopher Hill, Richard L. Greaves and the late Roger Sharrock. The most cursory glance at my notes will show what I owe to these experts. Furthermore, I owe the deepest debt of gratitude to Richard Greaves for constant encouragement and positive criticism of substantial portions my work in draft. Vera Camden, Ted Underwood, Stuart Sim and W. R. Owens have been generous with their help, and I am most grateful for their insights, suggestions and wise advice. I am deeply indebted to the work of a team of editors of the magnificent Oxford edition of Bunyan's *Miscellaneous Works*, now completed. The Ox-ford edition is both cause and effect of the upsurge in Bunyan research in recent years, producing rich fruit in the estimable journal, *Bunyan Studies*. Before the appearance of the Oxford *Miscellaneous Works*, the great standby of Bunyan studies for many years was the edition by George Offor: *The*

Works of John Bunyan in three volumes (Glasgow, 1854), reprinted by the Banner of Truth Trust of Edinburgh and Carlisle, PA.

My list of acknowledgements is, as always, long, and a great pleasure to make. I am grateful for help from the Bedfordshire Record Society, especially Joyce Godber. I have had every encouragement from the University of Lancaster, from its uncommonly generous sabbatical provisions and from the kindness of the Vice-chancellor Harry Hanham. My department and its heads, along with our research director Gordon Phillips and my internal assessor David Shotter, have provided a stimulating atmosphere for research, and I am particularly indebted to Ralph Gibson, Austin Woolrych, Sarah Barber, Bob Bliss (also for indispensable computer support), Harro Höpfl, Marcus Merriman, Sandy Grant, Keith Stringer, John Walton, Eric Evans, Stuart Mews and Angus Winchester. Members of the university have exercised great forebearance during my research absences and in my preoccupied state, including our departmental secretaries – especially Brenda Wright, Susan Waddington and June Cross – my undergraduate and research students, my College Principal Ralph Gibson, members of The County College, the editor of *European History Quarterly* Martin Blinkhorn, and my other colleagues on that journal. I am deeply grateful for the courteous efficiency of the Lancaster University Library staff, and above all to Thelma Goodman and her interlibrary loans staff, who have been patient with my importunities, and to John Illingworth who has gone to infinite trouble in meeting my difficult requests. At Keele University Press, Lucia Crothall, Nicola Pike and Richard Clark have been reservoirs of cheerful encouragement and quiet efficiency, and I owe much to my editor, Alan Sell.

From the wider scholarly community I have received encouragement and support from, amongst many: my research supervisor Sir John Plumb, John Bossy, Patrick Collinson, Ivan Roots, Geoffrey Nuttall, Hugh Barbour, Ken Carroll, David Lovejoy, John Punshon, John Hickey, Rob Stradling, Ronald Hutton and Nigel Smith, and from an angelic host of scholars and enthusiasts who descended on Lancaster in 1991 to celebrate the tercentenary of Bunyan's nearly exact contemporary, George Fox. My beloved family in South Wales have provided support and keen interest, and my sons Gerard and James and my daughter-in-law Rhiannon have given every help, from coffee and footnote scrutiny to computer advice and general morale-boosting. Above all, as we mark a great anniversary of our married life, I thank and dedicate this book, with my deepest love, to my wife Lorna, in some small tribute for her love and immeasurable support: Dwg dy fyd yn llawen gyda'th wraig annwyl holl ddyddiau bywyd dy oferedd ... *Pregethwr*, 9,9 *AMDG*: Lancaster, On the Feast of Corpus Christi, 1995.

ONE

John Bunyan: Biography and Autobiography

Our principal source for the earlier part of the life of John Bunyan is his autobiography, *Grace Abounding to the Chief of Sinners*, first published in 1666. This work, indispensable as it is for our understanding of Bunyan, has serious limitations in terms of our modern meaning of the word autobiography. For one thing, the core of the book is an account of a religious crisis that lasted for, at most, five years out of a sixty-year-long life. *Grace Abounding* is not a straightforward account of a life in all its circumstances, but the spiritual history of a self. Its purpose is to recount 'the merciful working of God upon my Soul'. Richard Greaves writes:

> Because of the relative paucity of biographical data for Bunyan, there is a natural tendency to treat *Grace Abounding* as a reliable source of information about Bunyan's life and psyche. While the book indisputably contains valuable historical facts, it is not a document that can bear the psychological and biographical interpretations often put upon it. *Grace Abounding* is an example of a literary genre with specifically pastoral intentions.[1]

Grace Abounding, especially in its episodic schematization, can also be regarded as the appropriation to one man's history of the Calvinist programme of the successive stages of conversion, a schema which Bunyan reduced to a cartographic form in *A Mapp Shewing the Order & Causes of Salvation & Damnation* of 1663 or 1664. These pastoral and theological emphases of the work mean (a) that the autobiography's arrangement is dictated by a preconceived scheme, and (b) that certain external and practical data receive less attention than would normally be given them in a biography or autobiography, as we understand the terms. Lack of personal detail, apart from the dominant spiritual narration, is a particularly serious omission from the point of view of modern biographical reconstruction, and the modern reader's interest in the human specifics of a life. Today's reader will undoubtedly be disappointed by the scantiness of Bunyan's recollections of his family and its circumstances, his relations with his parents, his schooling and even his formal religious training.

In recalling his parentage, Bunyan does not provide details of his parents: not even their names are given. He offers only a 'hint of my pedigree', and that only in order 'that thereby the goodness and bounty of God towards me, may be ... magnified'.[2] Bunyan is preparing the reader for a description of the way God goes to work on the most unpromising human material. If the reader expects Bunyan's promise of a 'pedigree' and 'my descent' to include an account of ancestry, he or she will be disappointed. Such a genealogy, going back to French settlers following the Norman Conquest, was lovingly and painstakingly reconstructed by Bunyan's great Victorian biographer, John Brown.[3]

However, the possession of such a record of ancestry was, in Bunyan's society, normally a characteristic of noble and gentle rank. In the opening lines of his autobiography Bunyan is at pains to deny any such rank: 'Wherefore I have not here, as others, to boast of Noble blood, or of a High-born state according to the flesh.'[4] Like Martin Luther, who also stressed his plebeian ancestry,[5] Bunyan was anxious to repudiate any aristocratic pretensions. Indeed, he went out of his way to emphasize that his origins were the opposite of noble. He was born poor, 'of a low and inconsiderable generation; my fathers house being of that rank that is meanest, and most despised of all the families in the Land'.[6]

Considerable discussion has gone on amongst Bunyan scholars as to the precise sociological meaning and accuracy of these remarks. What is clear is that Bunyan's parents were *not* of the 'meanest, and most despised of all the families in the Land'. That distinction would have to be applied to the recipients of relief, the paupers, vagabonds and criminals who abounded in the desperate 1620s, the decade of Bunyan's birth.[7] It is true that the Bunyans were slipping slowly down the social ladder, sharing the fate of numerous English families of the period who could claim yeoman origins. However, they were still a family of honest, residentially stable, self-supporting working artisans. The will left by Bunyan's father, an illiterate tinker, suggests wealth that was only a fraction of what was to be left by his successful son.[8] Nevertheless, neither the poverty nor the social debasement of the family should be exaggerated. Bunyan's parents, for example, were able to send him to school, possibly to grammar school, an investment characteristic of the middling strata of seventeenth-century English society. On the whole, Bunyan's remarks about the 'meanness and inconsiderableness of my Parents' may have to be regarded as hyperbole.[9]

Why would Bunyan, to whose Puritan frame of mind truth mattered vitally, have manipulated the record of his background? Is it possible that he was indulging in a piece of autobiographical self-deceit of a kind much favoured by self-made men in all ages: the dramatic magnification of initial disadvantages? This was certainly true of the ageing Luther, as he enjoyed the fame and relative financial security of his later years. In 1543, for instance, a guest at the Luther home remarked: 'manifest experience teaches us that those born to distinguished parents have accomplished something great'. Luther's father's origins could by no means be described as 'distinguished': born into the peasant caste, he had done well as a mining entrepreneur; palpably keen to claim personal credit for achieving 'something great', Luther emphasized the lowly aspect of his paternal antecedents: 'The contrary is true. I am the son of a peasant.'[10]

Was Bunyan, then, like Luther, inclined to highlight his career success by magnifying or inventing an unpromising start in life? Such an explanation for the exaggeration of his parents' poverty and social degradation – that his worldly success would stand out all the more sharply against a dark background of early deprivation – will not fit Bunyan's case. When *Grace Abounding* came out, its author was not a best-selling writer, but an imprisoned tinker-preacher, with a modest local notoriety and a certain reputation amongst the fragmented radical religious fraternity. His main reason for bending the facts about his childhood's material circumstances is the overriding religious nature and purpose of his autobiography. The centrality of the Christian religious inspiration of the work induced Bunyan to maximize the poverty and lowliness of his background. This was because of the role of poverty and obscurity in the Christian world-view. From Christ's 'Blessed are the poor in spirit' and Paul's 'not many wise after the flesh, not many mighty, not many noble are called',[11] Christianity has proclaimed an inversion of the normal social order and a belief in the moral superiority of the poor, humble and simple. This kind of thinking reached a high point in the medieval Franciscan cult of 'holy poverty'. Though the Protestant reformers rejected the cult of voluntary mendicancy, some of them reaffirmed the idea of God's poor. The reformer most influential in Bunyan's England, Calvin, the principal source of the religious tradition within which Bunyan operated, reasserted a moral preference – God's supposed preference – for the poor and poverty.[12]

Variants of Calvin's exaltation of the poor frequently appeared in England both before and during the Civil War period. The theme was present, for instance, in the series of parliamentary Fast Sermons, a typical example being Thomas Hodges' 1642 *A Glimpse of God's Glory*, with its identification of '[t]he crosses and meannesse (for the most part) of Gods people. A poore people, and afflicted, that is their character.'[13] Thus, Bunyan's later reports of a childhood of degradation and destitution should be seen in the context of a strong religious sense of the holiness of poverty.

Alongside social and economic information, the reader interested in fully rounded depictions of historical personalities naturally looks for some insights into the characters and views of the parents of the individuals in question. In a group of autobiographies or autobiographical fragments with which we may compare Bunyan's history of his life, information on parents is certainly included. In Luther's case, indeed, we have portraits of his parents, by Lucas Cranach, which bear out the impression that Luther gives in depicting his father and mother as hard-working characters, narrow, frugal, stern on themselves and on others.[14] In understanding Luther, we are enormously assisted by his account of his relationship with them. The autobiography of an English Puritan contemporary of Bunyan, Richard Baxter, also contains flashbacks, if not to both his parents, then at least to the writer's father. Baxter senior is drawn from life – a reformed gambler, a godly Micawber who begged, borrowed and bought (second-hand) pious books, and a Bible-reader lacking the force of personality to challenge the village revellers who disturbed his Sunday godly reading.[15]

Another of Bunyan's contemporaries, the Quaker founder George Fox, offers less in his autobiography than Baxter does about parental personalities. Fox's father emerges from the page as a Puritan stereotype, the godly weaver: 'My father's name was Christopher Fox; he was by profession a weaver, an honest man, and there was a seed of God in him. The neighbours called him "Righteous Christer".' The portrait is thinly drawn, and, perhaps, patronizing. However, this vignette shows, as does Baxter's fuller pen drawing of his father, that paternal influence and example were important channels through which the Puritan religious culture of early Stuart England was directed into the emergent personalities of the two individuals in question. Fox's reminiscences add a strong hint of maternal religious guidance. Through his mother, Fox claimed descent from Protestant England's aristocracy of martyrs commemorated by John Foxe in his *Actes and Monuments* (1563): 'My mother was an upright woman; her maiden name was Lago, of the family of the Lagos and of the stock of the martyrs.' Further detail was added to this sketch of the writer's mother by William Penn who, in a preface to Fox's *Journal*, developed the theme of her influence upon him, using memories that were probably conveyed orally by Fox himself. Fox's mother, Penn reported, was:

> a woman accomplished above most of her degree in the place where she lived … His mother taking notice of his singular temper and the gravity, wisdom, and piety that very early shined through him, refusing childish

and vain sports and company when very young, she was tender and indulgent over him, so that from her he met with little difficulty.[16]

Between them, Fox and Penn afford us a striking picture of the influence of an educated, godly mother as a moral and religious guide within the 'Puritan family'.[17] This recognition of parental influence over religious evolution was conditioned by the theological and anthropological convictions that the mature Fox shared with Penn. Fox's mother's role, as he came to see it, had been to nurture a 'seed of God' that had been planted in him, as it was in all men and women. There were all kinds of assumptions here – ones that Bunyan did not share – about the potential for indigenous holiness in men and women: 'When I came to eleven years of age, I knew pureness and righteousness, for while I was a child I was taught how to walk to be kept pure.'[18] Baxter, too, was specific about the didactic influence of a parent in the formation of religious experience. In line with the Calvinist tradition, which he modified but did not reject, Baxter had to lay the responsibility for his religious conversion on God. To that extent, Baxter and Bunyan were in agreement in their analyses of how conversion happened. However, Baxter distanced himself sufficiently from the doctrine of election to acknowledge that God worked cumulatively through human agencies: 'God made him [Baxter senior] the instrument of my first convictions, and approbation of a holy life, as well as the grosser sort of lives. When I was very young his serious speeches of God and the life to come possessed me with a fear of sinning.'[19]

Bunyan's more unalloyed Calvinism induced him to discount the importance of the human and natural educational agency of parents in a gradual religious development and conversion. In the absence of parental guidance in his path to godliness in youth, the absolute sufficiency of divine action in his regard would stand out all the more clearly. As Bunyan put it in the introductory passages of *Grace Abounding* :

> [I]t will not be amiss, if … I do … give you a hint of my pedigree, and manner of bringing up; that thereby the goodness and bounty of God towards me, may be the more advanced and magnified before the sons of men … [T]he Lord did work his gracious work of conversion upon my Soul.[20]

Thus, the earliest passages of Bunyan's memoirs – what they omit as well as what they include – were shaped just as much as Fox's were by mature doctrinal assumptions. The differences in those assumptions were marked, as between Bunyan and Fox, and, to a lesser extent, between Bunyan and Baxter. The rejection of a species of Calvinist determinism on the part of

Fox, in particular, allowed him to emphasize the role of human factors in an evolving religious nurture, leading without any major hiatus to childhood holiness. In contrast, Bunyan's underlying conviction of the minimal role of the human contribution in religious transactions inclined him not to seek evidence of early parental leadings on the road towards eventual sanctification. Conversion, for Bunyan, was a revolution of the personality as the result of God's working upon people: '*the Lord* did work his gracious work of conversion' (my emphasis).

However, Bunyan did admit the possibility of divine intervention in his religious formation through human mediation. Yet, he could not see himself, in the way Fox did, as having been brought gradually to a kind of natural holiness in childhood through the efforts of his parents. In Bunyan's scheme of things, the child and self-induced human holiness had to be left behind, and there was no smooth sequence of progressive improvement from childhood, as there was for Fox. Bunyan thought not in terms of continuous progressions, but of sudden, providentially induced turning points, along the lines of Calvin's *subita conversio*, his unexpected (or sudden) conversion. For Bunyan, one such crux was his marriage, when the religious influence of his wife and her father was brought to bear on him. The father in question was a Puritan martinet and a village patriarch, whose personality – more forcible than that of Baxter's father, and more fully described than Fox's 'Righteous Christer' – is conveyed with a detail that Bunyan withholds from the recall of his own father: 'She [Bunyan's first wife] also would be often telling me what a godly man her Father was, and how he would reprove and correct Vice, both in his house, and amongst his neighbours; what a strict and holy life he lived in his day, both in word and deed.'[21] Thus, indirectly, from his wife and from her legacy of Puritan piety and devotional books, Bunyan was to come under the influence of a Puritan father. In this way, he seems to have acknowledged some human instrumentality in his route to religion. However, if anything, this exposure to Puritan influences was, from his point of view, a wrong start, since it set him off on a false path of personal righteousness without God. The paradox of Bunyan's religious formation is that a course in pious reading during early manhood and marriage put him on what he discovered was a misleading trail of self-imputed holiness. In contrast, his earlier village boyhood upbringing, which was largely unregarded, natural and unsupervised, was, in a paradoxical sense, a better preparation for a drastic invasion of his sinner's persona by God, in a unilateral action which no humanly implanted holiness or piety of his own had anticipated. Indeed, from the point of view of *Grace Abounding* as a conversionist testimony to the seizure by God of a sinner with no claim to personal righteousness, Bunyan's boyhood (or his depiction of it) was ideal. He was, at least when not at school, allowed to run wild into a life – quite unlike that of the young Fox – of 'sports and gaming ... the very ring-leader of all the Youth that kept me company, into all manner of vice and ungodliness'.[22]

This apparently unsupervised childhood led the young Bunyan into alarming incidents, including a near-drowning in the Bedfordshire Ouse and a bold but ill-advised adventure in amateur dentistry involving an adder. Bunyan recounted these incidents to point up the ways of God towards him: his narrow escapes disclosed the guidance of a Providence which had also taken care of his much more important eternal welfare. For us, the escapades have the subsidiary, if unintended, value of throwing light on a childhood that was, at least in part, the natural development of a country boy. Religious and moral education seems to have played little part in this boyhood, at least in its earlier stages, or as far as the home was concerned; the parental home was not the doctrinal and ethical school that it was for Baxter and Fox. Bunyan's parents – his father in particular – seem to have been either too distracted, or too ignorant, or too unconcerned to provide the kind of guidance that Bunyan required, or later came to feel he had needed. Thus, a puzzled, anxious question from the young John Bunyan as to whether his family was descended from the chosen people of Israel elicited the blankly unhelpful paternal answer: *No, we were not:* wherefore then I fell in my spirit.' It sounds as if Bunyan *père* was not capable of dealing with such questions, or of understanding the anguish that lay behind them. Accompanying this parental inability to cope with a hypersensitive and overscrupulous youth was an indulgent renunciation of moral control. Bunyan came to resent his father's failure to 'learn [i.e. to teach] me to speak without this wicked way of swearing'. It may have been the case that a casual neglect marked Bunyan's early moral upbringing, but gave way to later disciplinarian pressures from school and church. The contrast between early indiscipline followed by tight repression led to severe conflict within Bunyan's personality as it moved towards manhood.[23]

Before we consider that theme further, we might note that a possible corollary of the partly indulgent, partly negligent early upbringing that Bunyan received was that he seems not to have experienced, or certainly does not record, any conflict with his parents, and particularly with his father.[24] In his disclosure of his protracted difficulties in coming to terms with God, we recognize close parallels with Luther's terror of the judicial 'righteousness of God'.[25] The horrifyingly punitive image of God in early modern Europe corresponded closely with the recommended model of disciplinarian fathers. Young man Luther's problems with God – a quaking terror so like that of the young Bunyan – have been interpreted in terms of his enforced submission to a harshly judicial father. Luther's father was reputedly implacable, and it is at least plausible that the son's fear of God the Father was a reflection of his dread of his severe and demanding earthly father. There is, however, no hint of such son–father conflict in Bunyan, nor can we find evidence in his recollections for the psychological origins of his obsessive fear of God which, indeed, had many resemblances to the young Luther's fearful hatred. In other words, whatever the validity of an hypothesis tracing Luther's attitude towards God to his terror of his father, there is no evidence that Bunyan's fear of God before his conversion arose from paternal intimidation.

Some writers, it is true, have speculated about Bunyan's resentment towards his father, over the latter's early remarriage after Bunyan's mother's death during his adolescence. Bunyan's mother died in June 1644 and his father remarried in August. It may well be that this gave rise to feelings of hostility on John Bunyan's part towards a father who, in hastily remarrying, might have appeared to be betraying a recently deceased mother. It is also possible that such resentment, whether or not it resulted in a transfer of indignation from Bunyan's father to God the Father, helped precipitate the protracted depression and religious crisis of Bunyan's young manhood. Admittedly, given the indispensability of a wife to the running of a household, seventeenth-century widowers usually did remarry quickly. If Bunyan experienced conscious or unconscious anger at his father's remarriage, his mother 'but two months dead', such emotions may have been widespread amongst young people in his society, common enough for a playwright to dramatize. That does not mean that those feelings were any less intense, either in Bunyan or his coevals. We may indeed speculate that any enmity that Bunyan, in his teens, may have felt towards his father and the latter's second marriage would have been likely, if not to provoke, then to exacerbate the violent psycho-religious crisis that Bunyan was about to undergo. However, there is no firm documentary evidence for concluding that the spiritual dejections that Bunyan encountered in his early twenties were induced in any way by his father, by his father's conduct or by his own relationship with his father.[26]

This is not to say that Bunyan's religious difficulties, and particularly his unbearable notions of God and of judgement, were unrelated to his family life. Once again, Luther provides us with clues about possible links between emotional and religious experience in early modern Europe. An immediate precipitant to Luther's entry into the monastery in 1505 – perhaps the most decisive event of his religious life – was the sudden death of a friend, and the intimations of his own mortality that this event brought with it.[27] For Bunyan, whatever the effects on him of his mother's death in June

1644, that of his sister in the following month must have brought home to him a particularly pressing awareness of death. Given the link made in seventeenth-century thinking between death and judgement, it would hardly be surprising if a serious personal religious crisis descended upon Bunyan following these family catastrophes of the mid-1640s. If we had to pinpoint the origins of Bunyan's *Anfechtung*, it would be in the tragic summer of his vulnerable sixteenth year.

Conflict as well as loss was a theme of Bunyan's adolescence and early adulthood. In his mid-teens he was recruited into one of the armies of the Civil War.[28] At the same time, there was a kind of civil war going on inside his own make-up, and the issues in that internal struggle reflected microcosmically some of the great matters in contention in the nation at large, as England painfully sought to establish what sort of society it was to be. One may speculate that a problem of contradiction arose in Bunyan, and did so because of the conflicting outside influences to which he was subject. These colliding influences were those, on the one hand, of home and its immediate village locality, and, on the other, of schooling and church indoctrination. Bunyan and, no doubt, many of his contemporaries were battlegrounds in a war of cultures and value systems. The battle was fought between the long-established, indeed essentially medieval, lifestyle, physical and instinctual, that was characteristic of popular culture, and the newer ethos of Puritanism, with its themes of caution, prudence, schooling and intellectuality. One part of Bunyan, the part he made use of in his later popular writings, was firmly rooted in traditional rural vernacular culture, thoroughly at home with its easy-going companionability, its rough speech and its insistent athleticism. As his recollections show, like generations of country boys he was physically resourceful and knowledgeable about wild animals. He was also alarmingly imprudent and, no doubt like village boys, prone to take the kinds of risks that proved courage and made possible his acceptance in his peer group. Much, if not all, of this youth culture, especially its foolhardy machismo, was foreign to the new outlook of Puritanism, though Bunyan was to make use of its exaltation of male valour in *The Pilgrim's Progress*. Urban rather than rural in its origins, the cultural revolution that underpinned English Puritanism tended to emphasize the 'bourgeois' virtues: caution rather than rash valour, intellectuality rather than instinct, restraint rather than gratification, mental rather than physical prowess, prudence rather than unheeding boldness. Prudence was particularly to the fore in the Puritan schedule of values. The doyen of English Puritan casuists William Perkins (1558–1602) devoted pages of his *Cases of Conscience* to an analysis of this virtue that was the 'high point in the life of man'.[29] Bunyan's earlier upbringing, home and village life were, in contrast, distinctly imprudent in their tone. Left largely to his own devices, it would appear, and without the repressive vigilance of the Puritan home, Bunyan gives the reader the impression of having been allowed to roam the countryside at will, with companions and with narrow escapes from danger. All this – Bunyan's unthinking 'natural life … according to the course of this world' – was far removed from that prudence that was at the heart of the Puritan world-view.[30]

Even so, it was not so much over the clash between prudence and imprudence that Bunyan encountered contradiction. The collision really came over the pull between athleticism and spirituality. A primary indicator of masculinity in Anglo-Saxon cultures, sportsmanship mattered enormously to the young Bunyan and to the village culture in which he grew up. It was not of such salient importance in the new, intellectualist culture of Puritanism and, a moderate though he was in these matters, Perkins was firm in his insistence that Sunday observance must come before sports: 'But as for the recreations and pastimes aforenamed, as bowling, and such like, they are not at this time to be used.'[31] Sunday stood at the point of collision between two cultures. The struggle for the possession of that day focused the whole conflict between merry-England gamesmanship and Puritan high seriousness, which, in turn, actualized a wider tussle about a whole agenda of social development: was the tone of English society to remain traditional, agricultural and bucolic, or was it to become industrious, serious-minded, urban and, in a word, capitalistic in its inspiration and aspirations?[32] In the tug of war for Sunday, those who were labelled Puritans strongly favoured an intellectualized and pietized Sabbath without physical recreation. Whatever rearguard action the defenders of the traditional Sunday fought against the new Sabbath was futile, as long as the most assertive and articulate elements within the country's political, social and clerical élites remained committed, as they were at the beginning of the seventeenth century, to a Puritanical programme for reorganizing English life.

Sabbatarianism was one of the badges of the godly in Stuart England. It was certainly more evident there than it was in the Calvinist-influenced Dutch Republic.[33] Anti-sabbatarianism, on the other hand, found no intellectual validation and was a cause in retreat, until, that is, it was given a powerful reinforcement and coherence, when it acquired the highest support – that of the crown. As part of a growing anti-Puritan offensive and responding to an initiative from a part of the country, Lancashire, where the civil war between the cultures was already acute, in 1618 James I published his Declaration of Sports. The Declaration upheld a nostalgic and sentimental vision of the traditional English Sunday, in which communal parish worship was followed by orderly games. Explicitly denouncing Puritans for their attempted suppression of 'honest mirth and recreation … exercise', the royal Declaration commended all the activities that the godly found so obnoxious on Sunday – 'dancing, either men or women, archery for men, leaping, vaulting … or any such harmless recreation': a roseate picture of a weekly sports day on every village green in England. Re-issued by Charles I, the Declaration made the Stuart crown the champion of an ancestral demotic culture, whose weekly festival was the ancient Sunday. Though the Civil Wars were undreamt of when Bunyan was growing up, this was already a culturally polarized society, and one in which two diametrically opposed value systems were at loggerheads. The wider conflict was fought over the little battleground of John Bunyan's personality.[34]

It was to be an important source of strength for the mature John Bunyan, as an author setting out to reach a mass audience, that he had deep roots in a pre-Puritan popular culture. During his youth, though, his familiarity with the language of vernacular culture and his enjoyment of its pursuits conflicted with the Puritan influences to which he became exposed, creating a damaging area of tension within his personality. He was particularly devoted to the folk games with which he had been brought up – the kinds of sports recommended in the Declaration. They were 'my play … my sports', and the time for playing them, in Stuart England's six-day working week, was Sunday afternoon, when Bunyan, interestingly employing the same verb as Perkins had used, would 'solace' himself with games. On one of those Sundays, Bunyan was playing a difficult-sounding competitive game called 'Cat'. The seemingly innocent pastime was made to appear to Bunyan as a 'vice', for indulgence in which Jesus in person was 'hotly displeased' with him.[35]

Bunyan was caught in the crossfire of the war of values. Though its actual impact was restricted, the Declaration of Sports endorsed the traditional sportive Sunday. However, in Bunyan's Elstow a different voice from that heard in the royal Declaration – a disputing voice – rang out: the authentic Puritan voice of the school of public moralism from Perkins onwards:

> But one day, (amongst all the Sermons our Parson made) his subject was, to treat of the Sabbath day, and of the evil of breaking that, either with labour, sports, or otherwise: (now I was, notwithstanding my Religion, one that took much delight in all manner of vice, and especially that was the Day that I did solace my self therewith.) Wherefore I fell in my conscience under his Sermon … and at that time I felt what guilt was … I was … greatly loaden therewith … with a great burden upon my spirit.[36]

Bunyan had convicted himself of one of the gravest faults in the godly calendar: that moral schizophrenia, hypocrisy ('notwithstanding my Religion'). His guilt shows us how those tensions that were fragmenting English society, were, on the level of a single, scrupulous provincial youth, tearing apart a personality, one that would have to be reintegrated if it were to survive.

Sabbath-keeping was but one aspect, albeit a most important one, of a broad programme being implemented in early Stuart England, and involving social and cultural innovation, 'godly discipline' and the conquest of human nature. The mastery of man's nature, considered in the Augustinian-Calvinist tradition to be deeply sinful, was a vital ingredient. Bunyan, for instance, had to overcome his love of games as part of what he calls his 'natural life'. Education played an indispensable part in the attempted Puritan overhaul of English society. It was viewed largely in terms of the conquest and suppression of nature – that human nature corrupted by the Fall. The unreformed nature of children was seen as being particularly close to mankind's unredeemed nature. Therefore, much of the purpose of schooling was the moral one of breaking and remaking the child's personality, with a view to correcting the inclinations of a sinful nature towards indolence, dirt, noise, violence, bad language and general disorder. As we have seen, Bunyan's childhood seems to have conformed to a thoroughly traditional, rustic, natural, open-air pattern, in which the boy was largely left to follow the bias of nature, growing up alongside village companions, sharing their speech, habits and games. However, his boyhood fell within the period of an 'educational revolution' in England, which reached far down the social scale, certainly extending to the artisan class to which Bunyan belonged. Indeed, Bunyan was profoundly affected by it, since it introduced him not only to the world of literacy, but also to the ethical and corrective elements in an education quite at variance with a boyhood largely free of restraint.[37]

The educational movement was directed not just at substantive curricular matters of subjects taught and learned. It was also aimed at the total transformation of children in a state of nature into adults in a state of order, if not of grace. The school that Bunyan may have attended – Houghton Conquest, Bedfordshire – was founded towards the end of the large-scale expansion of the grammar schools, during the 'educational revolution' – a massive increase in the provision of schools that was directly linked to Protestantism in the wider, cultural sense. Houghton Conquest School was closely linked to Puritan Cambridge and joined a group of foundations whose purpose, set out in their statutes, was the extinction through discipline of the natural child, and the implantation into the individual of a new standard of personality. Several traits received attention, including personal hygiene, docility, silence – none of which we immediately associate with the natural child – but one theme recurred constantly: swearing.[38]

Alongside the reform of Sunday, purification of speech – a crucial matter in a society with a largely oral culture – received concentrated attention from Stuart England's Protestant reformists. What was intended was nothing less than a Puritan campaign to transform the way in which English people spoke, and especially to remove the profane, if not the obscene, elements in their speech. In part, swear-words still found in ordinary speech and directly traceable to medieval popular piety – 'marry', 'mass', '[God'] sbody', '[God'] swounds', '[God'] steeth]', etc. – were objectionable because they were too redolent of popish religion.[39] In addition, besides being blasphemous or semi-blasphemous, the casual use of religious oaths expressed too much of that admixture between two worlds – the secular and the spiritual – that was a target for Puritan animus. Profane swearing was, like Sunday sport, a traditional practice against which Puritan reformers, as cultural innovators, set their faces. In so far as children picked up this customary trait of popular culture, one of the main aims of schooling was the determined eradication of the use of oaths and curses. Thus, school statutes such as those of Oundle (1566) ordered masters '[t]o cause the scholars to refrain from the detestable vice of swearing or ribald words ... [F]or every oath or ribald word ... the scholar to have three stripes'; at Dronfield (1579) it was ordained 'that scholars be corrected for swearing with the rod', and at St Bees (1583) 'if any of them [the pupils] shall use swearing ... they shall be sharply punished'.[40]

The young Bunyan thus moved into a school sector that was suffused with a Protestant reformist idealism, in which the use of bad language was regarded as a serious offence to be eradicated punitively. Yet, one part of Bunyan – the part with its roots in traditional vernacular culture – was particularly wedded to this habit: 'I had but few Equals ... both for cursing, swearing, lying and blaspheming the holy Name of God'. As with Sabbath observance, so with swearing, the young Bunyan faced a sharp conflict between popular custom and culture on the one hand and religious standards on the other. It is reasonable to assume that the conflict was intensified, if not created, by the collision between an earlier, free and easy home and local village life and a later, disciplinarian schooling, introducing norms set by the outside world. The collision, again resulting in guilt, became evident when Bunyan was 'about nine or ten years old', that is, possibly, around the time that he started school.[41]

The nature and extent of Bunyan's schooling need to be considered against the background of what was available to boys like him in earlier

seventeenth-century England. In addition, we shall need to set his recollections about his schooling in the context of certain religious preconceptions,
and in particular in the light of a radical Christian critique of advanced
learning. Concerning the educational facilities that were available to families like Bunyan's, we need to appreciate that literacy in Stuart England
was pursued by parents as an investment in their children with overridingly
practical aims, even if some individuals learned to read so as to enjoy books.
The acquisition of basic literacy and numeracy was a worthwhile attainment for farmers wanting to control written transactions and artisans who
wished to write bills and keep accounts. As an investment in economic
advancement, especially on the part of the middling or lower-middling
strata of society to which the Bunyans probably belonged, the duration
and scope of a child's (usually a boy's) schooling was overwhelmingly conditioned by financial considerations. Either fees had to be paid, or a child's
labour contribution to household income had to be discounted, or both.
A family needed to calculate carefully whether and for how long to release
a child for education, and the financial nature of the motives at work might
well set a terminus – even an abrupt one – to schooling, once set goals had
been attained. Likewise, a sudden downturn in a family's fortunes could
bring an immediate end to a spell of schooling.[42] Such points need to be
considered when we review Bunyan's remarks about his education. His
memoirs indicate that his family was typical of those in which the schooling of children was considered a worthwhile, if difficult, sacrifice: 'But yet
notwithstanding the meanness and inconsiderableness of my Parents, it
pleased God to put it into their hearts, to put me to School, to learn both
to Read and Write; the which I also attained, according to the rate of other
poor mens children.'[43] The suggestion of a financial struggle may imply
that schooling had to be abandoned once limited aims – reading and
writing – were achieved. The confident assertion that he attended a grammar school rested on lines from a collection of *Scriptural Poems*, whose
attribution to Bunyan Brown convincingly disputed.[44] That, of course,
does not necessarily mean that Bunyan did *not* attend a grammar school –
perhaps the one at Houghton Conquest.[45] In fact, three possibilities arise
with regard to his education. The first is that he went not to a grammar
school, but to a local 'petty school' linked to apprenticeships. The second
possibility is that he did attend a grammar school, but was soon whisked
away for work and did not go through the full curriculum of classical-
humanist learning. The third and least likely possibility is that he advanced
a considerable way along, or completed, a grammar-school education, but
for some reason chose to conceal the extent of his erudition.

On the whole, it would appear that Bunyan had a limited education, 'according to the rate of other poor mens children', missing out on fuller literacy in Latin and Greek, about whose absence from his mental furniture he was later to feel, by turns, defensive and touchily proud. Even so, a dialectical work that he published in the early 1670s, *The Doctrine of Justification by Faith*, uses the traditional, technical language of academic discourse in a way that casts doubt on his claim to have learned 'little': 'I did soon loose that little I learned, even most utterly.' Whatever the facts – elusive as they are – about Bunyan's education, it becomes clear that in his autobiography he was anxious to emphasize its scantiness: 'I never went to school to Aristotle or Plato' – these being the acknowledged twin chief representatives of pagan human learning.[46] What he was doing, in fact, was firmly setting himself within a tradition of denigrating merely human knowledge. Bunyan's interpretation of his education, like his analysis of his social background, was influenced as much by the 'facts' as by religious preconceptions – in this case those of Christian anti-academicism.

This particular set of attitudes has roots as old as Christianity itself. They may even be traced in Jesus's confrontations, as reported in the Gospels, with the scholarly élite of the Judaism of his day. St Paul recognized that his fellow Christians did not include many with academic qualifications – 'not many wise men after the flesh' – since 'God hath chosen the foolish things of the world to confound the wise'.[47] St Francis linked the renunciation of intellectual as well as material possessions to the imitation of Christ. With the Renaissance and the renewal of pagan scholarship, the fifteenth-century reforming Cardinal Nicholas of Cusa praised 'learned ignorance', while the reformer of Florence in the 1490s, Girolamo Savonarola, denounced humanist and classical scholarship, and was even more dismissive of Plato than Bunyan was. Brilliant academic though he was, Luther repudiated Scholasticism and 'that harlot reason'. The Leveller John Lilburne rebuked the pretensions of an academic élite, showing how the Apostles were without scholarly qualifications. The Digger Gerrard Winstanley linked intellectual subordination to academics and clerics with social, political and economic servitude. In line with a growing demand for a prophetic spirituality and divine illumination, Fox denied the value of the universities as preparation for the ministry, and radical sectarians in the1650s were particularly loud in their condemnation of academia. Needless to say, Puritanism, especially in its more conservative variants, also had a strong academic side, encouraged schooling, as we have seen, and was firmly established in Elizabethan Cambridge. Even so, we need to be aware, if we are properly to understand his own reflections on his schooling, of Bunyan's position within a tradition of radical Puritan suspicion of higher learning.[48]

If Bunyan tended to play down the quality of his education, this was partly so as to magnify the effect of God's 'work' upon him: 'the Lord did work his gracious work of conversion upon my Soul'.[49] This may suggest an illuminist view, as if Bunyan saw himself having personal prophetic inspiration in a direct relation to God. Richard Greaves puts into the mouth of an imaginary seventeenth-century radical Puritan the rhetorical question: 'what need of a university education was there for a tinker preacher like John Bunyan whose grace-bestowed faith gave him a sense of contemporaneity with the events about which he preached?' Indeed, Bunyan at times did sound much like one of the proponents of immediate, visionary inspiration, independent of Scripture, as when he heard a voice direct from heaven forbidding his games. Yet these prophetic tones were not entirely typical of Bunyan. Normally, he operated well within the mainstream Puritan tradition of reliance on the Scriptures. Though access to these did not require a university education – and for Bunyan the English Bible *was* Scripture – it did require education up to a certain level: that of the vernacular literacy that was the legacy of his schooling.[50]

Bunyan's literacy was to make possible for him a course of religious reading, with dramatic results. Its emphasis on the 'correction' of fallen nature, would mark a key stage in a phased progression from an early lack of control to later discipline. After what would seem to have been his father's indulgence had given way to the discipline of the schoolroom, probably in the traumatic year of his mother's death (1644), Bunyan was recruited into the army. This, in overwhelmingly Parliamentarian Bedfordshire, was undoubtedly the Parliamentarian army, emphatically a disciplinarian force. Whatever the teenage Bunyan picked up from the ardent Puritanism that was dominant in this army, he was also now subject to further forms of discipline: the 'disciplines of the wars', the regimentation and drilling, the unquestioning obedience to commands. After his demobilization, he had to face up to the new disciplines and responsibilities of married life in poverty, and was forced to give up 'all the Youth that kept me company'.[51]

Once again, we see that the overriding theme of Bunyan's young life was that of conflicting pressures, arising in part from the way in which discipline and constraint were loaded on to a youth whose boyhood had been, it would appear, ungoverned. The result of the clash of influences was an agonizing guilt and a kind of division of his personality that led Bunyan to seek an alternative identity. Unwittingly enough, in his autobiography he recalls a series of adolescent quests for an alternative self. At one point, as we have seen, he clutched at identification with the chosen people of Israel, who had been given a guarantee of the divine favour which his guilt told him he had forfeited: 'if I were one of this race, my Soul must needs be happy'. On another occasion, Bunyan's desire for a different identity induced a wish to be any member of creation other than the one he was: 'O how happy now was every creature over I was!' Another alternative identity was that of a devil – on the grounds that it was preferable to be an infernal tormentor than a soul tormented: '[T]hen I should often wish ... that I had been a Devil; supposing they were onely tormentors; that if it must needs be, that I indeed went thither, I might be rather a tormentor, then tormented my self.' In contrast with this apparent wish for the immunity bestowed by confirmed evil, there was a desire for the acceptability which the young Bunyan believed God conferred on clerics: 'counting all things holy that were therein [in the church] contained; and especially the Priest and Clerk most happy, and without doubt greatly blessed, because they were the Servants, as I then thought, of God'. Another possibility was the recovery of childlike innocence: 'I wished with all my heart that I might be a little childe again.' Other alternative identities included the Apostles – 'Would I had been in their cloaths, would I had been born *Peter*, would I had been born *John*' – and the animals: '[T]hey had not a sinful nature, they were not obnoxious in the sight of God; they were not to go to Hell fire after death.' Finally, in his quest to take on a new identity, Bunyan both envied and wished to achieve the serenity of the members of Bedford's gathered church: '[I]f I could, I would goe even into the very midst of them, and there also comfort myself with the heat of their Sun.'[52]

Thus, the acute divisions in Bunyan's personality, brought into being by the conflicting pressures of an upbringing in one ambience and an education in another and, arguably, exacerbated by family griefs and resentment, resulted in his seeking to replace his personality with some other identity. As a young monk, Luther cried out in the choir, 'I am not!'[53] This cry can be interpreted as one of self-rejection and of anxiety to replace the unsatisfactory self with the copy-book identity of the ideal monk. In similar fashion, Bunyan sought to reject his self, or the features of it that were in conflict with the norms inculcated by his education. How was he to find a self to put in place of the personality that he found flawed and divided?

Bunyan began the repair of his personality and the construction of a personal reintegration through piety and a kind of self-made holiness. First, there was a programme of pious reading centred on works of religious literature, brought by Bunyan's wife as legacies from the godliness of her paternal home. These books were Arthur Dent's popular work of exposition, *The Plaine Mans Path-way to Heaven*, first published in 1601 and frequently re-printed; and Lewis Bayly's *The Practice of Piety*, a Calvinist manual published before 1613. In addition to this reading, Bunyan, perhaps under the influence of his pious wife, took refuge in religiosity and scrupulosity. He became punctilious in his twice-daily church attendance, keen to associate with the recognized godly, and enmeshed in a romantic reverence for clerics and liturgies. This phase resembles Luther's pre-conversion period of pious observances: 'When I was a monk I was unwilling to omit any of the prayers ... I was very pious in the monastery ... I said mass and prayed ... I chose twenty-one saints and prayed to three every day when I celebrated mass; thus I completed the number every week.'[54] Calvin's recollections of his own comparable phase are less concrete than Luther's vivid recall of neurotic compulsions, but they convey the same sort of impression: 'I was ... strongly devoted to the superstitions of the Papacy' – that is, to the routinized salvific mechanisms of late medieval piety.[55] The young Wesley also went through a pre-conversion stage of compulsive appeasing rituals – his 'method'.[56]

We need to put in context Bunyan's memories of his 'great devotion' to 'the High-place, Priest, Clerk, Vestments, Service, and what else belonging to the Church'.[57] Bunyan's language makes it sound as if he was attending highly ornate religious services. In fact, his phase of placatory observances, after his time as a soldier, followed the official suppression of the Book of Common Prayer and its replacement by the plain Calvinistic worship of the Westminster Directory of 1645. However, though the new services were simpler than the Laudian ritualism of the 1630s, they were prescribed and clerically led. That is to say that, in retrospect, they became objectionable to Bunyan because of their formalism, in contrast to the spontaneous and congregational worship in the religious tradition in which he eventually found his spiritual home. He was to argue vehemently against all set prayers in *I Will Pray with the Spirit of 1662*.[58]

Bunyan's devout observances had the effect, for a while, of appeasing guilt. Thus, he was able for a period to combine the performance of 'my Religion' with the Sunday sports that were repugnant to the Puritan pressures he was encountering from a local Sabbatarian parson and, conceivably, from his wife. This attempt to reconcile contradictions and palliate guilt by performing rituals eventually broke down, to be followed by a period of collapse in which the contrarieties of his life were fully exposed. At last, a new synthesis was put in place. The remainder of *Grace Abounding* narrates a spiritual odyssey, a protracted dark night of the soul and Bunyan's emergence from it.

Indeed, throughout its length this autobiographical work is less an autobiography than a spiritual record, within a well-established Puritan genre.[59] *Grace Abounding* is certainly not a history of a man's own times. Therefore, important external events are virtually ignored. That the author was a soldier during the Civil Wars is revealed quite incidentally when

Bunyan recounts one of the providences that saved his early life:

> [W]hen I was a Souldier, I with others were drawn out to go to such a place to besiege it; but when I was just ready to go, one of the company desired to go in my room, to which, when I had consented he took my place; and coming to the siege, as he stood Sentinel, he was shot in the head with a Musket bullet and died.[60]

That tantalizing fragment, with no date and only 'such a place', is all we have from Bunyan of his military service in the climacteric conflict of his age. It is only incidentally a story about the English Civil War and really concerns God's dispensation to Bunyan; its very allusiveness has elicited a considerable amount of scholarship and ingenuity in order to supply the details that we would expect from a more straightforward autobiography about Bunyan's military service. But the spiritual autobiography as a literary genre imposed its own conventions; it was not a news bulletin or a record of recent history. Bunyan's deliberate negligence about momentous external events can be compared with Fox's attitude of total indifference to the Civil Wars which, in his *Journal*, he fails to note until 1651, by which time they were over.[61] In the cases of Fox and Bunyan, this oblivion over external events is explained by a preoccupation with internal drama: conflict in the outside world took second place to the resolution of civil wars within.

Bunyan's route into a converted life was opened up after his marriage, following his discharge from the army. We have seen that, so as to avert guilt, he entered into a phase of religious self-help characterized by compulsions. These included the meticulous performance of church rituals and also acts of self-denial similar in intent to, though not as extreme as, those that the young Luther practised in the monastery. These austerities represented attempts to placate an angry God by acts of self-sacrifice. They took the form of renouncing various physical activities and sports. A big and active man, Bunyan was used to regular outdoor exercise, and probably needed the release afforded by strenuous physical activity. As we have seen, he was certainly very attached to, and probably adept at, his sports and exercises – 'my best delights ... much delight in ringing ... my dancing, I was a full year before I could quite leave it'. Indeed, in a brief flurry of self-assertion Bunyan decided to keep his Sunday games and face the consequence of damnation. In the event, though, he gave up, one after another, the leisure pursuits that were anchored in the physical, extrovert, collective popular culture of his youth. From the point of view of physical and psychological well-being, this abandonment of a set of taxing and gregarious exercises – games on the village green, dancing and bell-ringing – may have compounded his problem of religious melancholia. Bunyan himself partly acknowledged that his guilt was out of proportion to his actual offences. He saw himself as one of a number of scrupulous personalities – 'poor creatures ... that though not much guilt attendeth the Soul, yet they continually have a secret conclusion within them, that there is no hopes for them'.[62]

Bunyan became convinced that his pastimes were sins. However, it is possible that he renounced them not only as perceived faults but, unconsciously, as pleasures to be offered up to God in expiation for a state of sin that he saw in himself. If this were so, Bunyan would have been endeavouring a self-help route to salvation reminiscent of medieval Catholic penitential practice. It is not surprising that he was to find in Luther, who was an enthusiastic, but eventually disillusioned, practitioner of penitential disciplines, one who directly 'spoke to his condition'. Bunyan's self-help phase, whose ethos violated the Protestant consensus on the sole divine responsibility for saving sinners, lasted about a year. In an almost incantatory way, he repeats references to the duration of that phase: 'Thus I continued about a year ... well, this I say, continued about a twelve-month, or more ... [W]ell, this I say, continued for about a twelve-month or more.'[63] It is possible to locate that 'twelve-month' in the early 1650s. However, Bunyan was as imprecise about the dating of his phase of self-help as he was insistent about its duration, as vague about the chronology of his religious crisis as Calvin and Luther were about the dating of their religious travails.[64] Though it is frustrating for a biographer not to have a time-table for such crucial experiences, we should realize that these are essentially internal processes that cannot, in their nature, be plotted according to an external calendar.

Bunyan had adopted an ethical righteousness, which impressed his neighbours with the dramatic nature of his apparent religious conversion, but which he came to feel was merely external. According to the Calvinist scheme of ultimate salvation – a scheme traced by Perkins and by other Puritan writers – sanctification came only as a result of divine election. Assurance of this was brought home to the individual member of the elect by an often painful and protracted process engineered by God. The process was a profound one, so that Bunyan's phase of personal righteousness came to appear to him as superficial and he saw himself as 'nothing but a poor painted Hypocrite'. True, he was an accomplished discourser of divinity, 'a brisk talker also my self in the matters of Religion', not unlike his character Talkative in *The Pilgrim's Progress*. But later he came to see himself as, in that phase of his life, no more than an empty rhetorician. In the gathered church in Bedford that Bunyan was to join, discourse was all-important, as it was throughout the whole Puritan movement, with its sermons and religious conversations. Yet, as in the testimonies of conversion required for entry into the gathered churches, the religious discourse had to be deeply felt, experiential and genuine. Bunyan indeed heard such godly discourse in Bedford, when he was going about his work as a tinker, from a group of 'three or four poor women' on whose talk he eavesdropped.[65]

This incident and the way he recounted it are deeply significant for our understanding of Bunyan. He describes the godly women as being 'poor', as well they may have been – though we have already seen something of the emphasis in the Christian tradition, and more markedly in radical Puritanism, on the sanctity of the poor and ignorant. As education and literacy penetrated down the layers of Stuart society, women were some of the last of their beneficiaries. Therefore, in the polarization, based on texts such as 1 Corinthians 1: 27–8, between self-appointed human claims to wisdom contrasted with God's endowment of the lowly with His spirit, women stood on the side of the truly favoured. A woman – his first wife – had already played a part in setting Bunyan on the road to godliness, and, as we shall see, the second part of *The Pilgrim's Progress* deals with the place of women in Christianity.[66]

On the grounds that the Bedford church came together under its minister John Gifford in 1650, Roger Sharrock calculated that Bunyan's encounter with the Bedford women must have occurred in the 'earliest days' of the history of that church.[67] Such a calculation would certainly fit the estimated chronology of Bunyan's conversion following his marriage in 1647, and place the key events in the early 1650s. However, we do not need to assume that the origins of Bedford's gathered church simply coincided with the inception of Gifford's ministry. The historical preamble to Bedford's church book makes it plain that the prototype at least of this church existed for some 'long time' before Gifford became pastor. The church was founded, by its rank and file of members, as a secret sodality in the time of 'ye bishops and their superstitions' (that is, before 1643), and eventually God 'placed Mr. John Gifford among them for their minister'.[68] Therefore, important as Gifford's ministerial leadership was, especially in giving the Bedford church a new sense of separate identity, we should also assume a high level of religious awareness on the part of the ordinary lay men and women who made up Bedford's community of gathered Christians. The talk that Bunyan heard during his momentous visit to Bedford was not a kind of reported sermon of Gifford, but personal, immediate, experiential religious speech: '[T]hey also discoursed of their own wretchedness of heart, of their unbelief, and did contemn, slight, and abhor their own righteousness, as filthy, and insufficient to do them any good.'[69]

'[I]nsufficient to do them any good': this overheard conversation not only carried the depth of sincerity that Bunyan's hitherto merely routine verbal professions had lacked, but it also enshrined key Reformation principles. Up to this point, Bunyan had been trying to save himself from damnation. The discourse of the godly Bedford women contained within it the essential Protestant realization that the responsibility and the initiative in salvation lay outside the individual, with God: 'their talk was about a new birth, the work of God on their hearts ... they talked how God had visited their souls with his love in the Lord Jesus'.[70] The Bedford conversations opened the wicket-gate for Bunyan's progress to a godliness that was authentic because it was not of his achieving.

Bunyan's *Grace Abounding* is, like *The Pilgrim's Progress*, about a progression, even a journey. Though the journey could be agonizingly difficult, for a member of the elect who had received God's 'effectual' call, the terminus of such a voyage, with its staging posts of faith, repentance, justification, forgiveness and sanctification, was pre-determined: glorification. As an itinerant tinker Bunyan, in the first half of the 1650s, was a man of journey, a denizen of the paths and the roadways: 'my Calling lying in the Countrey ... betwixt *Elstow* and *Bedford* ... to *Bedford*, to work on my calling ... as I was travelling into the Countrey'. These peripatetic work patterns brought Bunyan into contact with some of the new, and often profoundly disturbing, ideas circulating in the revolutionary England of the early 1650s – including the perfectionist or amoral notions of the Ranters. Fox, whose semi-perfectionist ideas bore some glancing similarity with Ranterism, encountered people identified with this ideology, or mood, in the same period. Bunyan's brief recollection of some exposure to Ranterism helps to give some chronology to his narrative. Perhaps Ranter amoralism even exercised some faint pull on Bunyan, but 'God ... did not suffer me to accept of such cursed principles'.[71]

In the event, Bunyan's encounter with Ranters and their thinking was a distraction from his main progress. The contact that was to matter most to him was with the godly congregation in Bedford and its leader John Gifford. Bunyan's approach to the Bedford congregation, and eventually to a religious and emotional stability, took place in a tripartite crisis, following the initial spell of 'about a twelve-month' of self-appointed virtue, 'my own righteousness'. These crisis phases, which contained within them less pronounced oscillations from depression to elation, were separated from one another by phases of tranquillity, the last of which brought the whole cycle to an end. The whole series of depressions and plateaux went on 'for some years together', perhaps lasting as long as the first half of the

1650s. The first phase fell in an undated period of about a year, after the collapse of Bunyan's experiments in self-induced holiness. It lasted from his first encounter with the women of the Bedford gathered church and his attainment of a certain provisional stability through Gifford's ministry. This phase ended in temporary stabilization, followed by a new swing into a phase of dejection, followed by a further recovery. [72]

A feature of the first crisis was 'hallucinatory' experience. One of these hallucinations was visual, and positive in its import. It was of the godly 'poor people at *Bedford* ... on the Sunny side of some high Mountain, there refreshing themselves with the pleasant beams of the Sun'. Bunyan had first come across the godly women of Bedford 'sitting at a door in the Sun', so that this vision can be seen as a re-capitulation of an actual experience. The other 'hallucinatory' experience was aural, and negative, in character. A voice, which Bunyan heard as being actual, threatened him with falling into Satan's power. An incidental feature of this first crisis was a quest for wonders, as when Bunyan was tempted to try miraculously to dry the puddles in a roadway. [73]

The question of believing, including faith in miraculous powers, raised the issue of whether or not Bunyan had faith. Since Reformation doctrine taught that the just were saved by faith, misgivings in this regard gave rise to the next chronic uncertainty, over Bunyan's predestination to be one of the elect. As yet, his theological development was not far advanced, so that he was capable of putting his problem over election in the simplistic terms of God's having already selected the quota of those he would save in the Bedford area: 'those good people of *Bedford* ... these being converted already, they were all that God would save in those parts, and that I came too late'. Equally, Bunyan was also led into a kind of elaborate, compulsive typologizing, as when he laboriously pursued Moses's division between clean and unclean beasts: 'I thought the *Hare* to be a type of those that talk of the Word, yet walk in ways of sin.'[74]

More encouragingly, during this first crisis Bunyan was edging towards a way of reading Scripture that was eventually to become helpful to him. At first, he recalled, he read the Bible for enjoyment, as a narrative. Gradually, however, he read it thematically and 'began to look into the Bible with new eyes ... and especially the Epistles of ... S. *Paul* '. This discovery of St Paul, aided by a Pauline commentary from Luther, was to be as decisive for Bunyan as Luther's own reading of Paul had been. The other aspect of his handling of Scripture at this time was less positive in its consequences. William James spoke of Bunyan's tendency to 'verbal automatisms'. There was certainly a marked inclination towards a kind of textualizing. Individual texts would constantly come into his mind, often having a powerful and sometimes threatening effect on him. His habit of viewing the Bible as a string of brief slogans was potentially dangerous. Because of conflicting messages coming from various – and not always harmonious – separate parts of the Bible, Bunyan was to fall even more into the grip of the sense of contradiction that was at the heart of his problem.[75]

During his first crisis phase, Bunyan's religious consciousness became strained to the utmost degree, so that, eventually, members of the Bedford church took pity on him and introduced him to Gifford's spiritual therapies. However, within this overall phase of doubt and guilt, there were less pronounced but more frequent swings between dejection and elation. We can reconstruct part of this pattern of alternation by running together a set of descriptions by Bunyan, spread out over a number of pages of his autobiography, of his moods, state of consciousness and often sudden changes of psychological condition:

> I had been so many weeks oppressed and cast down ... I was greatly lightened and encouraged in my Soul ... After this, that other doubt did come with strength upon me ... when I had been long vexed with this fear, and was scarce able to take one step more ... these words broke in upon my mind ... *and yet there is roome* ... These words ... were sweet words to me ... Nay, thought I, now I grow worse and worse, now am I farther from conversion than ever ... Yet that Word would sometime create in my heart a peaceable pause ... Now was my heart filled full of comfort and hope ... For about the space of month after, a very great storm came down upon me, which handled me twenty times worse then all I had met with before ... Yet at times I should have some strong and heart-affecting apprehensions of God.[76]

It was often the case that Bunyan was propelled into his despondent moods by his own speculations or by what he took to be diabolic temptations. In contrast, consolation and elation were generally derived from passages in the Scriptures. This pattern was not invariable, and there were times when Scripture, because of its own contradictions, 'did also tear and rend my soul'. For a while, Bunyan became a kind of battlefield for scriptural texts with conflicting import.[77]

The overall impression of this first phase of Bunyan's religious disturbance is one of depression that only occasionally lifted. Indeed, it almost seems as if he actually needed the despondent guilt that oppressed him so during this period, when he was 'afflicted with the sight and sence and terrour of my own wickedness, yet I was afraid to let this sence and sight go quite off my minde'. The continuing guilt meant that Bunyan still wished to renounce his identity for any other:

I could have changed heart with any body ... and now was I sorry that God had made me a man ... The beasts, birds, fishes, &c., I blessed their condition ... I blessed the condition of the Dogge and Toad, and counted the estate of everything that *God* had made far better than this dreadfull state of mine ... yea, gladly would I have been in the condition of Dog or Horse.[78]

Much of the intensity of Bunyan's spiritual trial in the early 1650s stemmed from the fact that he was facing his problems largely on his own: 'I sat by the fire in my house, and musing on my wretchedness ... I was travelling into the Countrey and musing on the wickedness and blasphemy of my heart.' As we have seen, his itinerant work brought him into contact with a variety of people and new ideas. On the other hand, much of his working life must have been spent in solitude, especially on the roads. Thus, he might be taken to conform to the stereotype of the artisan religious Dissenter, who has much opportunity, in the nature and course of his work, for religious reflection and self-observation. In Bunyan's case, his solitude permitted or encouraged textual cogitation, which sometimes became morbidly elaborate. During these largely solitary introspections, the Bedford church occupied the role, as it were, of a chorus witnessing Bunyan's dilemmas of the early 1650s: 'Sometimes I would tell my condition to the people of God; which when they heard, they would pity me'; 'I began to break my mind to those poor people in *Bedford*, and to tell them my condition: which, when they had heard, they told *Mr. Gifford* of me.'[79] Gifford's teaching was to be indispensable to Bunyan's recovery. He was his pastoral counsellor, as von Stauptiz had been the young Luther's, fulfilling the same role as that of numerous Puritan pastors since the days of Richard Greenham and William Perkins.[80] Perhaps Gifford was able to direct Bunyan towards the reassuring aspects of the Calvinist doctrine of election. After all, predestination could be a 'comfortable' doctrine, if one were able to appropriate to oneself its proper assurance and its positive aspects, even counting oneself amongst the elect, perhaps through being embraced in a congregation of 'visible saints'. The role of the Bedford church in Bunyan's spiritual healing must have been at least as important as the influence of Gifford. Bunyan perceived it as a gathering of the elect and membership of it as infinitely desirable.

One way in which the uncertainties of predestination could be stabilized was through the theory and practice of church covenants. These had been a feature of the life of English gathered and separatist churches since their inception in the sixteenth century. A church covenant could supply some predictive fixity to the otherwise inscrutable caprices of predestination; it might even make possible the identification, or self-identification, of the elect as the people of God in the church. The covenant between God and Israel in the Old Testament provided a model for agreements in which a church could commit itself to obey God's laws – walk in His ways – in return for which he would be a God to save His people. Thus, the Bedford church had come together in a covenanted fellowship – a 'covenant with God'. The logical exigencies of predestination were in no way abandoned, but its implications were pinned down. Through 'Holiness of life', the saints might obtain a kind of appropriation of election.[81]

If that were so, it was vitally important to be a member of God's church in whatever place it was established, since churches of saints attracted God's 'promises' of salvation. That is why Bunyan felt membership of the Bedford church to be a most enviable and desirable goal, exchanging solitary anguish for collective assurance. He became convinced that the Bedford church members who were gathered under Gifford's pastorate were part of the visible elect – 'these being converted already, they were all that God would save in those parts … How lovely now was every one in my eyes, that I thought to be converted men and women.'[82] His wish for a new identity now became focused on the ultimate, but attainable, enviability of sainthood, of membership in Bedford's gathered congregation. A scriptural text (Mark 3: 13) related how Christ 'went up into a Mountain, and called to him whom he would'. In both the Old and the New Testaments, mountains feature as meeting places between the human and the divine; around the time that Bunyan was undergoing his spiritual travail, Fox began his missionary crusade to the North of England with a vision from a hilltop. In Bunyan's case, the mountain motif appeared in a dream of the 'happiness of these poor people at *Bedford* … set on the Sunny side of some high Mountain, there refreshing themselves with the pleasant beams of the Sun, while I was shivering and shrinking in the cold'.[83]

Thus it was that, by means of both actual observation and a dream, Bunyan associated the gathered church with warmth, security and inclusion; non-membership of the church meant cold, exposure and exclusion. In a later letter entered into the Bedford church book with Bunyan's signature, a link was made between exclusion from the church and 'them that are naked and lodge without clothing, that have no covering in the cold'.[84] In his autobiography Bunyan's elaboration of his dream of the church on the mountainside dwells on his imagined struggle to squeeze himself into church membership:

> if I could, I would goe even into the very midst of them, and there also comfort myself with the heat of their Sun … if I could find some way or

passage, by which I might enter therein ... I made many offers to get in, but all in vain ... the Mountain signified the Church of the living God; the Sun that shone thereon, the comfortable shining of his mercifull face on them that were therein.[85]

It is no coincidence that, some time after Bunyan began to approach the Bedford church, his first phase of crisis came to an end. Gifford, he wrote, 'invited me to his house, where I should hear him confer with others about the dealings of God with the Soul', and 'I sat under the Ministry of holy Mr. *Gifford*, whose Doctrine, by Gods grace, was much for my stability ... [O]h! now, how was my Soul led from truth to truth by God.' Bunyan had gained access to 'them that were therein'.[86]

Bunyan's period of tranquillity between his first and second phase of crisis was brief. However, this interval was a productive one in terms of his overall development because it featured two important linked discoveries: of Christ and of Luther's writings. The 'discovery' of Christ aligned Bunyan with Luther, for Luther had found the key to the removal of sin in the Cross. According to Calvinist doctrine, the Atonement appropriated election to God's chosen. In Bunyan's discourse of the work and person of Christ during his recapitulation in *Grace Abounding* of his first crisis phase, there is no explicit mention of election. This passage of recall is a prose rhapsody in which the logical rigours of predestination are supplanted by emotive perceptions of the life and death of Jesus. Here, all Bunyan's scriptural references are to the New Testament. They refer to the real, human, living, crucified and risen Christ:

> [F]rom the birth and cradle of the Son of God, to his ascension and second coming ... from his conception and birth, even to his second coming to judgement ... from the Cradle to his Cross; to which, also ... I saw how gently he gave himself up to be hanged and nailed on it for my sins ... I have considered also the truth of his resurrection.[87]

As well as stressing the Cross, it is noteworthy that, like St Francis, who also set out to counter anti-incarnational theologies, Bunyan emphasizes Christ's cradle, the simple symbol of the Word's being made flesh. Recounting his own transitory doubts about Christ's real humanity (and divinity), Bunyan switches his Christological canticle to a sharp polemical attack on spiritualizing 'errors' about Christ. He fastens these doctrines on the Quakers, and the combative style of his rejection of tendencies to make Christ a kind of universal spiritual principle might seem to jar with the ecstatic tone of his previous prose hymn. However, the beliefs that he stigmatized threatened his grasp on a unique but fully human Christ whose blood had taken away man's – and Bunyan's – sins. Hence the urgency of his repudiation of any denial of the historical Incarnation and its consequences.[88]

Like John Wesley, Bunyan was profoundly influenced by Luther's *Commentary on St. Paul's Epistle to the Galatians*: 'I do prefer this book of Mr. *Luther* upon the Galathians, (excepting the Holy Bible) before all the books that ever I have seen, as most fit for a wounded Conscience.' Study of the Epistle to the Galatians brought Bunyan ever closer to Pauline teaching on the centrality of the Cross and the futility of the 'legal righteousness' of good works. The Epistle had a particular relevance for Bunyan because it was, in part, an account of conversion. Along with the Epistle to the Romans, it contains the central core of Paul's teaching 'that a man is not justified by the works of the law, but by the faith of Jesus Christ ... the just shall live by faith'. This doctrine had brought measureless comfort to Luther, who, like Bunyan after him, had for a while vainly attempted to placate God by the 'works of the law'.[89]

Vastly longer than Paul's brief Epistle to the Galatians, Luther's *Commentary* (he called it 'extremely verbose') was composed as a course of lectures in 1531, following the doctrinal stabilization of early Lutheranism with the previous year's Augsburg Confession. From its first translation into English in 1575, the *Commentary* became firmly lodged in the nation's repertoire of highly esteemed religious writings, and was reprinted on numerous occasions, including at least seven seventeenth-century editions. From Bunyan's graphic description of the crumbling text that he used – 'so old that it was ready to fall piece from piece, if I did but turn it over' – it sounds as if he had an early, if not the earliest, edition.[90] The *Commentary* conveyed, as it set out to do, a message of great comfort. First, 'man's weakness is so great, that in the terror of conscience and danger of death, we behold nothing else but our works, our worthiness and the law'. Next, Luther showed that the law of righteousness was 'not able to quiet a troubled conscience, but increaseth terrors and driveth it to desperation'. But: 'Believe in Christ Jesus crucified for thy sins ... This is the beginning of health and salvation. By this means we are delivered from sin, justified and made inheritors of everlasting life ... pacifying and quieting the conscience.' The sequence that Luther described fully reflected Bunyan's own experience, especially his realization of the futility of self-generated righteousness, and Luther conveyed 'comfort to the soule of man'. For these reasons, Bunyan took the *Commentary* to heart, 'as if his Book had been written out of my heart'.[91]

The stability thus won did not endure long. Bunyan now entered into a new crisis phase, lasting up to two and a half years and sub-divided, as the earlier one had been, by minor oscillations between despondency and elation. Perhaps because Bunyan does not account for his sudden descent from a plateau of stability, Tindall believed that the account of 'relapse from grace' was dramatized, as Bunyan placed his work within the hyperbolic literary conventions of enthusiastic religious literature. Perhaps so, though Bunyan's description of his second crisis phase has about it an unmistakable sense of deeply felt anguish. Indeed, recollections of his second major crisis lay bare his inner self with a candour that belies any merely literary composition. [92] In this new wave of anguish, Bunyan comes across as solitary and introverted, like Christian at the beginning of *The Pilgrim's Progress*, his fingers in his ears; his long-standing dejection and introversion must have made him both difficult and pitiable to live with. His isolation was compounded by his feeling of being severed from the church, association with which he so coveted. '[T]ortured on a Rack for whole dayes together', Bunyan was unable to eat and rose up from his meals to be alone. The solitary nature of his work created a lonely space into which he was thrown with his thoughts, his texts and his misery:

> [A]bout ten or eleven a Clock one day, as I was walking under a Hedge, full of sorrow and guilt God knows … one day I walked to a neighbouring Town, and sate down upon a Settle in the Street, and fell into a very deep pause about the most fearful state my sin had brought me to.

However, his solitude and introversion were much more than simply features of an independent way of working: Bunyan gives every indication of having been emotionally distanced from his family at this time, and also essentially alone in the midst of other men and women: 'Once as I was walking to and fro in a good mans Shop, bemoaning to myself in my sad and doleful state, afflicting myself with self abhorrence … one day as I was in a Meeting of Gods People, full of sadness and terrour.' [93]

The comfort that Bunyan had secured at the end of his first depression from his approach to the Bedford church was now threatened by his guilt: 'I did also desire the Prayers of the people of God for me, but I feared that God would give them no heart to do it.' Utterly isolated, Bunyan regressed to the sense of exclusion that had characterized his first great travail; therefore, the same metaphor of warmth and inclusion versus cold and exclusion recurred: 'Ah how safely did I see them walk, whom God had hedged in! they were within his care … Now did those blessed places, that spake of *Gods keeping his people*, shine like the Sun before me, though not to comfort me … all combined together to banish me out of the World.' Another feature of his renewed dejection was his wish for otherness, which we considered earlier: 'Oh, how gladly now would I have been anybody but myself! Anything but a man! and in any condition but mine own!'[94]

A further symptomatic feature of Bunyan's second major crisis period was the invasion of his mind by images of blood and bloodshed:

> *Cain* ... trembling under the heavy load of guilt that he had charged on him for the blood of his Brother *Abel* ...I should think with myself that *David* shed blood to cover his Adultery ... *Manasseh* ... made the Streets of *Jerusalem* run down with the blood of Innocents. These thought I are great sins, sins of a bloudy colour ... the avenger of blood pursued me ... now it remained that I enquire whether I have right to enter the City of Refuge. So I found, That he must not, *who lay in wait to shed blood.*[95]

The repetition of these images of blood arose from the centrality in Bunyan's thinking of the blood of Christ, shed for the remission of sins: 'that Blood that hath vertue enough to wash away' sins. Calvinist soteriology adopted and adapted the traditional 'Anselmian' version of redemption, according to which the Son atoned to the Father for humanity's inherited sin: a legal, 'forensic' transaction. Indeed, Calvinist theologians added to the legalistic interpretation of the Atonement by speaking of a 'covenant' between the Father and Christ for the redemption of the elect at large. There was, however, a tradition – one that had been strongly fostered in medieval piety – which was personalistic, devotional and emotive, rather than legal and forensic in its emphases. In this tradition the Crucifixion was seen as a personal act of love by Christ to the individual soul, an emotional and physical Passion to be depicted endlessly and meditated upon constantly, and a cruel death for which the individual sinner was in fact responsible. Bunyan shows strong leanings towards this individualistic and affective, rather than forensic and 'public' reading of the Passion. In his second crisis period he convinced himself that he was personally responsible for the shedding of Christ's blood, that he had forsaken Christ. Just as serenity at the end of his first extended crisis had come upon him because of his conviction 'that I loved Christ dearly', so his subsequent dejection arose from his belief in his betrayal of Christ. This was like St Peter's disownment, or, even worse, it resembled Judas's betrayal. Bunyan felt he had succumbed to a temptation to 'let [Christ] go again', 'to exchange him', in fact, like Judas, to '[s]ell Christ ... sell him'.[96]

In Bunyan's thinking, Christ had become a figure within his power, a vulnerable man of sorrows whose capacity, even to save, was severely limited, at least in Bunyan's regard. Christ could not save him because of the gravity of his sin – against Christ, a mental or emotional sin of betrayal, of failure to love. For Bunyan, this internal state of sin was worse than the objective sins of a sinner in deed, such as King David. Bunyan had now entered into a climate of intense emotionalism and subjectivity – like that of the medieval English mystics. It was an atmosphere in which Christ the triumphant salvific Pantocrater receded in favour of a suffering servant acquainted with grief and for whom Bunyan felt, or wished to feel, 'pity', a word full of the resonances of medieval affective 'piety'.[97]

Bunyan, then, was showing some of the traits of the classic contemplatives, and especially one of the difficulties that some of them faced – *accidia*, or spiritual dryness in prayer, compounded by anxiety. He had come to suspect that his state was that of the 'unpardonable sin', a theological concept of heavy oppressive power. Once again, his condition swung from despondency to relative peace. In fact, we should note that the alternation was not like the casebook 'manic depressive' one of swings from low to high states, but rather a fluctuation from low to calm moods. The pattern, as Bunyan recorded it, can be reconstructed, once again, if we bring together a number of separated passages from his autobiography:

[A]s tortured on a Rack for whole dayes together ... Now I began to conceive peace in my Soul ... I sunk in my spirits under exceeding grief again ... a great calm, in my Soul ... perswades me there might be hope ... then I began to mistrust, and to despair again ... I [had] encouragment to come to God by Christ ... a great easment to my mind, to wit, that my sin was pardonable ... I returned to my old fears again ... I went to bed at quiet ... But yet the Tempter left me not ... Thus was my Soul at this time, (and as I then did think for ever) set at liberty ... But before many weeks were over I began to dispond again.

At one particularly dangerous point, the speed at which his mood oscillated accelerated rapidly: '[M]y peace would be in and out sometimes twenty times a day: Comfort now, and Trouble presently; Peace now, and before I could go a furlong, as full of Fear and Guilt as ever heart could hold.'[98]

The mood swings were accompanied, if not caused, by what Bunyan saw as a kind of war of scriptural texts, further evidence of conflict and contradiction in and around him. Scripture was generally regarded as the very word of God, with its various writers, as Calvin said, merely secretaries of the Holy Spirit. Therefore, Scripture ought to speak with a single, consistent voice. Yet various passages of the Bible were in conflict one with another, and, in particular, some held out a promise of mercy, others a threat of judgement. Until Bunyan could reconcile these conflicting passages, he was at the mercy of their contradictions. The conflict was not a simple one between Old Testament texts of wrath and New Testament messages of mercy. For instance, Bunyan's seizure of an Old Testament promise of forgiveness, from Jeremiah, clashed with another Old Testament passage, from the story of Esau, indicating the withdrawal of God's mercy. Such rival scriptural excerpts had, as it were, autonomous and powerful personalities. They seemed sometimes to spring unbidden into Bunyan's consciousness and to have motor power to come and go, 'tarry' and 'break in': '[T]hat Scripture came into my heart … such a *great* word, it seemed to be writ in *great* letters, and gave such a justle to my fear and doubt, (I mean for the time it tarried with me, which was about a day) … these words did with great power suddainly break in upon me.'[99] With their apparently independent potency, scriptural texts threatened Bunyan: 'fearful and terrible Scriptures' would regard him 'grimly' or 'strike' him, 'kill'd' him or 'stood like a Spear against me'. Bunyan did not so much wrestle with intractable biblical passages: he saw them as forces struggling against him: 'How many Scriptures are there against me? … which of them would get the better of me.' At the same time, Bunyan viewed key Scriptures as warring agents contesting with one another: a particular text 'did work and struggle strangly in me for a while; at last, that about *Esaus* birthright began to wax weak' (the Esau text of the birthright was a recurrent nightmare). To some extent, Bunyan saw the ethos of the New Testament and its message of mercy as being in conflict with the Old and its theme of judgement: 'the Word of the Law and Wrath must give place to the Word of Life and Grace … *Moses* and *Elias* must both vanish, and leave Christ and his Saints alone.' He also saw himself as struggling with Satan for the possession of texts, referring to 'the slights that Satan used to take this Scripture from me'.[100] However, since for Bunyan all of Scripture was God's word, his difficulties with the Bible could not be resolved by a straightforward preference for one Testament over another – as Luther elevated the New Testament over the Old. The task facing him was one of reconciliation: 'a concurrance and agreement in the Scriptures … whether the Scriptures could agree in the salvation of my Soul'.[101]

Eventually, Bunyan achieved this vital task of reconciliation through arduous and methodologically traditional scriptural exegesis. There were obsessive features even in this exercise, as when he broke down a text into its component atoms: 'every word was a mighty word unto me; as *my*, and *grace*, and *sufficient*, and *for thee*'. In the end, though, he accomplished his 'concurrance and agreement' through extended step-by-step analysis in numbered sections, a process which he went over in *Grace Abounding*. He took a group of passages and analysed each potentially threatening excerpt systematically and, as necessary, in the light of other texts. This orderly, ratiocinative method made the terrible texts approachable: 'I began to take some measure of incouragement, to come close to them, to read them, and consider them.' Finally, Bunyan found that 'the Scriptures could agree in the salvation of my Soul'. The discovery was followed by a visionary realization that 'my Righteousness was Jesus Christ himself'. Bunyan had now emerged out of his second major religious crisis: 'Now did my chains fall off my Legs indeed, I was loosed from my affliction and irons, my temptations also fled away ... now went I also home rejoycing, for the grace and love of God.'[102]

The second crisis phase had been a particularly dangerous time for Bunyan. At one point, he had in mind the story of the suicide of Francis Spira, a classic *exemplum* about religious melancholia and its effects. He was also himself partly aware of the obsessive features of his make-up at this time: 'These things may seem ridiculous to others, even as ridiculous as they were in themselves, but to me they were most tormenting cogitations.' To some extent, the Scriptures, which seemed one upon another to be convicting him, also saved him from the ultimate despair, since he discovered a passage (Daniel 10: 14) that promised a terminus to his grief.[103]

If we were to consider *Grace Abounding* solely from the point of view of literary artistry, we might conclude that Bunyan ought to have brought his account of cyclic crisis to an end after recounting how he attained a second plateau of tranquillity, for 'about a twelve-month', through the reconciliation of conflicting scriptural texts. The autobiography does indeed round off the narration of resolved traumas with raptures about Christ, though Bunyan was still seized with 'exceeding dread and terrour' before God and Christ. Then Bunyan offers a detached analysis of the causes of the second phase of anguish: that he had under-estimated God and his need for Him. The internal drama concluded and analysed, Bunyan might have moved on to deal with the more external events of his life, his ministry and his imprisonment. However, he soon begins instead to recite a third stage of spiritual difficulty, which lasted about nine months. Though, of course, autobiographically authentic, this section is not entirely satisfactory from a purely literary point of view, since it largely repeats the description of earlier problems which now recurred.[104]

Bunyan's earlier problems over contradiction returned in the form of a further awareness of internal disagreements in the Scriptures. He relapsed into his earlier preoccupation with the scriptural 'sentences that stood against me'. He got out of this 'mire' only by putting the best and most hopeful construction on the 'Word of Promise', or simply by taking God's words in their plain sense, without torturing the text of the Scriptures until it, in turn, tortured him.[105]

Once again, the period of crisis was subdivided into lesser alternations between affliction and exhilaration or tranquillity:

> [O]ften in my greatest agonies ... Now was I got on high ... I was as one dead before Death came ... This did sweetly revive my Spirit ... yet suddenly there fell upon me a great cloud of darkness ... at this my former darkness and atheism fled away, and the blessed things of heaven were set within my view.

That last elation increased in intensity and led to final release: 'Christ was a precious Christ to my Soul that night; I could scarce lie in my Bed for joy, and peace, and triumph.' However, the alternations of gloom and alleviation had, once again, been both frequent and extreme. Sharp scruples were compounded by a grave physical illness – 'a Consumption' – a sickness which, doubtless, as with Luther, was intensified by mental anguish. A conscientious dilemma about approaching the Eucharist exacerbated the problem.[106] Throughout this, as during the two earlier bouts of misery, Bunyan continued to be haunted by the Scriptures. He was, however, now learning to manipulate the text so as to adjust the sense of problematic passages in the light of other, more reassuring phrases. For example, he could not find in his Bible the actual (and to him most helpful) words, '*I must go to Jesus*'. However, by putting together a group of other verses, he arrived at the gist of the phrase he was seeking to validate. Thus, he was discovering how to modify the terrifying totemistic rigidity that he had encountered in many individual scriptural passages and to make the Bible work the way he wanted it to – for him, not against him. He was also tending increasingly to give the New Testament and its ethos – reconciliation, forgiveness – priority over the Old Testament, in so far as its themes were justice and judgement: 'to see what might be the mind of God in a New-Testament stile'.[107]

In his attempt to find a scriptural location for the reassuring saying, '*I must go to Jesus*', Bunyan gives us a rare glimpse into his domestic life. He recalls that he asked his wife whether there was 'ever such a Scripture' as the words he sought. This indeed suggests that he saw his first wife as being conversant with the Bible. However, her answer – 'She said she could not tell' – indicates that she may have been beyond helping with the problems that her husband faced, especially his pronounced mood swings. Therefore, although 'with joy I told my Wife, O now I know, I know!', what he really wanted to do was convey his experience in 'the company of some of Gods people'.[108] Bunyan was now about to move into fuller integration with Bedford's local 'company of some of Gods people', a congregation whose rapid development in the1650s we should now briefly review.

In company with other gathered congregations in seventeenth-century England, Bedford's church, under the ministry of John Gifford, inserted into its records a brief account of its origins and evolution. The historical preamble of the minute book of the Bedford gathered church is imprecise as to dating. It may be that, some seven or so years before Gifford gave institutional shape to a covenanted church in the 1650s, there was a previous separatist congregation founded in Bedford, shortly after the outbreak of the first Civil War. However, the Bedford church's own historical notes strongly suggest that the church to which Gifford helped to give institutional identity, even though it may have been preceded by an organized fellowship around 1643, in fact emerged out of an earlier, looser association of individuals from the period when separatist anti-episcopalianism was given a sharper edge by the close alignment between episcopacy and ritualism under Archbishop Laud in the 1630s.[109] Even so, this local group of 'persons godly', not yet forming a 'visible Church Communion', may have retained links with the Established Church. Dissident groups certainly did this, under the 'semi-separatism' pioneered by Henry Jacob. Association with the Church of England took the particular form of attendance at services where godly but conformable ministers preached. Bedford's proto-church of semi-dissidents from the Church of England seems, in its first period, to have maintained such links, and only *'in some measure'* to have separated. When episcopacy broke down in 1643, this earlier fellowship may have coalesced into something more formally organized, but definite gatherings of the local godly can be dated only from 1650 onwards.[110]

A crucial role in the setting up of a covenanted church of visible saints in Bedford and the surrounding area was assumed by Gifford. He was a remarkable individual, a former Royalist army officer whose life before religious conversion and whose subsequent career made up an edifying narration of debauchery giving way to holiness. Gifford persuaded veteran 'saintes and brethren' to overcome their hesitations about forming a 'separate and close communion' and join in covenanted fellowship. Some of these individuals were well placed in local society. John Grew, for example, was twice mayor of Bedford and a justice of the peace; John Eston, also a justice, was three times mayor of the borough. Such cases help us to modify, if not negate, Bunyan's depiction of the church in Bedford as a community of 'poor' people.[111] Once again, we find that his preconceptions about the holiness of poverty influenced his perceptions.

Entrenched to a considerable extent in local society and politics, the Bedford church became enmeshed with local and national ecclesiastical structures. This 'separate' church lost much of its separateness in the 1650s. The parochial incumbency of St John's, once a medieval hospital chapel and in the gift of the town corporation, was made over to Gifford and his fellowship in 1653, and the congregation was thereby brought into the broad-based national church of the Cromwellian 1650s. As vicar, Gifford may well have had responsibilities to the parish of St John at large, as well as his pastorate of the select congregation worshipping on the premises of the parish church. Such an arrangement, often found in the Cromwellian church system, might explain Bunyan's later remarks that he began his preaching in Bedford 'in private', that is, to the more restricted gathered congregation rather than in the wider parish assembly.[112]

Such, then, was the church to which Bunyan gravitated during his spiritual trials of the first half of the 1650s – the church which he joined around 1655 and of whose ministry he became part after the middle of the decade. This church was long-established, at least in terms of its embryonic pre-history, was closely integrated into the life of the town, and became involved for a while in the local ecclesiastical system; it had a learned minister and a senior membership of spiritually experienced 'antient professors ... antient and grave Christians'. Calvinist in theology, Congregational (or 'Independent') in government, this church generally followed the principle of believers' baptism following conversion to newness of life.[113]

As for Bunyan, there is some hint of improvement in his material as well as his spiritual, circumstances after about 1655. Four children – two daughters, Mary and Elizabeth, and two sons, John and Thomas – were born before 1658. In 1655 there was a permanent move from the Bunyans' residence in his birthplace, the village of Elstow, to Bedford. The move probably had as much to do with changes (and perhaps an improvement) in Bunyan's work as with the need to be close to Gifford's congregation.

Because of the nature of *Grace Abounding* as a biography of a soul, it is difficult to find out much from the book about the conditions of Bunyan's employment. Incidental allusions to his journeys and contacts – 'one day I walked to a neighbouring Town ... in a good mans Shop' – help us to glimpse the life of a travelling tinker, and may suggest that his labour in his 'calling' simply went on alongside recurrent spiritual crisis. There is, however, one hint that Bunyan's swings from dejection to elevation threatened his work in the world, a foremost ethical priority in his Puritan code: 'such strange apprehensions of the Grace of God, that I could hardly bear up under it ... if that sense of it had abode long upon me, it would have made me uncapable for business'.[114]

The greater serenity that descended upon Bunyan after the mid-1650s released energies for creative activity, first preaching, then writing. As well as his 'calling' as a craftsman, Bunyan was to receive another 'call', from the Bedford church to serve in its ministry. In the autobiography, Bunyan recounted the steps in his emergence as a minister: five or six years after he had first been 'awakened', he was asked by a number of experienced members of the church to provide them all with a verbal account of God's dealings with him. This sounds like the kind of testimony of conversion that was delivered in gathered churches by each new entrant upon his or her reception. *Grace Abounding* is a vastly expanded version of such an experiential testimony. As we have seen, the autobiography conveys the depths of spiritual experience with moving narrative power. This quality of authenticity seems to have been readily recognized by the highly discerning leaders of the Bedford church, resulting in invitations to Bunyan to speak in 'Assemblies' as a preacher and to deliver words of 'Exhortation', 'at which ... they were both affected and comforted, and gave thanks to the Father of Mercies for the grace bestowed on me'.[115]

Bunyan's profound knowledge of Scripture and his combination of deep spiritual experience and articulacy in expressing it clearly made him an effective preacher. Bedford's church was the nucleus of other linked communities in the surrounding villages. When preaching members of the Bedford church went on tours to these neighhbouring communities, Bunyan at first accompanied them, as a trainee. At this stage, he spoke not 'in an open way' but 'more privately', 'amongst the good People'. That is to say, as in Bedford, where he had spoken 'in private', Bunyan was addressing gathered church groups of proven 'saints'. These well-received experiments in preaching led to a further call to a 'publick' preaching ministry, following the customary routines of prayer, fasting and an appointment by the collective 'call' of the church. The Bedford church book records the beginning of his ministry as a preacher (not a fully fledged pastor but, as we might say, a 'lay preacher') 'some time in the year 1656'. Bunyan himself records that his ministry was both to 'them that believed, but also to ... those who had not yet received the faith'. That is to say, he was an evangelist and a missionary. The movement to which he belonged was, at this time, very much a missionary one: hence the competition between himself and his church on the one hand and, on the other, a rival contemporary expansionist movement, the Quakers.[116]

Bunyan had initially responded to invitations to preach with shy misgivings: 'it did much dash and abash my spirit ... I did not, nor durst not make use of my Gift in an open way'. Despite these hesitations, the warm reception given to his preaching injected a powerful current of confidence into him. He discovered a natural 'secret pricking forward' to express his 'Gift'. Perhaps some of the contrast we see between the young Bunyan as a tortured neurotic and his middle-aged persona as a serene and benign 'Great-heart' can be accounted for by the cumulative therapeutic benefits of giving expression to talents, or to genius.[117]

Bunyan's *A brief Account of the Author's Call to the Work of the Ministry*, a supplement to *Grace Abounding*, is also an integral part of it, since it continues the discourse on God's dealings with the author. Though *A brief Account* deals with the conduct of a public ministry, it continues to examine internal states. This is because of the close relationship between Bunyan's public activity as a preacher and his internal condition as a Christian. Self-analysis is still to the fore, and it is clear from his account that Bunyan remained, at least in the earlier part of his public ministry, a prey to chronic religious anxiety:

> I was most sorely afflicted with the firy darts of the devil concerning my eternal state … I have been as one sent to them from the dead; I went my self in chains to preach to them in chains, and carried that fire in my own conscience that I perswaded them to beware of … when I have been to preach, I have gone full of guilt and terrour … I have been violently assaulted with thoughts of blasphemy.[118]

However, the activity of preaching was therapeutic: 'I have been at liberty in my mind until I have done my [preaching] work.' In the first phase of his preaching ministry, Bunyan emphasized the guilt that he still felt. This was like what Fox called 'pleading for sin'. Around 1658 the tenor of Bunyan's preaching changed in emphasis, from guilt to grace. Because, as he said, he preached what he felt – 'what I smartingly did feel' – there was a direct connection between his inner state and the content of his sermons. During the guilt-laden earlier period of his ministry, his preaching had the effect that his auditors were 'greatly afflicted in their minds at the apprehension of the greatness of their sin'. When a 'staid peace and comfort' settled on him around 1658, probably in part as a result of the self-confidence that came from his effectiveness as a preacher, he 'altered' his preaching – 'for still I preached what I saw and felt' – and preached 'blessed Grace'.[119]

The character of Bunyan's audiences may also have partly altered. As a preacher of guilt – brilliant, terrified and terrifying – Bunyan was addressing hearers who flocked into Bedford from 'the Countrey': 'they came in to hear the Word by hundreds, and that from all parts'. These auditors were probably members of the gathered churches and their fellow-travellers, coming to hear a preacher whose reputation was rising fast among the congregations. It seems that, as Bunyan's preaching shifted away from guilt, the character – and the locations – of his audiences changed. Whereas earlier they had come to him from the churches of saints, to Bedford, he now started to go out to wider auditories, throughout the county and, perhaps, in the wider region: '[M]y Ministry, was, to get into the darkest places in the *Countrey*, even amongst those people that were furthest off of profession ... because I found my spirit leaned most after awakening and converting Work'.[120]

The phrase 'darkest places in the *Countrey*' brings to mind the Puritan expression whose connotations have been examined by Hill: 'the dark corners of the land'. These were parts of the country seen as sunk in ignorance and needing a missionary approach. Though Bedfordshire was not notorious as one of those areas, Bunyan, in taking his gospel from the county town to its rural hinterland, was embarking on missionary work, and, indeed, joining the long procession of English itinerant preachers – like his contemporary Fox and his successor Wesley. His church acknowledged his shift to itinerancy and the demands it made on his time: 'brother Bunyan being taken off by the preaching of the Gospell ... our brother Bunyan being otherwise imployed'. It is also possible that the theological and soteriological emphases of his preaching altered in line with his new, essentially missionary, calling.[121]

W. T. Whitley drew attention to (and may have overstated) inhibitions about missionary work amongst Particular Baptists as a result of the doctrine of pre-determined election as developed in English Calvinism: 'their belief in absolute predestination emasculated all preaching for conversion'.[122] This means that, under the doctrine of specific election, the usefulness of broadcast preaching became questionable in the minds of some ultra-predestinarians amongst the Particular Baptists; the number of the elect was already made up and could hardly be expanded through even the most ardent preaching. In contrast, a non-predestinarian approach – that of Fox, for example – led to the conclusion that, since people had a choice of salvation or damnation and their manner of life affected the outcome, it was profoundly important to bring the Gospel to their attention and offer them the choice. In that case, a particular soteriological outlook resulted in active missionary preaching; with Bunyan, by a kind of reverse process, his work of evangelical preaching may even have re-shaped his soteriological outlook, softening the rigours of hyper-determinist predestinarianism, as he responded to the possibilities of decision-making on the part of his auditors – thereby, in turn, enhancing his homiletic appeal.

As Bunyan lessened his emphasis on guilt, the content of his preaching shifted subtly away from predestination. He seems to suggest that he modified the content of his preaching to suit the needs and character of his new audiences, who welcomed the missionary approach: 'I found my spirit leaned most after awakening and converting Work, and the Word that I carried did lean itself most that way.' Though the church he joined was suffused with Calvinist thinking, Bunyan had also been strongly influenced by Luther, for whom justifying faith was more important than election and for whom predestination was not as explicitly salient as it became for the Calvinist school, especially in England. A slight note of unconscious Arminianism seems to have crept into Bunyan's outlook and preaching, and indeed to have been inserted as a result of his preaching. His view of himself as 'Gods Instrument that shewed to them the Way of Salvation' does not, with its generous understanding of conversion and its pointer to freedom of choice, sound entirely consistent with the strictest predestinarian doctrines, least of all as these were developed, beyond Calvin's own positions, by his disciples, especially William Perkins, in England, in particular in the period from the 1580s to the 1620s. Any discernible move on Bunyan's part away from predestinarian doctrine should not be exaggerated. He must be placed firmly within the English Calvinistic tradition. It does appear, though, that during the height of his early career as a missionary preacher at large, in the later 1650s, Bunyan's 'preaching for conversion' was not 'emasculated' by 'belief in absolute predestination'.[123]

There is no mistaking Bunyan's success and popularity as a preacher at this time. The senior members of the Bedford congregation were right in detecting that his personal, fervent tone would reach others: 'they came in to hear the Word by hundreds'. The success of this preaching rested on its realism and its consequent power to stir others by reciting one man's experience. Even in the cold print of *Grace Abounding*, an enthralling personal drama is conveyed. Clearly, the oral recitation of his story made for riveting preaching. Apart from this appealing experiential tone, the doctrinal content attracted through its stark simplicity: 'the Doctrine of Life by Christ, without Works', the plain doric column of Reformation theology. Not only was this simplicity well geared to 'the darkest places in the *Countrey*', it was also entirely in line with Baptist attitudes to essentials and inessentials.[124]

It was indeed vital to all the churches within the English separatist tradition to adhere to basics and play down superficial and unimportant matters. At the beginning of the seventeenth century the English separatist expatriate churches in the Netherlands had been torn apart by division, often over trivial matters. Disagreement was a threat to the very survival of small congregations which were made up of believers well versed in dogma and its niceties. The danger could be averted by exalting the principle of 'fellowship' and by upholding tolerance of the ideas of other church members beyond a certain consensus on essentials. In his last message to the Bedford church, for instance, Gifford issued a warning against discord over minor matters. These things, he wrote, could cause 'separation from the Church about baptism, laying on of hands, annointing with oil, psalms, or any externals'.[125] Bunyan, too, was inclined to place a whole range of external practices and secondary beliefs under a heading of inessentials over which tolerance of disagreement was appropriate: 'I never cared to meddle with things that were controverted, and in dispute amongst the Saints, especially things of the lowest nature.'[126]

Such latitude was to characterize Bunyan throughout his ministerial career. It conditioned his attitude to the vexed question of believers' baptism as a prerequisite for membership in the church of which he was a leading member. His eirenic attitude can be seen in his 1672 work, *A Confession of My Faith, and A Reason of My Practice in Worship,* and in the controversy that flowed from it. As part of this broad outlook, Bunyan also rejected precise denominational labelling: 'I tell you I would be, and hope I am, A CHRISTIAN ... [A]s for those titles of Anabaptists, Independents, or the like, they came ... from hell and Babylon.'[127]

Bunyan's attitude to doctrinal tolerance and his avoidance of labelling brought him into conflict with members of the clerical and academic establishment of the 1650s. His openness on some questions of faith and practice contrasted with the intellectual precision sought by seventeenth-century academia with its ingrained habits of classifying and defining. Further, a much-discussed issue of the day – the right of unqualified 'mechanic' preachers to teach – was once more raised by Bunyan's activities. On one side of the dispute stood the more orthodox wings of English Puritanism, especially Presbyterianism, with its formidable intellectual resources. In opposition, there was a non- and anti-academic thrust in Puritanism, especially in its radical and separatist forms: we have already seen something of this in our earlier discussion of Bunyan's academic qualifications – or lack of them. This anti-academic movement gained ground in the 1650s, when all the bulwarks of the traditional establishment – legal, political, clerical, social and academic – were under attack. The message of emancipation, especially in the field of religion, was that unschooled orators might speak and teach. Such individuals – women as well as men – were open to ridicule from conservative foes, who called them 'tub-preachers', that is to say, artisans who presumed to supplant a highly trained graduate ministry.[128]

Bunyan was fully within this lineage of 'mechanic' preachers. They had a convincing defence to offer for preaching without formal qualifications. For one thing, the way in which they maintained themselves by the work of their hands (reminiscent of Paul the tentmaker) obviated any allegations of preaching for mercenary motives, or so as to exploit the lay people through tithes – as the professional 'hireling' ministry was often seen as doing. Some of these lay preachers justified their credentials in terms of prophecy and direct illumination. Bunyan stressed instead the training of a bitter spiritual travail and a deep knowledge of the Scriptures. Without a doubt, plebeian ministers, such as Bunyan, were well qualified to convey a simple message to numbers of ordinary people. Some members of the existing academically trained clergy were themselves sympathetic to the claims of the mechanic preachers. In the world-turned-upside-down atmosphere of England in the 1650s, much of academia was itself in revolt against academicism, and many of the clergy turned anticlerical. Fox, another classic artisan preacher, recorded conversions of existing ministers to his faith. In Bunyan's case, a distinguished don, William Dell – rector of Yeldon, Bedfordshire, fellow of one of Cambridge's leading Puritan seminaries, Emmanuel College, and eventually to become master of Gonville and Caius – made his pulpit available, saying (it was later alleged against him) 'he had rather hear a plain countryman speak in the church that came from the plough than the best orthodox minister that was in the country'.[129]

Even before his rapport with Dell, at the start of his ministry 'the Doctors and Priests of the Countrey [county] did open wide against' Bunyan. Eventually, in 1659 Bunyan and his preaching became the starting point for a fresh round in the continuing debate over professional versus charismatic qualifications for the ministry. When the Cambridge librarian and professor of Arabic, Thomas Smith, called into question Bunyan's commission to preach, another Cambridge man, Henry Denne, came to his defence. Denne emphasized the practical suitability of an artisan preacher to do the kind of missionary work that Bunyan specialized in – bringing the gospel to 'those people that were furthest off of profession'. Denne asked whether a 'congregation may not find some fitting men full of faith and the Holy Ghost to preach to … unbelieving heathens'.[130] This controversy, in which Denne took up Bunyan's defence, was in fact conducted with reference to those archetypal mechanic preachers, the Quakers. Smith's attack on Bunyan's preaching was entitled *The Quaker Disarmed* (1659) and Denne's riposte *The Quaker no Papist*. As a counter-revolutionary mood gained ground in the later 1650s, ultimately to lead to the Restoration, Quakers were identified by conservative opinion-makers as the epitome of the anarchy that had allegedly followed the execution of Charles I and the onset of religious toleration. Bunyan and the Quaker mechanic preachers were on the same side of the divide between defenders and assailants of the university-trained clergy. However, for all the similarity between Bunyan, with his supporters, and the Quakers on the issue of academic versus non-academic validation, they were in fact doctrinal opponents. Bunyan's first writings arose out of his theological dispute with Quakerism. In *Some Gospel-Truths Opened* (1656) and its sequel of the following year, *A Vindication of Some Gospel-Truths Opened*, Bunyan restated what he insisted was the scriptural truth of 'the *Divine and Human Nature of Christ Jesus*' against the spiritualizing trend that he detected in Quaker Christology.[131]

Bunyan composed his recollections of his missionary work around the themes of reception – 'they came in to hear the Word by hundreds' – or rejection – 'the wicked World hath raged' – of his message. Curiously enough, amongst the allegations against him was the charge that he was 'a Jesuit'. There was little in his theology to sustain such a claim: his preoccupation with sin and guilt certainly clashed with the Jesuits' alleged moral leniency. As we shall see, Bunyan's anti-Catholicism, though not hysterical, was of the standard seventeenth-century English Protestant kind. However, the propagandist charge that religious dissidents were papal agents in disguise was standard fare in the polemics of the period – one that Quakers (with rather more theological plausibility) also had to face. Bunyan also had to counter the accusations – and did so at length and vehemently – that his ministry created opportunities for sexual promiscuity. Much of his primness comes across in his denial of claims that he belonged, as it were, in an amoral 'world of the Ranters'. On this note of self-defence, Bunyan brings to a close his account of his public ministry as an essential part of his autobiography.[132]

The final section of Bunyan's account of himself deals with one of the most creative periods of his life, his imprisonment. *A brief Account of the Authors Imprisonment* forms, like the preceding narrative of his ministry, an integral part of *Grace Abounding* in its role as a spiritual autobiography. Bunyan's imprisonment and his account of it also enable us to locate him in the context of the drama going on around, as well as within him in the second half of the 1650s. Bunyan's church, if not Bunyan himself, was committed to a national radical movement which suffered its most serious defeat with the Restoration in 1660. Like other churches of its kind, the Bedford gathered church had a democratic ethos. Appointments of church officers were made in an entirely elective manner; Bunyan's own election to the pastorate, for instance, was brought about 'with joynt consent (signifyed by solemne lifting up of their hands)'. Women played a vital part in the life of the church: of the twelve founding members, eight were women. In the early 1650s the two members of the church who were on the corporation, aldermen John Eston and John Grew, brought the influence of the congregation's democratic ideals to bear in the council, in line with Gifford's egalitarian teachings: 'Let no respect of persons be in your comings-together. When you are met as a Church there's neither rich nor poor … ['T]is not a good practice to be offering places or seats when those who are rich come in.' It may also have been the case that anti-oligarchic council by-laws, identified in the reaction of the 1660s as 'Levelling Laws', were introduced in the 1650s thanks to the influence of the town's gathered church and its congregants who were council members.[133]

The commitment of the Bedford church to political radicalism in the nation at large is also evident in the 1650s. Eston and Grew, along with Gifford and Dell, signed a county-wide 'letter from the people of Bedford-shire' to Cromwell in 1653. With its call for men 'hateing covetousness' to 'govern these nations in righteousness', this letter pledged full support to the reformist, indeed partly messianic, Nominated Assembly of 1653. A few years later, a group of members of the Bedford church, again along with Dell, signed a petition, regarded by some of the establishment as seditious, against Cromwell's assuming the crown. The congregation unanimously expressed its relief when this threat to republicanism – 'the cause of God and the nation' – was averted.[134]

Nevertheless, the 1657 Humble Petition and Advice, which offered Cromwell the kingship, must be seen as part of a gathering conservative reaction in the later 1650s. Monarchy, including a possible Cromwellian monarchy, was coming to be regarded by conservatives as the most effective means of restoring lost subservience and hierarchy, whether in the church, the state or the family. Conservative Puritans, especially those labelled Presbyterians, bewailed the 'anarchy' of sects such as the Quakers, ushered in by what now appeared to be an ill-advised religious toleration. Bunyan himself was to be a victim of the accelerating conservatism of the late 1650s. For one thing, he was becoming the best-known individual in a church whose members, notably in 1653 and 1657, as well as through their influence in the council chamber, had shown their preference for liberty rather than order, equality rather than hierarchy and republicanism rather than monarchy. Moreover, the minister of the congregation, John Gifford, with his talk of 'the promises made to be accomplished in the latter dayes', had shown clear signs of the millenarianism that was increasingly identified with popular revolution.[135]

We shall have an opportunity later to explore Bunyan's social and political views more fully. It is worth noting that, of his nearly sixty published works, none directly concerns politics, and that one early production, the 1663 *Christian Behaviour* 'illustrates the conservatism of Bunyan's social views'. Conservative or not, there is every indication that Bunyan was not deeply interested in political questions, in view of the overwhelming priority of spiritual and religious issues in his scheme of things. However, he was a leader in a church which had taken a consistent radical line on political questions. Bunyan was also unmistakably a mechanic preacher. He himself confirmed such an identification around this time: in 1659 he recalled, 'I ... was brought up at my father's house in a very mean condition, among a company of poor countrymen'. Denne's defence of Bunyan in the same year, patronizing as it was, placed him in the ranks of the mechanic preachers, the 'tinker' who 'strives to mend souls as well as kettles and pans'. That is to say, Bunyan was identified with the educational and intellectual transformation that made up the real English revolution of the mid-seventeenth century. As a result of the expanded education and literacy that we considered earlier in this chapter, considerable numbers of a whole generation of plebeian English people had emancipated themselves intellectually from the ancient thraldoms of monarchy, nobility, gentry, clergy and academia. In part, Bunyan's offence was to be linked with that social and intellectual revolution and emancipation that flowered in the middle decades of the seventeenth century.[136]

The impact on Bunyan of the mounting campaign against the intellectual liberation of artisans and 'mechanicals' can be traced both in *Grace Abounding* and in the minutes of Bunyan's church. There was an orchestrated attempt to vilify him: 'It began therefore to be rumoured up and down among the People, that I was a Witch, a Jesuit, a Highway-man, and the like.' Apart from slander, there was recourse to law. In 1658 the Bedford church book recorded 'the indictment against brother Bunyan at the Assizes, for preaching at Eaton'.[137] It is not clear what the charge was on this occasion and the indictment itself was almost certainly abortive. In 1658 the moment was not yet opportune for a successful prosecution of an unauthorized plebeian preacher. However, Bunyan was arrested and imprisoned in 1660. The political circumstances and legal details of that cardinal moment in his career will be more fully examined when we consider the unfolding of his life after the Restoration. Here, we shall consider the account that Bunyan gives of his imprisonment in *Grace Abounding* in terms of the autobiography's narration of the dealings of God with an individual soul.

To sum up Bunyan's situation in the period before the Restoration, from the mid-1650s his protracted spiritual anguish was largely overcome. Lingering elements of disturbance seem to have been dispersed by the challenges and stimuli of evangelical preaching. As with Fox, once Bunyan's spiritual trial was over, the introspective solitary became a 'publick' figure. His preaching was well received, he gave considerable attention to improving its impact and he worried, not overmuch, about the evident and (in sharp contrast with his earlier self-loathing) entirely healthy self-esteem, conferred upon him by the expression of his 'Gifts'. He was increasingly called in for personal counselling of church members, a role in which the psychic sensitivity gained from his own experiences must have been particularly useful.[138] With his temporal 'calling' also demanding his attention, Bunyan was fully occupied. On the domestic front, his first wife died in 1658 and, with four children to look after, he conformed to the usual seventeenth-century pattern (as his father had) of a speedy remarriage, in 1659. Then, in 1660 came the cataclysm of a restoration of the Anglican monarchy, which, for Bunyan, meant imprisonment and the end of his highly visible preaching activities. He was not to be punished for what he had done or not done in the past, but was presented with options for his future. He was offered a plain choice, and the decision was his: cease preaching and avoid gaol, or preach and accept it: 'the Justices did sentence me … because I refused to Conform'. We need to consider the possibility of a kind of egoism in Bunyan's acceptance of imprisonment, and in particular his response to the possibility, in close confinement, of educational and spiritual development.[139]

Indeed, for Bunyan, prison did turn into a vital educational experience in personal maturation, just as it had for John Lilburne, who had made use of his imprisonment for self-discovery.[140] Bunyan's prison education took him into deeper meanings in Scripture :

> I have continued with much content … I have also received, among many things, much conviction, instruction, and understanding … I never had in all my life so great an inlet into the Word of God as now; them Scriptures that I saw nothing in before, are made in this place and state to shine upon me; Jesus Christ also was never more real and apparent then now … I have had sweet sights of the forgiveness of my sins in this place … I have seen that here, that I am perswaded I shall never, while in this world, be able to express.[141]

Thus, prison was a rewarding experience for Bunyan because, alongside his deeper insights into Scripture, he gained perceptions of the ineffable. As part of his contemplation of the Bible, he pondered Matthew 10: 37, which he rendered as, '*He that loveth father or mother, son or daughter, more than me, is not worthy of me*'. Standing in the way of Bunyan's wholehearted appreciation of the spiritual and educational benefits of prison was his awareness of his family. He was inclined to discount this as a worldly property and pleasure, which he needed to renounce along with his liberty:

'even to reckon my Self, my wife, my Children, my health, my enjoyments, and all, as dead to me, and my self as dead to them'. He saw temptation in the pull of natural affections: 'I found myself a man, and compassed with infirmities; the parting with my Wife and poor Children hath oft been to me in this place as the pulling the flesh from my bones ... because I am somewhat too fond of these great mercies.'[142] Like Christian in *The Pilgrim's Progress*, with his four children who were 'very dear' to him, Bunyan had to abandon family as a pre-condition of his progress to his goal. Alongside his affections, Bunyan recalled his parental duties. He was poignantly aware of the needs of his blind ten-year old daughter Mary who was especially dear to him because of her vulnerability:

> Poor Child! thought I, what sorrow art thou like to have for thy portion in this world? Thou must be beaten, must beg, suffer hunger, cold, nakedness, and a thousand calamities, though I cannot now endure the wind should blow upon thee; but yet ... thought I, I must venture you all with God.[143]

What considerations might have weighed so heavily with Bunyan that he could contemplate the abandonment of his family to a fate so starkly depicted? In the first place, there was trust in Providence inspired by Scripture – '*Leave thy fatherless children ... Verily it shall be well with thy remnant*' – perhaps accompanied by confidence that his church would help look after his dependants during his absence. However, the main reason Bunyan gives for accepting imprisonment and thereby forsaking his family was not trust in God in the 'concernments' of this world. Nor, in accepting imprisonment, was Bunyan calculating the personal benefits of retirement and contemplation, a lengthy coenobitic retreat. He had no illusions about the practical horrors of his incarceration for himself and his loved ones. Outweighing these awarenesses, and giving him no real alternative to going to gaol, was his 'dread of the torments of Hell' if he capitulated. Today some might see a kind of selfishness in Bunyan's anxiety to avoid his damnation by a jealous God. Seen from a modern point of view, Bunyan was ducking the demands of parenthood, and for the sake of afterlife prospects which many, if not most, regard today as, at best, metaphors. A modern judgement might be that Bunyan's primary responsibility as a man and, indeed, as a Christian was to his family and their welfare. However, Bunyan was not a modern man. Though his paternal affection was painfully strong, the termini of heaven and hell were as real to him as any temporal consequences. It is also the case that he had recently emerged from a chronic psychic crisis over his perceived 'betrayal' of Christ and could not face a second, and inevitably more disastrous, trauma, to be brought on this time by a more objectively identifiable betrayal were he to renounce his preaching activities.[144] Like Luther, who in 1521 could face the prospect of burning almost calmly, rather than recant the beliefs that meant everything to him, Bunyan could accept prison as the price of the avoidance of a relapse into the deepest pit of misery.

Bunyan draws *Grace Abounding* towards a close at the point where he has achieved the status of a martyr. The Conclusion, with its numerically sub-divided sections, brings to an orderly end this majestic spiritual autobiography, whose Preface apologized for its lack of literary artistry: the work is in fact constructed with a high degree of craft. [145] It seems clear that this Preface to *Grace Abounding* is in fact the final addition to the entire production and forms a distinct creation. The Conclusion is of a piece with the main body of the work, and retains much of its tone of tension and anguish. There are references, for instance, to 'my spirit so filled with darkness', and Bunyan once more recalls the almost physical force of those scriptural texts which, in the autobiography, he had imagined warring over him: 'I have sometimes seen more in a line of the Bible then I could well tell how to stand under.' There is, again, the sharp recollection of swings from depression to spiritual exultation: 'Of all tears, they are the best that are made by the Blood of Christ; and of all joy, that is the sweetest that is mixt with mourning over Christ; O 'tis a goodly thing to be on our knees, with Christ in our arms.' These passages are reminiscent of the raptures of the medieval mystics, with Bunyan himself in a *pietà* scene.[146]

In contrast, the resonances of the autobiography's Preface are serene, and when spiritual extremes are recalled, it is a case of the recollection of emotion in tranquillity: '*I can remember my fears, and doubts, and sad moneths, with comfort.*' The contrast in tone is explained by the difference between the persona that Bunyan adopts in the Conclusion from that in the Preface. In the former, the author is still essentially what he had been throughout the autobiography – an anguished, if justified, sinner: 'I find to this day seven abominations in my heart.' In the Preface, on the other hand, he adopts the cadences of one who has been tested in the fire and annealed and whose example would be of benefit 'to those whom God hath counted him [Bunyan] worthy to beget to Faith'. It is the tone of a pastoral letter from a father in God to disciples from whom he is separated. Not only is its voice pastoral, it is also paternal, Johannine: '*Children, Grace be with you* ... The father to the children shall make known the truth of God ... *My dear Children.*' Not surprisingly, there is an allusion to the progenitor of the Christian pastoral epistle written at a distance from its recipients: '*I thank God upon every Remembrance of you ... It was Pauls accustomed manner.*'[147]

In the Preface, then, Bunyan chose a tone of voice – level, magisterial – rather different from the tense style, 'fascinating in its excited, nervous prose and pathological obsessiveness', that he had deployed throughout most of *Grace Abounding*. Indeed, he was fully aware of the various styles and voices open to him. One was '*a stile much higher then this in which I have here discoursed*' in the body of the autobiography. Perhaps this reference to his capacity for a more elevated prose needs to be taken into account when we consider his remarks about his formal education. It seems that Bunyan did not use a plain style because it was the only one available to him. Indeed, the Preface points to an elaboration and complexity – indeed, a 'conceit' – of metaphor, contrasting with the simplicity and immediacy of the figures of speech in the main text of the work.[148] However, simplicity and immediacy were carefully selected by Bunyan as an artist, so as to advance the purposes of his work and to reflect its nature. The autobiography, as well as being just that, also had two other personae – testament and sermon – and each of these suggested a certain stylistic approach. In the first place, the work should be seen as a composed literary version of those testimonies of conversion which preceded membership in the gathered churches. The author's purpose was '*to open before his Judges, the manner of his Conversion*' – the '*Judges*' being, in the first instance, those existing members of the church who were qualified to evaluate the authenticity of the experience being recounted. Expanded, set down in writing and published, this edifying account would be of considerable help and comfort to readers in a state of mind similar to that which Bunyan described. With such a readership in mind, he employs an intimate, conversational tone, based on the speech conventions used when unfolding a religious experience to a small, attentive audience: 'I thought verily, as I have told you' and 'Well, about two or three dayes after.' The effectiveness of this kind of person-to-person mode – of the seminar rather than the lecture theatre – is increased by Bunyan's use of a rapid and dramatic speech rhythm, heightening the emotional impact of the content in passages of special intensity, for example: 'Gold! could it have been gotten for Gold, what could I have given for it … converted men and women! they shone, they walked like a people that carried the broad Seal of Heaven about them' and '[S]aid the Tempter, Your sin is unpardonable. Well, said I, I will pray. 'Tis no boot, said he. Yet, said I, I will pray.'[149] The dialogue exchanges have a particularly gripping speed and urgency: Bunyan is already honing the realism and rapidity of dialogue that gives such force to works such as *The Pilgrim's Progress* and *The Life and Death of Mr. Badman*.

As well as being based stylistically on the format of an orally delivered experiential confession preceding church membership, *Grace Abounding* can also be considered as a kind of extended sermon – perhaps like those based on his own experiences that he delivered in the period before his arrest and imprisonment. Looking at it in this way, we find that many of the devices of language that Bunyan uses, especially his powerful, surprising images, were of a kind that a skilled preacher would employ when attempting to bring his material within the direct ken of his auditors. We know, from Bunyan's own account of his preaching, that he studied to give it maximum meaning to his hearers, with a view to increasing its missionary impact. Thus, as Sharrock says, in later editions of *Grace Abounding* he was moved by 'a desire to embellish experiences artistically, and to draw from his past fresh incidents likely to encourage and evangelize'. Bunyan analysed his own sermon technique from the viewpoint of the freshness and vividness of allusion: 'I never endeavoured to … make use of other men's lives … I have also observed, that a word cast in by the by hath done more execution in a Sermon then all that was spoken besides.'[150]

The individual style adopted by Bunyan in *Grace Abounding* did not preclude the most lavish use of Scripture. However, it is instructive to see the manner in which he employs scriptural citations in the body of the work, and one way to do this is to contrast a scriptural excursus in the Preface with the routine deployment of biblical allusions in the main body of the text. Since the Preface has the character of a cover-letter written to fellow-members of the church, Bunyan is confident enough to develop within it an elaborate allegory, which assumes extensive scriptural knowledge on the part of that group of readers. In the main body of the autobiography, in contrast, when Bunyan cites the Scriptures, as he does constantly, he does so literally and didactically and does not assume much, or any, prior biblical knowledge. That is to say, considered as a sermon, *Grace Abounding* fell within the established tradition of Puritan educational homiletics in introducing audiences to numerous passages from the word of God. The preacher could hardly use the Scriptures as a quarry for figures of speech if he was, in fact, providing in his sermon an introduction to the Bible for novices. However, since a sermon without similes would lose all the vitality that Bunyan aimed to inject into his preaching, he needed to use analogies – but only those well within the range of experience of his wider public, even of scripturally uninstructed members of a missionary audience or readership. Frequently, in fact, the images are grounded in rural life and work: '[His heart] was as a clog on the leg of a Bird to hinder her from flying … [I] did compare my self in the case of such a Child, whom some Gypsie hath by force took up under her apron, and is carrying from Friend and Country; kick sometimes I did.' Apart from these rustic analogies, Bunyan constructed an image that probably came from his brief spell of military service: 'I was often as if I had run upon the pikes, and as if the Lord had thrust at me.' Another figure is derived from the vagaries of Stuart coinage: 'those Graces of God that now were green in me, were yet but like those crack'd-Groats and Four-pence-half-pennies that rich men carry in their Purses, when their Gold is in their Trunks at home.'[151]

Images like that of the rich man carrying debased coins show considerable conscious artistry, though some others of Bunyan's figures of speech suggest less of art than of the subconscious. This applies particularly to his images of childhood. We have just looked at one of those – the haunting depiction of the kidnapped child. In another child metaphor, Bunyan likens Satan's insistent and eventually successful tempting to the 'continual rocking [that] will lull a crying Child asleep'. The third in this series of metaphors from childhood is particularly searing: 'I did liken myself in this condition unto the case of some Child that was fallen into a Mill-pit, who though it could make some shift to scrable and spraul in the water, yet because it could find neither hold for hand nor foot, therefore at last it must die in that condition.' In all these similes the child is used as the symbol for vulnerability and even intense danger. It is possible that the use of such analogies was suggested, at least to Bunyan's subconscious mind, by the peril that he envisaged his own family, and especially his blind daughter, to be facing during his imprisonment.[152]

Notes

1. John Bunyan, *Grace Abounding to the Chief of Sinners* (London, 1666; ed. Roger Sharrock, Oxford, 1962), p. 5. Newey adds: 'In *Grace Abounding*, probably the best-known example of Puritan autobiography, Bunyan presents his past with a mixture of interpretative formality and intimate fidelity to fact, circumstantial and especially psychological details being gathered into a demonstration of spiritual progress under Providence as Bunyan strives to identify in his own life a steady advance towards a state of convinced election, a goal often anticipated by hopeful stirrings of the heart but also frequently deferred by temptation and backslidings.' Vincent Newey, 'Wordsworth, Bunyan and the Puritan mind', *English Literary History* 41 (1974), p. 216. For a brief, useful introduction, see Paul Delaney, *British Autobiography in the Seventeenth Century* (London, 1969), pp. 88–93; see also Owen C. Watkins, *The Puritan Experience* (London, 1972), ch. 7. For an introduction to the political and religious background to Bunyan's life, see I. M. Green, 'Bunyan in Context' and Richard L. Greaves, 'John Bunyan:

The Present State of Historical Scholarship', in M. van Os and G. J. Schutte (eds), *Bunyan in England and Abroad* (Amsterdam, 1990), pp. 1–27 and 29.

2. *Grace Abounding*, p. 5.

3. John Brown, *John Bunyan: His Life, Times and Work* (2nd edn, London, 1886), pp. 21–8.

4. *Grace Abounding*, p. 5.

5. Richard Friedenthal, *Luther* (trans. John Nowell; London, 1967), p. 8.

6. *Grace Abounding*, p. 5. Hill suggests that Bunyan's ancestors had been driven into poverty through land sales: Christopher Hill, *The English Bible and the Seventeenth-Century Revolution* (London, 1993), p. 439.

7. See Paul Slack, *Poverty and Policy in Tudor and Stuart England* (London and New York, 1988), pp. 93, 95, 99.

8. Brown, *Bunyan*, pp. 301, 350–1.

9. *Grace Abounding*, p. 5.

10. Jaroslav Pelikan and Helmut T. Lehmann (eds), *Luther's Works* (55 vols; St Louis and Philadelphia, 1960–86), vol. 54: Theodore G. Tappert (ed. and trans.), *Table Talk* (Philadelphia, 1967), p. 458.

11. Matthew 5: 3; 1 Corinthians 1: 26.

12. Ronald S. Wallace, *Calvin's Doctrine of the Christian Life* (Edinburgh and London, 1959), p. 177.

13. Robin Jeffs (ed.), *The English Revolution Fast Sermons to Parliament* (27 vols; London, 1970–1), vol. 4, p. 33.

14. Tappert (ed.), *Table Talk*, pp. 178, 188.

15. N. H. Keeble (ed.), *The Autobiography of Richard Baxter* (abridged J. M. Lloyd Thomas, London and Melbourne, 1974), pp. 4–7.

16. John L. Nickalls (ed.), *The Journal of George Fox* (Cambridge, 1952), pp. xxxix, 1.

17. See Levin L. Schüking, *The Puritan Family: A Social Study from the Literary Sources* (trans. Brian Battershaw; London, 1969), ch. III.

18. Nickalls (ed.), *Journal of George Fox*, p. 1.

19. Keeble (ed.), *Autobiography of Richard Baxter*, pp. 4–5.

20. *Grace Abounding*, p. 5. For Bunyan, Fox and conversion, see Hugh Barbour, 'The "Openings" of Fox and Bunyan', in Michael Mullett (ed.), *New Light on George Fox 1624–1691: A Collection of Essays* (York, 1994), pp. 129–43.

21. *Grace Abounding*, p. 8.

22. *Ibid.*, p. 7.

23. *Ibid.*, pp. 9, 12; see also Vincent Newey, '"With the Eyes of my Understanding": Bunyan's Experience and Acts of Interpretation', in N. H. Keeble (ed.), *John Bunyan: Conventicle and Parnassus* (Oxford, 1988), p. 192.

24. For an analysis of Bunyan's problems in psychological terms, see William James, *The Varieties of Religious Experience: A Study in Human Nature* (38th impression; London, New York and Toronto, 1935), p. 157.

25. Compare, for example, Bunyan's 'Now I should find my minde to flee from

God, as from the face of a dreadful Judge' (*Grace Abounding*, p. 52) with Luther's 'That expression "righteousness of God" was like a thunderbolt in my heart … this righteousness was an avenging anger, namely the wrath of God' (Tappert (ed.), *Table Talk*, pp. 308–9). Luther recalled his punitive parents (*ibid.*, pp. 234–5). For discussion of a possible connection between Luther's view of God and his experiences of his father, see Erik H. Erikson, *Young Man Luther: A Study of Psychoanalysis and History* (London, 1959), esp. p. 67.

26. Brown, *Bunyan*, p. 41. *Hamlet*, I, ii; For speculation that Bunyan's father's remarriage was a 'brutal blow', see Jack Lindsay, *John Bunyan: Maker of Myths* (London, 1937; reprinted New York, 1969), pp. 10–11. For remarriage in seventeenth-century England, see Keith Wrightson, *English Society 1580–1680* (London, 1982), p. 103.

27. Julius Köstler, *Life of Luther* (London, 1883), p. 38.

28. Anne Laurence 'Bunyan and the Parliamentary Army', in Anne Laurence, W. R. Owens and Stuart Sim (eds), *John Bunyan and his England 1628–1688* (London and Ronceverte, WV, 1990), pp. 17–29.

29. Thomas F. Merrill (ed.), *William Perkins 1558–1602: English Puritanist* (Nieuwkoop, 1966), pp. 166ff.

30. *Grace Abounding*, pp. 7–8, 5. For the upbringing of children in seventeenth-century England, and in particular the discussion of whether or not children were loved, see Lawrence Stone, *The Family, Sex and Marriage in England 1500–1800* (London, 1977), pp. 112–13; A. Macfarlane, *Marriage and Love in England : Modes of Reproduction 1300–1840* (Oxford, 1985), p. 524; Patrick Collinson, 'The Protestant Family', in his *The Birthpangs of Protestant England: Religious and Cultural Change in the Sixteenth and Seventeenth Centuries* (Houndsmills, 1988), ch. 3. See also R. Houlbrooke, *The English Family 1450–1700* (London, 1984), and C. Shammas, 'The Domestic Environment in Early Modern England and America', *Journal of Social History* 14 (1980), pp. 3–24.

31. Merrill, *William Perkins*, p 160. English Calvinism's rigour in this regard was a departure from Calvin's own use of freedom, as in his playing of bowls on Sunday, to which activity Perkins took special exception; see David S. Katz, *Sabbath and Sectarianism in Seventeenth-Century England* (Leiden, New York, Copenhagen, Cologne, 1988), p. 4. See also Richard L. Greaves, 'The Origins of English Sabbatarian Thought', *Sixteenth Century Journal* 12 (1981), pp. 19–35.

32. See Christopher Hill, 'The Uses of Sabbatarianism', in his *Society and Puritanism in Pre-Revolutionary England* (London, 1964), pp. 145–218.

33. Keith L. Sprunger, 'English and Dutch Sabbatarianism and the Development of Puritan Social Theology, 1600–1660', *Church History* 51 (1982), pp. 24–38.

34. For the Declaration of Sports, as re-issued and extended by Charles I, see S. R. Gardiner (ed.), *The Constitutional Documents of the Puritan Revolu-*

tion 1625–1660 (3rd revised edn; Oxford, 1958), pp. 99–103; see also R. Hutton, *The Rise and Fall of Merry England: The English Ritual Year 1400–1700* (London, 1994).

35. *Grace Abounding*, pp. 6–11.
36. *Ibid.*, pp. 9–10; Hutton, *The Rise and Fall of Merry England*, pp. 170–1.
37. Joseph E. Illick, 'Child-rearing in Seventeenth-Century England and America', in Lloyd deMause (ed.), *The History of Childhood* (London, 1976), pp. 303–50.
38. For the 'educational revolution' and the expansion of literacy in the period *c.*1560–1640, see Lawrence Stone, 'The Educational Revolution in England, 1540–1640', *Past and Present* 38 (1964), pp. 41–80; Peter Clark, 'The Ownership of Books in England, 1560–1640: The Examples of Some Kentish Townsfolk', in Lawrence Stone (ed.), *Schooling and Society: Studies in the History of Education* (Baltimore, MD, and London, 1976), pp. 95–111; David Cressy, 'Levels of Illiteracy in England 1530–1730', *Historical Journal* 20 (1977), pp. 1–23; David Cressy, 'Literacy in Seventeenth-Century England: More Evidence', *Journal of Interdisciplinary History* 8 (1977), pp. 141–50; Margaret Spufford, 'The Schooling of the Peasantry in Cambridgeshire 1575–1700', in Joan Thirsk (ed.), *Land, Church and People: Essays Presented to Professor H. P. R. Finberg* (Reading, 1970), pp. 112–47. For what may have been Bunyan's school, see *The Victoria History of the County of Bedford* (3 vols; London, 1972), vol. 2, p. 180.
39. Jonson's plays, for instance, contain a steady stream of casual cursing, essentially derived from medieval piety and used as emphatic overtures to speech: 'Marry, sir, your brother … mass, I know not well … 'sdeath, you will not draw then?' (*Every Man in his Humour*, III, vi, vii). The use on the stage of such popish profanities cannot have improved the already strained relationship between the godly and the playwrights. However, one of Jonson's characters in *Every Man* uses an up-market form of un-profane humanistic swearing: 'By Pharaoh's foot', 'body of Caesar' (III, v).
40. Foster Watson, *The English Grammar Schools to 1660: Their Curriculum and Practice* (Cambridge, 1908), pp. 132–6.
41. *Grace Abounding*, p. 6.
42. Cressy, 'Levels of Illiteracy', pp. 1–23.
43. *Grace Abounding*, p. 5.
44. Brown, *Bunyan*, pp. 39–40.
45. *Ibid.*, p. 41.
46. *Grace Abounding*, p. 5; Brown, *Bunyan*, pp. 39–41. A grammar-school education, albeit attenuated, would certainly have equipped Bunyan for further study. Sharrock thought that his coherent and grammatical prose suggested a grammar schooling: Roger Sharrock, 'Bunyan and the book', in Keeble (ed.), *John Bunyan*, p. 74; Wakefield speaks of the 'Calvinist scholasticism which was his theological milieu': Gordon Wakefield, '"To be a Pilgrim": Bunyan and the Christian Life', in *ibid.*, pp. 113–14.

47. 1 Corinthians 1: 26–7.

48. On St Francis, see John Moorman, *A History of the Franciscan Order* (Oxford, 1968), p. 123; for Nicholas of Cusa, see Jasper Hopkins, *Nicholas of Cusa on Learned Ignorance: A Translation and an Appraisal of de Docta Ignorantia* (2nd edn; Minneapolis, MN, 1985), pp. 52–3; for Savonarola, Luther and Lilburne, see Michael A. Mullett, *Radical Religious Movements in Early Modern Europe* (London, 1980), pp. 28, 52, 62; for Winstanley, see Gerrard Winstanley, *The Law of Freedom in a Platform or, True Magistracy Restored* (New York, 1973), pp. 52–3, 70–1.

    For Puritanism and education, and especially Puritan anti-intellectualism, see: Richard L. Greaves, *The Puritan Revolution and Educational Thought: Background for Reform* (New Brunswick, NJ, 1969), esp. pp. 132–6 – elsewhere (in 'A Tinker's Dissent, a Pilgrim's Conscience', *Church History* 5 (1987), pp. 8–13), Greaves shows that Bunyan underestimated his formal education so as to expand his audience and magnify the Spirit's influence on him; Leo F. Solt, 'Anti-Intellectualism in the Puritan Revolution', *Church History* 24 (1956), pp. 306–16; William York Tindall, *John Bunyan: Mechanick Preacher* (New York, 1964), esp. pp. 79–90; and John Morgan, *Godly Learning: Puritan Attitudes towards Reason, Learning and Education* (Cambridge, 1986).

49. *Grace Abounding*, p. 5.

50. *Ibid.*, p. 10; Greaves, *Puritan Revolution*, pp. 118, 119. For attitudes to direct spiritual illumination, see G. F. Nuttall, *The Holy Spirit in Puritan Faith and Experience* (Oxford, 1947), ch. 3.

51. *Grace Abounding*, p. 7.

52. *Ibid.*, pp. 9, 59, 6, 9, 12, 25, 29, 19. On Bunyan's wishing to be of the people of Israel, Monica Furlong suggests that there may have been a confusion in his mind between being of the 'Israelites' and being descended from the 'Egyptians, to whom travelling tinkers, with their gypsy associations, were sometimes said to be kin': Monica Furlong, *Puritan's Progress: A Study of John Bunyan* (London, Sydney, Auckland and Toronto, 1975), p. 48.

53. Erikson, *Young Man Luther*, ch. 2, esp. pp. 34, 35–6; see also Vera J. Camden, 'Blasphemy and the Problem of the Self in *Grace Abounding*', *Bunyan Studies* 1, 2 (1989), esp. pp. 14–15.

54. Tappert (ed.), *Table Talk*, pp. 85, 95, 340. For Bunyan's wide and diverse reading in addition to Dent and Bayly, see Greaves, 'The Present State of Historical Scholarship', pp. 31–2, and Roger Sharrock, 'Bunyan Studies Today: An Evaluation' in van Os and Schutte (eds), *Bunyan in England and Abroad*, pp. 1–5; for Dent, see Maurice Hussey, 'John Bunyan and Arthur Dent', *Theology* 52 (1949), pp. 459–63.

55. T. H. L. Parker, *John Calvin* (London, 1975), appendix 2, p. 163.

56. *The Works of the Rev. John Wesley, A. M., Sometimes Fellow of Lincoln College, Oxford* (14 vols; London, 1840–20), vol. I, pp. 13, 16–17.

57. *Grace Abounding*, p. 9.

58. See below, pp. 151–8.

59. Delaney, *British Autobiography*, sections v and vi; Watkins, *The Puritan Experience*, ch. 7, for an excellent study of *Grace Abounding*.

60. *Grace Abounding*, p. 8.

61. Nickalls (ed.), *Journal of George Fox*, pp. 65, 67. For the chronology of *Grace Abounding* and an interesting suggestion that Bunyan's problems lay in 'temporal time' and the solution to them in 'an immortality not known in terms of time … the realities of the transtemporal', see E. Beatrice Batson, *John Bunyan: Allegory and Imagination* (London and Canberra, 1984), p. 19; see also Roger Sharrock, 'Temptation and Understanding in *Grace Abounding*', *Bunyan Studies* 1 (1988), pp. 11–12.

62. *Grace Abounding*, pp. 10–14, 11. For the date of Bunyan's demobilization, see Laurence, 'Bunyan and the Parliamentary Army', pp. 28–9. For Bunyan's physical type, see *A Brief Character of Mr. John Bunyan*, in *Grace Abounding*, appendix B, p. 174. The anatomist of melancholy, Robert Burton, using the same word – 'solace' – that Bunyan was to employ, spoke of 'May-games, Feasts, Wakes and merry meetings, to solace themselves, the very being in the Country', and, as a therapist, commended 'the King's declaration' and folk games to help 'such as are troubled in mind': Robert Burton, *The Anatomy of Melancholy* (New York, 1948), pp. 439, 446, 451–2. For guilt and *Grace Abounding*, see John Stachniewski, *The Persecuting Imagination: English Puritanism and the Literature of Despair* (Oxford, 1991), and for an interpretation of Bunyan's 'ringing', see *ibid.*, pp. 156–8. For Bunyan's use of the word 'guilt' meaning the committing of an offence, in contrast to the modern meaning of a subjective sense of offence, see Robert Claiborne, *English: Its Life and Times* (London, 1994), p. 75.

63. *Grace Abounding*, pp. 12–13.

64. Tappert (ed.), *Table Talk*, pp. 193–4 and n. 65; John Calvin, 'The Author's Preface to the Commentary on the Book of Psalms', in John Dillenberger (ed.), *John Calvin: Selections from his Writings* (Missoula, MT, 1975), p. 26. Anne Hawkins, in 'The Double Conversion in Bunyan's *Grace Abounding*', *Philological Quarterly* 61 (1982), pp. 259–76, describes Bunyan's as 'a kind of conversion which is by definition diffuse, repetitive and cumulative', (running counter to our expectation that conversions will be, like those described by Paul and Augustine, sudden and complete). For accounts of conversion, see Norman Pettit, *Grace and Conversion in Puritan Spiritual Life* (New Haven, CT, 1966), Patricia Caldwell, *Puritan Conversion Literature: The Beginning of American Expression* (Cambridge, 1993) and Nigel Smith, *Perfection Proclaimed: Language and Literature in English Radical Religion 1640–1660* (Oxford, 1989), pp. 33ff. For Bunyan's experiential chronology and the way he used it 'impressionistically' and with didactic artistry, see M. R. Watson, 'The Drama of *Grace Abounding*',

English Studies 46 (1965), pp. 471–82. Some further clarification on the chronology of Bunyan's conversion is provided in his *Doctrine of the Law and Grace Unfolded*: see below, pp. 144–5.

65. *Grace Abounding*, pp. 13, 14. For the idea, in Perkins, of mapping out 'A Chart of Salvation and Damnation', see H. C. Porter, *Puritanism in Tudor England* (London and Basingstoke, 1970), pp. 295–7.

66. For the position of women in the radical Puritan tradition to which Bunyan gravitated, see, *inter alia*, Claire Cross, '"He-Goats Before the Flocks": A Note on the Part Played by Women in the Founding of some Civil War Churches', in G. J. Cuming and D. Baker (eds), *Studies in Church History*, vol. 8 (Cambridge, 1972), pp. 195–202; and Keith Thomas, 'Women and the Civil War Sects', *Past and Present* 13 (1958), pp. 42–62.

67. *Grace Abounding*, notes, p. 137.

68. Bedford Church Book, quoted in Brown, *Bunyan*, p. 81.

69. *Grace Abounding*, p. 14.

70. *Ibid.*

71. *Ibid.*, pp. 14–36, 17; Nickalls (ed.), *Journal of George Fox*, pp. 47, 80–1, 113, 181–3; for the Ranters and their radical antinomianism, see A. L. Morton, *The World of the Ranters: Religious Radicalism in the English Revolution* (London, 1970) and Jerome Friedman, *Blasphemy, Immorality, Anarchy: The Ranters and the English Revolution* (Athens, OH, and London, 1986). J. C. Davis, in *Fear, Myth and History: The Ranters and the Historians* (Cambridge, 1986), claims that the Ranters were largely a fabrication of conservative propaganda in the 1650s; for this, and Bunyan and the Ranters, see Greaves, 'The Present State of Historical Scholarship', pp. 32–3.

72. *Grace Abounding*, pp. 14, 17, 33, 37.

73. *Ibid.*, pp. 19, 14, 30.

74. *Ibid.*, pp. 22, 24; Leviticus, ch. 1.

75. *Grace Abounding*, p. 17; James, *Varieties of Religious Experience*, p. 157.

76. *Grace Abounding*, pp. 21–3, 26, 30, 31, 34.

77. *Ibid.*, p. 33; see also Brainerd Stranahan, 'Bunyan's Special Talent: Biblical Texts as "Events" in *Grace Abounding* and *The Pilgrim's Progress*', *English Literary Renaissance* 11 (1981), pp. 329–36; for Bunyan's 'disclaiming locutions', presenting him as the passive experiencer of dynamic scriptural passages – according to conventions of Puritan spiritual autobiography, see Peter J. Carlton, 'Bunyan's Language, Convention, Authority', *English Literary History* 51 (1984), pp. 17–32; Sharrock, 'Temptation and Understanding', p. 6.

78. *Grace Abounding*, pp. 28, 27–33. In his important article locating Bunyan's recounted experiences within the traditions of Puritan literary self-disclosure, 'Spiritual Experience and Spiritual Autobiography', *The Baptist Quarterly* 32 (1988), pp. 393–402, Roger Pooley shows an 'incidental parallel' with William Perkins's reference to the relative enviability of 'A Dog or a Toad';

this seems a striking coincidence of similarity – unless perhaps Bunyan had read Perkins.

79. *Grace Abounding*, pp. 36, 26, 25.

80. For Greenham and the tradition of 'comforting wounded consciences', see Patrick Collinson, *The Elizabethan Puritan Movement* (London, 1967), pp. 128, 349.

81. Bedford Church Book, quoted in Brown, *Bunyan*, p. 194. For the theology of church covenants, see, for example, the Elizabethan separatist Henry Barrow, who explained that the true church was 'a companie and fellowship of faithful and holie people gathered', and 'To this societie is the covenant and all the promises made of peace, of love, and of salvation': Leland H. Carlson (ed.), *Elizabethan Nonconformist Texts, Volume III: The Writings of Henry Barrow 1587–1590* (London, 1962), pp. 214–15.

82. *Grace Abounding*, pp. 22, 24.

83. Nickalls (ed.), *Journal of George Fox*, pp. 103–4 ; *Grace Abounding*, p. 19.

84. Brown, *Bunyan*, p. 211.

85. *Grace Abounding*, pp. 19–20. For Milton's images of cold and warmth, see Lolette Kuby, 'The World is Half the Devil's: Cold–Warmth Imagery in *Paradise Lost*', *English Literary History* 41 (1974), pp. 182–91. Hill links Bunyan's dream to images of private property and trespass: 'In *Grace Abounding* Bunyan recorded dreaming of the congregation as a walled estate, into which he had to force his way': Hill, *The English Bible*, p. 149.

86. *Grace Abounding*, pp. 25, 37.

87. *Ibid.*, pp. 37–8.

88. Compare Bunyan's insistence on the historical reality of the Atonement won through the Crucifixion: see below, pp. 128, 131–2.

89. *Grace Abounding*, p. 41; Galatians 2: 16; 3: 11. Paul's influence on Bunyan was profound: see Margaret Olofson Thikstun, 'The Preface to Bunyan's *Grace Abounding* as Pauline Epistle', *Notes and Queries* 230 (1985), pp. 180–2.

90. *A Commentary on St. Paul's Epistle to the Galatians Based on Lectures Delivered by Martin Luther*, revised translation based on the English version of 1575, with introduction by Philip S. Watson (2nd impression; London, 1956), pp. 1–15, 17. I am grateful to my friend Ralph Gibson for the gift of the copy, a far better preserved one than Bunyan's, from his late father's library; *Grace Abounding*, p. 40. For Bunyan and Luther, see John R. Knott, jun., *The Sword and the Spirit: Puritan Responses to the Bible* (Chicago and London, 1971), pp. 132–4; also John Bossy, 'One More Allegory', *Bunyan Studies* 2, 1 (1990), pp. 79–80.

91. *Commentary on St Paul's Epistle*, pp. 22, 23, 136, 139; *Grace Abounding*, p.41.

92. Tindall, *John Bunyan*, pp. 34–5; *Grace Abounding*, pp. 41–3.

93. *Ibid.*, pp. 42, 44, 58, 52, 65.

94. *Ibid.*, pp. 55, 47, 59, 45.

95. *Ibid.*, pp. 50, 51, 68–9.

96. *Ibid.*, pp. 51, 41, 42. For an analysis of the 'forensic' approach to the Atonement in Calvinism, see F. Lyall, 'Of Metaphors and Analogies: Legal Language and Covenant Theology', *Scottish Journal of Theology* 32 (1979), pp. 1–17.

97. For an example from one of the great medieval mystics of feelings, very close to Bunyan's, of reciprocated 'pity' between Christ and the soul, see P. Franklin Chambers, *Juliana of Norwich: An Introductory Appreciation and an Interpretative Anthology* (London, 1955), pp. 91, 108.

98. *Grace Abounding*, pp. 42–65. For a classic analysis of spiritual aridity, see Cassian of Marseilles, 'Of Accidie', in Helen Waddell (trans. and intro.), *The Desert Fathers* (London, 1936; reprinted 1977), pp. 229–32. I am grateful to my friend Gordon Phillips for bringing this passage to my attention.

99. *Grace Abounding*, pp. 62, 64, 65. For Calvin's view of the authority of Scripture, see Parker, *John Calvin*, p. 77.

100. *Grace Abounding*, pp. 66–71; see also Sharrock, 'Temptation and Understanding', p. 6.

101. *Grace Abounding*, pp. 61, 66.

102. *Ibid.*, pp. 65, 70, 66, 72.

103. *Ibid.*, pp. 49 (and notes, p. 146), 57, 62.

104. *Ibid.*, pp. 72–82.

105. *Ibid.*, p. 77.

106. *Ibid.*, pp. 77–82.

107. *Ibid.*, p. 71.

108. *Ibid.*, p. 82. Bunyan also gives an insight into his relationship with his wife and his compassion for her during labour pains (*ibid.*, p. 75).

109. Bedford Church Book, quoted in Brown, *Bunyan*, pp. 76–7.

110. For Jacob's ecclesiology, see Michael Watts, *The Dissenters: From the Reformation to the French Revolution* (Oxford, 1978), pp. 51–6; my emphasis in the quotation, from Brown, *Bunyan*, p. 81.

111. *Ibid.*, pp. 85–7. For Bunyan, the Puritanism of the 1650s and the Bedford church, see B. R. White, '"The Fellowship of Believers": Bunyan and Puritanism', in Keeble (ed.), *John Bunyan*, pp. 1–19.

112. *Grace Abounding*, p. 83.

113. Brown, *Bunyan*, pp. 84–5.

114. *Grace Abounding*, pp. 58, 52, 78.

115. *Ibid.*, p. 83; see also Pooley, 'Spiritual Experience', pp. 393–402.

116. *Grace Abounding*, p. 83 and appendix A, p. 164.

117. *Grace Abounding*, p. 83. Towards the end of the book, Bunyan embarks on a discourse about 'Gifts and Abilities' and concludes, 'let all men therefore prize a little with the fear of the Lord (Gifts indeed are desirable)' (*ibid.*, pp. 91–2).

118. *Ibid.*, pp. 83, 85, 86, 90.

119. Nickalls (ed.), *Journal of George Fox*, p. 18; *Grace Abounding*, pp. 84–6.

For the change in emphasis in Bunyan's preaching 'as he made a more positive offering of hope', see Graham Midgley's 'Introduction' in Roger Sharrock (ed.), *The Miscellaneous Works of John Bunyan* (13 vols; Oxford, 1976–94), vol. V, p. xv.

120. *Grace Abounding*, pp. 84, 89.

121. Christopher Hill, 'Puritans and the Dark Corners of the Land' in his *Change and Continuity in Seventeenth-Century England* (London, 1974), pp. 3–47; *Grace Abounding*, appendix A, p. 164.

122. W. T. Whitley, *A History of British Baptists* (London, 1923), p. 306.

123. *Grace Abounding*, pp. 89, 85. For the tendency in English Calvinism to emphasize the difficulty of conversion, countered by the Arminian reaction stressing freedom to choose, see J. Sears McGee, *The Godly Man in Stuart England: Anglicans, Puritans and the Two Tables, 1620–1670* (New Haven, CT, and London, 1976), pp. 59–64; and for the elaboration of a full programme of predestination, especially on the part of William Perkins, who was, in turn, strongly influenced by Calvin's successor Beza, see Nicholas Tyacke, *Anti-Calvinists: The Rise of English Arminianism c.1590–1640* (Oxford, 1987), pp. 1–4, 29. Highlighting Luther's influence on Bunyan, Green ('Bunyan in context', pp. 12–13) examines his 'dilemma that was probably common among Calvinist pastors: how to find the right balance between on the one hand telling a congregation that all their efforts were useless as a means of achieving salvation, and the other urging them to do their utmost to honour God, to edify their families and friends, and to make their election sure'.

124. *Grace Abounding*, p. 87.

125. B. R. White, *The English Separatist Tradition: From the Marian Martyrs to the Pilgrim Fathers* (London, 1975), ch. 5; G. F. Nuttall, *Visible Saints The Congregational Way 1640–1660* (Oxford, 1957), ch. 2; for Gifford's warning, see Brown, *Bunyan*, p. 95; for Bunyan's open view of baptism, see below, pp. 177–81.

126. *Grace Abounding*, p. 87.

127. Brown, *Bunyan*, p. 239.

128. Tindall, *John Bunyan*, ch. 4.

129. Nickalls (ed.), *Journal of George Fox*, pp. 115, 123–4; Dell, quoted in Brown, *Bunyan*, pp. 117–18; for Dell, see Richard L. Greaves and Robert Zaller (eds), *Biographical Dictionary of British Radicals in the Seventeenth Century* (3 vols; Brighton, 1982–4), vol. I, pp. 221–2.

130. *Grace Abounding*, pp. 87, 89. For Denne, see Greaves and Zaller (eds), *Dictionary of British Radicals*, I, pp. 223–4; Denne, quoted in Brown, *Bunyan*, p. 123.

131. See *Grace Abounding*, p. 39, for Bunyan's list of 'errors of the *Quakers*'; Barry Reay, *The Quakers and the English Revolution* (Hounslow, 1985); for the *Gospel-Truths* debate, see Chapter 3 below.

132. *Grace Abounding*, pp. 84, 89; for other allegations that Protestant radicals

were in fact covert Catholics, see J. Kent, 'The "Papist" Charge against the Interregnum Quakers', *Journal of Religious History* 12 (1983), pp. 180–90. The charge that adult baptism of women provided sexual opportunities for their baptisers provided rich copy for anti-sectarian propagandists such as Thomas Edwards; singling out the Baptist minister Samuel Oates (father of Titus), Edwards wrote of a 'young lusty fellow' who 'hath traded cheifly with young women and young maids, dipping many of them, though all is fish that comes to his net': Thomas Edwards, *Gangraena: or A Catalogue and Discovery of many of the Errours, Heresies, Blasphemies and pernicious Practices of the Sectarians of this time* (London, 1646; reprinted Exeter, 1977), p. 146.

133. Bedford Church Book, quoted in *Grace Abounding*, appendix A, p. 167. For democratic trends in the Bedford corporation, see Michael Mullett, '"Deprived of our Former Place": The Internal Politics of Bedford, 1660–1688', *Bedfordshire Historical Record Society* 59 (1980), pp. 8–9, 110–11.

134. Brown, *Bunyan*, pp. 94–6, 101–2, 107–9.

135. Gifford, quoted in *Grace Abounding*, p. xx.

136. *Ibid.*, p. xii; Christopher Hill, *The World Turned Upside Down: Radical Ideas in the English Revolution* (London, 1972), esp. ch. 18.

137. In Brown, *Bunyan*, p. 127; 'Eaton' is Eaton Socon, Bedfordshire, a few miles north-east of Bedford; *Grace Abounding*, p. 93.

138. Bedford Church Book, quoted in *Grace Abounding*, appendix A, p. 164.

139. *Grace Abounding*, pp. 95–6.

140. For Lilburne's development in prison, see Mullett, *Radical Religious Movements*, p. 52.

141. *Grace Abounding*, p. 96.

142. *Ibid.*, pp. 97, 98.

143. *Ibid.*

144. *Ibid.*, pp. 98–9.

145. *Ibid.*, pp. 102–3.

146. *Ibid.*, p. 102. For Michelangelo's inclusion of himself – as Nicodemus – in a sculpted *pietà*, see Umberto Baldini, *L'opera completa di Michelangelo scultore* (Milan, 1973), plate 59. I am grateful to Richard L. Greaves for suggesting this comparison.

147. *Grace Abounding*, pp. 1–3, 102; Thikstun, 'The Preface to *Grace Abounding*', pp. 180–2.

148. Hawkins, 'The Double Conversion', p. 260; *Grace Abounding*, p. 3.

149. *Grace Abounding*, pp. 2, 30, 67, 24, 63.

150. *Ibid.*, Sharrock's Introduction, p.xxxi; pp. 87–8; also see Pooley, 'Spiritual Experience', pp. 393–402.

151. *Grace Abounding*, pp. 26, 32, 78, 73.

152. *Ibid.*, pp. 35, 62.

TWO
Bunyan's Life: 1660–1688

By the time of his arrest late in 1660, Bunyan had acquired a certain degree of fame, or notoriety. He had made a start to his career as an author with *Some Gospel-Truths Opened* (1656) and its partner in anti-Quaker polemic, *A Vindication of Some Gospel-Truths Opened* (1657), along with *A Few Sighs from Hell* (1658) and *The Doctrine of the Law and Grace Unfolded* (1659). In the anti-Quaker works, Bunyan upheld orthodox doctrines of the historical reality of Jesus Christ, and in *The Doctrine of the Law and Grace Unfolded* he extended this sense of Christ's actuality into a resounding, emotive restatement of the Reformation doctrine of the Crucifixion of Christ as the sufficient recompense for sins: 'I saw through grace that it was the blood shed on Mount Calvary that did save and redeem sinners.'[1] Such perceptions were closely related to the content of his preaching of grace and redemption at around this time. His strong sense of human sinfulness, and of mankind's incapacity on its own to elude it, placed him on the orthodox Protestant side of a line on the other side of which were ranged more advanced radicals – the Quakers in particular. Indeed, in 1659 Bunyan was involved in the anti-Quaker propaganda backlash, when he composed a pamphlet, since lost, associating the Quakers with allegations of witchcraft in Cambridgeshire.[2]

If Bunyan can in this way be seen as theologically conservative, how do we account for his harassment by conservative forces in the late 1650s, climaxing in his imprisonment in 1660? The answer may possibly lie in part in the tone and content of one of those writings of the late 1650s, *A Few Sighs from Hell* (1658), and in particular its social (rather than its more strictly theological) message. Restating his own plebeian origins – 'my low and contemptible descent in the world' – and using as his text Christ's parable of Dives and Lazarus (Luke 16: 19–31) – a focus since medieval times for sermons of social criticism and radicalism – Bunyan unmistakably attacked the rich. The work brought together the themes, familiar enough in mid-seventeenth-century England, of social justice and apocalyptic revenge: '[T]here ... is a time coming, O ye surly dogged persecutors of the saints, that they shall slight you as much as ever you slighted them ... The righteous ... shall wash his feet in the blood of the wicked ... the time is coming, when they [the rich] will both sigh and cry.'[3] In the kind of tones once used by medieval preachers, Bunyan denounced the linked sins of luxury and exploitation: 'Methinks to see how the great ones of the world will go strutting up and down the streets sometimes, it makes me wonder' and '[H]ow many pounds do some men spend in a year on their dogs, when in the meanwhile the poor saints of God may starve for hunger?'[4] He had a good deal also to say about the financial abuses of the market – ' swearing, lying, couzening, stealing, covetousness, extortion, oppression, forgery, bribery, flattery, or any other way, to get more'[5] – but he concentrated much of his intense social anger on tenurial grievances, with clear implications for the then current issue of enclosures and evictions, against which recent riots had taken place in the East Midlands: 'They will build houses for their dogs, when the Saints must be glad to wander ... and if they be in any of their houses for the hire thereof, they will warn them out, or eject them, or pull down the house over their heads, rather than not rid themselves of such Tenants.'[6] In this last passage, Bunyan does not seem to be saying that landlords oppressed the 'saints' in any sectarian sense of the word, but that the poor and oppressed were by definition God's chosen ones, as described in the original parable of Dives and Lazarus. Poverty was holy, and God had 'chosen the poor, despised and base things of this world'. The possession of wealth, on the other hand, was almost a sin in itself, and the rich 'most liable to be puffed up with pride'. The attack, though focusing on a landowning, rent-collecting gentry, was also extended to take in the comfortably off professional clergy and intelligentsia, who studied 'Hebrew, Greeke, and Latine ... *Aristotle, Plato*'.[7]

A Few Sighs from Hell, then, carried clear messages of social protest, apocalyptic inversion and revenge of the poor against the rich, singling out the gentry. It was a dangerous book, not least for its author, who recorded the threats that the work evoked, threats that might well be realized when those who were the targets of the book's strictures were once more firmly back in the saddle of power.[8]

By the end of the 1650s people like Bunyan could be regarded as epitomizing the world turned upside down of the Interregnum. Even a Quaker identified Bunyan's repudiation of the stereotyped role of an artisan, and cited him as one 'who goes up and down to preach and lookest upon thy self higher than the Priest'.[9] As part of a programme of restoring the obedient society, the makers of the Restoration settlement included the reimposition of religious unanimity and the acceptance of a Church of England that preached a doctrine of submission and was dominated by the landed ruling class. It was true that Charles II favoured tolerance and aimed at reconciliation through the recognition of religious pluralism under the law. Indeed, the king, for whom Bunyan was to discover a fund of loyalty partly on the basis of his role as a tribune against the intolerance of the gentry identified in *A Few Sighs from Hell* as exploiters, had pledged himself to an open religious policy in his Declaration of Breda of April 1660, on the eve of his return to England. This was, however, to no avail and the details of the Restoration settlement, above all of the religious settlement, were actually hammered out, centrally in Parliament and locally in the counties, by the Cavalier-Anglican gentry and their allies amongst the clergy. During the Interregnum most of the the royalist gentry had stayed at home, bearing the wounds, literal and metaphorical, of military service and defeat, hardened and embittered by the stigma of 'malignancy', the fines and impoundings, the loss of lands which, in many cases, was never made good. To these men, all the sects of non-Anglican Protestants and, above all, the left-wing Puritans, were social and political revolutionaries, enemies of property, deference and obedience. Whatever Charles II's intentions, the requirements of law and order demanded that such deviants be made to conform to the Church of England or face punishment and suppression. The situation in Bedfordshire, and Bunyan's part in it, provide a microcosm of processes that were taking place around the country during, and indeed before, the Restoration.[10] As it was achieved and consolidated, the Restoration was an Anglican triumph, engineered by the gentry, and Bedfordshire gives a local example of the initiatives that were used in the re-establishment of the Church, in the form of the order given by the county's magistrates, in the month before Bunyan was arrested, that the Prayer Book be used once more in the churches of the county.[11] Through such measures, Anglican clergy and laity at the local level cut through the intricacies of national debate in the early Restoration period about the shape of the eventual religious settlement, and were simply asserting the fact of an Anglican victory. Bunyan was one victim of the Cavalier-Anglican gentry's seizure of the initiative.

He was also a victim of a particularly (but not uniquely) envenomed atmosphere in his native county – Bedfordshire society was sharply polarized. As we have already seen, radicals in the county had persistently campaigned for left-wing causes in the1650s, and in 1659 – the make-or-break year for the English Revolution – a petition of 'Divers freeholders and others' put forward a set of far-reaching demands: abolition of the tithe; extensive law reform; religious toleration; and control of the militia by the radicals. Much of the inspiration for Bedfordshire's militancy came from the county town. Bedford's freemen had been fighting a protracted campaign against the rise of oligarchy in the borough's government. The artisans – small-scale producers for a local market and including hatters, cobblers, cordwainers and maltsters, all of whom provided the backbone of Nonconformity in the area – aimed to use local government to protect their economic interests under an essentially medieval and pre-capitalist system of protective regulations. The resumption of anti-democratic and oligarchic trends in the Bedford corporation in and after 1660 coincided with the swamping of the town's government by the local Anglican gentry. The social chasm could hardly have been wider. Bedford was a centre for small artisans, of the 'meanest sort', the kind of people who looked to democracy in the corporation to defend their interests as independent manufacturers for local consumption. Set against them were county magistrates, such as the ferociously anti-Nonconformist Sir George Blundell of Cardington Manor, a Restoration knight who was admitted with a selection of fellow squires into the burgessdom of Bedford in 1661, in an attempt to check the borough's record of plebeian and Nonconformist radicalism.[12]

In Bedfordshire's adversarial atmosphere of 1660–1, the Bunyan of *A Few Sighs from Hell* typified the social radicalism and intellectual self-assurance of Bedford's 'levelling' freemen and the religious radicalism which, as conservatives complained, spread out like an infection from the towns to the country parishes and villages. The man responsible for his arrest, Francis Wingate of Harlington, can also be taken as an archetype – of rural gentry rather than urban freemen, of religious assent rather than sectarian dissent, and of a vindictive and triumphant royalism now once more in the ascendant, in Bedfordshire and throughout the shires of England. Wingate was certainly one of those Cavalier county squires who could claim his share of privations for the sake of king and church. Though he himself had not fought in the Civil Wars, his widowed mother had had to pay heavy charges and fines for her royalism, and it would be hard to believe that Wingate did not harbour a grievance against the whole Puritan fraternity that seemed to have been responsible for his family's misfortunes.[13]

In their hunt for the ringleaders of dissent, men like Wingate were motivated not only by revenge, but also by fear. Fear of the radicals – such as the Quakers and the millenarian Fifth Monarchists – continued to characterize the political atmosphere for at least the first half of the 1660s. Indeed, such fears were surely justified by the violent attempts of radical Puritan activists in the early 1660s to reverse the Restoration. Bunyan's arrest and imprisonment, then, have to be seen in the context of a hunt for suspected subversives, prompted by insecurity over the Restoration in the light of the continuation of Puritan militancy from 1659 into the early years of Charles II's reign. Was it also the case that paranoia about left-wing Puritan subversion induced the authorities to ignore the forms of common law and the liberties of the subject? In Bunyan's case, Hill writes that his 'trial and sentence to prison was less a judicial than a political act', and Lindsay claimed that 'the action that was taken against Bunyan was entirely illegal'.[14] Indeed, at first sight, it may appear that Bunyan's arrest, and especially his continued imprisonment after 1661, violated English law and that he was a victim of the suspension of due process in favour of emergency powers because of a fear of terrorism in the aftermath of the Restoration.

Bunyan's own account of his arrest and imprisonment enables us to evaluate the actions taken against him from the point of view of their legality or otherwise. It is clear from this account that feelings of panic prevailed in those responsible for ruling post-Restoration Bedfordshire. In particular, Wingate feared that Bunyan and local separatists 'did intend to do some fearful business, to the destruction of the country [county]'.[15] It remains to be seen whether this nervousness led to a bending of the laws. *A Relation of the Imprisonment of Mr. John Bunyan* is divided into five parts: an account of his arrest and investigation; a narrative of his examination and indictment by justices; a recapitulation of his discussion with the clerk to the justices; a recitation of his wife's appeal to the judges; and a narrative sequel. Bunyan was arrested under the 1593 Act of Elizabeth I's reign: 'an Act to retain the Queen's majesty's subjects in their due obedience'. Bunyan was clearly in breach of this law, which had been renewed under Charles I. A warrant was issued for his arrest and he was taken at the start of a meeting for worship at Samsell near Harlington, Bedfordshire, where he had been invited to preach. He had undoubtedly committed the offences covered by the statute, which penalized persons who absented themselves from parish worship for over a month and who 'willingly join in, or be present at, any such assemblies, conventicles or meetings, under colour or pretence of any such exercise of religion, contrary the laws and statutes of this realm'.[16]

Bunyan, then, as an absentee from parish worship, had, by opening the service at Samsell, violated the 1593 Act. Furthermore, as we shall see from his account of his imprisonment, the authorities were well within the law in offering him an option of conformity to the Established Church, or, ultimately, of banishment (or death), following indictment and a kind of cooling-off spell in prison, 'there to remain [for up to three months] without bail or mainprise, until [he should] conform'. Failing reconciliation to the Established Church, 'before the justices of the peace in the open quarter-sessions of the … county', the accused was to 'abjure this realm of

England, and all other the Queen's majesty's dominions for ever' or face death. Bunyan was arrested and was to be imprisoned under a sweeping, but undoubtedly legal, measure. Whether it was just in the wider sense, the 1593 Act was a law of the land – as well as being the kind of emergency legislation that suited the needs of England's restored rulers in the heated atmosphere of 1660.[17]

In the preliminary hearing, Wingate was in a position to offer bail, and did so:

> He wished me to get me sureties to be bound for me, or else he would send me to the jail.
>
> My sureties being ready, I call'd them in, and when the bond for my appearance was made, he told them, that they was bound to keep me from preaching; and that if I did preach, their bonds would be forfeited. To which I answered, that then I should break them.

This offer, motivated by a desire above all to silence Bunyan – 'if you will promise to call the people no more together, you shall have your liberty' – left the outcome of the situation entirely within his hands: by refusing the conditions for bail, he *chose* to go to prison.[18]

Bunyan's examination turned into a discussion with Wingate himself and with two other *dramatis personae*: a priest, Lindale, and a lawyer, Foster. The conversation concerned the legal trouble that Bunyan might have avoided had he made a simple act of verbal submission. In fact, the whole process based on the Elizabethan statute turned on the question of obedience. The measure was drawn up so as 'to retain the Queen's majesty's subjects *in their due obedience*'. Its harsh penalties – banishment, forfeiture of property, death – could be avoided simply by submission: 'I have grievously offended God in contemning her Majesty's godly and lawful government and authority ... I do promise and protest ... That from henceforth I will from time to time obey.'[19] The word 'submission' is repeated regularly in the statute and, although reconciliation to authority would have been to many an attractive option when compared with banishment, the capitulation had to be made with an unequivocating and deliberately humiliating publicity, at parish worship, and carefully recorded.

The theme of submission was to the fore in Bunyan's dialogue with Wingate. However, in these exchanges the concept was aired not so much in terms of the Elizabethan statute's insistence on acknowledgement of the government of the realm, but rather in terms of the acceptance of hierarchy and of stereotyped social roles. These themes were developed by two representatives of the social hierarchy present at Wingate's home and by their walk-on roles in the drama of Bunyan's appearance before the magistrate. The first of these, the parson Dr Lindale, tried to score points about the unsuitability of preaching by craftsmen. The issue was the same as that raised in the previous year when Henry Denne had defended the tinker's right to teach the gospel. The next of Bunyan's interlocutors was the magistrate's brother-in-law, the Bedford lawyer Dr William Foster. He was hardly less maladroit than Lindale, and his class preconceptions led him seriously to underestimate Bunyan's intelligence. Foster did, however, focus on that central issue of obedience and submission: 'you shall have your liberty to go home ... if you will be but ruled'. He also articulated the traditional hierarchical view of the proper roles – the 'callings' – of the various strata of the social order: 'He said, that [preaching] was none of my work; I must follow my calling.' In addition, in referring to the 'callings' typical of Bunyan's auditors, – '[h]e told me, that I made people neglect their calling' – he alleged the ignorance thought to characterize a plebeian audience: 'He said again, that there was none but a company of poor simple ignorant people that come to hear me.' This claim played straight into Bunyan's hands as he delivered the stock response of the artisan preacher in the ongoing debate with the religious establishment: 'those that are most commonly counted foolish by the world, are the wisest before God'.[20]

Bunyan's ripostes to his interlocutors showed the lack of deference that was at the heart of the matter as far as upholders of hierarchical society were concerned. As for the claim of the professional intelligentsia that manual workers were unqualified to maintain a religious position, Bunyan's polemical skill and scriptural knowledge exploded that myth. In recounting his interrogations he gives an excellent account of his conduct of his defence. Like Fox recording the triumphant court appearance that he made at Lancaster in 1652,[21] Bunyan was in charge of the narrative and could render it more or less as he chose. The unfolding of the encounters has a dramatic quality – life imitating theatre. Three 'tempters', Wingate, Lindale and Foster – the squire, the parson and the lawyer, the stereotypical triple pillars of the establishment – came 'on stage' in succession, each of them attempting unsuccessfully to break down the defences of the hero: *Samson Agonistes* in a Bedfordshire manor house. One of this procession of would-be seducers makes a particularly striking entry. Foster's arrival in the narrative, in an atmosphere of candlelit menace, with Bunyan's arrest now accompanied by honeyed betrayal and even a traitor's kiss, carries resonances of another arrest, another trial:

Well, when I came to the justice again, there was Mr. *Foster* of Bedford, who coming out of another room, and seeing of me by the light of the

candle ... he said unto me, who is there, *John Bunyan?*[1] with such seeming affection, as if he would have leaped in my neck and kissed me.[22]

The addition of a footnote, '[1]A right Judas', by labouring a comparison,
spoils an effect better hinted at: in any case, the Church lawyer Foster could
hardly be described as a 'Judas' towards Bunyan. In his recapitulation
of these scenes, Bunyan shows himself aiming for a Christlike mien, and
eventually checking his own aptness in dialogue exchanges by adopting a
dignified refusal to defend himself or to go on the attack: 'I was as sparing
of my speech as I could.'[23]

Refusing to compromise by accepting bail on the conditions set out,
Bunyan was imprisoned until the next Bedfordshire quarter sessions, in
January 1661. Bunyan named four justices '&c.' (there were five) as being
present at the quarter sessions. The group – Sir Henry Chester of Tils-
worth, Sir George Blundell of Cardington Manor, Sir William Beecher of
Howbury and Thomas Snagg of Marston Manor – had strong Royalist
credentials and included men who had suffered for the king's cause, and
who had been knighted after the Restoration.[24] The presiding justice, Sir
John Kelyng of Southill, was 'a prominent local Royalist' squire, a professional lawyer, and was made a serjeant-at-law in 1660. He was also a classic
case of a man whose privations during the 'late anarchy' (he had suffered
lengthy imprisonment during the 1640s for his stand against Parliament's
Militia Ordinance) had made an extreme advocate of the furthest extension
of state powers at the expense of the individual subject and of established
protective institutions, including Parliament and the law. A prosecutor of
the regicides and of the millenarian Sir Henry Vane, knighted after Bunyan's
trial, a member of the Cavalier Parliament for Bedfordshire and a future
draftsman of the 1662 Act of Uniformity, Kelyng was a man who did well
out of the Restoration. His ultra-Royalist views – he became notorious for
ridiculing the hitherto sacrosanct Magna Carta as 'Magna Farta' – coincided with his career interests as a state lawyer. The high point in that
career came with his appointment as Chief Justice of the King's Bench. In
a 1663 trial of Quakers in that court, Kelyng revealed the hectoring, deeply
partisan and authoritarian court-room style which later post-Restoration
judges, above all George Jeffreys, were to adopt. Kelyng made his own
contribution to the equation of sectarian Puritanism with treason – ' Their
end is Rebellion and Blood' – and he also acquired notoriety for bullying
juries and arbitrarily suppressing the, admittedly archaic, custom of benefit
of clergy, which frequently acted as a bar to capital punishment. Choleric,
rough and crude in view and speech, Kelyng, whose death, according to
the biographer of the Chief Justices, came 'to the great relief of all who

had any regard for the due administration of justice', has been seen as the model for Bunyan's violent judicial tyrant, Lord Hategood in *The Pilgrim's Progress*.[25]

What possible chance of a fair hearing did a religious and social dissident like John Bunyan have before a court presided over by a reactionary zealot like Kelyng?[26] In point of fact, Kelyng's conduct as chairman of the bench ('the judge in that court') was remarkably restrained. Many seventeenth-century trials – in a period when questions of politics and religion frequently came before the courts – assumed the character of public debates over ideological issues. In the case of Bunyan's trial, the issues being debated were the propriety of separatist as opposed to Anglican worship, the legitimacy of the Book of Common Prayer and, in some detail, the value of prescribed as opposed to extempore prayer. Though most of these issues had been gone over many times in the continuing debate between Conformists and Non-conformists, the discussions in the Bedford courtroom were civilized, intricate and serious. True, one of the justices behaved obtusely, with a question aimed at Bunyan: 'who is your God? Beelzebub?', while another of the magistrates tried to introduce a note of levity by asking, 'in a laughing way', about extempore prayers being written out in advance of meetings for worship – a flippancy totally out of place when a man was on trial, possibly for his life. However, none of these excesses was committed by Kelyng. As the presiding justice, he went out of his way to set a fair and judicious tone for the proceedings. Throughout, there was certainly a vivid contrast between his conduct at Bunyan's trial and his behaviour three years later in proceedings against Quakers at the Old Bailey, when he boasted of how he had earlier 'hanged up four or five of the Speakers or Praters; whom we found to be the chief Leaders of the Rebellion'.[27]

In his dealings with Bunyan, Kelyng relied on reasoned argument rather than force. He spoke feelingly of his own religious principles and claimed that the Anglicans had the better of the religious argument, so that the doctrines of the Church of England needed no artificial support. Thus, in reply to a colleague on the bench who thought some of Bunyan's remarks threatening, Kelyng said, 'No, no, never fear him, we are better established than so; he can do no harm', an observation which, it might be thought, undermined the whole idea of trying a religious dissident – unless it is realized that, as references to 'armour' when Bunyan was arrested show, sectarian conventicles were widely viewed as planning sessions for conspiracy.[28]

Thus, Kelyng's attitude towards Bunyan was fair-minded and courteous. Bunyan himself recalled phrases such as 'let me a little open that Scripture to you', and '[h]e said I should have liberty' [to develop arguments], and '[s]o I proceeded' – on occasion in courtroom speeches of up to sixteen lines of modern printed text. At one point, not only Kelyng but apparently all the justices agreed with a remark made by Bunyan on a favourite theme of his, 'pray[ing] with the spirit' (about which he was to publish at length in 1662): 'They said, that was true.' Later, Kelyng concurred emphatically with remarks by Bunyan about praying with feeling. In one exchange, Bunyan, obviously carried away by the atmosphere of free debate rather than of trial, started attacking the Book of Common Prayer: '*Keel.* He said, we were commanded to pray. *Bun.* I said, but not by the Common Prayer-book ... I said that those prayers in the Common Prayerbook, was such as was made by other men, and not by the motions of the Holy Ghost.' For a while, Kelyng overlooked what might have been viewed as insults to the Prayer Book. When finally he did check Bunyan over this, he did so to protect not so much the liturgy, as the prisoner at the bar: '[S]aid he, let me give you one caution; take heed of speaking irreverently of the Common Prayer-book. For if you do so, *you will bring great damage upon yourself.*' [29] Just once, Kelyng's notorious choler got the better of him. When Bunyan had concluded a particularly rhapsodic encomium of separatist worship, Kelyng 'called this pedlers French, saying that I must leave off my canting'.[30] Apart from this lapse, though, Kelyng maintained his dignified demeanour on the bench and engaged Bunyan in a balanced discussion. However, he drew this to a close with an admission of his own defective scriptural knowledge. Bunyan was now reminded, with evident shock on his part, that what he was involved in was a court appearance, not a verbal duel: Kelyng 'said to me, then you confess the indictment, do you not? Now, and not till now, I saw I was indicted.' Despite the abrupt switch from a dialectical to a forensic mode and the harsher language he used when he delivered sentence, Kelyng's course of action at the climax of the proceedings remained lawful and in full conformity with the provisions of the statute under which the trial was being held:

> Then said he, hear your judgment. You must be had back again to prison, and there lie for three months following; at three months end, if you do not submit to go to church to hear divine service, and leave your preaching, you must be banished the realm: And if, after such a day as shall be appointed you to be gone, you shall be found in this realm ... you must stretch by the neck for it.[31]

Bunyan's subsequent encounter with the next representative of officialdom, clerk of the peace Paul Cobb, was the most ambiguous and, in its consequences, the most mysterious of his dealings with the legal and political establishment. Of a local gentry family which had a distinguished record in the government of Bedford and its ecclesiastical administration, Cobb was to show his Anglican and loyalist credentials in his office of clerk to the commissioners empowered under the 1661 Corporations Act to eliminate Dissenters from Bedford corporation. The climax of his Royalist – indeed, of his Tory – career came in 1684, at the height of the Tory Reaction, when, as mayor, Cobb was chiefly responsible for surrendering Bedford's charter in return for a new, Tory-oriented grant.[32] However, in 1661 Cobb's task was the much more modest one of trying to secure Bunyan's conformity. Cobb's interview with Bunyan was in fact demanded by a clause in the statute to the effect that an offender be 'required by ... any justice of the peace of the county' to make submission. Cobb acted as the justices' agent – 'sent by the Justices to admonish me, and demand of me submittance to the church of *England*'.[33]

As well as throwing further light on the legal circumstances of Bunyan's imprisonment, the dialogue with Cobb is instructive in revealing some of Bunyan's abiding political principles – that the powers that be are ordained by God and must be obeyed, but that neither obedience nor authority should be absolute. Bunyan, who had been studying the 1593 Act in gaol, was prepared for an analysis of it with Cobb. He tried to argue that the statute had been originally aimed, not against secessionist worshippers, but against political subversives. Cobb countered with the standard Cavalier-Anglican view that conventicles were covers for subversion, and he cited the recent news of Thomas Venner's Fifth Monarchist rising in London in January 1661.[34] However, the argument about the political content of conventicles was beside the point, since the 1593 Act was concerned to repress religious secession as such, albeit for undermining the royal supremacy.

The political loyalism that Bunyan voiced in his talk with Cobb seems to bear out Sharrock's claim that he 'remained a staunch and consistent supporter of civil obedience'.[35] Like Fox, who contrasted the king's commitment to toleration with the harshness of those who administered the laws in his name,[36] Bunyan may have begun to put his trust in the Charles II of the Declaration of Breda as a counterweight to Cavalier intolerance. He gave Cobb a pledge of personal 'loyalty to my Prince, both by word and deed'. In addition, he offered a reference to 1 Peter 2: 13–14, which refers to obedience to 'governors, as unto them that are sent ... for the punishment of evildoers'; the choice of citation may suggest that, like some sixteenth-century Continental Anabaptists and seventeenth-century English Baptists, he saw the state primarily as an engine for the repression of sin, and consequently as having less to do with the saints, who thus owed the state a more passive kind of allegiance. That implied diffidence towards constituted authority was less than Cobb wanted from him. Later in his

life, and partly as a result of Charles II's intervention on behalf of Nonconformists, which led to his release from prison in 1672, Bunyan was to
develop a more positive commitment to kingship, whereas early in the
Restoration period, when viable republican government could readily be
remembered, Bunyan may have taken the view that all forms of established
government were valid and 'all righteous laws, and that whether there was
a King or no'. Cobb, who saw only kingly government as 'ordained of
God', sought a more unqualified monarchist undertaking.[37]

Much of the interest in Bunyan's dialogue with Cobb lies in its inter-
personal dimension. Cobb tried to use winning ways, asking after Bunyan's
health and addressing his social inferior as 'neighbour':[38] Bunyan found
his attitude 'civil and meek'. This does not mean that the proprieties of
deference were set aside. Cobb summoned Bunyan into his presence in
the gaol and the speech conventions of the deferential society were strictly
observed. However, under the surface of social etiquette, the underlying
relationship between the court official and the prisoner shifted, subtly but
unmistakably, as Cobb, a gentleman but not ' a man that can dispute', became
the auditory – almost the pupil – to Bunyan the teacher. Bunyan's learning
was on parade, with a citation from John Wyclif (though this came via
John Foxe). Bunyan even adopted the teacher's method of explaining a
point by a 'similitude', deploying his skills in devising parables, and proceeded to deliver a lecture on the work of Christ as mediator. However, the
discussion of doctrinal points had little to do with the matter in hand. Cobb
at one point introduced the topic of heresy and the discernment thereof:
'But will you be willing … that two indifferent persons shall determine the
case [of doctrine], and will you stand to their judgment.' This, like the
parallel subject of whether or not conventicles hatched political subversion,
was nothing to the point, since the 1593 Act took no account of the theological views advanced in illicit meetings for religious worship: those
meetings were illegal because they were autonomous, not because they were
unorthodox. So, despite the euphoric summation that Bunyan gave to his
encounter with Cobb – 'O! that we might meet in Heaven!' – this had been
a meeting somewhat at cross purposes. It certainly yielded no results in
terms of securing Bunyan's submission.[39]

The ensuing appeal of Bunyan's wife, Elizabeth, to the judges on assize
has links with some of the conventions of popular culture. A desperate
appeal, a last gamble, by a distressed wife to the representatives of law and
authority had something of the ballad about it, but the scene in which
Elizabeth Bunyan played the heroine was in fact quite often enacted in
reality. John Lilburne's wife besieged Parliament at the time of his first
imprisonment, as did the wife of the Baptist minister John James, convicted

of treason in 1661, and in 1660 Fox's future wife, Margaret Fell, petitioned Charles II for his release.[40] Such scenes had even more narrative power when dramatic antitheses were in operation. In a society acutely conscious of status according to age, gender and wealth, Elizabeth Bunyan, the young wife of an imprisoned tinker, was about to approach the senior male bastions of the law, chiefly recruited from the country's social élite. Cobb saw Bunyan on 3 April 1661, twelve weeks after his appearance at the quarter sessions and nineteen weeks in all since his arrest at Samsell and examination by Wingate. The king's coronation on 23 April 1661 carried with it, through a kind of arbitrary prerogative of mercy, a 'general pardon', or reprieve, of prisoners. In the same month, a further, and critical, stage in Bunyan's trials should have been reached, as it marked the expiry of the three-month period initiated by Kelyng and his colleagues. Bunyan's continuing refusal to submit should have meant that the sentence of banishment would now come into effect. However, it seems that the legal picture was confused by the fact that the coronation reprieves and Bunyan's sentence of banishment both fell due in the same month. Although Bunyan was not exiled, neither did he gain a reprieve. He was left in prison, while his wife tried to persuade the judges at the assizes to release him. The local legal establishment took the view that Bunyan did not qualify for the royal reprieve because he already stood convicted and would instead have to apply for a pardon. This question of whether he had been convicted seemed, to Bunyan and his wife at least, to remain open. He himself, like many another prisoner, especially those whose fates remain undetermined, had to become something of a legal expert, acquiring a knowledge of legal vocabulary and concepts that he was to deploy in a late work, *The Advocateship of Jesus Christ* (though, as we shall see, he used legal terms and concepts dexterously in the pre-Restoration *The Doctrine of the Law and Grace Unfolded*). He may have briefed his wife, and tended to see her as his messenger: 'I did, by my wife, present a petition.' However, Bunyan's second wife was herself articulate, resourceful and courageous. She also seems to have had that working knowledge of the law that it behoved the early modern English poor to possess as part of their survival equipment.[41]

The two judges holding the midsummer assizes at Bedford in August 1661 held opposed views on religious and political issues. Sir Thomas Twisden (or Twysden) was a 'staunch loyalist' who acted as a witness in the trials of the Regicides and who, like Kelyng, became a serjeant-at-law at the Restoration. In contrast, Sir Matthew Hale was inclined to Puritan opinions and was favourable to Dissenters; in Baxter's words, 'He was most precisely just … the pillar of justice, the refuge of the subject who feared oppression.'[42]

Hale 'very mildly received' a petition from Elizabeth Bunyan for her husband to be given a hearing at the assizes, but though Hale was sympathetic, he was also pessimistic about a successful outcome. It was incumbent on the petitioning couple, and on Elizabeth in particular, to be persistent, even if this tactic risked annoying the judges by its importunity – as it certainly incensed the short-tempered Twisden. The latter put forward an interpretation of Bunyan's case which was undoubtedly hostile, but also incontrovertible under the terms the 1593 Act, so much so that Hale was bound to endorse it. Twisden told Elizabeth that her husband 'was a convicted person, and could not be released, until [he] would promise to preach no more'. When Elizabeth tried to win Hale's support – in the intimidating atmosphere of a crowded, all-male gathering of squires and lawyers in a Bedford inn – she found that he had to support Twisden's reading of Bunyan's plight under the statute: 'Woman, I told thee before I could do thee no good; because they have taken that for a conviction which thy husband spoke at the sessions: And unless there be something done to undo that, I can do thee no good.' Two arguments that Elizabeth Bunyan employed against her husband's conviction would not stand up. Her claim that he had been imprisoned wrongly because he was arrested 'before there were any proclamation against the meetings' was beside the point, since the statute of 1593 was valid law and did not need to be activated by proclamation.[43] As for her claim that the original indictment was 'false', though its rhetoric was loaded against her husband, it was substantively accurate: Bunyan *had* 'abstained from coming to church to hear divine service' and, given the 1593 Act's implicit definition of divine worship to mean parish worship according to the 1559 Act of Uniformity, his claim that he 'was a common frequenter of the Church of God' was regarded as inadmissible.[44]

Likewise, Bunyan had undoubtedly upheld what the law regarded as 'several unlawful meetings and conventicles', and his attempt, notably before Cobb, to prove that these were not treasonable or a cover 'to do evil in their meetings' once again missed the point, which was that the law looked upon all religious conventicles as 'unlawful', regardless of the opinions voiced in them, and in themselves being 'to the great disturbance and distraction of the good subjects of this kingdom'.[45] There was, though, enough ambiguity in the statute's polemical phrasing 'under colour or pretence of exercise of religion' for Bunyan to claim that his religious meetings were not dissimulated to be for purposes of religious worship – and, on this basis, Hale advised an appeal, preferably through a writ of error.[46]

When the August 1661 assizes reviewed Bunyan's earlier conviction and the sentence of banishment, the judges, including Hale, were, on balance, right in concluding that Bunyan had been lawfully sentenced: if his conviction was shaky in natural justice, that was the fault of the draconian 1593 statute. Elizabeth Bunyan sought to convey the impression that her husband had been caught out on 'but a word of discourse that they took for a conviction', and Hale thought there was enough in that to form the basis for one of three kinds of appeal. However, in the earlier quarter sessions, Bunyan had been made aware of a transition, albeit swift, from 'discourse' to 'indictment': '[Kelyng] said to me, then you confess the indictment, do you not?'[47] In fact, the sessions had begun, quite properly, with the indictment, and, after protracted 'discourse', Bunyan's eventual replies to the indictment were sufficient, under the terms of the statute, to convict him: 'this I confess, we have had many meetings together'. Kelyng then delivered sentence, and Bunyan resumed: 'if I was out of prison to day, I would preach the Gospel again to-morrow'.[48] Neither at the sessions nor in a subsequent official interview had Bunyan made the submission that the law required. The fact that the quarter sessions had been run correctly as far as the law in question was concerned ensured that those at the assizes who wanted to secure Bunyan's conviction – especially Sir Henry Chester, who had taken part in the quarter sessions – reverted constantly to the authoritative record of those earlier proceedings.[49]

As the legal argument thus swung against Elizabeth Bunyan, and the statute book as well as the quarter sessions record pushed the door closed against a judicial review, she threw herself on the mercy of the judges: 'my Lord, I have four small children'. The compassionate Hale responded warmly to this approach and, as it were, colluded in her poignant portrayal of a desperate situation: 'Alas poor woman!' The hardliners Twisden and Chester, on the other hand, did their best to depict Bunyan as a profiteer from illicit preaching. The wearisome debate about a tinker preaching was briefly broached again, but Elizabeth made a striking, if not entirely well-advised, point about the class bias built into English law: 'because he is a Tinker, and a poor man; therefore he is despised, and cannot have justice'. She also gave hints of an eschatological reckoning, and by clear implication condemned an unholy court: 'when the righteous judge shall appear, it will be known, that his doctrine is not the doctrine of the Devil'.[50] Elizabeth Bunyan's heroic and at times heart-rending appeal thus clarified the issues in her husband's case and the episode revealed the depths of Cavalier-Anglican prejudice against Bunyan and his ilk.

A prisoner, by definition, loses control, and indeed often knowledge, of many of the circumstances constraining him. This certainly applied to Bunyan, who admitted, with regard to manoeuvres affecting his fate, 'I do not know of all their [the authorities'] carriages towards me.' Indeed, he put the worst construction upon these 'carriages' and blamed some of the local authorities, now singling out Cobb, for his plight. Of course, the Bedfordshire magistrates had indeed taken the decision to invoke the 1593 Act, but Bunyan's mental difficulty was that, as an English Protestant, influenced by the view of Elizabeth as the quintessential godly prince, he was not prepared to accept that it was her state that had created the statute under which he was convicted: 'I would not entertain so much uncharitableness of that parliament in the 35th of *Elizabeth*, or of the Queen herself, as to think they did by that law intend the oppressing of any of God's ordinances ... but men may, in the wresting of it, turn it against the way of God.'[51]

Following the August 1661 assizes Bunyan remained in prison, at least for part of the time. Seventeenth-century English gaols could be very casually run, and Bunyan, evidently through simple inefficiency, was given 'some liberty'. In fact, he used this liberty not just to come and go in the Bedford area, but to rove as far afield as London, and even to preach: 'I followed my wonted course of preaching.' London, with its guildhalls for hire and its large Nonconformist population, became the national headquarters for Dissenting churches after the Restoration. Like Fox and Baxter, Bunyan was to become closely linked to the capital and these early excursions may have been connected with the development of a church network, based on the integration of individual congregations into a wider associational structure.[52] From the viewpoint of the authorities, such journeys could readily have been interpreted, especially around the time of Venner's rising, as liaison work for a subversive Nonconformist underground. Convinced that he 'went thither to plot and raise division, and make insurrection', the magistrates were, not surprisingly, 'angry' at his visits and threatened to dismiss the Bedford gaoler, evidently an easy-going character who, probably after a reprimand, tried to make up for his lapse with greater vigilance.[53] Not only had Bunyan been travelling at large, giving rise to suspicions that he had been organizing insurgency, but he had resumed preaching, the original grounds of his prosecution. In addition, the actual content of his preaching was deeply incriminating, through its attacks on the restored Church of England: 'exhorting them to be stedfast in the faith of Jesus Christ, and to take heed that they touched not the Common Prayer'.[54]

We can see why Bunyan felt that he needed to preach along these lines. Maintaining a 'stedfast' position was the most important task facing the Bedford gathered church after 1660. At the best of times, that church, like all the other Nonconformist congregations, was faced with the constant threat of erosion, if not extinction, of membership through apostasy, often encouraged by the moral strictness of those churches. There were always individuals drifting away – 'withdrawing from Church assemblys'. However, after the Restoration the greatest single threat to the membership of the

gathered congregation was the Church of England and the temptation facing church members of 'conformity to the world's way of worship' – [m]any
of the friends having in these troublous times withdrawne themselves from
close walking with the Church'. The problem was intensified, now that
deference and obedience were back in style, by the sectaries' image of political subversion. The allegation of treason was made by a Bedford church
member in the course of a difficult church disciplinary case, in which Bunyan was closely involved. Humphrey Merrill, who had convinced himself
that the Bedford congregation was implicated in rebellion, was reconciled
to the Established Church at the quarter sessions. Given this kind of direct
danger to the congregation, it was vital to preachers like Bunyan to uphold
a message of fidelity and avoidance of conformity.[55]

However, although this thrust in Bunyan's preaching answered the
needs of his church in the period after the Restoration, it did not help his
case that he had resumed preaching, targetting the Prayer Book. Having in
this way compounded an offence, Bunyan would have faced a difficult time
at an assize hearing. Perhaps it is in this context that we should consider
the role, ambiguous and ultimately unascertainable, of Paul Cobb in the
run-up to autumn 1662, when Bunyan believed he was again due to face
the judiciary. Cobb prevented Bunyan from making an appearance at those
assizes. There are two possible reasons for this action. One explanation
envisages Cobb as being fundamentally hostile to Bunyan and seeking to
prevent a likely acquittal by impeding his appearance in court. The other
hypothesis is that Cobb, by keeping Bunyan out of court, was in fact protecting him from the consequences of a full trial at the assizes.

Let us first examine the possibility that Cobb decided to keep Bunyan
in prison out of malice, preventing an assize trial that Bunyan hoped would
lead to an acquittal. Abandoning his earlier enthusiasm for Cobb, Bunyan
came to believe that he was sedulously working for his downfall. As Bunyan recalled, he himself had prevailed on the gaoler and won the favour of
a judge and the high sheriff of the county so as to have his name inserted
in the schedule of prisoners to go on trial at the assizes. However, 'the
Justices and the Clerk of the peace, did so work it about, that I, notwithstanding, was defered, and might not appear ... [T]he Clerk of the peace
did discover himself to be one of my greatest opposers.' Cobb, Bunyan
alleged, browbeat the gaoler, who seems, after his earlier negligence in
letting Bunyan wander, to have been anxious to give no further offence.
Cobb deleted Bunyan's name and offence from the calendar prepared for
the assizes, and instead entered a brief memo to the effect that '*John Bunyan*
was committed in prison; being lawfully convicted for upholding of unlawful meetings and conventicles.' Bunyan claimed that Cobb gained the ear

of the assize clerk and the local justices in support of his manoeuvres and threatened the gaoler with having to pay Bunyan's fees and with a complaint of misconduct, which would have led to the official's dismissal.[56]

Why should Cobb have gone to such trouble to keep Bunyan away from the assizes? It is possible that a clique of justices, with Cobb as their agent, were keen to keep the fluent and persuasive Bunyan out of an open court in which he might well have been cleared. We may also speculate that Cobb and his associates feared the possibility of a hearing for Bunyan that might show up earlier legal faults and, even more seriously, lead to his release.[57] This line of approach, and in particular the argument that Cobb was trying to keep Bunyan out of a court that would acquit him, seems to me to rest on questionable assumptions about the 1593 Act and indeed about the political atmosphere of the early Restoration period. The statute was a legal dragnet, which, intentionally, left no room for the acquittal of recalcitrant prisoners of conscience. And Bunyan was recalcitrant: at the August 1661 assizes, when his wife had put in her unsuccessful plea that he be heard, the most sympathetic of the judges had, rightly, been pessimistic about an acquittal, or had suggested that it lay in Bunyan's own hands: 'And unless there be something done to undo that [i.e. the earlier conviction] I can do thee no good.'[58] The most effective 'something done to undo that' would, of course, have been the act of submission which would have ended the whole process, but which Bunyan consistently refused to make. At the assizes that Bunyan wished to attend the law would have required that he be asked a variant of the fatal question that Twisden had earlier directed at his wife: 'will your husband leave preaching?' And it was, surely, inevitable that Bunyan would reply with a variant of the answer that his wife had made to Twisden on his behalf: 'he dares not leave preaching'.[59] No writ of error could then have been able to prevent the awful consequences that Kelyng had so graphically described at the quarter sessions. Cobb, then, was protecting Bunyan from the legal consequences of his own resolve. There were few, if any, grounds for supposing that Bunyan's appearance in court would have had any other result than the endorsement of Kelyng's earlier judgement. Bunyan himself was optimistic, ingenuous and, perhaps, ignorant of the overall political and legal situation, in believing that a court appearance would result in his acquittal. He blamed Cobb for barring his access to the bench, but he himself admitted that he did not know the whole position.[60]

Perhaps Bunyan might have guessed at some other motive than malevolence in Cobb's stratagems. For one thing, there was the evidence of Cobb's earlier attitude. He had referred three times in his interview with Bunyan to 'much good' that Bunyan might do, as a kind of auxiliary religious counsellor, within the confines of the Church; he had warned Bunyan of the dire consequences to himself of persisting in his courses; and he had used a 'civil and meek' manner. Furthermore, Bunyan became aware that Cobb had deleted his name from the calendar in such a way as to favour him: 'he also took the kalender and blotted out my accusation, as my Jailor had writ it ... [M]y Jailor himself, as I afterwards learned, had put in my accusation worse than in itself it was by far.'[61] Thus it appears that Cobb was prepared even to deceive the judges on Bunyan's behalf. Cobb may have felt that the impending sentence of banishment, with a reserve option of execution, under a particularly harsh statute that was not widely used after the Restoration,[62] was not only cruel, but was sure to make a martyr of a popular preacher who could be silenced with much less heroism through indefinite imprisonment. Knowing what we do of Cobb's political and religious outlook, we can guess that he would have wanted to suppress the opinions of this incorrigible dissident, and close confinement provided the means. Bunyan's family would suffer by his incarceration, but so would they by his banishment, and even more by his death. Imprisonment need not be for ever, and it was just possible that its harsh medicine might produce the desired submission. We may conclude that, for a mixture of motives, Cobb made possible Bunyan's survival.

As Bunyan began what were to be twelve years of imprisonment, his church entered a period of acute challenge, in which the psychological shock of the re-instatement of the Anglican monarchy had to be absorbed, attitudes to the restored Church of England and to shattering political events had to be evolved and articulated, a threatened haemorrhage of church membership had to be staunched and the continued existence of the community had to be organized. All this had to be undertaken in a new mood of rejection, of displacement and of alienation of the gathered church from its social surroundings. Thus, a sense of social isolation begins to be reflected in the Bedford church records, in a powerful scriptural vocabulary of estrangement: 'in the face of the Canaanites that dwell in the Land ... the customs of the people are vaine'.[63] Even so, this perception of a hostile outer world was not entirely well grounded, since, when persecution was stepped up against them, the church members could count on support from the local community.

The Restoration did not immediately see the Bedford church lose its political interests. Strongly political prayers were said by the congregation both before and after the Restoration, and the borough's mayor, John Eston senior, was a church member at the time of the king's return. However, the political prayers were becoming passive in tone – prayers for the welfare of rulers – and the sense of informed commitment and participation that we see in church records in 1659, when there were prayers of gratitude for the suppression of Booth's royalist rising, faded. The position of conscientious Dissenters such as Eston in borough corporations was to be made untenable by the 1661 Corporations Act, requiring an Anglican monopoly of municipal office. After August 1660 the democratic reforms of the corporation introduced in the 1640s and 1650s – the 'Levelling' Acts of 1647, 1650 and 1651, which had thrown wide open the formerly privileged burgessdom – were annulled, and the corporation was flooded with new entries from the gentry and aristocratic ruling class of the shire (including Sir John Kelyng), in preparation for a new royal charter in 1663.

For members of the Bedford gathered church, all these changes formed a study in contrast. The democratic by-laws that had helped to give a political voice to the kind of artisan-freemen – the 'meanest sort', who formed a major element of the membership of the congregation – were abrogated without the church's ability to resist. This systematic demotion and marginalization of a whole social and religious community within local society were epitomized in its expulsion from the parish church where in the 1650s it had occupied a central place in the town's religious life. The phrase 'deprived of our former place', entered in the church minutes to record the expulsion from the building in September 1660, could well have been used to sum up the whole experience of Bunyan's church, as its members were pushed from the centre to the margins of local life within a few months of the king's recall. The primary focus of consequent resentment was the restored Church of England whose 'superstitious and idolatrous worship' was upheld 'with force and cruelty'. However, such religious antagonism could not be divorced from its political context. When a leading member of the church, Samuel Fenn, reflected publicly on the crown, he singled out for attack the royal supremacy over the Established Church, 'gravely to deprive our Lord the King ... of his title and authority'. So, since the separatist approach to the Church of England and its relationship with the monarchy had disturbing implications for the social and governmental system, the Bedford congregation continued to be closely watched as a group of potentially dangerous oppositionists. Indeed, local magistrates continued through the 1660s to react nervously to the Dissenters and in 1655 the justices put the 'watch and ward' on special alert, with instructions to investigate conventicles.[64]

The mood and mentality of the Bedford gathered church in the 1660s, a decade laden with a sense of catastrophe on the part of English Dissent, can best be summed up in Hill's term, 'the experience of defeat'. The feelings of collective failure that overwhelm any heavily defeated ideological grouping were all the more intense for the English Dissenting churches, inasmuch as they had a conviction of divine support. Indeed, we can see Bunyan's congregation constructing a new awareness of God's abiding presence on their side amidst the mutability of temporal affairs and the 'slippery and unstable nature that is in earthly things'. Those words were written in a letter of consolation to a church member, one Harrington, driven from home by persecution. It fact, it was persecution that made possible the necessary psychological recovery of Dissent, as it undertook the transition from godly rule to second-class citizenship, and as it adjusted to the cataclysm of 1660. The scriptural model for the movement was now no longer Joshua, but Job; patience was to be the exercise of saints, God's choice was to be seen imparted to His suffering servants and, as Bunyan wrote, 'it was a mercy to suffer upon so good account'. Bunyan's experience, which was certainly no harsher than that of many Dissenters who met death in prison, shows us a religious community evolving through persecution into heroism.[65]

There remained the possibility of a recourse from present woes in millenarian expectancy, and the vindication at the second coming of those martyrs who, as the handbook of Christian messianism puts it, 'overcame ... by the blood of the Lamb' (Revelation 12: 11).[66] In her appearance before the judges Elizabeth Bunyan gave evidence of her own expectation of a messianic deliverance. Bunyan's church had had its own dealings in the1650s with outright millenarians such as George Cokayne. Indeed, it would have been hard for the congregation to escape the millenarianism that suffused English public life and, above all, the thinking of the sects, in that climacteric decade of eschatological expectancy. In the 1660s the doctrine of the millennium, evolved originally in the books of Daniel and Revelation to convey consolation in persecution and a conviction of ultimate victory, might have provided considerable emotional support for Bunyan and his congregation. The problem was, not only that the millennium was becoming intellectually unfashionable, but that it became associated with political radicalism and, indeed, terrorism. In Venner's rising against the Restoration, the Fifth Monarchists began their work with the shooting, in St Paul's, of an individual who failed to say he was for 'King Jesus' rather than King Charles, and the insurgents went on to murder large numbers.[67] It was, as we have seen, this incident that Paul Cobb had in mind when he spoke to Bunyan of 'the late insurrection at *London* ... [when] they intended no less than the ruin of the kingdom and commonwealth'.[68]

Thus, Venner's millenarian uprising seemed to bear out the depiction of Puritan dissidents as violent extremists, to justify arrests such as Bunyan's and to vindicate the anti-Nonconformist penal code being put in place from

1661 onwards. Millenarianism, and the expression of messianic hopes, consolatory as these might be to persecuted individuals and groups such as Bunyan and his church, were dangerous. Indeed, around this time the Quakers were transforming the doctrine of the millennium from an activist programme for the near future into a quietist vision of the 'Lamb's war'.[69] In the 1660s Bunyan trod a delicate path between expressing a consoling messianic hope and the avoidance of extremist or activist conclusions. He emphatically repudiated Venner's guerilla tactics, and his statement to Cobb – 'That practice of theirs, I abhor' – must be regarded as his sincerely held view of violent revolutionary messianism. Even so, Bunyan undoubtedly looked forward to a literal second coming of Christ in glory to rescue, and then to rule with, the oppressed saints. This hope was expressed, in a particularly vivid and condensed way, in his versified *Prison Meditations* of 1663:[70]

> *Just* thus it is, we suffer here
>   For him a little pain,
> Who, when he doth again appear
>   Will with him let us reign.

In the same year, Bunyan produced a major commentary on the Book of Revelations, *The Holy City, or, the New Jerusalem*.[71] In this, he dealt with the political ramifications of the messianic programme – its consequences to existing states – in passages dealing with kings, kingdoms and nations. At first, the message for these categories seems reassuring enough. The kingdom of God posed no threat to existing powers:

> The Governours of this World need not at all to feare a disturbance from her, or a diminishing of ought they have ... It is a false report then that the Governours of the Nations have received against this City, this *New Jerusalem*, if they believe, that according to the Tale that is told them, she is and hath been of old a Rebellious City, and destructive to Kings, and a Diminisher of their Revenues. I say, these things are lying words.

However, the import of these reassurances is subsequently undermined by much more disturbing messages: that the world's rulers have persecuted the saints of God, that they have been seduced by Babylon, the symbol of evil, that they will be recalcitrant to the setting up of the Heavenly City, and that they will be subjugated to the Kingdom of God after the humble have come to it willingly:

Alas, all the injuries that the Kings and Great Ones of the Earth have done to the *Church* and *Spouse* of Christ in these days of the New Testament … [B]efore this City is set up … most of the Kings and the great ones of the Earth will be found imployed and taken up in another work, than to fall in love with Mount *Zion* … [T]hey [the Kings of the Earth] … are conquered by the Grace of Christ, and Wisdom of the Son of God. *They shall make war with the Lamb, but the Lamb shall overcome them; for he is King of kings, and Lord of lords* … Now they shall all give way to the Government of the King of kings … *The Kingdoms of this world are become the Kingdoms of the Lord and of his Christ* … *The Kingdom and Dominion, and the greatness of the Kingdom … shall be given to the People of the Saints.*

It is hard to see how Bunyan could square these predictions with reassuring sounds about a Kingdom of God that posed no threat to earthly realms. He was at this time as convinced as any of the radical millenarians of the imminence of the apocalypse – 'Alas, it is now towards the end of the world'. He was sure that the *eschaton* would be one of deliverance – 'then the Prisoners shall be set at liberty' – and he looked forward to a Parousia of vengeance: '*he will avenge the blood of his Servants*'. As for the identity of that elect – those who 'build up the temple' – the lineal heirs of the medieval martyrs and the leaders of the Reformation were the members of the gathered churches: 'These be they that are for having the Church *a select company of visible Believers.*' In opposition to these saints, the 'Kings of the Earth … will be shaking the sharp end of their weapons against the Son of God, continually labouring to keep him out of his Throne, and from having that rule in the Church, and in the World as becomes him who is the head of the body.'[72]

In *The Holy City*, a classic of the literature of apocalyptic confrontation, the world's existing regimes are assembled in battle order in an Armageddon against the kingdom of God and the saints. This was not the 'mild and sedentary chiliasm' of Tindall's description, despite Bunyan's avowed intent to make the doctrine of the millennium politically innocuous. Bunyan, in fact, drew enough hope out of the existing apocalyptic corpus to make it consolatory, and sufficient menace to give it a subversive tone. It is true that his eschatological views, and in particular his view of the role of kings in the final drama, were to be subjected to extensive modification during his life, and in a work of the early 1680s, *Of Antichrist, and His Ruine*, he was to accord Protestant kings a leading role in bringing down the Antichrist. One would agree with Roger Sharrock that revolutionary millenarianism is absent from *The Holy City*, as it is from *Of Antichrist, and His Ruine*, and

with Aileen Ross – at least as far as *Of Antichrist, and His Ruine* is concerned – that 'far from being a political or social revolutionary, the Bedford
preacher was essentially a conservative, orthodox Christian, and his millenarianism a progressive, hopeful, peaceable view of human history'.[73] However,
in 1663, a long-term prisoner as a consequence of the Restoration, Bunyan
felt estranged from worldly powers and expressed that sense of alienation
in a highly charged apocalyptic.

Bunyan's portfolio of writings comprising ten works of poetry and prose
that were published in the 1660s, plus other works possibly composed
in that decade and published later, may occasion surprise that a prisoner
could also be a nationally known author, though prison authorship and
publication from a prison cell were by no means uncommon, notably in
John Lilburne's case. Perhaps what is more surprising is that Bunyan was
able to surmount the inconveniences, especially the overcrowding, of prison
in order to write: at times of increased persecution, the small county gaol
where he was lodged might fill up with more than fifty religious dissidents,
besides the usual quota of ordinary lawbreakers. Normally, such conditions
of overcrowding would hardly be conducive to sustained writing. However,
Bunyan's fellow-prisoners were largely made up of like-minded fellow-
Dissenters. Through some of them, such as Nehemiah Cox (from 1670),
and through visitors, Bunyan was able to maintain close links with his own
congregation and to help organize Nonconformity in the county. Indeed,
confinement alongside co-religionists, far from acting as a barrier, stimu-
lated his creativity: *The Holy City* originated as a sermon to other prisoners.
Christopher Hill also speculates that sharing imprisonment with some
local Quakers dulled the edge of the hostility that Bunyan had shown
towards their movement in the 1650s.[74] Apart from the stimulus of such
contacts, Bunyan had, as basic reference books, the Bible and Foxe's *Book
of Martyrs*.[75]

Bunyan was also able to do some limited work for the church: he acted
as a pastoral counsellor to a woman oppressed by guilt, and in August and
September 1661 he was deputed to try to dissuade members threatening
to lapse, the individuals in question possibly being directed to visit him in
prison.[76] However, Bunyan's activity on behalf of his church was, obviously,
restricted by the circumstances of his imprisonment. This loss was all the
more serious in that the congregation was now without its young pastor,
Gifford's successor John Burton, who died in 1660. His imprisonment
apart, Bunyan was the obvious choice to succeed Burton in the pastorate
and he took up that office after his liberation. However, in the early part
of Bunyan's imprisonment his church restricted its activities considerably.
Indeed, as persecution mounted with the gathering Cavalier reaction in the

early 1660s, the church sought cover, and its minute book is silent for five and a half years between 1663 and entries for September and October 1668, the latter indicating that Bunyan was then at large, at least unofficially.[77]

It has sometimes been claimed that, even before that date, Bunyan was at liberty. This was allegedly in 1666, according to a slightly confused account given by the continuator of Bunyan's autobiography, Charles Doe:

> [Bunyan was] confined in *Bedford* Goal for the space of six Years, till the Act of Indulgence to Dissenters being allowed, he obtained his Freedom by the Intercession of some in Trust and Power, that took pity on his Sufferings; but within six Years afterwards he was again taken up, viz., in the Year 1666, and was then confined for six years more.[78]

Apart from confusing the text on which Bunyan was preaching at the time of his re-arrest with the one that he was using when he was first apprehended in 1660, Doe probably erred in writing 'within Six years afterwards', instead of the more intelligible 'within six months afterwards he was again taken up.' These solecisms apart, though, Doe's account suggests that a kind of personal amnesty led to Bunyan's release in 1666, the year when *Grace Abounding* was first published.

Bunyan was certainly free in 1668, as the Bedford church book testifies: 'that brother Bunyan and brother Harrington send for brother Merrill and admonish him'.[79] The possibilities, then, are either that he was released twice in the course of the 1660s – in 1666 and 1668 – or that he was at liberty in only one of these years. If we had to choose one year when Bunyan's imprisonment was interrupted for some time, it would be 1668; arguments in favour of 1666, advanced by writers following Doe, hardly stand up. Neither the outbreak of the plague in that year, nor the fact that Lord Chancellor Clarendon was losing his grip would have set Bunyan free: the year 1666, when Bunyan's books were seized in a raid on his publisher's premises, was not a promising one for him. On the other hand, church book minutes recording his activity and movements in autumn 1668 were entered at the time and are, for that reason, authoritative. If the broader situation is relevant, then by 1668 the decidedly Anglican Clarendon had been succeeded by Charles II's tolerationist Cabal and, more to the point, the 1664 Conventicle Act had lapsed. Although Bunyan had not been imprisoned under that Act, its expiry marked a period of relative ease for Dissenters, and also one in which, as the now-resumed Bedford church records show, his work for the church increased steadily, even though he was still theoretically a prisoner. Of course, it may have been the case that he was released twice, or several times, during the 1660s and early 1670s, and that his eventual release in 1672 was anticipated in the previous decade. On the whole, though, it would appear that his imprisonment had a fairly protracted interruption only once: in 1668.[80]

Thereafter, Bunyan's imprisonment seems to have become more and more nominal and he was able to take on an increasing load of church work, culminating in his election to the pastorate. For some time the need for a settled ministry in the Bedford church had been apparent. After the death of Burton in 1660, the congregation adopted a joint pastorate, its attempts to secure a single leader having been thwarted. The period without a single pastor coincided with a phase of persecution and crisis for the church. The absence of a 'fit pastor' and of 'a spirit of government among us' was bewailed by one member, and others evidently shared his view that the maintenance of discipline and ministry was imperilled by the deficiency. In the rather less repressive conditions of the early 1670s, the church once more went about appointing a pastor. Bunyan was now extremely well qualified for the position. He had used prison as a centre from which to co-ordinate the organization of the church in Bedfordshire. A nationally known religious writer, he had given plentiful evidence of his constancy, sincerity and ministerial gifts. Even so, the choice of a pastor was not a foregone conclusion, representing the most important collective decision that a congregation could make, and the steps in Bunyan's election were carefully paced.[81] There was a proposal on 24 November 1671 at a church meeting at Hanes, Bedfordshire, followed by prayer meetings in branches of the church in Bedford, Gamlinghay and Hayes, to pray concerning 'the choyce of brother Bunyan to office'. In the event, Bunyan's election and induction took place on 21 January 1672:

> After much seeking God by prayer, and sober conference formerly had, the congregation did at this meeting with joynt consent (signifyed by solemne lifting up of their hands) call forth and appoint our brother John Bunyan to the pastoral office or eldership. And he accepting thereof gave up himself to serve Christ and his church in that charge and received of the elders the right hand of fellowship.[82]

In thus resuming the full range of its procedures, the Bedford church seemed to be signalling its emergence from its post-Restoration critical period. In the course of the 1670s, the church was to show considerable demographic strength, enhanced by the administrative work of Bunyan and a group of colleagues. Returns of Dissenters in the Church of England's official survey, the Compton Census of 1676, reveal the relative numerical health of Nonconformity in Bedford and Bedfordshire. The town's most populous parish – Bunyan's parish, St Paul's – had 605 Conformists and 70 Nonconformists, which, in any national terms, was a high proportion at 11.5 per cent. Bedford's five parishes contained an overall population of 1,117, plus 121 Nonconformists (9.7 per cent). For purposes of random comparison, Coventry's two surveyed parishes, with an overall population of 1,871, had 167 Nonconformists (8.9 per cent), Stamford's population of 1,577 had 17 Nonconformists (1.07 per cent), Southampton, with 1,618 non-Dissenters, had 296 Nonconformists (15.7 per cent), and Hereford, with a total of 1,755, had 58 Nonconformists (3.3 per cent). Compared with an average of 7.24 per cent of Dissenters representing wide variations in a group of arbitrarily selected towns, Bedford's proportion of 9.7 per cent is distinctly on the high side.[83]

The Nonconformists' own reasonably accurate census, the Evans List of 1715–18, shows the continuing comparative popularity of Dissent in Bunyan's county. The Evans List gives Bedfordshire a total of 9.33 per cent Dissenters – compared, for instance, with 8.26 per cent in Wiltshire, 4.45 per cent in Staffordshire, or 2.65 per cent in Lincolnshire. However, Bedfordshire stands out in the Evans List as having the highest number of Calvinistic (Particular) Baptists in England (without counting Monmouthshire) – 5.17 per cent, compared with the next highest totals of 4.26 per cent in Bristol/Somerset, 4.08 per cent in Hertfordshire, and a national average of 0.74 per cent. Clearly, then, not only was Nonconformity relatively strong in numerical terms in Bedford and Bedfordshire, but the variant of it to which Bunyan was aligned acquired an impressive *point d'appui* in the area.[84]

Furthermore, evidence suggests that, following the Restoration, the Bedford church gained adherents. Even in the dark year of 1663 the church was able to record '[f]ifteen Members added in three months during a time of violent persecution'. By 1668 the vicar of St Paul's was writing that 'the separatists increase daily'. Some members, especially those who were lukewarm about or hostile to the church's ethos, particularly its radical political image, drifted away or were excommunicated. However, given the perils of separatist membership, it is likely that new entrants tended to be active and committed. Efforts were also made to prevent further losses of members: in 1661 the town was divided up into three areas allocated to leading members to watch over congregants; in 1669 a letter-writing campaign was undertaken to keep up the enthusiasm of those members living at a distance from Bedford, such dispersion being a persistent problem in maintaining the membership of Nonconformist churches. These organizational strategies came to fruition in the 1670s.[85]

In and around Bedford there was a detectable lack of enthusiasm in enforcing the penal laws, especially from the 1660s onwards, which was partly caused by and partly the result of the relative strength of Dissent in the locality. It is true that the area had its hardliners, such as Sir George Blundell of Cardington Manor who cheerfully distrained on Quaker goods and who admitted that he 'would sell a cow for a shilling rather than that the work should not go forward'. The authorities also expected support from 'certain Gentlemen of the Town'. However, much of the impetus behind persecution came from the Established Church, and especially from Dr William Foster, a lay lawyer and an ecclesiastical official, commissary of the archdeacon's court and chancellor of the diocese of Lincoln. Foster held four church courts in Bedford between May 1668 and October 1669 and devoted his attention to harassing Nonconformists. He prodded a churchwarden into enforcing the new Conventicle Act in 1670, resulting in large-scale non-co-operation. Foster also issued a warrant for the arrest of two members of Bunyan's congregation, Samuel Fenn and Thomas Cooper, in 1669, and another for the re-arrest of Bunyan in the mid-1670s. As Mr Emmison wrote, drawing attention to the indispensable role of the Church and of Foster personally in maintaining a momentum of persecution in Bedford, '[t]he interesting fact … is that the warrant [for Bunyan's arrest] was drawn up under ecclesiastical, as opposed to lay, direction'.[86]

Foster was acting in some isolation in Bedford in enforcing post-Restoration repressive laws, especially once the perceived threat of sectarian Dissent as a revolutionary movement started to fade locally after 1665. But even the Established Church itself, or at least its lesser officials, seemed to be letting Foster down: churchwardens refused to act on information of conventicles. Meanwhile, individuals sentenced to banishment under the Conventicle Acts stayed in Bedford for years. Then in 1670, when the churchwarden Thomas Battison, goaded by Foster, tried to break up a conventicle, the town emptied of inhabitants to 'avoid his call' for aid. This was a borough with considerable support for the sectarians, especially from working people – the 'Tradesmen, Journeymen, Labourers and Servants' – as distinct from those 'gentlemen of the Town' who may have provided some support for the penal laws when pushed. This relative tolerance that extended to Bunyan's church should be taken into account when we consider the 'organizational response' of Bunyan and his fellow separatists to their tribulations and to their opportunities.[87]

Richard Greaves has shown that '[i]n the 1670s John Bunyan and his Nonconformist colleagues put into effect an "organizational plan" developed during the imprisonment years prior to 1672'.[88] The plan provided a panel of preachers for the villages of north Bedfordshire and equipped local Dissent with a resilient structure, which was able both to withstand

the persecution that was certainly forthcoming and to produce a missionary response in the event of toleration. Individuals committed to Bedford
gaol with Bunyan in the 1660s included radical religious leaders of the
1650s, such as John Donne of Pertenhall and Keysoe. The second Conventicle Act and its enforcement by William Foster brought together in the
prison a nucleus of up to nine individuals who planned an underground
network for local Dissent which functioned for the following two decades.
The first fruit of this planning, though, was a highly orchestrated response
to the Declaration of Indulgence of 1672. Licences were applied for, by
Bunyan and his associate Thomas Taylor, on behalf of five individual Bedfordshire churches with their local branches, and of these, predictably, the
Bedford church put in the largest number of applications.

A striking fact about these preachers and organizers is that they were
heavily recruited from that same artisan class to which Bunyan belonged –
heelmaker, blacksmith, cordwainer, saddler, weaver, and so on – along with
some small shopkeepers or merchants, husbandmen or yeomen, and the
ordained minister John Gibb of Newport Pagnell (son of a Bedford craftsman). A group of these north Bedfordshire Dissenters was admitted to
membership of the Bedford church in the late 1660s and early 1670s,
forming a new generation of leaders shaped by the experience or prospect
of post-Restoration persecution. A notable feature of the organizational
structure was a system of liaison through visitors and formally appointed
missionaries. In this way the erosion of local congregations through isolation might be averted.[89]

Bunyan emerges from Greaves's close analysis as the co-ordinator of an
impressive church organization. He was able to do for Bedfordshire Dissent
what Fox was doing, on a wider canvas, for Quakerism: constructing a network. The longer-term results of these efforts can be seen in the remarkable
strength of Particular Baptist Nonconformity in Bedfordshire into the
eighteenth century. It seems, though, that this work must have soaked up
much of Bunyan's time and energy. His silence as a published author
between 1666 and 1671 or 1672 may be explained in various ways – that
he was working on material, especially *The Pilgrim's Progress*, that later
saw the light of day; that repression and the raid on his publisher in
1666 discouraged publication; or that he was mutely contemplating 'the
approach of the millennium'. However, as Greaves writes: 'The silence is
better attributed to Bunyan's preaching forays and organizational work in
these years.'[90]

The culmination of these years of preparation came in 1671 when Bunyan was elected to the pastorate and then in 1672 when he was allowed by
the Declaration of Indulgence to assume his role openly.[91] Despite some

reservations about the ambitious exercise of the royal prerogative that was involved in the Declaration and about the (restricted) inclusion of Catholics in its benefits, Nonconformists generally welcomed the measure and, after a decade and more of repression, applied for licences to conduct worship. Twenty-five of these were issued in Bedfordshire (compared, for example, with sixteen in Buckinghamshire, twenty-five in Cambridgeshire, twenty in Hertfordshire and fifteen in Huntingdonshire). In Bedfordshire, most unusually, the overwhelming preponderance – nineteen out of twenty-five applications – was submitted on behalf of communities identified, broadly, as 'Congregational', including Bunyan's own licence to preach, at the house of Josias Roughead in Bedford. Other licensees included such men as Thomas Cooper, John Donne, Simon Hayes and John Wright, identified by Greaves as fellow-prisoners of Bunyan and fellow-organizers with him in the period up to 1672. Though in other parts of the country Congregationals tended to take second place to Presbyterians in the number of licences issued, the tag 'Congregational' – the generic, embracing term that was doubtless deliberately chosen to avoid divisiveness – dominated the Bedfordshire applications, confirming an impression of the group's organizational efficiency and of a co-ordinated response to the opportunities presented by the Declaration of Indulgence. An additional list – of premises with a licence, without the name of a 'teacher', but only that of the owner of the property in question – shows an overwhelming Congregational predominance in Bedfordshire, with thirteen out of fifteen licences awarded to that denomination.[92]

A follow-up to the Declaration of Indulgence had a particular bearing on Bunyan. No Quakers applied for licences. For them, worship was inherently free, and the state had no moral right either to prevent or to permit the worship of God. However, in 1672 hundreds of Quakers were still languishing in gaol under various penal statutes. One of their leaders, George Whitehead, successfully applied to the king for their release and subsequently advised the freeing of other Dissenters under a royal pardon. It was through this 'Quaker pardon' that Bunyan was freed in May 1672, with a formal royal pardon granted in September.[93] Immediately upon his release, Bunyan set to work at his ministerial and administrative duties in the church, as well as re-building his livelihood. He co-ordinated applications for licences to preach, making twenty-five submissions for other preachers and thirty requests for buildings to be registered for worship. He travelled extensively, kept up connections with satellite congregations of the Bedford church, visited other gathered churches in Cambridgeshire, Hertfordshire and Huntingdonshire, and obtained permission to preach in Leicestershire.[94]

As a result of a Quaker initiative, Bunyan was thus able to resume his full church ministry. What were his views on the Quakers in the 1670s, two decades after his early theological combat with them? Clearly, changes had taken place: although many of the basic differences between his theology and that of the Quakers still remained, in some areas the potential for antipathy had diminished. The intense and, to Bunyan's way of thinking, unacceptable feeling of identity with Christ that we find in early Quakers, such as James Nayler, faded after the Restoration into a rather more 'respectable' Quakerism that would have met with fewer objections from the Christologically conservative Bunyan. Indeed, all the Nonconformist sects drew closer together after the Restoration, sharing a common persecution. In the 1650s Bunyan's Quaker opponent Edward Burrough had castigated the Bedfordshire Independents of Bunyan's persuasion for acting as paid agents in a national, state-financed establishment of religion. Though the charge might have stuck when it was made, after 1660 the Bedford separatists became a self-supporting church, free of state maintenance and with no paid ministers – like the Quakers. While differences in areas such as this faded, Bunyan got to know Quakers better on a personal level, meeting many of them in prison.[95]

In the 1670s Bunyan emerged as a figure of reconciliation, especially with respect to differences within his own church. It is hard to categorize that church as, strictly speaking, Baptist. Although it upheld believers', that is, effectively, adult baptism, and although Bunyan himself may have undergone such a baptism upon his entry into the congregation, the Bedford church did not make believers' baptism a condition of full communicant membership, but upheld Gifford's teaching that there should be no 'separation from the Church about baptism'. True to this tradition, in a work published in 1673, *Differences in Judgment about Water-Baptism, No Bar to Communion*, Bunyan argued that such disagreements should be 'no bar to Communion within the Church'. That work was part of a polemical exchange in which Bunyan argued for an open approach to these differences over baptism. However, in this controversial encounter he was trying to avoid controversy and to find a broad measure of agreement with Baptists, in whose ranks he counted himself: 'I go under that name myself.' Throughout, though, Bunyan was attempting to make the basis of his Christianity as broad as possible, avoiding labels when these were merely divisive.[96]

Bunyan's emergence as an eirenic thinker and writer can also be seen in his approach to the Church of England, even though this was, on the face of it, cast in terms of controversy. In the early 1670s Bunyan went on the offensive against an Anglican writer, one of the emergent Latitudinarian school, a Bedfordshire man, Edward Fowler, rector of Northill. In a 1671 work, *The Design of Christianity*, Fowler allegedly put forward doctrines of salvation through human effort – ideas which seemed to Bunyan to undermine the very foundations of Protestantism, including the Protestantism of the Church of England. Therefore, in his *A Defence of the Doctrine of Justification, by Faith in Jesus Christ* (1672) Bunyan, in the somewhat odd position of the dissident upholding orthodoxy, attacked what he saw as the revisionist notions of human sufficiency and confidence in good works which he claimed to detect in Fowler. Bunyan attacked Fowler personally, according to the polemical conventions of the time. However, it might be said that in this controversy Bunyan was actually defending several of the Thirty-nine Articles and the Church of England's Protestant fundamentals – its 'wholesome Doctrine' – against innovation. When Fowler (or his curate) replied, in the vituperative *Dirt Wip't Off* (1672), dredging up weary clichés about the unfittedness of a self-educated man to write, Bunyan ignored the matter: his concerns were increasingly with the affairs of his own church. Even so, his relative openness to the Church of England can perhaps be seen in the baptism of his son Joseph in the parish church in November 1672.[97] For the Bunyans, this would have amounted to little more than the registration of a birth. However, it perhaps suggests an attitude to the Church of England that was less hostile than that usually found in the recorded proceedings of his congregation.

As a minister, Bunyan now had to defend his reputation against allegations of sexual misconduct, of a kind commonly made against unofficial charismatic preachers. A whiff of sexual scandal in 1674 played into the hands of Bunyan's foes and prompted him, Brown suggested, to insert into later editions of *Grace Abounding* a retrospective repudiation of the allegations of sexual impropriety that had been levelled against him in the 1650s. The woman at the centre of the rumours, Agnes Beaumont, had been received into Bunyan's church in 1672. She told her story, in vivid, vernacular prose, with irregular spelling that probably reflected her south Midland dialect pronunciation, in a *Narrative of the Persecution of Agnes Beaumont in 1674*.[98] The case is interesting for the light it sheds on male and parental power over women in seventeenth-century England and on the extent of women's freedom in religious matters. An articulate and religiously sensitive woman, Beaumont wrote feelingly in her *Narrative* of her life of prayer and her love of 'the Lords table'. Drawn magnetically to congregational worship, she related how she had had to plead with her father for permission to attend a meeting at Gamlinghay in Cambridgeshire, and how he grudgingly gave his consent on condition that she perform her household tasks before leaving home. Beaumont's *Narrative* reveals not only how much a seventeenth-century woman might be subject to male permission even to travel from home, but also how she might be totally dependent on men for transport. In the 'deep of Winter', she pleaded unsuccessfully with her brother, a church member, for a horse to take her to a meeting. Her intense need to be present at worship and her anguish at the prospect of being denied it come across sharply in her narration: 'now my way is hedged up wth thornes. And their I weighted, and lookt, many a long looke ... wth my heart full of feares least I should not goe.' Beaumont's literary approach, with its vivid metaphors and its sharp recollections of incident, dialogue and states of feeling, remind us of Bunyan's style in *Grace Abounding*. Both Beaumont and Bunyan were influenced in their writing by the conventions of discourse in the gathered church.

Beaumont was very much under the influence of Bunyan as a religious teacher. Stranded, she was surprised by his unexpected arrival at her brother's house, on his own way to the meeting. The idea that Beaumont was in love with Bunyan is given some credence by her shy ploy of getting her brother to act as a go-between with the preacher to get her a lift on his horse. More likely, she was acutely anxious to attend the worship; as her brother said to Bunyan: 'If yow doe not Cary her, yow will breake her heart.' Bunyan was reluctant to take her, and a gruff and cold side of him is glimpsed: 'he Answered my Brother very roughly, and said, "Noe not I, I will not Cary her." These was Cutting words to me indeed, wch made mee weepe bitterly.'[99] In a prim and inquisitive society, an unwed woman on horseback behind a married man amounted to a compromising situation, of the kind that Bunyan had to avoid, girt as he was by enemies out to trap him. Believing strongly in parental authority, he had to take account of Beaumont's father's rights over his daughter: 'if I should cary yow, yor father would be greivous Angrey wth me'. Eventually, Bunyan was prevailed on to give her a ride, infuriating her father. There is no mistaking her pleasure in her ride. Not only was she managing to get to the meeting, but she was riding behind the best-known religious leader in her region, 'and proud to thincke I should ride behind Such A man as he was ... And sometimes he would be speaking to mee About the things of god as we went Along.'[100] Beaumont's *Narrative* includes, like all good travelogues, at least one character met along the way – the clergyman, Lane of Edworth. At the sight of Bunyan in an ambiguous situation, Lane was 'as if he would have staird his Eyes Out'. However, Beaumont's soaring spiritual lyric indicates that her love was not for Bunyan but for 'Iesus Christ; how faine would I have dyed in the place, yt I might have gone the next way to him, my blessed Saviour. A sence of my sinns, and of his dying love, made me love him, and long to be with him.'[101] Beaumont next recounted her weary, wet, anxious, cold journey home after the meeting, 'plosshing through the durt over shoes' and culminating in a dismal arrival at her father's house, all in darkness and locked against her. A brief discussion at his bedroom window showed Beaumont senior to be implacable: 'Where yow have beene all day, goe at Night.' She spent a freezing night in the barn and was eventually readmitted to the house, on condition that she renounce Bunyan and the congregation. The whole incident provides the clearest instance of male totalitarianism, moral blackmail and the denial of religious rights – in this case those of a woman of highly tuned sensibilities. Religious repression in seventeenth-century England's patriarchal society was a matter not just of statutes and magistrates, but also one of everyday domestic tyranny.

There was worse to come, as the Beaumont affair switched from tension to tragedy. Following a weekend of bitter conflict, Beaumont's father died suddenly of a seizure, probably as a result of anger over his daughter's going to the meeting in Bunyan's company. Parson Lane reported seeing her with Bunyan, and a thwarted suitor alleged that Bunyan and Beaumont had conspired to poison her father. She was acquitted of the charge by a coroner's inquest.[102] However, such publicity was bound to damage Bunyan, and Beaumont's *Narrative*, with its addendum denying that Bunyan was a widower wishing to make her his wife, seems to have been written partly with a view to clearing his name.

As the continuator of Bunyan's autobiography, Charles Doe made no mention of the Beaumont affair, even though it was of some importance in Bunyan's life and the account of it was appended to editions of *Grace Abounding* from 1680 onwards.[103] However, it is important to realize part of Doe's purpose. Knowledge of the Beaumont incident was already available through the 1680 addendum, but it may have been the case that Doe ignored the episode because he was remoulding Bunyan as a kind of model for bourgeois Nonconformity after the Glorious Revolution. This ideal type of Dissenter was a prudent, low-risk personality, a respectable, affluent, domesticated and sedate *paterfamilias* – the kind of individual in whose life even a suggestion of scandal, as in the Beaumont affair, played no part. As Doe wrote of Bunyan: '[T]his person managed all his affairs with such exactness as if he had made it his study above all other things, not to give occasion of offence ... In his Family he kept up a very strict Discipline, in Prayer and Exhtortations.'[104] Such a paragon of probity sat awkwardly with the charismatic firebrand who had got involved in a dubious situation with a woman less than half his age on the snowy roads of north Bedfordshire in 1674.

In his continuation, Doe also touched on Bunyan's relations with the authorities, and especially with the Church of England. Here again, his purpose seems to have been to fashion a character suitable for a post-Revolution readership. In particular, Doe may have sought to present Bunyan as a consensual figure, operating in a climate of agreement in which moderate Nonconformists saw eye to eye with liberal Anglicans on the basis of a shared Protestantism. Probably for this reason, and possibly also to obscure from post-Revolution readers the fact that in 1672 Bunyan had been the beneficiary of an exercise of royal prerogative which, from the point of view of James II's similar experiments, would have proved an embarrassment to Bunyan's reputation as Doe wished to reconstruct it, Doe emphasized the role of a moderate-minded bishop, Thomas Barlow of Lincoln, and a group of other like-minded clerics in obtaining Bunyan's release from prison in 1672. Bunyan's patience under duress, Doe wrote, prompted 'Dr. *Barlow* the then Bishop of *Lincoln*, and other Churchmen, to pity his hard and unreasonable sufferings, so far as to stand very much his Friends, in procuring his Enlargement.'[105] The real picture is perhaps more complex. Barlow did not obtain Bunyan's release in 1672, because he was not then bishop of the diocese of Lincoln in which Bunyan lived. Moreover, Bunyan might easily be depicted not as the beneficiary of Anglican benevolence, but the victim of sustained Anglican intolerance in the 1670s. Fowler relentlessly attacked 'the very Pestilent Schismatick', pillorying Bunyan's alleged ignorance, and a propaganda campaign of vilification was launched by Lane in 1674. Above all, Bunyan was an outstanding victim of a new wave of ecclesiastical aggression in the mid-1670s and was imprisoned again as a result of it. Doe represented this reimprisonment as the operation of a malign but impersonal fate: 'another short affliction ... fell to his share'.[106] In fact, Bunyan was locked up again as a consequence of a new drive by clerical zealots against religious dissidents.

There was an emphatic reassertion of the Anglican interest, especially as a political force, after 1672, as the clergy increasingly took on the role of a pressure group, close to the centres of power, operating to defend the Church of England's position. In March 1673 the king succumbed to pressure to revoke what was portrayed as the unconstitutional Declaration of Indulgence. The Cabal administration that had backed the tolerationist policies broke up, to be succeeded by the markedly Anglican leadership of the Lord Treasurer Danby. A reaffirmation of Anglicanism took place. The bishops, led by Archbishop Sancroft and encouraged by Danby and by their success in having the Declaration cancelled, worked with resolution and co-ordination. In January 1675 they advised the king 'to take effectual care for the suppression of conventicles', and in the following month all the licences issued under the Declaration were recalled. Just as Bunyan had been released as a consequence of royal policy contained in the

Declaration, so he was to be imprisoned again as a result of the reassertion of the Established Church's hegemony.[107] Indeed, Bunyan was proceeded against not under statute – the 1670 Conventicle Act, for instance, which targeted the leaders of Nonconformist worship – but under ecclesiastical law, in a quite remarkable assertion of the remaining legal powers of the Established Church. William Johnson, Dr Foster's clerk and deputy registrar, apparently made out a warrant, which was endorsed by Bedfordshire magistrates in March 1675, for Bunyan's arrest. Bunyan somehow evaded this warrant, but a summons to appear before the archdeacon's court was subsequently issued against him by Foster under the ancient writ for the arrest of excommunicates, *de excommunicato capiendo*. Thus, as a result once more of the almost unilateral initiative of Foster as an ecclesiastical official, Bunyan again found himself a prisoner. He spent six months in gaol and was released in June 1677.[108]

Despite this chain of events, Bunyan's relations with the Established Church were not marked on either side simply by unremitting hostility. For one thing, in his polemical encounter with Fowler, Bunyan aimed at a theological *rapprochement* with traditional Anglican Protestantism – as we saw above. For another thing, the Established Church was a broad one, comprising hardliners such as the lay official Foster, but also comparative liberals such as the diocesan Barlow. Unfortunately, Charles Doe has been responsible for a certain amount of confusion over Barlow and his role *vis-à-vis* Bunyan. Doe gave the misleading impression, perpetuated by Asty in his life of the Congregational leader John Owen, that Barlow intervened to rescue Bunyan after his first term of imprisonment, between 1660 and 1672. This error then led Barlow's biographer in the *Dictionary of National Biography* to deny that he could have intervened on Bunyan's behalf, since he did not become bishop of Lincoln until 1675. However, though Doe was wrong about the date of Barlow's intervention, he was right about the basic fact, and the bishop of Lincoln was probably instrumental in securing Bunyan's release after his second term of imprisonment. Barlow's action, then, helps us to understand that Bunyan's fortunes were caught up in conflicting pressures within the Church of England as neo-Laudian uniformists, dominant in the institution since the Restoration, began to share its territory with a new school seeking a measure of Protestant unity with Dissenters.[109]

There has been some discussion over whether or not Bunyan wrote the first part of *The Pilgrim's Progress* during his second imprisonment, in the 1670s. This can be quickly resolved. The work is, as Bunyan makes clear, a prison writing, but perhaps could not have been started and finished in a six-month incarceration. Hill comments that whether Bunyan wrote the work in 1660–72 or in 1676–7 'doesn't matter much, but for what it is worth my preference would be for the earlier period'.[110] Perhaps Bunyan put finishing touches to the book in 1676–7, before its entry in the Stationers' Register in December 1677.

Bunyan's father Thomas died early in 1676, poor, though not destitute. We have no way of assessing the impact of this death on Bunyan himself. In his work on practical morality, *Christian Behaviour* (1663),[111] Bunyan discussed the duties of parents towards their children and those of children towards their parents. In a passage addressed to fathers, and headed, tellingly, '*Touching the Master of a Family*', Bunyan deals with fathers 'governing' their households and exercising religious leadership in families, controlling their reading and thinking. Children needed to be handled with 'Gentleness and Patience … love, pitty and compunction of spirit', but Bunyan's emphasis was in fact entirely on authority and discipline: 'If thou art driven to the Rod, then I. Strike advisedly in cool blood … Be often indeavouring to fasten on their consciences … their Death and Judgment to come.'[112] Bunyan's theory of the family does not seem too far removed from the domestic regimen of Agnes Beaumont's father. Indeed, if Doe is to be believed, Bunyan put into practice his principles of paternal dictatorship: 'In his Family he kept up a very strict Discipline.'[113] In common with the consensus of his period, Bunyan envisaged fathers in terms of authority, command and discipline rather than of intimacy and affection. His review of the 'Duty' of children towards parents begins with the obligations of obedience and deference. It is true that he also provides the occasional glimpse of a warmer, more personal and emotional relationship between children and parents, especially when children have themselves become parents and have come to know the agonies and joys of parenthood. Even so, Bunyan's analysis of parent–child relations in *Christian Behaviour* is mostly conditioned by formal and doctrinal considerations and by a somewhat judicial concept of 'recompense' by children for debts to their parents. There is little in this work on the family to suggest that Bunyan had a particularly close relationship of love and friendship with his father.

Throughout the 1670s, his brief imprisonment apart, Bunyan continued his ministerial work. He wrote *The Heavenly Foot-man*, a work which, as Graham Midgley says, has 'an assured and consistent literary mastery', pointing towards *The Pilgrim's Progress*, in 1671 (published 1698). Other productions included *The Barren Fig-Tree* (1673), an anti-Quaker work; *Light for Them that Sit in Darkness* (1675); and a catechism, *Instruction for the Ignorant* (also 1675).[114] He was also responsible for the continuing development of his church, and especially its evolution as a covenanted, godly, disciplined community, with a strict, clearly understood collective morality and 'brief confession of faith'. The upright life demanded of church members required stern disciplinary action, including expulsions of individuals for such offences as drunkenness, uncontrolled debt and card-playing.[115] Doe also recalled a gentler side, with Bunyan absorbed in visiting and consoling the sick and in reconciling families. Bunyan also consolidated his leadership of the church. The learned elder, Nehemiah Cox, with his well-advertised knowledge of Greek and Hebrew, may have tried to mount a revolt of some kind against Bunyan's governance and was called on to repent the 'rents and devisions' he had made in the congregation.[116] Indeed, it would have become less and less easy to challenge Bunyan's leadership and prestige. In his region his work in church government and organization now 'gave him the Epethete of *Bishop Bunyan*'. His fame extended to the capital; as Doe puts it:

> He often came up to *London*, and there went among the Congregations of the Nonconformists, and used his Talent to the great good liking of the Hearers; and even some, to whom he had been misrepresented, upon the account of his Education, were convinced of his Worth and Knowledge in Sacred Things, as perceiving him to be a man of sound Judgment, delivering himself, plainly and powerfully.

Doe went on to explain that many who came to hear Bunyan 'for novelty sake' went away edified and 'wondered, as the *Jews* did at the Apostles', at Bunyan's immediate revelation.[117]

Doe's remarks underscore Bunyan's links with the headquarters of English Nonconformity in London. We know that Bunyan delivered sermons to metropolitan congregations in Addle Street, in Stepney and in Southwark, as well as joining some of the intellectual giants of Dissent in delivering the prestigious Pinners' Hall sermons begun in 1672. Even so, and despite the fame of *The Pilgrim's Progress*, Doe's recollections make it plain that Bunyan continued to be regarded as an entertaining curiosity, as a formally unqualified, unordained natural or charismatic orator – the attitude eventually to be summed up in a London obituary notice: 'died Bunian … a man said to be gifted in that way [of preaching] though once a cobbler'.[118] The most famous London pulpit that Bunyan occupied was that of the Independent leader John Owen.[119] Once the academic star of Independency, Owen encapsulated the attitude towards Bunyan and his ilk that was still widespread in the 1670s and 1680s; it consisted of a mixture of condescension and astonishment at the 'Talent' – the inexplicable untrained gift – of the 'tinker'. Owen's remark to Charles II (who had enquired about Bunyan's fame) that he, Owen, would willingly exchange his learning for the tinker's ability to stir hearts[120] reminds us that in that caste-conscious society people could still not think about Bunyan except in terms of class, and of the apparent paradox of a plebeian who could think. In fact, Bunyan's vivid, demotic preaching realized the targets of 'plain speech' now sought by even the most erudite divines.

Through such figures as Owen, Bunyan drew closer to the religious mainstream of Nonconformity and away from the strict sectarian principles of those Baptists who insisted on communion only for baptized believers. That world of relatively liberal Nonconformity was held together, and its connections with moderate Anglicans such as Bishop Barlow were facilitated, by a marked anti-Catholicism. In the year of the publication of the first part of *The Pilgrim's Progress*, English anti-popery ran riot with revelations of an alleged so-called Popish Plot.[121] Bunyan shared in the anti-popery that lay at the heart of English Protestant culture, nourished by his favourite non-scriptural reading, the *Book of Martyrs*. His messianist work, *The Holy City,* written for the expected apocalyptic year, 1666, described the downfall of the papacy, 'the *Man of sin*, that *Son of Perdition* ... Antichristian *Babylon*'.[122] He was certainly aware of the atmosphere of paranoia and panic following 1678, when the new Whig party sedulously used the press to whip up fears of Catholic atrocities following a French or Spanish invasion and a violent displacement through the assassination of Charles II in favour of his Catholic brother and heir presumptive, James, Duke of York. Writing in the 1680s, he remembered: 'then we began to fear cutting of throats ... and of seeing our children dashed in pieces before our faces'.[123] All this was out of the familiar stock-in-trade of seventeenth-century English anti-popery, based in part on recorded atrocities committed by Catholics in the French Wars of Religion, the Revolt in the Netherlands and the Irish Rebellion. More immediately, Bunyan's horrific images of the prospect of a Catholic take-over were undoubtedly adapted from a best-selling piece of Whig journalism of the period of the Exclusionist campaign to secure Protestantism through denying the Duke of York his claim to the throne. This piece was probably written by Robert Ferguson, a Scots radical Whig and agent of the Whig leader, Lord Shaftesbury. The tract, with the title, *An Appeal from the Country to the City for the preservation of his Majesty's person*, included the following phrases, from which Bunyan borrowed for his own later evocation of the atmosphere of anti-popery around 1679: 'you behold ... troops of papists ... dashing your little children's brains out against the walls ... and cutting your own throats'.[124]

Though Bunyan subsequently recalled those phrases to intrude a retrospective note of scepticism about the Whig hysteria of the Exclusion crisis, it would hardly be surprising if, at the time of the Popish Plot itself, in common with the great majority of his fellow-Dissenters, he did not take to heart inflammatory messages such as Ferguson's. Indeed, his links with the Whigs and even with Ferguson at that time may have been closer than mere readership of Ferguson's outpourings. Ferguson was an ardent admirer of and assistant to Owen, whom he brought into Shaftesbury's circle, and Bunyan and Owen became quite close.[125] Though Bunyan was not centrally concerned with politics, he had personal links with the first Whigs. When we read his later recollections, albeit perhaps written in a mood of disillusionment with politics *per se*, of London's 'good Lord mayors, honest sheriffs',[126] we should remember that Bunyan was looking back on a time when the Whigs exercised a tight control on the London mayoralty, while the city's electorate voted into the shrievalty Whig zealots such as the Dissenter Slingsby Bethel, satirized as 'Shimei' by the Tory poet Dryden and a committed republican.[127]

Away from the capital, Bedfordshire and Bedford became Whig strongholds. In the election to the first Exclusion Parliament in 1679, the loyalist Lord Aylesbury's son, Thomas Bruce, could not withstand the local power of the Russell Earls of Bedford, Whig standard-bearers in national as well as in local politics. Whiggery in Bedfordshire, however, as the county's Parliamentarian and Puritan past would suggest, was far from being merely an adjunct of Russell patronal influence and of local deference to it; it was a spontaneous popular force, and when 3,000 men, along with the mayor and corporation of Bedford, came out to meet Lord William Russell before the general election of 1681, when the Whig members were returned unopposed, they were not acting as Russell clients but as an independent political movement which the Russells served and promoted. Thus, the county freeholders presented Russell with a manifesto containing six policy points which included repeal of the 1593 Act.[128]

As for Bedford borough, with its extensive freeman and inhabitant householder franchise, its adherence to the Whig cause was, if anything, even more pronounced than that of the shire electorate. The town returned, in apparently uncontested elections, two Whig members to each of the Exclusion Parliaments. As a freeman, residing and practising his trade in Bedford, Bunyan would have had a vote in parliamentary elections. If he used it, with the borough's elections not fought, he cannot have cast it in any other way than for the party that had made the cause of Nonconformity its own, the Whigs.[129] If, as we may assume, he adopted a Whig stance during the Exclusion crisis, where did he belong within the broad spectrum – ranging from acceptance of the monarchy to outright republicanism – of Whiggery? What was his political position during the Tory Reaction following the ascendancy of the Whigs? Finally, how might his political views have affected his attitude to James II and his overtures towards Dissent in 1687–8? As for the colour of his politics during the Exclusion period, Bunyan belonged within a tradition, going back to Tudor times and, above all, to Foxe, of loyalty to the monarchy for its historic role in delivering England from popery and introducing the Reformation and, messianically, in destroying Antichrist.[130] While, as William Lamont has shown, the messianic vision of English kingship became dimmed in the course of the seventeenth century, Bunyan was a political traditionalist with whom there remained a strong Protestant predisposition to acclaim the monarchy, especially in its millenarian role.[131] Others who shared that view, at the height of the Exclusion crisis included the Whig Baptist Hanserd Knollys and the co-author of the Popish Plot, Israel Tonge, both of whom looked to Charles II to crush the papal Antichrist: Whig royalism.[132] It may even have been the case that underlying Nonconformist support for the exclusion of the Duke of York from the succession was the realization that, as a popish king, he would not be able to carry out the cherished task.

Bunyan uttered his political credo of personal loyalty to the monarch at the beginning of the Restoration period: 'I look upon it as my duty to behave myself under the King's government, both as becomes a man and a christian; and if an occasion was offered me, I should willingly manifest my loyalty to my Prince both by word and deed.'[133] His own position within the apocalyptic anti-papal tradition of English Protestant royalism is unmistakable, his loyalty to the crown closely linked to his expectation of the indispensability of kings in bringing down Antichrist: 'the Destruction of her Flesh shall come by the Sword as managed in the Hands of Kings ... Kings, I say, must be the Men that must down with Antichrist'.[134]

For all the earlier record of the Bedford church of support for the Commonwealth and the allegations of subversion that clung to it after 1660, following the Restoration, and apart from the note of apocalyptic alienation sounded in The Holy City, Bunyan took a royalist line.[135] He had every reason to do so, especially in view of his belief in religious toleration, and every reason to detest the social, ecclesiastical and legal establishment apart from the king. In 1660 he had been arrested not by order of the king, but on the initiative of a local Cavalier landowner, who deliberately flouted the policies of religious toleration that Charles had set out so clearly in the Declaration of Breda. For a while, Bunyan pinned his hopes on a royal pardon, only to see the legal and social establishment thwart its application to his case. In the early Restoration years, just after Bunyan had begun his ordeal, in his Declaration of Indulgence of 1662, Charles was checked by the Cavalier-Anglican ruling class in his bid to uphold the promises he had made at Breda, thereby offering an alternative to a steadily mounting volume of intolerance expressed in the statutes of a Parliament dominated by landed gentry who were fully supported in their bigotry by the bulk of the Anglican clergy. In 1672 Bunyan was released as a result of another Declaration of Indulgence, though in 1675 an attempt was made by a group of Bedfordshire magistrates to rearrest him, and in 1676 he was imprisoned again, this time as the result of an ecclesiastical prosecution. Bunyan, then, was likely to distinguish between the king, to whom for both ideological and more personal reasons he had every reason to give his allegiance, and the landed Cavalier ruling class, the Established Church and, later, the Tories, all of which groups he had every reason to detest. This stance – this discernment of allegiances – was later to dictate his attitude to James II as the king attempted to break down the Tory-Anglican monopoly of power in England. During the Tory Reaction, the evidence that Bunyan's royalism remained genuine – calling into question Tindall's claim that he 'cherished a deep and natural hatred of … [the] king' – is particularly convincing when it comes from a treatise which, remaining unpublished during Bunyan's lifetime, expresses political ideas that were not put on for display, *Of Antichrist, and His Ruine*.[136] In this work from the period of the Tory Reaction, commending the Jews of the Old Testament who carried 'it very tenderly and lovingly to those Kings that at present they were under', Bunyan appealed to his (eventual) readers to 'let the King have verily a place in your Hearts, and with Heart and Mouth give God Thanks for him … Pray for the long Life of the King.' In what should be read as a rebuke to fellow-Nonconformists who had been attracted to extremism during the Whig ascendancy and were drawn to terrorism in the subsequent Tory Reaction, Bunyan described himself as 'one of those old-fashion Professors, that *covet to fear God, and honour the king*'.[137]

Throughout the hectic periods of the Whig dominance of political life (1679–81) and the dramatic swing to the Tories that followed (1681–6), Bunyan was phenomenally active as an author, including the production of three of his most substantial works, *The Life and Death of Mr. Badman* (1680), *The Second Part of The Pilgrim's Progress* (1683), and *The Holy War* (1684). His preaching work extended between Bedfordshire and its region, and London, and he continued to deal as an author with ecclesiological issues and as a minister with the organization, discipline and pastoral care of his church. As persecution of Nonconformists mounted during the Tory Reaction, he responded, in *Seasonable Counsel* (1684), with a fresh appeal for loyalty to the king. As Charles II's death in 1685 made way for the Catholic James II, Bunyan continued to be preoccupied with church affairs and, though he may have responded to James's accession guardedly, he certainly avoided any association with the Duke of Monmouth's ill-advised attempt to dislodge the king in the summer of 1685. Then, when James began his dismantling of the penal laws in April 1687, Bunyan responded more positively and, as Richard Greaves writes, 'availed himself of the opportunity to press ahead with his ministerial work'.[138]

Bunyan's established predisposition to think well of English kings may have helped condition his response to James II and his overtures to Nonconformity in 1687–8. Many Whigs and Dissenters allied with the king in 1687–8, when he pursued what was, in some respects, a Whig policy with regard to toleration for the Dissenters and also, J. R. Jones argues, the creation of a 'synthetic ruling class', centred on the commercial and urban sectors and their economic interests; Bunyan was likely to have been one of these new allies. Others included people like Lord Brandon, a Whig who took over the lord lieutenancy of Lancashire so as to forward the royal policy of repealing the Test and Corporation Acts, the twin pillars of the Tory-Anglican hegemony. On the more strictly religious front, James's active Nonconformist supporters included William Penn, who tried, with some success, to bring the Society of Friends around in support of the king's innovative policies. Many Dissenting congregations pressured their ministers to accept James's Declarations of Indulgence, and the Quakers responded to the opportunity to build a group of meeting houses in 1688. In Coventry the main Nonconformist denominations jointly addressed the king with warm thanks for indulgence.[139] Such records of complicity with a king who was systematically represented in retrospect as a popish tyrant had to be carefully scrutinized and, where necessary, revised when the history of the Nonconformists' relations with him came to be written up after his deposition in 1688; William Penn was found to be marginalized amongst Quakers. Bunyan's biographer Doe played his part in recasting the account of the Dissenters' responses to James II. Doe's recollections point firmly away from Bunyan's collaboration with the king. According to Doe, Bunyan was approached, as a leader of Dissent, with a view to obtaining his support for James's plans to emancipate the non-Anglican religious communities of Protestant Nonconformists and Catholic recusants. But he saw through the king's design to get Dissenters to back such a restoration of Catholicism as would eventually sink the Nonconformist, and the whole Protestant, interest:

When in the late Reign, Liberty of Conscience was unexpectedly given and indulged to all Dissenters of all Perswasions; his piercing wit penetrated the Veil, and found it was not for the Dissenters sake they were so suddenly freed from the Prosecutions that had long lain heavy upon them, and set, in a manner, on an equal foot with the Church of *England*, which the Papists were undermining, and about to subvert.[140]

Bunyan, in Doe's interpretation, came to the same sort of prescient conclusions that the anti-Catholic and constitutionalist politician, Lord Halifax, propounded in his 1687 *Letter to a Dissenter*: that the Nonconformists should be wary of supporting pro-Catholic policies which, by advancing Romanism, would subvert and ultimately destroy all forms of Protestantism. When it came to the more specific promotion of the king's policies, through preparing for a general election which James intended would result in a Parliament pledged to repeal the penal laws and the Test Acts, Doe recalled how diffident Bunyan had been about the whole operation:

> During these things, there were Regulators sent into all Cities and Towns corporate, to new model the Government in the Magistracy, &c., by turning out some, and putting in others; against this, Mr. *Bunyan* expressed his Zeal with some wearines [wariness?], as foreseeing the bad consequence that would attend it, and laboured with his Congregation, to prevent their being imposed on in this kind, and when a great man in those days coming to *Bedford*, upon some such errand, sent for him, as 'tis supposed, to give him a place of publick Trust; he would by no means come at him, but sent his Excuse.[141]

Doe depicts Bunyan as having been approached by a royal agent with a view to getting this influential Nonconformist to join the king's new-modelled corporation (purged of its Tory-Anglican stalwarts). From that position, he and other Dissenters would be expected to lend support, in the Bedford constituency, as others were intended to do throughout England and Wales, to preparations for a general election to return a Parliament with an anti-Tory majority mandated to repeal the penal laws. The 'great man' in Bunyan's account was undoubtedly the Catholic Lord Lieutenant of Bedfordshire, the Earl of Peterborough, who was busy furthering the king's policies.[142]

Was Doe's attempt thus to distance Bunyan from James's measures accurate? In his attempt to project a Bunyan suitable for a post-Revolution readership, Doe stressed that he drew back from the king's plans that would 'subvert' the Church of England. Yet Bunyan surely had no good motive to defend the Established Church, at least not at the price of foregoing a much-needed liberty of worship and civil rights. And even Doe had to admit that Bunyan had availed himself of a royal indulgence that was, from the strict constitutionalist point of view, illegal and, from the Anglican standpoint, in itself an attack on the rights of the Established Church: 'Mr. *Bunyan*, following the Examples of others, did lay hold of this Liberty, as an acceptable thing in it self, knowing that God is the only Lord of Conscience.'[143]

While Bunyan was thus portrayed as having responded only passively to the royal Declarations of Indulgence, Doe went on to claim that he tried actively to dissuade his congregation from complicity with the policy of ejecting from corporations those Anglicans who were unwilling to fall in with the king's plans, replacing them with Dissenters and, where available, Catholics. Yet if Bunyan tried in this way to counsel his hearers against compliance, he was singularly unsuccessful. In March 1688 a new draft of royal nominees to make up the numbers of the purged corporation in a 'regulation' included two members of Bunyan's congregation, and a further regulation led to the admission of at least four recorded members of the church.[144] If Doe was right, Bunyan would have been isolated from his flock, or at least from a group of politically active members of it who flouted his pastoral advice. Is it possible, though, that Bunyan was rather more co-operative than Doe, with his post-Revolution, anti-James II stance, tried to make out? In November 1687 one of the most enthusiastic local proponents of royal policy, John Eston, whose father had been a founding member of Bunyan's congregation, wrote to Peterborough that Bunyan and other Nonconformist leaders 'were unanimous for electing members who would vote for the repeal of the Test and Penal Laws'. Although ultimate answers are elusive, it seems that Bunyan was rather more supportive of James's policies than Doe would have liked to admit.[145]

Bunyan was now in the last year of his life and, dying on 31 August 1688, was unable to witness the reversal of policy by James II in the autumn and the king's capitulation to William of Orange in the winter of 1688. He died during a spell in London, the place with which his life as a national Dissenting leader was now so much bound up. He caught a fatal chill as a result of an excursion to Reading, to reconcile a family quarrel. Thus the cause of his death – a sudden illness contracted as a result of the pastoral work of family peacemaking – almost exactly mirrored the circumstances of the death of his early mentor, Luther. After providing for his family – 'he had disposed all things to the best' for his widow Elizabeth (d.1692) and five surviving children – 'he resign'd his Soul into the hands of his most merciful Redeemer' and was buried in the necropolis of London Nonconformity, Bunhill Fields.[146]

Notes

1. In John Brown, *John Bunyan: His Life, Times and Work* (2nd edn; London, 1886), p. 125.
2. For the details, see William York Tindall, *John Bunyan: Mechanick Preacher* (New York, 1964), appendix, pp. 217–22; and T. L. Underwood (ed.) *Miscellaneous Works of John Bunyan*, vol. I (Oxford, 1980), pp. xxviii–xxix. For this case and Bunyan's activities in 1659, see Richard L. Greaves's 'Introduction' to *I Will Pray with the Spirit*, in *Miscellaneous Works of John Bunyan*, vol. II (Oxford, 1976), pp. xxviii–xxxix.
3. John Bunyan, *A Few Sighs from Hell*, in Underwood (ed.), *Miscellaneous Works of John Bunyan*, vol. I, pp. 231–382 and xxxv–lvi; also in G. Offor (ed.), *The Works of John Bunyan* (3 vols; Glasgow, 1854), vol. III, pp. 673–724.
4. *A Few Sighs from Hell*, pp. 252, 257. Sharrock drew attention to the features of the 'traditional homily' and the 'old oral culture' in *A Few Sighs from Hell*: Roger Sharrock, 'Bunyan and the Book', in N. H. Keeble (ed.), *John Bunyan: Conventicle and Parnassus* (Oxford, 1988), p. 73. See also Underwood (ed.), *Miscellaneous Works of John Bunyan*, vol. I, p. liii.

   From the vast array of medieval English sermons of social 'satire and complaint', compare Bunyan's strictures to denunciations of 'the evil princes of the world, the kings, earls and other lords of estates, who lived with pride and with great circumstance and equipage, who used to keep many hounds and numerous and evil retinue … who nourished their own bodies in delicacies and the pleasures of gluttony and lust, who ruled their subjects harshly and cruelly to obtain the aforesaid luxuries'; or compare the preacher imagining the cries of the poor: 'O just God, mighty judge, the game was not fairly divided between them [the rich] and us. Their satiety was our famine; their merriment was our wretchedness … Their plenty was our scarcity': in G. R. Owst, *Literature and the Pulpit in Medieval England: A Neglected Chapter in the History of English Letters & of the English People* (2nd revised edn; Oxford, 1961), pp. 293, 301.
5. *A Few Sighs from Hell*, p. 340; Compare Calvin's condemnation of the characteristic sins of the market place: 'It is evident that nobody trades without lies and deceits … [Y]ou can see the cheats that everyone adopts to put one over on his trading partner; eveyone is out only to rob and to enrich himself at the expense of others; deceptions are carried out everywhere; one diddles you, another offers dud goods': my translation from A. Biéler, *La Pensée économique et sociale de Calvin* (Paris, 1961), p. 391.
6. *A Few Sighs from Hell*, pp. 257, xxxviiii–xliii.
7. *Ibid.*, pp. 253–4.
8. Christopher Hill, *A Turbulent, Seditious and Factious People: John Bunyan and his Church* (Oxford, 1988), p. 89. In *The English Bible and the Seventeenth-Century Revolution* (London, 1993), p. 78, Hill writes that *A*

Few Sighs from Hell 'must have contributed greatly to the Bedfordshire gentry's determination to silence [Bunyan] as soon as they got the chance'. For a consideration of Bunyan's 'class awareness' (and the limits to his social radicalism), see Richard L. Greaves, 'John Bunyan: The Present State of Scholarship', in M. van Os and G. J. Schutte (eds), *Bunyan in England and Abroad* (Amsterdam, 1990), pp. 33–5.

9. In Tindall, *John Bunyan*, p. 321.

10. For the Declaration, see Arthur Bryant (ed.), *The Letters, Speeches and Declarations of King Charles II* (London, 1935), pp. 84–5. For the 'Anglican Restoration', see Robert S. Bosher, *The Making of the Restoration Settlement: The Influence of the Laudians* (revised edn; Westminster, 1957), esp. ch. 4; also I. M. Green, *The Re-establishment of the Church of England* (Oxford, 1978), esp. ch. 9 for the gentry's role; for the sheltering of the Church of England by Royalist gentry during the Interregnum, see Robert Beddard, 'The Restoration Church', in J. R. Jones (ed.), *The Restored Monarchy 1660–1688* (London, 1979), pp. 155–8.

11. Jack Lindsay, *John Bunyan: Maker of Myths* (London, 1937; reprinted New York, 1969), p. 115.

12. Michael Mullett, '"Deprived of our Former Place": The Internal Politics of Bedford, 1660–1688', *Bedfordshire Historical Record Society* 59 (1980), pp. 2–6.

13. For the Wingates, see Brown, *Bunyan*, p. 134, and *Victoria County History, Bedfordshire*, vol. II, pp. 362, 363; vol. III, p. 381. For the gentry and repression, along with the circumstances of Bunyan's arrest and imprisonment, see Gerald R. Cragg, *Puritanism in the Period of the Great Persecution* (Cambridge, 1957), pp. 44–5 ff.

14. Hill, *Turbulent, Seditious and Factious People*, p. 115; Lindsay, *John Bunyan*, p. 115. For the background see Richard L. Greaves, *Deliver Us From Evil: The Radical Underground in Britain 1660–1663* (New York and Oxford, 1986).

15. 'A Relation of the Imprisonment of Mr. John Bunyan ... in NOVEMBER 1660 ... (London, 1665)', in *Grace Abounding*, p. 105; see also Roger Sharrock, 'The origins of A Relation of the Imprisonment of Mr. John Bunyan', *Review of English Studies* 10 (1959), pp. 250–6.

16. Danby Pickering (ed.), *The Statutes at Large* (23 vols; London, 1762–6), vol. VI: *From the First year of Q. Mary, to the Thirty-fifth Year of Q. Elizabeth, inclusive*, p. 423.

17. For the passage of the 1593 Act and the fears expressed at the time that its catch-all clauses 'might entrap the best subjects', see J. E. Neale, *Elizabeth and her Parliaments* (London, 1957), pp. 286–94.

18. 'Relation of the Imprisonment', pp. 107, 109. Pickering (ed.), *Statutes at Large*, vol. VI, p. 423. Talon brought out the choice presented to Bunyan between imprisonment and submission: 'He might have regained his physical liberty at the price of spiritual servitude; if he gave up preaching, he was

told, he would be allowed to go back to his family.' Yet Bunyan was not a martyr for martyrdom's sake – 'the subtlest form of pride': Henri Talon, *John Bunyan* (London, 1964), p. 9.

19. Pickering (ed.), *Statutes at Large*, vol. VI, pp. 424–5 (my emphasis).

20. 'Relation of the Imprisonment', pp. 109, 110, 111.

21. John L. Nickalls (ed.), *The Journal of George Fox* (Cambridge, 1952), pp. 133–7.

22. 'Relation of the Imprisonment', p. 109.

23. *Ibid.*, p. 108.

24. *Grace Abounding*, p. 160.

25. For Kelyng, see Eric Stockdale, 'Sir John Kelyng, Chief Justice of the King's Bench 1665–1671', *Bedfordshire Historical Record Society* 59 (1980), pp. 43–53. For Kelyng's unconstitutional attitudes (despite the value of his *Reports*) see Sir William Searle Holdsworth, *A History of English Law* (17 vols; London, 1922–66), vol. VI, pp. 501, 560.

26. For the quarter sessions trial see 'Relation of the Imprisonment', pp. 113–19.

27. *Ibid.*, pp. 117, 114. Kelyng, quoted in Stockdale, 'Sir John Kelyng', p. 48.

28. 'Relation of the Imprisonment', p. 116. Kelyng's claim that the Book of Common Prayer needed no special protection since it 'hath been ever since the Apostles time' seems bizarre – unless, perhaps, he had in mind the Prayer Book's antiquity by virtue of its descent from the English variant of the Missal.

29. *Ibid.*, pp. 115–7 (my emphasis); for a profound analysis of Bunyan's encounter with Kelyng in terms of the former's 'anti-hermeneutics of experience', see Thomas H. Luxon, *Literal Figures: Puritan Allegory and the Reformed Crisis in Representation* (Chicago and London, 1995), pp. 138–41.

30. 'Relation of the Imprisonment', p. 117. Kelyng's use of the term 'pedlar's French' – 'the jargon of thieves and vagabonds' – to describe Bunyan's religious rhetoric seems eccentric. Pointing to a fanciful belief in the existence of an elaborate criminal culture, with an argot of its own, the phrase was linked to another – 'the canting tongue' – and both were used of any convoluted speech. 'Cant' also meant 'to talk in an affectedly solemn or hypocritical way', 'a hypocritical or affected style of speech; the language peculiar to a sect … affected use of religious phrases or sentiments'. Jeffreys used the term 'cant' against Baxter to express his view of Nonconformists as whining, equivocating hypocrites: ' "Aye", said Jeffreys, "this is your presbyterian cant" ': quoted in *Chambers Twentieth Century Dictionary*: 'Cant'; N. H. Keeble (ed.), *The Autobiography of Richard Baxter* (London and Melbourne, 1974), p. 262; *Grace Abounding*, p. 160.

31. 'Relation of the Imprisonment', p. 118; for Bunyan's treatment of the proceedings as being 'more like debates about the meaning of Scripture than points of law', see Roger Pooley, 'Plain and Simple: Bunyan and Style' in Keeble (ed.), *John Bunyan*, p. 106.

32. Mullett, ' "Deprived of our Former Place" ', p. 16.

33. For Bunyan's dialogue with Cobb, see 'Relation of the Imprisonment', pp. 119–25.

34. For Venner's rising, see Bernard Capp, *The Fifth Monarchy Men: A Study in Seventeenth-Century English Millenarianism* (London, 1972), pp. 199–200; Champlin Burrage, 'Fifth Monarchy Insurrection', *English Historical review* 26 (1910), pp. 739–46; Greaves, *Deliver Us From Evil*, pp. 50–7. For Bunyan's repudiation of Venner, see Richard L. Greaves (ed.), *Miscellaneous Works of John Bunyan*, vol. XI (Oxford, 1985), p. xl; for contemporaneous reactions, see below, n. 67.

35. *Grace Abounding*, p. 161.

36. Fox, on trial in 1664, said, 'we have the word of a King for tender consciences besides his speeches and declarations at Breda. Dost thou own the King? If thou love the King, why doth thou break his word, and not own his declarations and speeches to tender consciences? ... I honour all men, much more the King': Nickalls (ed.), *Journal of George Fox*, pp. 467, 469.

37. 'Relation of the Imprisonment', pp. 120, 124. Compare Bunyan's views with reflections on the state by a sixteenth-century Anabaptist: '[W]e see how governmental authority grew and from whence it came, namely, from the wrath of God ... [I]t is evident that governmental authority is not of grace, but is given in disfavour and anger ... [T]he government is a picture, sign and reminder of man's departure from God ... [G]overnmental authority [has] its place outside Christ, but not in Christ': *Account of our Religion, Doctrine and Faith Given by Peter Rideman of the Brothers whom Men Call Hutterites* (2nd English edn; Rifton, NY, 1970), pp. 104–5. For a later view of the relationship between sin and the setting up of the state, see the joint statement of Independents and Baptists in 1647, supporting the magistracy as being ordained by God for controlling sinful man, in B. R. White, *The English Baptists of the Seventeenth Century* (London, 1983), p. 75.

38. Cobb never called Bunyan by what was then the honorific 'Mr' but by the socially calibrated 'goodman'. Bunyan addressed Cobb as 'Mr', and, though Cobb never once called Bunyan 'Sir', Bunyan addressed him by that title ten times in the course of their conversation. It is also worth noting how pronouns were used throughout these exchanges: Bunyan was usually addressed by the respectful 'you' (Kelyng once called him 'thou', when reminding him that he was a tinker), but later Bunyan's wife was spoken to as 'thee' by Hale, the term perhaps being used to denote kindness (as to children), as well as class and gender inferiority. Bunyan himself respected the formal conventions of speech – much more so than Fox, who, at his trial in 1664, insisted on addressing all and sundry with an egalitarian 'thou', but took great exception to being spoken to (by Twisden) with a demeaning 'sirrah': 'Relation of the Imprisonment', pp. 113–25; Nickalls (ed.), *Journal of George Fox*, pp. 466–9.

39. 'Relation of the Imprisonment', pp. 123, 125.

40. Pauline Gregg, *Free-born John: A Biography of John Lilburne* (London,

1961), pp. 102–3; Nickalls (ed.), *Journal of George Fox*, p. 383; White, *The English Baptists*, p. 99.

41. For the *'Discourse between my Wife and the Judges'*, see 'Relation of the Imprisonment', pp. 125–9. For popular knowledge of the law, see Hill, *Turbulent, Seditious and Factious People*, p. 124.

42. For Twisden, a Royalist but also a survivor, who had come through the Interregnum without much damage to himself, see *The Dictionary of National Biography*, vol. XIX, pp. 1336–7. For his 'angry' treatment of Fox and Margaret Fell in 1660, see Nickalls (ed.), *Journal of George Fox*, p. 390, and for Fox's getting the better of him in 1664, see *ibid.*, pp. 466–9. For Hale, who 'remained throughout his life attached to his early puritanism', who worked for the comprehension within the Church of moderate Nonconformists and who 'showed a certain tenderness towards the dissenters in his administration of the Conventicle Acts', see *Dictionary of National Biography*, vol. VIII, pp. 902, 908; for Baxter's tribute, *ibid.*, p. 904. Holdsworth wrote a lavish encomium of him in *A History of English Law*, vol. VI, pp. 574–97.

43. 'Relation of the Imprisonment', pp. 125, 126. For the proclamation of 10 January 1661, passed in the emergency of Venner's rising, see N. H. Keeble, *The Literary Culture of Nonconformity in Late Seventeenth-Century England* (Leicester, 1987), p. 29.

44. The indictment reads: 'That John Bunyan of the town of Bedford, labourer, being a person of such and such conditions, he hath (since such a time) devilishly and perniciously abstained from coming to church to hear divine service, and is a common upholder of several unlawful meetings and conventicles, to the great disturbance and distraction of the good subjects of this kingdom, contrary to the laws of our sovereign lord the king, &c.' 'Relation of the Imprisonment', pp. 113, 114.

45. *Ibid.*, pp. 113, 120.

46. Pickering (ed.), *Statutes at Large*, vol. VI, p. 424. For technical errors in writs and how they might be exploited, see Nickalls (ed.), *Journal of George Fox*, p. 705; see also Alfred W. Braithwaite, ' "Errors in the Indictment" and Pardons: The Case of Theophilus Green', *Journal of the Friends Historical Society* 49 (1959–61), pp. 24–30.

47. 'Relation of the Imprisonment', pp. 127, 118.

48. *Ibid.*, p. 118.

49. *Ibid.*, pp. 126–7

50. *Ibid.*, pp. 127, 128.

51. *Ibid.*, pp. 130, 121: compare the opinion of London conventiclers in 1641 that the Act 'was not a true law, for it was made by bishops': see Michael Watts, *The Dissenters: From the Reformation to the French Revolution* (Oxford, 1978), p. 78.

52. 'Relation of the Imprisonment', p. 129; White, *The English Baptists*, pp. 64–70.

53. 'Relation of the Imprisonment', p. 130.
54. *Ibid.*, p. 129.
55. Bedford Church Book, quoted in Mullett, '"Deprived of our Former Place"', p. 5.
56. 'Relation of the Imprisonment', pp. 130–1.
57. Compare Sharrock's view that 'the plausible Paul Cobb, possibly acting as agent of the local squirearchy, had [Bunyan's] name taken out of the list of felons and stopped his case from coming up' – so as to avert a likely acquittal and release: Roger Sharrock, *John Bunyan* (London, 1954; reissued 1968), p. 42.
58. 'Relation of the Imprisonment', p. 126.
59. *Ibid.*, p. 127.
60. *Ibid.*, p. 130.
61. *Ibid.*, pp. 130–1.
62. In 1664 Charles II pardoned twelve Buckinghamshire Dissenters, sentenced under the 1593 Act: see Watts, *The Dissenters*, p. 224.
63. Bedford Church Book, in Mullett, '"Deprived of our Former Place"', p. 7.
64. *Ibid.*, pp. 7–9, 4, 5, 7.
65. Christopher Hill, *The Experience of Defeat: Milton and Some Contemporaries* (London, 1987); Bedford Church Book, in Mullett, '"Deprived of our Former Place"', p. 6; 'Relation of the Imprisonment', p. 106.
66. For the now substantial literature on millenarian and messianic expectancy in seventeenth-century England, see, *inter alia*: Brian W. Ball, *A Great Expectation: Eschatological Thought in English Protestantism to 1660* (Leiden, 1975); David Brady, 'The Number of the Beast in Seventeenth-Century England', *The Evangelical Quarterly* 45 (1973), pp. 219–40; B. S. Capp, 'The Millennium and Eschatology in England', *Past and Present* 57 (1972), pp. 156–62; Paul Christianson, 'From Expectation to Militance: Reformers and Babylon in the First Two Years of the Long Parliament', *Journal of Ecclesiastical History* 24 (1973), pp. 225–44; Christopher Hill, *Antichrist in Seventeenth-Century England* (Oxford, 1971); Willliam Lamont, 'Richard Baxter, the Apocalypse and the Mad Major', *Past and Present* 57 (1972), pp. 68–90.
67. The incident was recorded, with considerable shock, by Baxter, Burnet, Evelyn and Pepys. Baxter recalled how 'about twenty or two-and-twenty furious fanatics, called Fifth Monarchy men (one Venner, a wine-cooper, and his church that he preached unto), being transported with enthusiastic pride, did rise up in arms and fought in the streets like madmen against all that stood in their way, till they were some killed and the rest taken and executed': Keeble (ed.), *Autobiography of Richard Baxter*, p. 159. Burnet reported, 'one Venner, a violent Fifth Monarchy man, got together some of the most furious of the party, well armed ... They scoured the streets before them, and killed many, while some were afraid and all were amazed at this extravagance': Bishop Gilbert Burnet, *History of His Own Time* (abridged

Thomas Stackhouse; London and Melbourne, 1986), p.37. Evelyn recorded 'a bloudy Insurrection of some fifty-monarchy Enthusiasts', inspired by 'madnesse and unwarrantable zeale': E. S. de Beer (ed.), *The Diary of John Evelyn* (London, New York and Toronto, 1959), p. 415. Pepys recalled how the news of the uprising was brought to him in bed, 'that there hath been a great stirr in the City this night by the Fanatiques'; after an evening out, Pepys's party 'were in many places strictly examined, more then in the worst of times, there being great fears of these fanatiques rising again'. Robert Laham (ed.), *The Shorter Pepys* (Harmondsworth, 1987), p. 109. For Venner, see Richard L. Greaves and Robert Zaller (eds), *Biographical Dictionary of British Radicals in the Seventeeth Century* (3 vols; Brighton, 1982–4) vol. III, pp. 268–70.

68. 'Relation of the Imprisonment', p. 120.
69. See, for example, Hugh Barbour and J. William Frost, *The Quakers* (New York, Westport, CT, and London, 1988), pp. 45–6.
70. 'Relation of the Imprisonment', p. 120; John Bunyan, *Prison Meditations Directed to the Heart of Suffering Saints and Reigning Sinners*, in Graham Midgley (ed.), *Miscellaneous Works of John Bunyan*, vol. VI (Oxford, 1980), p. 49; also in Offor (ed.), *Works of John Bunyan*, vol. I, pp. 63–6.
71. John Bunyan, *The Holy City: Or, The New Jerusalem*, in J. Sears McGee (ed.), *Miscellaneous Works of John Bunyan*, vol. III (Oxford, 1987), pp. 69–196 and xxxii–xlv; also in Offor (ed.), *Works of John Bunyan*, vol. III, pp. 397–459.
72. *The Holy City*, pp. 96, 135, 164–5, 166–9.
73. Tindall, *John Bunyan*, p. 132; Aileen M. Ross, 'Paradise Regained: The Development of John Bunyan's Millenarianism', in van Os and Schutte (eds), *Bunyan in England and Abroad*, p. 73; Sharrock, 'Bunyan and the Book', p. 78.
74. Hill, *Turbulent, Seditious and Factious People*, p. 122.
75. Brown, *Bunyan*, p. 163; for Bunyan's other – and extensive – reading, see Richard L. Greaves, *John Bunyan and English Nonconformity* (London and Rio Grande, OH, 1992), pp. 39–41.
76. Bedford Church Book, cited in *Grace Abounding*, p. 166.
77. Brown, *Bunyan*, pp. 188–9.
78. 'A Continuation of Mr. Bunyan's Life', in *Grace Abounding*, pp. 171–2.
79. Bedford Church Book, in *ibid.*, p. 166.
80. *Ibid.*, p. 167; Brown, *Bunyan*, pp. 183–4; for proof that Bunyan 'was not released and re-arrested in 1666', see Richard L. Greaves, 'The Spirit and the Sword: Bunyan and the Stuart State', in Greaves, *John Bunyan and English Nonconformity*, p. 104, n. 16.
81. See the excerpts from the Bedford Church Book, in Brown, *Bunyan*, pp. 199, 226–9.
82. In *ibid.*, p. 228.
83. Figures calculated on the basis of Anne Whiteman (with Mary Clapinson)

(ed.), *The Compton Census of 1676: A Critical Edition* (London, 1986), pp. 88, 251, 324, 351, 450 and Introduction, pp. lxxvii–lxxix.

84. For calculations based on the Evans List, see Watts, *The Dissenters*, table XII, p. 509.

85. *Ibid.*, pp. 385–6, 286–9; Mullett, '"Deprived of our Former Place"', pp. 4–7.

86. *Ibid.*

87. *Ibid.*; for checks on persecution, see I. M. Green, 'Bunyan in Context', in van Os and Schutte (eds), *Bunyan in England and Abroad*, pp. 9–10.

88. Richard L. Greaves, 'The Organizational Response of Nonconformity to Repression and Indulgence: The Case of Bedfordshire', *Church History* 44 (1975), p. 472.

89. *Ibid.*, pp. 472–84.

90. *Ibid.*, p. 472; see also Tindall, *John Bunyan*, p. 132.

91. For the Declaration, see Frank Bate, *The Declaration of Indulgence 1672: A Study in the Rise of Organised Dissent* (Liverpool, 1908), esp. ch. 5.

92. *Ibid.*, appendix VII, p. xvi; Greaves, 'Organizational Response', p. 474.

93. Bate, *Declaration of Indulgence*, pp. lix, 100.

94. Hill, *Turbulent, Seditious and Factious People*, p. 149; Greaves, 'Organizational Response', pp. 475–6 and ff.; Brown, *Bunyan*, p. 233.

95. Hill, *Turbulent, Seditious and Factious People*, p. 79.

96. Brown, *Bunyan*, pp. 239–41; for further discussion, see below pp. 177–81.

97. Brown, *Bunyan*, pp. 186–7; John Bunyan, *A Defence of the Doctrine of Justification, by Faith,* in T. L. Underwood (ed.), *Miscellaneous Works of John Bunyan*, vol. IV (Oxford, 1989), pp. 7–130, and xx–xxv; also in Offor (ed.), *Works of John Bunyan*, vol. II, pp. 278–334; see also Isabel Rivers, 'Grace, Holiness and the Pursuit of Happiness: Bunyan and Latitudinarianism', in Keeble (ed.), *John Bunyan*, pp. 45–69.

98. In *Grace Abounding*, pp. 176–9.

99. *Ibid.*, pp. 176, 177.

100. *Ibid.*, p. 177.

101. *Ibid*, pp. 177, 178.

102. *Ibid.*, pp. 178, 179.

103. *Ibid.*, p. xxxvii.

104. *Ibid.*, p. 172.

105. *Ibid.*, p. 168; for Barlow, see *Dictionary of National Biography*, vol. I, p. 1147.

106. In *Grace Abounding*, p. 172.

107. Bate, *Declaration of Indulgence*, pp. 140–1. For Bunyan's second imprisonment, and Barlow's role, see Roger Sharrock and Blanton Wharey (eds), *The Pilgrim's Progress* (Oxford, 1960), pp. xxvii–xxix.

108. Sharrock, *John Bunyan*, pp. 48–9. For Bunyan's life from 1675 to 1677, including church administration and his London connections, see Richard L. Greaves (ed.), *Miscellaneous Works of John Bunyan*, vol. VIII (Oxford, 1979), pp. xvi–xxx.

109. Brown, *Bunyan*, pp. 255–6; in *Grace Abounding*, pp. 168 and xxvi; Mullett, '"Deprived of our Former Place"', p. 7.

110. Hill, *Turbulent, Seditious and Factious People*, p .197.

111. John Bunyan, *Christian Behaviour; Being The Fruits of true Christianity*, in McGee (ed.), *Miscellaneous Works of John Bunyan*, vol. III, pp. 9–62 and xxix–xxxi; also in Offor (ed.), *Works of John Bunyan*, vol. II, pp. 549–74.

112. *Christian Behaviour*, pp. 22, 29, 30.

113. In *Grace Abounding*, p. 172.

114. John Bunyan, *The Heavenly Foot-man* and *The Barren Fig-Tree*, in Graham Midgley (ed.), *Miscellaneous Works of John Bunyan*, vol. V (Oxford, 1986), pp. 137–78, 9–64; and Introductions, pp. xlix–li, xiii–xliii; and 'Note on the text', pp. 134–5; also available in Offor (ed.), *Works of John Bunyan*, vol. I, pp. 378–94, 561–85. John Bunyan, *Light for Them That Sit in Darkness*, in Greaves (ed.), *Miscellaneous Works of John Bunyan*, vol. VIII, pp. 49–160; also in Offor (ed.), *Works of John Bunyan*, vol. I, pp. 391–436. For *Instruction for the Ignorant*, see below, pp. 182–5.

115. For examples of church discipline, see Michael Mullett, *Sources for the History of English Nonconformity 1660–1830* (London, 1991), pp. 36–7.

116. In *Grace Abounding*, p.169; Bedford Church Book, in Brown, *Bunyan*, pp. 248–9. Cox became a Baptist leader in his own right: W. T. Whitley, *A History of British Baptists* (London, 1923), pp. 131–2, 150.

117. In *Grace Abounding*, pp. 169, 170–1.

118. In Brown, *Bunyan*, pp. 383–4. Surprise that 'a man with Bunyan's social and educational background could have come to compose such a famous and widely read book' (as *The Pilgrim's Progress*) continued into the nineteenth century: W. R. Owens, 'The Reception of *The Pilgrim's Progress* in England', in van Os and Schutte (eds), *Bunyan in England and Abroad*, pp. 98–9.

119. For Owen, who helped Bunyan to find a publisher, see Greaves and Zaller (eds), *Dictionary of British Radicals*, vol. II, pp. 282–4, and Peter Toon, *God's Statesman: The Life and Work of John Owen, Pastor, Educator, Theologian* (Exeter, 1971).

120. Brown, *Bunyan*, p. 382.

121. For anti-popery see John Miller, *Popery and Politics in England 1660–1688* (Cambridge, 1973), esp. ch. 8; for the Popish Plot see J. P. Kenyon, *The Popish Plot* (London, 1972); for Bunyan's life between the time of the Plot and 1684, including his work for the church in Bedfordshire ('a fine balance of spiritual awareness and organizational aptitude') and his response to political events, see Richard L. Greaves (ed.), *Miscellaneous Works of John Bunyan*, vol. IX (Oxford, 1981), pp. xv–xxv.

122. *The Holy City*, pp. 134–5; Richard L. Greaves, 'John Bunyan and the Changing Face of Popery', in Greaves, *John Bunyan and English Nonconformity*, pp. 127–40.

123. John Bunyan, *Israel's Hope Encouraged*, in W. R. Owens (ed.), *Miscellaneous Works of John Bunyan*, vol. XIII (Oxford, 1994), pp. 5–95, 21; also

available in Offor (ed.), *Works of John Bunyan*, vol. I, pp. 577–620.

124. In J. P. Kenyon (ed.), *The Stuart Constitution: Documents and Commentary* (Cambridge, 1966), p. 467.

125. For Ferguson, his links with Owen and the latter's espousal of radical Whig politics and active resistance, see Richard L. Greaves, *Secrets of the Kingdom: British Radicals from the Popish Plot to the Revolution of 1688–1689* (Stanford, CA, 1992), pp. xi, 19, 42–8, 93–4, 121–2, 165–6; for Ferguson's literary theory of metaphor and allegory and its closeness to Bunyan' practice, see Barbara A. Johnson, 'Falling into Allegory: The "Apology" to *The Pilgrim's Progress* and Bunyan's Scriptural Methodology', in Collmer (ed.), *Bunyan in Our Time*, pp. 134–6.

126. *Israel's Hope Encouraged*, p. 21.

127. John Dryden, *Absalom and Achitophel* (James and Helen Kinsley (eds); London, 1961), ll. 583–629, and notes, p. 56; Tim Harris, *London Crowds in the Reign of Charles II: Propaganda and Politics from the Restoration until the Exclusion Crisis* (Cambridge, 1987), p. 183; K. H. D. Haley, *The First Earl of Shaftesbury* (Oxford, 1968), pp. 581–2, 563–4; see also below, pp. 279–280.

128. Basil Duke Henning, *The House of Commons 1660–1690* (3 vols; London, 1983), vol. I, pp. 125–6.

129. *Ibid.*, p. 127; Mullett, '"Deprived of our Former Place"', pp. 19–20.

130. See William Haller, *Foxe's Book of Martyrs and the Elect Nation* (London, 1963).

131. William Lamont, *Godly Rule: Politics and Religion, 1603–1660* (London, 1969), ch. 2.

132. W. R. Owens, '"Antichrist Must Be Pulled Down": Bunyan and the millennium', in Anne Laurence, W. R. Owens and Stuart Sim (eds), *John Bunyan and His England, 1628–1688* (London and Ronceverte, WV, 1990), p. 93.

133. 'Relation of the Imprisonment', p. 120.

134. John Bunyan, *Of Antichrist, and His Ruine*, in Owens (ed.), *Miscellaneous Works of John Bunyan*, vol. XIII, pp. 421–504, 485, 488; also available in Offor (ed.), *Works of John Bunyan*, vol. II, pp. 42–82.

135. Greaves, 'The Spirit and the Sword', pp. 102–26.

136. Greaves dates the writing of *Of Antichrist, and His Ruine* to no later than 1683: see Richard L. Greaves, 'Amid the Holy War: Bunyan and the Ethic of Suffering', in Laurence *et al.* (eds), *John Bunyan*, p. 67; see also Owens (ed.), *Miscellaneous Works of John Bunyan*, vol. XIII, pp. xxiv–xxxiv; for a further exploration of Bunyan's political views during the 1680s, see below, pp. 264–7, 273–4, 275, 277–80, 281–4.

137. *Of Antichrist, and His Ruine*, pp. 487–9; for Bunyan's life and writings during the Tory Reaction and the reign of James II, see Greaves (ed.), *Miscellaneous Works of John Bunyan*, vol. IX, pp. xv–xxv; vol. XI, pp. xv–xxi.

138. *Ibid.*, p. xv.

139. For the Whigs and James II, see J. R. Jones, *The Revolution of 1688 in*

England (London, 1972), pp. 138–40; for Penn and James II, see Vincent Buranelli, *The King and the Quaker: A Study of William Penn and James II* (Philadelphia, PA, 1962).

140. In *Grace Abounding*, pp. 169–70.
141. *Ibid.*, p. 170.
142. Mullett, '"Deprived of our Former Place"', pp. 29–31.
143. In *Grace Abounding*, p. 170.
144. Mullett, '"Deprived of our Former Place"', pp. 29–31.
145. Greaves (ed.), *Miscellanous Works of John Bunyan*, vol. XI, p. xx.
146. In *Grace Abounding*, p. 173; Brown, *Bunyan*, pp. 389–90.

THREE
Bunyan's Earlier Writings

Having reviewed Bunyan's career, we now begin to consider his literary output, starting with a group of key early writings: *Some Gospel-Truths Opened* (1656), *A Vindication of the Book Called, Some Gospel-Truths Opened* (1657), *The Doctrine of the Law and Grace Unfolded* (1659), *Profitable Meditations* (1661), *I Will Pray with the Spirit* (1662), *One Thing is Needful* (1665), and *Ebal and Gerizzim* (1665). The chapter that follows is structured in separate sections, each examining one or two works. The purpose of this chapter is to show how Bunyan's mainstream Protestant theological position was established in published work, in some cases crystallizing out of controversy, and to examine his evolution as a meditative writer; we shall also consider the development of his literary technique, in poetry as well as prose.

Some Gospel-Truths Opened and Bunyan's anti-Quaker offensive

Two expansionist missionary movements collided in Bedfordshire in the mid-1650s. The Quakers had already made deep evangelical inroads, especially in the North – in the Lake Counties and the Yorkshire Dales.[1] Quakerism, with its belief in a divine light latent in every man and woman, presented a challenge to the insistence in orthodox Calvinism, to which Bunyan subscribed, on sin, damnation and predestination. The challenge was localized in Bedfordshire with the establishment in the county of a Quaker missionary base, under the gentry patronage of John Cook at Beckington Park, where a Quaker Yearly Meeting was held in 1658. In the event, Bedfordshire showed only a modest number of about 560 Friends by 1718, compared with over 2,800 Particular Baptists.[2] However, that eventual, and rather disappointing, outcome was not to be anticipated in the mid-1650s, when the nascent Quaker movement was dynamic rather than sedate and when, with its influential gentry support and theology of hope, it must have seemed to pose a grave threat to the Calvinist evangelism in which Bunyan had embarked in Bedfordshire. Returns made in 1669, showing the results of the Friends' 'vigorous evangelistic efforts', recorded seventeen Quaker meetings, compared with eleven of Baptists, four of Independents and two of Presbyterians.[3]

The polemical literature arising out of Bunyan's defence of his mission territory against the Quaker offensive gives a strong impression of inter-personal confrontations. These began when the Quaker controversialist Edward Burrough heard a sermon by Bunyan at Pavenham, Bedfordshire, in April 1656, followed by further addresses by Bunyan, John Burton and other church members in May. In one of these sessions, Bunyan was challenged by a female Quaker evangelist. The substance of the polemical assault epitomized the Friends' alleged indifference towards the Scriptures and assailed Bunyan's acceptance of the Bible as the inspired word of God that had made possible his rescue from despair: 'throw away the Scriptures'; in *Grace Abounding* Bunyan registered his belief that the Quakers main-tained 'That the holy Scriptures were not the Word of God.'[4] Bunyan's response to this Quaker challenge took the form of his first book, *Some Gospel-Truths Opened*.[5] The title makes clear the work's local provenance: it was written by 'John Bunyan of Bedford', and the fact that one of the London imprints of the book was to be sold by the bookseller Matthias Cowley of nearby Newport Pagnell, Buckinghamshire, underlines its local significance. As well as being addressed to issues that had arisen in a particular area (a theme taken up by Edward Burrough in his counter-offensive addressed to 'especially you in Bedfordshire'), the work dealt with a situation very much of its time.

Assuming the persona of a critic of current modernity and a custodian of traditional doctrines, Bunyan set out in *Gospel-Truths* to confute errors which, as the title put it, 'at this day ... break loose'. The contemporary references pinpoint the then current religious situation in England, or a perception of it, focusing on the bewildering varieties of religious experi-ence which many underwent in a short time-span, 'posting most furiously in a burning zeal':

> Now ... a company of loose ranters, and light notionists, with here and there a legalist, which were shaking in their principles from time to time, sometimes on this religion, sometimes on that ... so many giddy-headed professors in these days, that do stagger to and fro like a company of drunkards ... in these distracted and dangerous times.

John Burton added his own reflections on the current situation, in a com-mendatory epistle to Bunyan's work, with references to Socinians, and to

'*Familists, Ranters, Quakers* or others'.[6] As well as containing these allusions to the situation at the height of England's revolution of the 1650s, Bunyan's *Gospel-Truths* is a highly personal work, in two senses: it alludes to his own experience; and it is the outcome, in its style and its substance, of his incipient career as a preacher and pastoral counsellor.

The allusions in *Gospel-Truths* to Bunyan's recent life, and especially to his conversion, are plentiful. Though less overtly, and to a lesser extent than in *Grace Abounding*, Bunyan draws on his own spiritual travail to write 'as he smartingly did feel'. This experiential approach enabled him to capture the unreliability of 'carnal security' and of trusting in 'thy own righteousness', the futility of which he had discovered and which he detected in Quakerism. His own recent plight had shown him that 'thy obedience, thy zeal, thy self-denial, thy holiness, righteousness' were in fact 'but sin in the sight of the great God'. In opposition to any view of inherent goodness, Bunyan recalled his own crucial recognition that 'God's grace is sufficient for thee'.[7]

As well as being a piece of experiential writing, *Gospel-Truths* is a personal work of its author in his now established role of preacher. A coda to the work concerned the debate about preaching for fees, but this issue involved the stipendiary minister John Burton more than it did Bunyan himself, and Bunyan the preacher is more evident in the tone of this book, which reflects him as 'preacher of the Gospel'. His preaching style comes through the printed prose most clearly in the form of dialogue, with the reader being addressed in the way that Bunyan was accustomed to speak to his audiences: 'Ah Friends, put a red hot oven and stubble together, and what work will there be ... Ah poor soul.' The effect of the dialogue mode is heightened through the use of striking figures of speech, such as the stark image of worldly people who pursue temporal satisfaction like 'a fool to the correction of the stocks, till a dart strike through his liver'. A question-and-answer format, as if to an actual auditory, is employed effectively: 'Ay, but when didst thou see thyself a lost creature ... ? Why do you doubt of it? ... Do you believe it?' The device is all the more successful when the same question is hammered home repeatedly: 'Art thou born again?' – this asked five times. Stylistic impact is also achieved with the repetition of phrases that become almost incantations, like the oft-repeated 'Jesus the Son of Mary, who was espoused to Joseph the Carpenter' (with its variant), or the haunting reiterated recollection of the Crucifixion 'without the gates' of Jerusalem.[8]

Bunyan's role as a missionary preacher and as a pastoral adviser is also evident in the content as well as in the style of *Gospel-Truths*. The proclaimed purpose of the treatise is to mount an attack on the belief, attributed to Quakers, in salvation by human means, based on free will and good works. Even so, there are points in the book when Bunyan, speaking with his preacher's voice, seems to play down predestination and to make way for some role for individual choice and effort. Bunyan's work of evangelization, in appealing to his audiences to change their lives, may have had some effect in this toning down of his attitude to predestination. Thus, at one juncture in *Gospel-Truths*, he discusses the struggle against temptation as if its protagonist were not a predestined soul, but rather a combatant in a battle for life. At another point, heaven is presented as an attainable goal and hell as an avoidable destination: 'here is the ... way to have the one, and the way to escape the other'; the reader is also invited to 'strive' and 'labour' for saving faith – a stress on choice and personal effort not entirely compatible with the 'eternal decrees'.[9]

Thus *Gospel-Truths* may be seen as the outcome of a particular series of events in Bedfordshire in the mid-1650s and also as the product, stylistically and substantively, of a phase in Bunyan's life, when his work as a missionary preacher had a strong influence upon his doctrinal outlook. However, *Gospel-Truths* is not only the result of temporary and local circumstances but also aims to present a set of what Bunyan regarded as eternal verities. The principles in question were derived immediately from the Reformation, at longer range from a school of Christian thought going back to Augustine and, ultimately, to Paul. The keynotes are a repudiation of free will, of good works and legal righteousness in attaining salvation, and a reliance instead on God and the merits of Christ alone to this end. Whereas in *Gospel-Truths* Bunyan, as a preacher and practical counsellor, may have shown occasional tendencies towards some acceptance of human 'labour' in achieving redemption, in the same work, as a theologian, he presented an impeccably Lutheran, Augustinian, anti-Pelagian and Pauline case, summed up in an early passage: 'thou art not profited by the works of the law ... salvation was ... fully, and completely wrought out for poor sinners by the man Christ Jesus'.[10] Bunyan needed to stress the humanity of Christ – whether or not his Quaker opponents actually denied this – to complete his view of justification: his soteriology dictated the shape of his Christology.

A standard version of the doctrine of justification by faith alone, without the 'works of the law', was set out by Luther in his *Commentary on Galations*, which Bunyan studied with great profit prior to his conversion. According to this formulation, God imputed the merits of Christ's saving death to the sinner and the appropriation of those benefits was accomplished by faith, which enabled the sinner to 'lay hold' of Christ's redemptive achievements. This salvific faith was a divine gift, and a selective one, because, if it were not, all would be saved, since faith was viewed not only as indispensable, but as automatic in effecting salvation. From this proceeded a theory of predestination.

Bunyan saw predestination as part of a scheme worked out over time, according to which God foreknew the Fall of man, and arranged for His Son to rectify its effects by means of a saving death which had the effect of a 'purchase'. This then qualified Christ to acquire a certain number of His own, whom He had ransomed from damnation in advance by His death. The redemptive fruits of the Son's death were foreknown to the Father so that He was able to credit the Son with the number of the elect in His 'account' long before the salvific event was to take place: that was how pre-destination actually worked. The contractual model and the terms used by Bunyan – 'purchase', 'bargain' and 'account' – were partly explanatory metaphors (rather like George Herbert's audacious likening of the Re-demption to a grant of a new lease of land), but they also pointed to a view of actual transactions – a 'forensic' treaty between God and His Son, dealings that were seen as having taken place historically, even if they occurred before history.[11] The terms of the treaty were:

(1) that to redeem mankind, the Saviour should become man and 'should take upon him flesh and blood' – this immediately obviated for Bunyan any merely spiritual, non-incarnational Christology;

(2) that the same Saviour should 'bring *everlasting* righteousness to justify sinners withal';

(3) that the terms, whose fulfilment was foreknown, were considered discharged by the Father before the 'bargain' was actually sealed in blood, making possible the pre-determination of the 'prisoners, poor souls' to be ransomed from the eternal death otherwise decreed for sin as a result of the Fall. The relentlessly transactional model – 'on such and such conditions as are before-mentioned' – is softened by a perception on Bunyan's part that the whole operation arose from the way that 'God brings out of his love that which he and his son have concluded upon'.[12]

The treaty made, the Father gradually disclosed its terms, partly through 'types' or analogies, to a succession of Old Testament figures, from Adam, Noah, Abraham and Moses to the Prophets, Bunyan here taking up a Cal-vinian view of the integral relationship of the Old Testament to the New. At this point in the work, Bunyan is able to convey an intense sense of expectancy, leading up the arrival of Christ as redeemer in the fullness of time. It was vital, and was included in the first clause of the original redemptive treaty, that this redeemer be fully man as well as fully God. Here, Bunyan sets out the so-called Anselmian schema, named after its explicator, Anselm, Archbishop of Canterbury (c. 1033–1109), who, in his *Cur Deus Homo* (*Why God Became Man*, 1097–1100), had argued that, since humanity in the representative figures of Adam and Eve had offended God through sin, a man (in the person of Christ) must expiate the offence, but that, since the offence was committed against the infinite majesty of God, only God could annul it. In Bunyan's Anselmian formulation, Christ had to be true God and true man, with a human body bearing the weight of expiatory death for sins; the infinite God required the 'infinite satisfaction', and 'True God, and true man … the divine nature [of Christ] did inable him to undergoe in his humane nature, all that sin, curse, and wrath that was laid upon him for us.'[13]

Any view of Christ that took away from His humanity – by treating Him as a spirit, by regarding Him as essentially a spiritual presence in the believer, or by down-playing the historical events of His life, death and physical resurrection – threatened Bunyan's confidence in salvation as an achievement of which the believer could be sure, since it took place outside of himself, by God in Christ, releasing the sinner from the burdens of the law and works. The need to vindicate the historicity and humanity of Christ and His saving work – whether or not these were actually being denied by appreciable numbers of people – launched Bunyan into an extended operation of 'proving' Christological data. Like Bunyan's explication of Anselmian soteriology, his dialectical method of establishing his beliefs about Christ is intellectually impressive and certainly belies the patronizing picture of the rustic *ingénu* given by Burton in his prefatory epistle.[14] The success of Bunyan's Scripture-based argumentation depends on acceptance of the Old Testament as an integral prelude to the New. Even more, Bunyan's dialectical success required a view of the New Testament as both a set of propositions and an autonomous testimony to their veracity.[15] Bunyan's heavy reliance on Scripture did not prevent his using its text somewhat freely on occasions. To take one example, Christ's open-ended words about His identity – 'Ye say that I am' – are turned by Bunyan into a kind of 'I say that I am'. Bunyan also takes considerable liberties with the New Testament text by introducing extensive additional dialogues into speeches such as that of the angel of the Resurrection and even into Christ's discourses.[16]

All this exegesis – by turns impressive, authoritative and ingenious – was subjected to the central purpose of *Gospel-Truths*: the establishment of the historical actuality of the incarnation, redeeming death, resurrection and ascension of Jesus Christ. If this task was not entirely necessary in terms of the immediate polemical encounter – Bunyan's 'proving' data were accepted by his opponent Burrough on behalf of the Quakers – Bunyan's conclusions about the entirely vicarious justification of sinners rested on the acceptance of premises about Christ as an historic redeeming agent outside individual men and women. That said, although Bunyan asserted the historical Christ as a saviour who had achieved mankind's redemption at a fixed point in time, he may have been less interested in the historical Jesus – and he was certainly not concerned with him in the role of exemplar, as, for example, in the medieval *imitatio Christi* tradition. For Bunyan, it was indeed 'blasphemy for any to presume to imitate him'.[17]

The argument about Christ in *Gospel-Truths* can also be seen as an argument about man. Bunyan had tried and found wanting the formula which, according to him, Quakers accepted, of a human righteousness guided by a light of conscience and not merely imputed from outside. Justification by faith in the work of the historic Christ as an external redemptive force had been accepted by Bunyan, ultimately because it offered an escape from the oppressive futility of reliance on legal and human righteousness. Bunyan's emphasis on externality – his rejection of inner good conscience or of any inherent human capacity for righteousness – was reflected in his constantly repeated phrase about 'that blood that was shed without the gate', 'without' being his shorthand for the vicarious nature of redemption.[18]

Although *Gospel-Truths* would have worked as a free-standing statement of Reformation principles, especially that of justification by faith, which had recently rescued Bunyan psychologically and spiritually, the work arose out of a polemical encounter and had a strongly adversarial tone. This tone was generated partly by a defensive denominational reaction to the Quaker attack on the paid ministry, which the Bedford gathered congregation had accepted as a feature of their place within the national church of the 1650s. However, that issue was more of a matter for Burton than for Bunyan. Indeed, Bunyan was clearly uneasy in justifying a salaried ministry, and happier in defending his own, Quaker-like self-financed ministerial work. Even so, he did adopt an aggressive overall approach to the Quakers, in defence of Reformed theology under attack. Assuming the mantle – a 'conservative' one for this 'radical' figure – of a defender of orthodoxy against heresy, Bunyan launched his attack against 'those fond hypocrites' (elsewhere 'blind Pharisees', 'painted hypocrites') 'called Quakers'. In a savagely satiric passage, Bunyan derided the obsessive practices and prohibitions into which, he believed, the Quaker belief in the possibility of human righteousness might lead: 'Now ... quakers are changed to the laws of the world ... Now they must wear no hatbands; now they must live with bread and water.'[19] Bunyan's verbal abuse of Quakers, his linking of them with 'Ranters ... drunkards', his attribution to them of a purely spiritualist Christology and his brutal attacks on beliefs that the Friends really did hold, such as the spirit of Christ within and the positive value of an inner light of conscience, were certain to evoke a Quaker response (though Bunyan receives only passing mention in a list of Quakerism's literary adversaries).[20]

Bunyan's *Gospel-Truths* soon came to the notice of the 23-year-old Quaker Edward Burrough, who produced, as a retort, his *The True Faith of the Gospel of Peace Contended for*,[21] as unintentionally ironic a title as could be imagined for such an embattled work by so redoubtable a controversialist. Burrough's riposte, like the Bunyan tract that had provoked it, arose out of local confrontations.[22] Bunyan's first blow, in what would turn out to be a contest of several bouts, took in the Quakers as part of an assorted array of radicals from the new left of English religious life of the mid-seventeenth century. Burrough's reply, in contrast, was specifically aimed at Bunyan and, to a lesser extent, at 'his fellow [Burton] who have joyned themselves to the broken army of Magog'. Burrough's language of vituperation, with which his work opens, reveals an already practised master, far exceeding Bunyan's in its sustained force: 'How long ye crafty Fowlers will you prey upon the Innocent ... [Y]our Dens are in Darkness and your mischief is hatched upon your beds of secret whoredoms ... thou blind Sot.' The personal attack is particularly directed at the Bedford church's acceptance of a salaried ministry, 'for Hire, for Gifts and Rewards ... for so much a year for preaching' – a point that Bunyan tried to answer, not altogether satisfactorily, in his reply to Burrough.[23] For all its *ad hominem* venom, *The True Faith* addressed a number of serious theological issues. Bunyan attempted to depict the Quakers as part of an extremist radical fringe. Burrough, while borrowing Bunyan's own kind of self-image of a thoughtful, if not academically qualified, lay Christian, oppressed by a self-interested clerical caste, presented the Quaker movement in terms of its balance between theological extremes.[24]

The sensational incident of October 1656, when the Quaker concept of Christ within helped induce James Nayler to imitate, at Bristol, Christ's Palm Sunday entry into Jerusalem, may still have lain in the future when Burrough wrote *The True Faith*. Even so, it was important to him, in his confrontation with Bunyan, to demonstrate the balance in Quaker Christology, and this he did with considerable success. He was, in fact, able to show that Bunyan had caricatured the Quakers, bracketing them with the notorious Ranters, as upholders of an anti-incarnational, subjectivist, spiritualizing perception of Christ, which Bunyan wanted to vilify, but which most Friends did not in fact maintain: 'We prize the Lord Jesus Christ

God man … thou goes on proving, *That he is the Saviour that was born of Mary, &c,* which thing we never denied.'[25]

Even so, and having established the Quakers' basic orthodoxy with regard to the 'historical' Christ, Burrough made room for the idea, distinctive but not peculiar to the Quakers, of a 'Christ Jesus within' – a concept whose dismissal by Bunyan in *Gospel-Truths* arguably impoverished his Christology. On the questions of conscience, law, justification and good works, Burrough was also able to present a picture of balance in Quakerism, suggesting that Bunyan's viewpoints were extreme and led to inadmissible conclusions such as antinomianism, or a merely verbal faith. Burrough carefully explained his attachment to the Reformation keystone, the all-sufficiency of the Cross of Christ: 'nor is [salvation] wrought by any other, but by Jesus Christ fully and compleatly'. Nevertheless, this stress on imputed justification needed to be balanced by a positive acceptance of law and works, in contrast to the negative view of these that Bunyan had tended to adopt in *Gospel-Truths*. Burrough detected clear possibilities for antinomianism in Bunyan's rigidly predestinarian views and his belief in justification without the works of the law: 'thou and thy Generation would leap over the law'. He went on to argue that personal commitment to a more than external and imputed sinlessness was required, since the law was not 'fulfilled for them, who are yet transgressors of it in themselves'. For Burrough, faith by profession only, without works, was dead, and the just were saved by faith with works – 'according to their deeds'. The pattern for such saving good deeds was Christ Himself, and Burrough deployed his own variant of the 'imitation of Christ' tradition; or rather, he perceived an inner Christ whose light 'hath lightened every man that comes into the world', and who produced in the Christian the good works that faith ought to yield up: 'Christ Jesus wrought in them mightily, and it was he that wrought in them to will and to do.'[26]

Burrough was here presenting the Quaker consensus as it was emerging in the 1650s and as it had evolved, thanks to Fox, in a repudiation of the determinism and 'pleading for sin' that Fox had found in the Calvinism of his Puritan background. Alongside his ability to combine an appreciation of an historical, redeeming Christ with a sense of His continuing presence within His followers, Burrough can be seen as restoring a doctrinal equilibrium that had been lost in the Luthero-Calvinist preoccupation with justification independent of human effort: a balance of works with faith, of personal holiness alongside imputed merit, of space for the operation of human conscience. True, Burrough's suggestion of a purely human, indeed, almost incidental causality for the Crucifixion – 'Christ Jesus was hanged … because they wickedly judged him to be a blasphemer' – may have threatened his consensual image by endangering the Anselmian model which explained the Cross according to a majestic divine plan; however, as we have seen, Burrough insisted that only the Cross could forgive sin.[27]

All in all, then, Burrough offered a view of Quakerism that set it within one Christian tradition, even if that one was not entirely Bunyan's. Burrough did not have Bunyan's command of Scripture (though he insisted that the Quakers took the Bible literally[28]) and his language lacked Bunyan's clarity and precision – perhaps intentionally so. However, he had presented his beliefs convincingly enough, and since seventeenth-century controversialists seldom abandoned the field until some point of exhaustion had been reached, his answer to *Gospel-Truths* was sure to evoke a counter-blast.

Bunyan's *A Vindication of the Book Called, Some Gospel-Truths Opened* was more pointed in its targeting than *Gospel-Truths* itself.[29] Whereas in the earlier work Bunyan had identified a loose alignment of doctrinal radicals, in the *Vindication* he was more concerned with 'the doctrine of the Quakers' and specifically with his now personal antagonist 'the Author, Edward Borrough', the 'unruly spirit', accused of 'corrupting my words, and then … calling me liar'. Thus, where *Gospel-Truths* could be viewed as an authoritative statement of Reformation principles, valid even if divorced from its polemical context, the *Vindication* is more evidently part of an inter-denominational and inter-personal debate. Bunyan's tone of Christian friendliness in this work – 'And now my friend, in love to thy soul' – is belied by a thoroughly pugnacious style, and content, Burrough being firmly identified as Bunyan's 'adversary'. The obverse of the attack on Burrough in particular, and the Quakers in general, is a stout solidarity with Bunyan's own group and a defence of his minster, Burton, who contributed to a somewhat laconic recommendation to the *Vindication*.[30]

Bunyan's debating technique in the *Vindication* consisted of an attempt to push Burrough into a tight dialectical trap in which the latter's protestation that Quakers '*prise the Lord Jesus Christ*' in an orthodox scriptural way was brushed aside ('by words in generall we may be deceived') unless he took a kind of loyalty oath to Protestant dogmas of justification by faith, by Christ alone, without the law. Bunyan could not accept that the Quakers were orthodox with regard to the nature of Christ as a unique hypostatic union, existing beyond the believer, unless they subscribed to his view of the saving work of Christ, performed in historical time on behalf of the sinner by a being who totally transcended him or her. This had the merit of making clear two sharply opposed positions, and at one point Bunyan could only remark on the obvious fact that, while he held one opinion, Burrough held another: '[W]hereas, thou sayest, this conscience, or law

... works in all men either to justifie or condemne. I do plainly deny, that either conscience, or the law can justifie.'[31] In the end, Bunyan still felt that he was right, despite Burrough's repudiation of the link, to lump together Quakers and Ranters in his Edwards-like schedule of recent 'heresies' and 'strong delusions'. In doing so, he once again assumed the role of defender of orthodox Protestantism against 'novelty' (though he did not make the 'papist charge' against the Friends that their doctrine smacked of Catholicism's alleged works-righteousness). The doctrines of the Quakers, Bunyan believed, were in fact those of the Ranters, and he would have been in essential agreement with Baxter on that point: 'Their doctrines were mostly the same with the Ranters.'[32]

This work of Bunyan's, like its predecessor, covered a number of topics, such as his expectation of an imminent and physical second coming. However, his two-part publishing début had been essentially concerned with his doctrine of redemption, and he rounded the work off with: 'think you should be justified by the blood of the Son of *Mary* shed on the Crosse without the gate'. He felt that this insistence on an historic, objective saving person and event had to be strenuously protected from any attempt to set up a rival spiritualized Christ, either alongside or as an alternative to the external redeeming one. A full appreciation of Christ's saving action required a sense of His total otherness from the justified sinner, precluding the Quakers' understanding of a Christ within. Christ was external to man in the same way as His atoning death took place outside Jerusalem. Bunyan's repudiation of an interior Christ could be vehement: 'there is no such thing as the spirit of Christ in every man'.[33] Thus he set out the full extent of his differences with Quakerism.

Burrough, seconded by Fox in the *Mystery of the Great Whore Unfolded* (1657), returned to the fray with *Truth (the Strongest of all) Witnessed Forth*, the tumultuous title breathing challenge and the kind of destructive *odium theologicum* that made its own contribution to the eventual collapse of Puritanism's 'good old cause' at the end of the 1650s.[34] The spleen evident in Burrough's title – against 'JOHN BUNION (one of Gog's Army)' and his 'foule dirty lyes and slanders' – is fully sustained in the text, with its further attacks on 'John Bunion, thou and thy false Witnesses ... Remember and repent for the day of your visitation is upon you ... thy slanderous and lying and perverting Tongue.' Yet the new terms of abuse could not conceal the increasingly stale doctrinal content, mostly concerned with what Bunyan and his associates had or had not said in and around Bedford, with the inner light, justification, Christ within, Quakers and Ranters, Bunyan and Burton, and so on.[35]

The fundamental differences between Bunyan and Burrough, already sufficiently clarified by the former in his *Vindication*, made the continuation of the dialogue increasingly pointless. Though in his next work, *The Doctrine of the Law and Grace Unfolded*, he defended his respect for the law, Bunyan produced no direct reply to *Truth Witnessed Forth*. It was not that he was particularly averse to controversy. He had taken up the cudgels with every appearance of enthusiasm in his riposte to Burrough, and he subsequently operated again as a controversialist in his debates with Fowler, with closed-communion Baptists, with advocates of women's meetings and with seventh-day sabbatarians.[36] That said, in *Gospel-Truths* Bunyan had set out not so much a polemical case, as what he took to be the basics of incarnational Christianity and Protestant soteriology. Unlike Burrough, Bunyan was not the spokesman for a new movement struggling for living room. Perhaps, too, at bottom he lacked the unquenchable thirst for embattled controversy of the 'son of thunder', Burrough. 'No picker of quarrels' in his extraordinarily self-deceptive assessment of himself, Burrough aimed sixteen of his writings against named opponents, and turned from his assault on Bunyan to an attack on 'Four and twenty Arguments' by Baxter. Bunyan, meanwhile, gravitated towards works on social justice and on non-controversial dogmatics. Nevertheless, the debate with Burrough reveals important features of Bunyan's thought, especially his scriptural literalism and his firm attachment to justification by faith alone.[37]

The Doctrine of the Law and Grace Unfolded

Following the appearance of *A Vindication* in 1657, Bunyan published *A Few Sighs from Hell*, a work we have already considered. Then, in 1659 came *The Doctrine of the Law and Grace Unfolded*, which Richard Greaves describes as Bunyan's 'principal exposition of covenant theology'.[38] Like *Gospel-Truths*, *The Doctrine of the Law and Grace* is an extended sermon – 'honest preaching' by a 'Gospel Minister'. Its theme is the contrast between the two covenants, of the law and of grace. The treatise develops ideas set out in *Gospel-Truths* and offers a defence of Bunyan against the charge made by Burrough that his attitude 'slights the Law'. In fact, throughout the work Bunyan takes the law most seriously, showing its links with sin. The individual must be deeply aware of both, not only in the purely cerebral way that Bunyan recalled in his pre-conversion self in *Grace Abounding*, but in a deep, heartfelt, 'experimental' (or, as we would say, 'experiential') way. Indeed, the individual must recognize the fullness of evil in himself and see himself as 'the biggest sinner in the world', an idea running through *Grace Abounding* and encapsulated in its full title.

Rightly, such a sinner could be only crushed by the 'terrour and amaze-ment' of the law which convicts. To convey that sense of the terror of justice, Bunyan employs once more the story of Dives and Lazarus which he had made the basis of *A Few Sighs from Hell* and which, in Luke's Gospel (16: 17, 19–21) develops out of Christ's discourse on the permanent valid-ity of the law. References such as this to the New Testament characterize this work throughout. Bunyan's reliance on Scripture as an objective authority can be seen as a sort of parallel with his trust in salvation outside of himself, won through action taken by Christ, with no human involve-ment. Bunyan claims no educational resources of his own, apart from Scripture. This is where he introduces recollections of his apparently meagre schooling. But this very lack of academic qualifications is viewed as possessing positive advantages in furthering his evangelical purposes, since a work 'empty of Fantastical expressions, and without light, vain, whimsical Scholar-like terms', but with 'plain, yet sound, true, and home sayings' would be best guaranteed to convey its message to a wide read-ership.[39]

In this work Bunyan aims to address those for whom hope is held out, those who, in the classic distinction that he is about to unfold between a covenant of the law with works and a covenant of grace, belong under grace. Unrepentant sinners, on the other hand, were placed in the category of those who sinned against the law, and therefore belonged under the law and its awful curse. Although the law was indeed praiseworthy, grace was infinitely superior to it. Bunyan had a powerful sense of the oppressive-ness of the law: for instance, Adam and Eve and their descendants were sentenced for breaches of the law which had still to be given explicitly to Moses. Thus, he conveys his understanding of the law as being enor-mously dangerous, for those who try to obey it as a means to an end as well as for those who disobey it.[40] To explain the onus of the law, Bunyan depicts it as both massively weighty and vastly ramified, so that 'if any man doth transgress against any one of these ten [commandments], he doth commit treason' against them all, while ignorance of the true nature of the law was a feature of being under its sway. The law was fault-finding to the last degree, so that even the least distraction in prayer would 'bring eternall vengeance upon thee'. For support, Bunyan refers his reader to '*Dod* upon the Commandments'. John Dod's and Robert Cleaver's *A Plain and Familiar Exposition of the Ten Commandments* (1603) was another of those popularizing – 'Plain and Familiar' – Elizabethan and Jacobean works of Calvinist dogmatics and piety which, like those of Dent and Bayly, had a strong influence on Bunyan. His belief in the inseparability of the Ten Commandments is found in Dod and Cleaver, as is his preoccupation with the contrast between what they called '[t]he law and the gracious promise'.[41]

Bunyan saw his unremitting exposure of the harsh covenant of law and works as necessary if he was to shake people free from the deceits of self-righteousness by imagined good works. Here, his method is strongly reminiscent of that used earlier by Perkins. In his 1590 open letter to *All Ignorant People that Desire to be Instructed* (compare the title of Bunyan's *Instruction for the Ignorant*, 1675), Perkins listed no fewer than thirty-two common errors about salvation, a corpus of popular Pelagianism which, judging from the vernacular tone in which he renders these opinions, he seems to have encountered in the course of his pastoral work. These errors of presumption included 'That ye can keep the commandments, as well as God will give you leave' and 'That is an easier thing to please God than to please our neighbour'. We should see both Bunyan and Perkins as aiming to use a pastoral shock treatment, dwelling on the implacability of the law so as to dispel reassuring but complacent and fatal fallacies about the possibility of meeting its demands.[42]

The 'shock treatment' required, for its effectiveness, a dramatic depiction of God's relentlessness under the law: 'he hath no regard on thee, no pitty for thee' – no pity, that is, for those who remain in the deluding covenant of works and law. The analogy is with an imagined legal system of perfect justice alone, without the quality of mercy, a system in which justice, dispensed by a 'just Judge', 'will execute upon the offender'. God is that just and merciless judge, more merciless than a human magistrate, since whereas the latter, 'corrupted and perverted', might offer pardons without full satisfaction made, God's law is so perfect that pardons granted must be accompanied by entire satisfaction for the offences pardoned.[43]

Did Bunyan set up two Gods, one constrained by His own law, the other dispensing mercy? In one aspect, Bunyan's God seems a primitive figure, angry and vengeful, as well as imprisoned by the rules of 'his Justice … his Word'. He bays for sacrificial blood, 'thy own blood, or the blood of some other man (for it calls for no less)', demanding 'irrecoverable ruine on them that transgress'. This Moloch-like figure, while primeval and anthropomorphic, is also relatively weak, since He is represented as the agent of the justice that makes Him so merciless. He is indeed viewed as being caught up in the toils of a legal system which has taken on a powerful life of its own, restricting the godhead, an oppressive, indeed hateful autonomous force. Although the law is viewed as a servant 'sent by his Lord to see and pry' – an intrusive detective-prosecutor – the 'master–servant' relationship seems ambiguous, or even inverted, since there seem to be limits placed upon God's freedom of action, imposed by the law: God '*cannot* … regard' the offender. Entrapping both God and the human race, the law must, in Bunyan's mind, have a let-out. The merciless 'justice' of retributive law must somehow be set aside, and God become a God to escape its restrictions.[44]

Before exploring that possibility, Bunyan relentlessly presses home his argument about the literal impossibility of the law and its fulfilment. The unfairness of the law is seen in the way it convicts not only 'prophane and ungodly wretches', as would be expected, but also those who lead 'a holy, righteous, religious life', who are 'as sure to be damned as the other that are more profane and loose': the righteousness of God condemns the self-righteous. The apparently despairing view that even those who 'are reformed, and abstain from the sins against the Law ... will be damned' is pursued with ferocious rigour. Belief in an even partial personal righteousness, through which God would 'let us be saved by Christ', is consigned to the vaults of Romanist Pelagianism, 'the darkest dungeon in Popery'. Bunyan shows how even the repentant, the sermon-hearers, those who join 'a visible company of professors of Christ', far way from the 'rudiments and traditions of men', might yet be under the covenant that brought death, that of the law and works. Indeed, such godly persons – the very saints – faced a particular temptation to human righteousness by congratulating themselves on the perfection of their church-order.[45] Bunyan deliberately adopts this kind of apparent extremism over the implacability of the law because of his design to leave no room whatsoever for any possibility of humanly engineered justification through the law and works, thereby creating the maximum possible conceptual space for the antithetical alternative, free grace alone. Next, he opens up this alternative possibility, having systematically closed off the route by way of inherent human righteousness. This he does by introducing the prospect of vicarious, unmerited justification, in which God and the law are placated for sin, but only through the merits of Christ, which are appropriated to the believer in a living faith: 'the whole stress of the salvation of your souls [is] upon the merits of another man (namely Jesus)'.[46]

To the objection that the Gospel held out 'conditional promises' of salvation, Bunyan replied that the only condition was faith, and that, since faith was all-sufficient, no other condition was conceivable. It is interesting with Bunyan, as with Luther, to see what the nature of this saving faith was – and it was certainly much more than assent to a set of propositions. In this respect, Bunyan's use of tenses and pronouns is revealing. First, the tense is the present: 'that my sins be forgiven me'. That is to say, although he emphasized the historical actuality of the saving drama in his controversy with Burrough – that sins were forgiven 'on Mount *Calvary* ... some sixteen hundred years ago' – a merely historical, merely mental faith in the proposition would not suffice; living faith had to be 'not only of your heads and fancies, but of your very souls'. Linked to that sense of present forgiveness, the pronouns used have the immediacy of the first-person: 'my sins forgiven me ... O man! thou must go quite back again; thou art out of the way'. If, to use Donne's 'commercial metaphor', humanity was damned 'in grosse', it was saved 'by retail', and forgiveness is thus bestowed on the individual, each one anew. This personal tone has echoes of other evocations in the English evangelical tradition of personal forgiveness; compare, for instance, Bunyan's 'my sins forgiven me' with Charles Wesley's:

> And can it be that I should gain
> An interest in the Saviour's blood!
> Dy'd He for Me who caus'd his Pain!
> For Me? who Him to Death pursu'd?
> Amazing Love! How can it be
> That Thou my God shouldst die for Me?[47]

It seems significant that when Bunyan discusses the dispensing of the justice of God, he considers its impact on the whole impersonal mass of humanity, with a few historical types. In contrast, the mercy of God is poured out to the individual. Even so, the individual plays no part in his or her own salvation, not even by acquiring faith as a precondition of it, lest faith be seen as a personal redeeming achievement, a 'good work'. In point of fact, faith is not really the condition of the individual's salvation, but only an instrumental third factor in channelling the effects of God's love and of Christ's merits already ('afore') secured: 'Faith ... is not the Saviour' – grace is. Bunyan's soteriology, then, might be described as salvation by grace alone, a formula that certainly got round any suggestion that, having discounted the possibility that people might meet the conditions of their salvation through works of righteousness, he has introduced a new 'condition' to be met – faith.[48]

Given this elevated appreciation of the role of grace, it is entirely appropriate that, in a new section on the 'doctrine of grace', Bunyan should launch into a rhapsodic prose hymn to 'unchangeable grace'. The whole scenery has been shifted. Whereas Bunyan's God of justice made demands and imposed exactions of revenge and blood, the God of mercy he now unveils – freed, as it were, from subservience to His own laws – gives, and his free gifts range from conversion and pardon to everlasting life. The recipients of these unmerited gifts have no rights – as they would have in a sale or bargain – so that Bunyan carefully chooses the word 'priviledges' to describe the benefits to them of the covenant of grace. Indeed, it is a covenant made not with mankind, but between other parties on mankind's behalf. Because Bunyan wants to play down the idea of any meaningful covenant between God and humankind – as opposed to the efficacious one between the Father and Christ – he uses considerable freedom in interpreting Old Testament covenants between God and man, downgrading their reality (as for example, that with David) as little more than types of the primary covenant between the Father and the Son. Indeed, Bunyan even has to play fast and loose with accepted chronologies, since the traditional 'first' covenant, the one between God and Israel in the Old Law, was such only in that it was the first given to man. It came after a vastly more significant first covenant in which God, in His mercy, now totally transformed from Bunyan's provisional projection of wrathful revenger, actually makes anterior provision for sin: 'Oh! God thought of the salvation of man before there was any transgression of man'. And the emphasis shifts from justice and vengeance to mercy and love. In the full power of His divinity – 'let God be God!' – God in His mercy pre-arranges the redemptive history of mankind, by striking a bargain.[49]

It is difficult for us, especially, perhaps, with our altered, or even impoverished metaphorical imaginations, to know the extent to which, in his discussion of a covenant and a bargain, Bunyan had in mind a simile or an actual exchange. Certainly, analogies of contract came naturally to him as a member of a stratum of society – self-employed artisans – in which agreements to perform set pieces of work for stated prices were everyday events. In a still largely pre-literate society, these bargains were typically verbal and sealed with a handshake; thus, Bunyan has Christ shake 'hands with the Father in making of the Covenant'. In Bunyan's depiction of the divine transaction, the image adopted was, in fact that, of a sale, in which Christ offered as His 'price' His blood, in return for the commodity – the 'bargain' – which was the choice of those to be saved 'before time'.[50]

Bunyan's development of the transactional imagery is certainly elaborate. The metaphor of a sale by treaty is fully explored, with a list of the terms that the divine worker has to fulfil – incarnation, becoming a curse, death, satisfaction, righteousness, victory over death – and, on the Father's side, raising up Christ upon satisfaction given and releasing the fruits of victory to sinners. The Father is the 'creditor', the Son the 'debtor': some might find the pecuniary metaphor taken to extremes: 'the *creditor* looks that his *money* should be brought into his house'. A secondary metaphorical coda is derived from English civil law, which provided back-up for contracts, and criminal law, which imposed punitive sanctions for felonies. Bunyan introduces bail, bondsmen, the issuing of processes, and sureties, with Christ himself depicted as the only surety or '*bonds-man*' competent to oversee the fulfilment of His own part of the undertaking. Meanwhile, the 'criminal law' executes Jesus: 'and scrued his very heart blood out of his precious heart'.[51]

The suffering servant portrayed here puts us in mind of the later medieval 'Christ-of-pity' genre: 'my bloody sweat, my bloody wounds, my cursed death ... [T]hey made the blood run down his blessed face'. This is accompanied by an extraordinarily powerful evocation of Christ's desolation and abandonment, introduced so as to establish the fact that Christ died 'a *cursed* death', with all the pain of hell, to atone for sin. If these were 'medieval' themes – and certainly ones found in medieval poetry, and in the iconography of the Passion which strongly survived, and was, indeed, revived under Arminian auspices, in English churches during Bunyan's boyhood – equally 'medieval' in feel is the intimation that sinners, by their offences, intensified Christ's pains: 'canst thou finde in thy heart to labour *more* sins upon his back?'[52] There may be some contradiction between these themes of 'affective' piety, which contained the possibility that the sinner could somehow lessen Christ's pains by being moved to choose to avoid sin, and the more forensic and pre-determined model, which left the individual sinner out of the account except as a member of a race for whose sin full allowance had already been made in a 'bargain' struck before time. Fittingly, Bunyan concludes this section – which, although it involves a highly intellectualized examination of 'Type' and 'Antitype', is also suffused with an emotional response to Christ – on a note of passionate appreciation: 'O blessed Jesus!' He moves on to explore Christ's sacerdotal office – 'O what a New Covenant high Priest have we!' – in an essay heavily dependent on the New Testament's hymn to Christ's high priesthood, the Epistle to the Hebrews. Here, too, Bunyan shows his skill in a sustained exercise in Old Testament typology.[53]

In a subsequent extended passage, Bunyan deals with the need for the annihilation of self-pretence and self-righteousness. Those brought to grace were not the 'good', but pardoned sinners: '*drunkards, whoremasters, liars*'. The intimate tone that Bunyan now uses rests on personal reminiscences and the powerful recall of spiritual states: 'And indeed to speak my own experience'. These individual experiences have value in illustrating processes taking place more widely in men and women: fear of backsliding sets the soul in the path of effectual prayer; awareness of the limited utility of the law establishes knowledge of its real advantages. Calling, perhaps, on his own, more secular, wartime experiences, Bunyan evokes the image of the law as a 'great gun well charged against his soul': a fitting figure for the sort of destruction – the kind wreaked by a culverin – that must be done to self, to self-righteousness and to self-inspired faith. Amidst the devastation, there are left only the 'righteousness of God' (Luther's talisman) and 'a crucified Christ'. Such passages – Bunyan's 'pinch of the whole discourse', as autobiographically real as any in *Grace Abounding* – are intense, personal and passionate in ways that his reflections on the forensic dimensions of the covenants are not.[54]

Bunyan is not generally considered to be a mystical writer. His approach tends to be concrete rather than contemplative, his images realistic – as when he builds, brilliantly, upon the foundations of the parable of the prodigal son a new parable of the utter destitution of the sinner 'killed' to everything but Christ: 'Oh! then … give me Christ on any terms whatsoever he cost'. Christ is sought unconditionally, unhesitatingly and desperately, without any 'indenting'. Yet for all these sharply observed images from life – wartime artillery, artisans and apprentices 'indenting' for contracts – there is in Bunyan's awareness of the need for self-annihilation – the 'great gun well charged against the soul' – something of the mystic's quest for nothingness, as there is a mystical flavour to his appreciation of the weakness and impoverishment of the sinner meeting the strength and richness of Christ.[55]

Bunyan's literary skill is next deployed in a stark contrast between the destitute and, indeed, destroyed soul and its reincarnation into a 'glorious, perfect, and never-fading life', imputed to it in recognition of Christ's saving work. This flight is given buoyancy by Bunyan's further autobiographical recollections – of his rapturous realization that '*Thy righteousness is in heaven*' and of his consumption ('some distemper of body') and fear of death.[56] The autobiographical excursus, a kind of sketch for *Grace Abounding* – 'Something of the Authors experience' – may provide some help with the dating and phasing of Bunyan's religious travail of the 1650s:

> But being through grace kept close with God (in some measure) in prayer, and the rest of the ordinances; but went about a year and upwards, without any sound evidence as from God to my soul, touching the salvation as comes by Jesus Christ. But … then the Lord (just before the men called Quakers came into the Countrey) did set me down so blessedly in the Doctrine of Jesus Christ.

This inclusion of 'just before the … Quakers came' may have been intended primarily to mark the sharp contrast between a realization of Christ's objective historical reality that had been vouchsafed to Bunyan and the purely internalist Christology he needed to attack, ascribing it to the Quakers. But the phrase may allow us at least to speculate about the dating of Bunyan's spiritual dramas of the 1650s. The Quaker William Dewsbury came to Bedfordshire in 1654 and, if Bunyan had that visit in mind, his decisive conversion came 'about a year and upwards' after his reception into the Bedford church, in 1653 ('in prayer, and the rest of the ordinances'), and just before Dewsbury's arrival. Alternatively, Bunyan was recalling the more noteworthy appearance of Edward Burrough in 1656, when Bunyan had his stormy encounter with this Quaker spokesman. At that time, Bunyan was already a noted preacher in his region and was about to become an author. Even so, his religious development may still have been incomplete. He may have received deeper insights into the 'Doctrine of Jesus Christ' late in 1655 or early in 1656, preparing him for his encounter with the Quakers, for a preaching of greater hope and for the authorship of the key works on justification that we have been considering.[57]

In this early work, Bunyan's literary technique is still relatively un-formed, and his anxiety to instruct, or to deploy an essentially homiletic style, led him to repeat himself extensively, as in his return to an attempt to refute popular errors, as he saw them, about the ease of redemption by human effort and in his renewed insistence that only Christ saved sinners – that those who aimed to come to Christ through their own righteousness in fact made Him redundant. Instead, argued Bunyan, one must approach Christ full of one's evil, as a chief of sinners, indeed 'as the basest in the world … a blood-red sinner … a halter about thy neck'.[58] At the same time, Bunyan inclined to a doctrine of the sinlessness of the elect; it was, he wrote, a gross error to hold that ' a man may be a child of God to day, and a childe of the Devil to morrow'. Such matters had been pre-determined – even though Bunyan struggled to avoid a logically unassailable conclusion that those irreversibly secured for salvation 'need not care what they do'. However, there *was* a possible sin – indeed, the only unpardonable sin – that, if not the elect, then those 'formerly enlightened into the nature of the Gospel', could commit. This was the mental sin of underestimating the ben-efits of Christ – '*to trample upon the blood of Christ shed on the Cross*' – by seeking, once more, to attain one's own salvation. It appeared that the believer could 'wilfully' damn himself – or herself – by voluntarily reverting from the covenant of grace to that of works. A corollary of Bunyan's view of people willing themselves out of the covenant of grace by a sin of lack of confidence in Christ is the voluntarism implicit in his view of a person's taking an initiative towards Christ: 'if thou wouldest be saved thou mayest come to Christ'. Such possibilities of personal choice loom ever larger as we approach the conclusion of *Law and Grace*: 'Shall I have my sins, and lose my soul? … Would not heaven be better to me then my sins?' Bun-yan's overriding homiletic purpose here – 'to stir thee up to mend thy pace towards heaven' – seems to undermine his high Calvinist scheme of predestined election or reprobation. Particularly towards the end of *Law and Grace* Bunyan the preacher displaces Bunyan the theologian to confront his readers with options of choice that ought not, according to the logic of his determinist soteriology, to exist.[59]

Profitable Meditations

Bunyan's next work, *Profitable Meditations*,[60] was published during his first imprisonment. However, unlike his later verse work, *Prison Meditations*, *Profitable Meditations* contains no reference to the fact of his being imprisoned; if written in gaol, the work may have been composed during the early casual period of his incarceration, when, as we saw, he was left remarkably free. *Profitable Meditations* represents Bunyan's first experiment in writing verse, a medium which he was to explore with increasing skill. The verse pattern was that of the ballad, an art form which enjoyed enormous popularity in seventeenth-century England. By that time, though a medium designed for oral delivery, it was increasingly committed to print and sold cheaply, often recounting memorable and sensational events. Ballad was perhaps the verse form closest to poetry's origins as song. A fixed and simple metre and rigid adherence to rhyme were essential attributes of the genre, and Bunyan's faithful observance of the obligation to rhyme would even induce him on one occasion to invent a word, near in sound to the one required, so as to maintain a rhyme.[61] Bunyan was deeply immersed in the English vernacular culture of the earlier seventeenth century, of which ballads were such a vital part. Much of this popular culture contained archaic features, especially chivalric themes abandoned in upper-class culture but 'handed down' for popular consumption. He recorded his youthful fascination with chivalric ballads and, from his unconverted days, recalled his preference for such entertainments over the Scripture: 'Alas! What is the Scripture? Give me a ballad, a news-book, George on horseback, or Bevis of Southampton; give me some book ... that tells of old fables'; there are even signs that he was first drawn to the Scriptures themselves for their adventure stories – 'the historical part thereof'. However, even when the converted Bunyan stopped reading ballads, their literary conventions left a deep impress on him. Fast-paced tales of derring-do, of adventurous journeys and encounters – the very stuff of the ballads – provided the models for *The Pilgrim's Progress*. Also, the formal arrangement of the ballad, and above all its relentless rhymed quatrains, gave Bunyan his stylistic base for *Profitable Meditations*, his first popular, and his first enjoyable, work.[62]

Despite Bunyan's apologies for using this form, the ballad was far too powerful and too useful a medium to be rejected for use, especially by so popular an evangelist as he had become. The 'godly' ballad, as Duffy and Watt both show, was a recognized subspecies, providing an example, not of the replacement of 'popular' culture by 'godly' culture, but a case of the integration of the two, and of the profane being put to sacred use. An example from a religious tradition quite different from Bunyan's, that of Lancashire Catholic recusancy, will provide an example of this cultural cross-fertilization. The piece in question, 'A songe of foure preistes that suffered death at Lancaster; to the tune of Daintie come thou to me' (c. 1615) contains features of the ballad, as adapted to a religious purpose: a note-worthy and stirring story, a popular love-song tune 're-cycled' for purposes of religious propaganda, the quatrain structure, and rhyme at all costs, even at the sacrifice of coherent syntax:

> In this our English Coast much blessed blood is shed
> two hunded preistes almost in our time martered
> And manie lay men dye with joyfull sufferance
> many moe in prison lye gods cause for to advance.

Criticism of the ballad, including the 'godly' ballad, in terms of its elevated poetic inspiration or lack of it, are not particularly pertinent. The form was practical, perhaps mechanical, and designed for conveying intelligible and memorable messages. Bunyan found it a most useful implement.[63]

Fusing vernacular form with godly content, *Profitable Meditations* typi-fies Bunyan's writings in being firmly anchored in Scripture. His technique was to place references to scriptural texts, sometimes four to a quatrain, alongside the lines of verse which, supposedly, were based on those texts. Sometimes, as Graham Midgley points out, there are erroneous references. At other times the links between verse and Scripture seem slender. To take one example, Bunyan's lines: 'And with his Snares he doth so catch their feet, / That they with joy unto his place do go' are referred to 2 Corinthians 4: 4, which runs: 'In whom the god of this world hath blinded the minds of them which believe not, lest the light of the glorious gospel of Christ, who is the image of God, should shine unto them.' Thus the poem is not to be considered as simply a series of scriptural texts in versified form; the texts do not always have a natural relationship with the verse, and, if the texts were removed, the poem would not be in any way affected.[64]

Although *Profitable Meditations* can be considered as verse in its own right, Bunyan still felt the need to apologize, or to appear to apologize, for writing in this medium. The traditions of the godly ballad were, as we have seen, so well established in early-modern England as to make Bunyan's excuses formal and perfunctory. However, he did excuse the medium by explaining that the 'delight' taken in metrical verse and the facility it created for memorizing material made it a useful tool. This utilitarian consideration, especially that of rote learning, dictated the particular verse form that Bunyan adopted, the simple a, b, a, b rhyme scheme.[65]

Profitable Meditations divides up into ten sections (with some subsectioning) and a brief conclusion. The central part of the work, sections IV to VIII, consists of dialogues, and various discourses also feature in other parts. Therefore, we can consider this work partly as a dramatic poem. The discourses are generally between two parties (there is also converse between Christ and a group of 'the Wicked'). These apart, the *dramatis personae* are, in the order of their appearing, Satan, a tempted soul, Christ, a sinner, a doubting soul, Death and a saint. The unity of the whole is maintained by giving a sequential numbering to the 184 stanzas (with some mis-numbering in the original edition).[66]

A study '*Of Man by Nature*' in twelve stanzas forms part of the didactic section of the poem, before the central dramatic discourses begin. Section II, '*Of the Sufferings of Christ*' in fourteen stanzas, sets out a doctrine of redemption. A celebration of man, untypical of Bunyan and found in the first section – '… Man, so wise / And noble by Creation …' – gives way to an awareness of the true plight of 'poor man'. The perception of the Atonement as the outcome of a forensic transaction – 'And buy him to Himself with heav'nly price' – is supplemented by a devotional approach reminiscent, as in *The Doctrine of the Law and Grace Unfolded*, of the pity expressed in late medieval English Passion poetry for the physical agony and spiritual desolation of the crucified Christ:

> The pains he bore were more than we can think,
> Which by his bloody sweat and wounds we see.

Echoes of ideas that were by then set deep in Bunyan's consciousness, such as the law that 'doth me assail' and the unpardonable sin, are more tersely expressed than in *Law and Grace*.[67]

Amongst Bunyan's dialogues, a markedly successful one is that between Satan and a 'tempted soul'. The representation of Satan's role as tempter reached its highest point in seventeenth-century English literature with Milton's *Paradise Lost*. A secularized version of the part of the satanic tempter was devised by Dryden in his portrayal of Achitophel (the Whig leader Shaftesbury) tempting Absalom (Charles II's illegitimate son Monmouth) to commit the ultimate political sin of treason against his father. In both of these literary versions, the satanic figures use all the devices of rhetoric in their attempts to persuade, devices of which Bunyan's Satan, too, is in full command. Whereas Milton's and Dryden's tempters try to persuade their victims to commit Satan's sins of pride – ambition and disobedience – Bunyan's Satan tempts people to commit the sin of despair. The tempted soul rebuts the tempter by simple confidence and faith in Christ.[68]

The possibilities for dramatic tension contained in scenes of temptation must arise from the unpredictabilities of free choice. In his temptation scenes Bunyan emphasizes free choice with particular clarity. In 'A Discourse between Christ and a Sinner' Christ takes over from Satan as a kind of tempter, His interlocutor being as resistant to His persuasions as the 'tempted Soul' was to those of Satan. Christ, too, employs rhetoric to further His purpose. His appeal is based on the emotions, echoing the medieval genre, the 'complaints of Christ' that were intended to move the hearts of sinners towards Him through His recitation of His own sufferings:

> Doth not my bleeding Wounds and Mercies sweet …
> Affect thy heart? behold my Hands and Feet.

Since choice is being emphasized here – the acceptance or rejection of Christ – stress on the determinants of predestination is diminished. Indeed, Bunyan actually depicts the sinner placing all his or her hopes on predestination – quite erroneously:

> I need not yet forsake my wordly gain,
> 'Tis *Grace*, not *Works*, that brings to Heaven above.

Not only does the sinner have to make a personal choice but he or she has to conclude a prompt selection of Christ or sin, thus lending a special note of dramatic urgency to this instalment of dialogue. Bunyan for once breaks with his quatrain form to introduce a choric aphorism, making a general point about the lot of those who plead to be allowed to delay the fatal choice:

> The man's a Fool that makes this Plea;
> And yet thus foolish many be.[69]

A later dialogue, the nineteen-stanza 'A Discourse between Death and a Sinner', with its vivid personification of death, has much of the feel of a medieval morality play or a sermon exemplum, in which Death, terrifyingly, confronts the man or woman at ease in the world: '*Death*. Friend, I come to thee, with me thou must go.' As in medieval depictions, a contrast is introduced between the pride of life and the horror of death: '[*Sinner*] Touch not my Beauty, nor my fine array.' Death is persistent, with all the ghastly force and black humour of the *danse macabre* scenes and, exactly as in medieval sermonic exempla, thwarts all attempts to buy him off:

> [*Death*] Thou must be gone, the Worms do lack their food ...
> [*Sinner*] I'le give you Gold, if you'l depart away ...
> [*Death*] 'Tis not thy Gold I care for, Come away.

Amidst scenes of considerable pathos – 'You see my Wife and Children weeping stand' – Death, utterly inflexible and pitiless, is linked with his ally – his 'brother' – hell, creating an atmosphere of terror as powerful as, say, the damnation scene in Marlowe's *Doctor Faustus*: 'My soul sees fire, and hellish Devils too.'[70] The impression created here of death as omnipotent and horrifying – a mood characteristic of medieval representations culminating in Bruegel's version – is carried over into the next dialogue, the ten stanzas of '*A Discourse between* Death *and a* Saint':

> *Death.* I am the King of Terrors, that's my name.
> I throw down Kingdoms, none can me withstand.[71]

As we shall see, Bunyan returns to this image of sovereign death in *Prison Meditations*. However, Death's boasts in *Profitable Meditations* are in vain, for the despair and terror of the exchange between Death and the sinner give way to the serene, indeed, impregnable, confidence of the saint. In a particularly effective polemical sally, the saint uses the evidence of the Resurrection to rebut Death's claim that he has vanquished the saint's champion, Christ.

'*Of the day of Judgment*' is treated in two parts, in which Bunyan develops the theme of the second coming, suggesting that Christ has chosen the salvation of the elect – 'but ... a few', whom he 'did mark' – but that the damned actually will their own damnation. Put another way, the saved are undeserving of salvation, the damned merit damnation. The unregenerate choose, and achieve, their fate: 'How oft did you your back upon me turn?' To those who have deliberately rejected Him, Christ is inflexible and vengeful, resembling in a way the earlier figure of pitiless death: '... I no Mercy will you show'.[72]

A penultimate section, of antiphonal dialogue between a 'Saint in Heaven' and a 'Sinner in Hell', runs to twenty-three stanzas. The saint does seem an appallingly complacent individual:

> I lived in the World as well as you,
> And served Sin, until I heard the Word.

The dialogue brings out once more what seems to be, in this work of drama, tension and choice, Bunyan's view that salvation was indeed unmerited, while damnation was willed and deserved: '[*Sinner*] The fault was mine, his Grace I did refuse.' Throughout this poem, it is this sense of crucial decisions and potentially tragic turning points that makes it a compelling Everyman play, whose outcomes are by no means all foreknown, and in which the exigencies of didactic and dramatic writing relax the constraints of orthodox soteriology. The sinner cries out:

> O sad! that I had clos'd with Christ; or would
> I had not heard of Him at all, then I
> Had either saved been, or else I should
> Have had less torment to Eternity.

On a final, calmer recessional note, a two-stanza conclusion urges the reader to look up to God.[73]

I Will Pray with the Spirit[74]

In his evocation of wordless prayer and 'the groanings of the Spirit' in *Law and Grace*, Bunyan had pointed towards the theme of praying spiritually. In the same work an anticipation of this theme is also traceable in his deprecation of the false assurance that the self-righteous put in 'prayers, reading, hearing, baptisme, breaking of bread, or the like'.[75] Opposition to pre-arranged formulae and rituals, especially when un-accompanied by inner disposition, characterized Bunyan and his church. In sharp contrast, a classic instance of prescribed prayer, set for days of the week and seasons of the year, was the Book of Common Prayer. This difference in approach to prayer was at the heart of Bunyan's argument with Kelyng in1661. In *I Will Pray with the Spirit*, Bunyan sets out to perform two tasks, both in part arising out of his debate with Kelyng: the defence of valid prayer and an attack against invalid prayer, using the Book of Common Prayer as the archetype of the latter. At times, however, Bunyan puts forward relatively superficial and historically grounded objections to particular features of the Book of Common Prayer, objections which sit ill with his total rejection of the underlying liturgical principles on which the Prayer Book was based. Taking as his text the chapter in 1 Corinthians, in which Paul evinces some scepticism about the vogue during his own day of speaking in tongues as opposed to prayer that was both spiritual and intelligible, Bunyan set down the testimony against fixed forms of prayer that he had maintained on illicit preaching forays during the earlier period of his imprisonment: 'I followed my wonted course of preaching ... exhorting them ... to take heed they touched not the Common Prayer, &c'. Bunyan's position on the Common Prayer, alongside many other Puritan sectaries, was to deny the whole principle of prayers ordained in any way except spiritually. In *I Will Pray*, Bunyan set out an interpretation of prayer consistent with the view of God and humanity that he had worked out in *Law and Grace*. That is to say, formal liturgical prayers could be seen as human works designed to placate God through man-made means. Bunyan's spontaneous spiritual prayer, in contrast, was effected by the all-powerful God in the believer, 'by the strength or assistance of the Spirit'.[76]

I Will Pray has the classic form of a seventeenth-century sermon, with its initial text (from 1 Corinthians 14: 15), the customary unfolding of the 'method' to be followed, in four parts, and the final 'Use and Application of what shall be spoken'. The 'use' in a sermon applied what was preached to the more practical concerns of life. Bunyan had already developed the application of the 'use' in *Law and Grace*.[77] A preliminary explanation of prayer, in affective and experiential terms, establishes the stance that Bunyan will take on this issue throughout the treatise. He reveals a deft polemical skill in offering an apparently unexceptionable definition of prayer, which surely commands the reader's assent, just as such an innocuous description had won over Kelyng in the Bedford trial: 'a sincere, sensible [sensitive], affectionate [affective] pouring out of the heart or soul'. However, Bunyan's apparently unexceptionable definition led him, in a more exclusive spirit, to rule out prescribed formal prayers as 'a few babling, prating, complementory [sc. complimentary] expressions', thus precluding the possibility that any set prayers could be true prayers at all. This implied attack on the Book of Common Prayer was rapidly made explicit. Bunyan's treatise is soon identified as both a positive, pastorally oriented exploration of the true nature of prayer and a highly contentious attack on one tradition of praying – that epitomized in the Book of Common Prayer. Real experiential prayer, Bunyan writes, made a 'better Common Prayer-Book, than that which is taken out of the Papistical Mass-Book; being the Scraps and Fragments of the devices of some Popes, some Friars, and I wot not what'.[78]

Citing Foxe for support (somewhat illicitly, since Foxe had attacked the Mass, but not the Prayer Book as being derived from it), Bunyan appears to join himself to a well-established tradition of Puritan onslaught on the Book of Common Prayer as being based on the Missal; for example, John Field's *A View of Popish Abuses* of 1572 had identified the Prayer Book as 'an unperfect book, culled and picked out of that popish dunghill, the mass book, full of all abominations'. Thus Bunyan's opinion that the Book of Common Prayer was 'taken out of the Papistical Mass-Book' seems, on the face of it, well within the tradition of Puritan critique as represented by Field. However, Field stood near the head waters of a long stream of disparagement, but, for all the vehemence of critical language, far from out-and-out rejection, of the Prayer Book – a tradition that saw it as 'unperfect', which accepted its underlying liturgical ethos and which viewed it as being both seriously in need of, and essentially amenable to, reform. Baxter, with his anxious expectation of further amendment of the liturgy in 1660, was fully representative of that selectively critical, Reformist, classic Nonconformist outlook. Bunyan, in contrast, had nothing positive to offer on the reform of the Prayer Book in a more Protestant direction and his tactical objections to the Anglican liturgy were beside the point, since, as an irreconcilable dissident rather than a reformist critic, he was at odds with the Prayer Book not so much on the grounds of its historical filiation from the Sarum rite of the Mass, but on those of its underlying nature as prescribed prayer.[79]

What, then, is Bunyan's fundamental approach to prayer – embracing those assumptions that would have made the most Protestant set prayer book in Christendom unacceptable to him? His analysis of the nature of prayer is ratiocinative in method, but his conclusion approaches a unitive mysticism: God 'looks on that man' who is a 'member of Christ' as 'part of his Body ... united to him by election, conversion, illumination, the Spirit being conveyed into the heart of that poor man by God'. Thus, the initiative in prayer, as in all else that matters to Bunyan, comes from God; prayer is not to be seen as an autonomous human exercise and it is this that rules out prescribed prayer, since it is based on human invention. The concept of prayer as God's work in the believer means that, despite evident mystical leanings, Bunyan insists that prayer must be guided by God's word in Scripture – 'it is blasphemy, or at best, vain babling, when the Petition is beside the Book' – the model being Christ in the garden, who refused to pray for His release other than according to the fulfilment of Scripture.[80]

Bunyan's sharp polarization of right against wrong in approaches to prayer is echoed in a radical contrast between the people of God in the gathered church – 'blameless and harmless, the Sons of God' – and the outside world, 'a crooked and perverse Nation'. This can be parallelled by the mentality of social estrangement evident in the proceedings of the Bedford church around the time of the writing of *I Will Pray*. In turn, this mood of alienation took in a new disillusionment with temporal solutions, in contrast with the political activism that the godly in Bedfordshire had manifested during the Interregnum. Following the Restoration there was an entirely understandable rejection of worldly and political methods on the part of members of this church. In Bunyan's case there came a knowledge – a kind of positive passivity – that the 'perfect peace' of the church could not be attained on this earth but only 'until she be in Heaven', though in fact this peace had already been promised and ensured, 'purchased with [Christ's] blood'. Thus, in recommending prayer for the welfare of the church, Bunyan proposes petitioning for something that has, in fact, already been fully guaranteed. That is precisely what his view of prayer is, one that is also entirely in line with his overall view of God's majesty and omnipotence: the saints prayed for that 'which the Father hath given', and a 'Petition' that was 'beside the Will of God' was 'not to be answered'. Bunyan seems, then, to have been discounting not just prescribed but petitionary prayer as such. For him, prayer was an act of submission 'according to that Will of God'. Indeed, so inadmissible was prayer, other than according to the sovereign will of God, that true prayer was induced in the individual by 'God's Spirit' Paul (*'the Spirit it self maketh intercession for us'*) being cited in support.[81]

Thus, Bunyan unfolded a theory of prayer based on a distinctive view of God. Together with the tradition of Puritan criticism of the Book of Common Prayer, which he purported to take up, he traced a direct textual connection from the Prayer Book to the Missal. However, this was only secondary to the main issue, for written into both these textually related liturgies were shared underlying assumptions about the kind of God who could be reached and influenced by petitionary prayer: God as the supreme patron. Thus, collects in the Missal 'For Rain', 'For Fair Weather', 'In Time of Cattle Plague', 'For the Deliverance from Death in Time of Pestilence', 'For Peace' and so on rested on the same kind of assumptions about God, humanity, nature and their interrelations as were to be found in collects of the Book of Common Prayer: 'In the time of Dearth and Famine' (for 'cheapness and plenty'), 'For Rain' ('Send us … moderate rain and showers'), 'For Fair Weather', and the rest. The fundamental preconceptions underpinning those two sets of prayers coming from a common intercessory tradition were that God's mind was not finally made up, that He was susceptible to human persuasions, that His actions could be influenced and deflected, and that He intervened in natural, meteorological, social and economic events. In sharp contrast stood Bunyan's view of the futility or impertinence of petitioning an absolute and omnipotent God for anything that He had not already pre-ordained. Different theologies – indeed different world-views – call forth different liturgies.[82]

Bunyan, then, was basically at odds not with the text of the Prayer Book, but with its innermost pre-suppositions. Nevertheless, he continued to concentrate his attack on relatively superficial features, such as the observance of festivals: 'setting such a Prayer for such a day, and that twenty years before it comes. One for *Christmass,* another for *Easter* ... For each Saints day also, they have them ready for the generations yet unborn to say.' Here again it would appear that Bunyan, as with his attack on other identifiable 'popish' features of the Prayer Book's text, was once more placing himself in the more moderate Puritan tradition of isolating those objectionable features of the book that stood in need of reform, but accepting either the basic value of the Prayer Book or, at least, the value of set liturgies. The long-standing Reformist objection to festivals was set out in the 1580s in the Articles of Reformation of Ministry in the Puritan-inspired 'The Seconde Parte of a Register', which had demanded 'that the book of common prayer be amended in such points as it is faulty in; with cutting off all the services of the holy days'. Of course, the prayers set for times and seasons, themselves of Catholic origin, encapsulated the idea of un-spontaneous prescribed prayer, of human composition, that Bunyan repudiated. Even so, given the much more fundamental unacceptability and unreformability of the Book of Common Prayer in terms of his whole theological and religious outlook, we might ask what concern it was of his whether or not the Church of England's liturgy had or did not have prayers set well in advance of seasonal occasions. Perhaps something of this nature was in Kelyng's mind when he warned Bunyan against criticizing the Prayer Book – as if Kelyng were advising Bunyan to mind his own business: 'take heed of speaking irreverently of the Common Prayer-book'.[83]

Kelyng warned that such careless talk would land Bunyan in trouble, a prediction that was well-grounded, and it is perfectly possible that Bunyan stayed in gaol for so long in the 1660s because of the kind of outspokenness about the Book of Common Prayer that we have been considering here. It is also arguable that Bunyan's polemical attacks on the Prayer Book, bitter, satirical and splenetic as they were, marred, from a 'literary' point of view, the spiritual exaltation of his treatise on prayer, descending from rapture to rancour. Given that Bunyan was not really of the Nonconformist school of reform-minded Prayer-Book critique, why did he bother to attack particular features of the Prayer Book, or make the Anglican liturgy his business at all? Pique and bitterness apart, he did so for four reasons: first, the Prayer Book was made his business by a legal requirement that he must use it; second, the kind of praying he loathed – petitionary and pre-arranged – reached an apogee in the liturgy of the Church of England; third, this early in the Restoration period he had not acquired a sufficiently sectarian frame of mind to be indifferent to the nature of the public worship of the Church in which he had been reared; and, fourth, in his preaching and writing in the early 1660s he needed to dissuade would-be apostates from deserting the gathered churches by deterring them from accepting the blandishments of the public liturgy.

The extent of Bunyan's conceptual divorce from the kind of worship that reached its fullest realization in England in parish services becomes further apparent in a discourse on prayer grounded in his 'own Experience': 'as for my heart, when I go to pray, I find it so loth to go to God'. It becomes clear that the prayer that Bunyan envisages as the best was solitary and individual – 'between God and the Soul in secret' – rather than congregational, and that for Bunyan, in this as in other respects, the provisions of the church were of secondary importance. In contrast, the prayer of the Church of England was expressly 'common', that is to say, congregational, parochial, holistic, social and indeed national, observing communal times and seasons, interceding for collective needs.[84]

Bunyan's solitary prayer was also, at its best, wordless and 'unexpressable', and, as we have seen, he repudiated any praying that was set out in advance. Sooner or later, this would require him to deal with the vexed question of the validity of one particular 'set' form of oral prayer, the Lord's Prayer. Bunyan comes to this topic by way of a treatment of providing religious instruction for children, and the specific question of teaching them what was generally regarded as an essential component of a child's Christian education, the Lord's Prayer. In view of his denigration of prescribed prayer, Bunyan has to deal with the objection that Christ had commanded, in the form of the 'Our Father', the use of a prescribed prayer and that, therefore, a 'stinted Form of Prayer' was generally valid. Bunyan got round this objection by denying that the Lord's Prayer was prescribed. He maintained instead that Christ commended two different versions of the Lord's Prayer and that since, by definition, a prescribed prayer was unvarying, the Lord's Prayer did not fall into this category. In Bunyan's Authorized Version the most obvious variation between the two texts of the prayer, in Matthew 6 and Luke 11, is the inclusion in the former, but not the latter, of the doxology, 'For thine is the kingdom, the power, and the glory, for ever'. This interpolation in the Authorized Version has a fascinating history: it was not found in the earliest Greek texts or in the Latin Vulgate. Tyndale, the father of English Reformation translations of the Scriptures into the vernacular, derived his version from Erasmus's New Testament, which had been based, in its turn, on a relatively late Greek text incorporating the doxology. Bunyan was to know none of these things. The Bible that he had was the one he regarded as the word of God in English, and the variations between the two passages furnished him not with material for an essay in textual criticism, but with convincing proof that Christ had expressly ruled out prescribed prayer by recommending two variants of the same invocation. Bunyan also adduced the argument that Christ, in giving the Lord's Prayer, was outlining a suggested model for praying, rather than one hard-and-fast form of words: 'After this manner therefore pray ye' – or, as we might say, 'Pray along these lines'.[85]

I Will Pray with the Spirit has lasting value as a devotional and pastoral treatise. There is sensitive handling of wounded souls and an unfolding of the comfort to be taken by those in despair in the face of a spiritual state ostensibly without hope: 'There is a sense of senslesness, according to thy sense then, that thou hast of the need of any thing, so pray ... and if thou art sensible of thy senslesness, pray the Lord to make thee sensible.' As well as operating as a sublime spiritual manual of lasting use – Bunyan in the voice of Juliana of Norwich or Thomas à Kempis – *I Will Pray* is a tract for its times, pugnacious and sardonic. Here, the voice of Bunyan's caustic anticlericalism is that of a Marprelate, a Langland or a Chaucer, with the depiction of 'Your Trencher-Chaplains, that thrust themselves into great mens Families ... in truth the great business is their own Bellies.' Though operating within a long-standing tradition of anticlerical criticism and satire, the work is a particular product of that period following the Restoration, when the Elizabethan Book of Common Prayer was re-imposed by a triumphalist Church of England and a Cavalier Parliament, with its 'popish' features, which the godly had been criticizing for more than a century, re-asserted and indeed deliberately accentuated. Bunyan's highly contemporary criticisms of the Book of Common Prayer and of its upholders were the fruit of the most direct personal experience; his recital of the way those who rejected the 'Traditions of men' contained in the Prayer Book 'must be driven out of the Land, or the World' contain the clearest references to the options held out in the Act of 1593, terminal options which Bunyan avoided only by means of protracted imprisonment. Restored neo-Laudian episcopacy was linked to popery in Bunyan's impassioned critique: it was the 'Pope, Bishop, or other' who commanded forms of worship that were not required by God. But if Bunyan thus attacked the Church using such long-established Puritan charges, he also showed inclinations towards a *rapprochement* within non-Anglican Protestantism, including an appreciation of an understanding of the nature of prayer that was usually associated with his earlier polemical foes, the Quakers. He also refers to the 'silencing of God's dear Ministers', and if he means by this to allude to the whole body of Puritan clerics of all denominations ejected under the terms of the Act of Uniformity in 1662, then there is the possibility of his reaching out in this work to the wider community of Nonconformity. Many Nonconformists beyond the Bedford church would have agreed with the strictures that Bunyan delivered against a form of worship that had 'nothing but Tradition of men, and the strength of Persecution to uphold, or plead for it' – a charge which, in sterner terms, re-appeared in a minute of the Bedford congregation in 1671 against 'that superstitious, and idolatrous worship that with force, and cruelty is maintained'.[86]

One Thing is Needful

Following *I Will Pray with the Spirit*, Bunyan returned to verse in *Prison Meditations* (1663), which we have considered in the context of his eschatology, and to prose in *Christian Behaviour* (also 1663), which we looked at from the point of view of his attitude to the governance of families. In *A Mapp Shewing the Order & Causes of Salvation & Damnation* (1663 or 1664) Bunyan adopted the kind of scheme taken up by Perkins, the construction of a route-chart to redemption.[87] Then, perhaps in 1665, Bunyan reverted to verse with *One Thing is Needful*, a work in which, abandoning the ballad form, his poetic technique made major strides.[88]

The poem concerns the traditional 'four last things' – death, judgement, hell and heaven – which provided Bunyan with the four-fold structure of his poem. Two of these 'last things', death and judgement, are directly linked, and other two, heaven and hell, directly counterposed. The apportionment of stanzas to the themes, conditioned by didactic considerations, is uneven: fifty-one are concerned with death, fifty-two with judgement, eighty-two with heaven and ninety-seven with hell, reflecting Bunyan's dominant concern that his readers avoid that last destination.[89] Death appears initially:

> … as a King Rampant and stout …
> He Conquers all.[89]

This theme of all-conquering and sovereign death had already been introduced in *Profitable Meditations*. Following originally medieval iconographic, homiletic, dramatic and literary depictions, most of which, as Watt shows, were still surviving strongly in Stuart England, Bunyan makes death into a personality, in fact a powerful ruler, a lord of kings, as in medieval versions such as the fifteenth-century *danse-macabre*, *Knight, King, Clerk Wend to Death*:

> I wende to dede, a kyng y-wys;
> What helps honour or warldes blys?

In equally traditional fashion, Bunyan's figure of death is a great leveller:

> *Death* favours none, he lays at all,
> Of all sorts and degree.

A further traditional ingredient, surfacing strongly in Bunyan, was of death as the antidote to vanity, the *memento mori* motif found in medieval English verse:

> Seyng a man ys butt a sakeof stercory [excrement]
> And schall retorne to wormys mete.
> What cam off Alysaunder the grett?
> And of strong samson who can tell?
> Were nott wormys ordeyned ther fleshe for to frett?

Bunyan likewise captures the physical horror of mortal corruption:

> Beauty *Death* turns to rottenness,
> And Youth to wrinckled Face.

He is also influenced by the still-vibrant iconographic tradition, one hardly affected by alleged Protestant 'iconophobia', of depicting death with his emblems, those of the passage of time, of annihilation and of internment: 'The Glass that runs, the Sythe and Spade'. As Huston Diehl points out, Protestant Reformation religious teaching made extensive use of such well-established symbolism. Indeed, Tudor and Stuart funereal art was especially rich in images of death accompanied by his emblems and implements. Bunyan's 'All must tast of his Dart' is especially indebted to the English emblem school, including Francis Quarles.[90]

In line with his sensitivity to mental and emotional states, Bunyan is concerned to emphasize the individual's awareness and fear of his or her mortality. This corresponds to a long-range trend in western culture to individualize and emotionalize death, a development traced by Philippe

Ariès. Bunyan does indeed give considerable attention to the state of mind of the individual facing death. However, in late-medieval depictions, the deathbed, if one were fortunate, was a place of efficacious repentance and a sacramental preparation for death as a successful journey, including the opportunity, courtesy of the Church, for a final absolving confession and other fortifying sacraments. As he was later to show in *Mr. Badman* (1680), Bunyan rejected such last-minute dramas out of hand. In *One Thing is Needful* his dying man was in a much simpler, starker plight, the conclusion foregone:

> So his poor Soul doth faint away
> Without hope or relief.

The individual in question had chosen a life of sin, and the hour of his death was too late a time to amend that, least of all by sacramental aids. Even so, the place of predestination in all this is far from clear. Bunyan is sure that the saved are the elect, obtaining:

> … that rest
> Which none can win but only they
> Whom God hath call'd, and blest.

However, the general tenor of the poem is to emphasize individual choice, during the whole of life rather than on the deathbed. Bunyan's evocation of his dying sinner's plight has the purpose of persuading his readers to reject sin or otherwise face the anguished death that he graphically portrays.[91]

   Choice rather than predestination is equally to the fore in Bunyan's next section, *Of Judgment*, as these examples show:

> The living, too, run here and there,
> Who made him not their Choice …
> My sins have brought me to this plight,
> I threw my self away …
> For every one must now receive
> According to their wayes.

Emphasis on election at this point – that is, on a pre-judgement made long ago on the whole of mankind, thereby reducing, if not eliminating, the determinative function of judgement following death – would not have suited

Bunyan's literary and instructive purposes of using the drama of death, judgement, hell and heaven to convey his moral lesson that individuals should avoid sin so as to escape sentencing.[92] As in his section on death, in his stanzas on judgement Bunyan, is primarily concerned with the individual and the verdict upon him or her:

> But every heart shall op'ned be
> Before this Judg most high …
> Into that gulf my sins have brought
> Me justly to possess.

However, his principal source for imagining judgement is the Book of Revelations, upon which five passages in his section *Of Judgment* are based, along with the so-called 'Little Apocalypse' in Mark 13. The emphasis in these New Testament apocalyptic passages concerned with judgement is on an eschatological verdict in a *dies irae*, a final collective sentence on the vast masses of mankind. On the basis of the kind of scenario set out in Revelation 7: 9 – 'and, lo, a great multitude, which no man could number of all nations and kindreds, and people, and tongues, stood before the throne, and before the Lamb, clothed with white robes, and palms in their hands', Bunyan placed the fate of the individual soul within a general judgement of 'whole thousands'. The entire judicial action, prosecution and sentence, is conducted by the deity, without the role of prosecutor that was entrusted to the archangel Michael in medieval depictions.[93]

In this poem Bunyan proceeds for much of the time by way of analogy and allegory. One obvious allegory for the Last Judgement was that of earthly justice. As Diehl says, depictions of the Judgement in courtrooms had the twofold purpose of reminding Christians of the ultimate sentence, and also of legitimating earthly courts of law by showing them as reflections of God's court of justice. Possibly as a result of his recent experiences with the English legal system, Bunyan was not powerfully seized by an analogy between human and divine justice. His one courtroom image in this poem – 'These Prisoners have no bail' – did not occur in his section on judgement, but rather in his passage on hell.[94]

In dealing with death, Bunyan had before him the observed reality of one of the few universal human experiences; in his treatment of the Judgement he had literary models from the New Testament to guide him; and for his writing on hell there was a homiletic and literary tradition which combined highly physicalized detail with horror. For his account of heaven, however, Bunyan emphasized its ineffability – and consequent indescribability:

> The glory and the comliness,
> By deepest thought none may
> With heart or mouth fully express.

The result tends to be that Bunyan is reduced, if not to describing heaven in terms of his incapacity to describe it, then simply to restating how beautiful it is:

> Its State also is marvellous
> For baeuty to behold,
> All goodness there is plentious,
> And better far than Gold.

As is to be expected from Bunyan's preoccupation with the internal human condition, his heaven means the satisfaction not of physical or aesthetic, but rather of spiritual, mental and emotional needs. Spiritually and intellectually, heaven yields vital information about the fulfilment of God's 'Attributes', that is, the reconciliation of His justice with His mercy 'when Christ was slain'. Heaven, then, means the final revelation of truth – 'All Mysteries shall here be seen' – with the full disclosure of Christ as 'Prophet, Priest, and King'. On the emotional level, heaven offers the bliss of meeting again with (godly) relatives – 'The Wife, the Child, and Father dear' – and those who were instrumental in a person's conversion.[95]

Genre conventions required symmetry in the depiction of such themes as heaven and hell: a feature of one situation, for example, the permanence of eternal felicity, needed to find its counterpart – in this case, the eternity of infernal misery. Just like heaven, hell is so limitless in its range of experience as to be ultimately indescribable:

> So fearfull, that none can relate
> The pangs that there are born.

However, no writer can go on indefinitely telling his readers that he cannot describe what he relates, and Bunyan finds a way – a scriptural way – of describing hell, by means of analogy. He offers three analogues found 'in the Word'.[96] The first of these is a 'burning Lake'. The fact that Bunyan has used here exactly the same term as Milton in Book I of *Paradise Lost* means, not that Milton has quarried Bunyan, but that both authors have gone to a common scriptural storehouse, Revelation 19: 20 and 20: 10, with the horrific image of 'a lake of fire burning with brimstone'. This burning hell is a place of unendurable pain, which God Himself explains:

> O damned men! this is your fate,
> The day of grace is done ...
> Me you offended with your sin.[97]

Bunyan's second analogue for hell is prison, an image with some scriptural resonances in Matthew 5: 25 and in 1 Peter 3: 19. His third image, a pit, has stronger scriptural support, especially as a symbol for abandonment and the grave, as in Psalms and Isaiah, and of descent, as in Christ's 'descent into hell'. The image of the pit seems to have had a terrifying hold on Bunyan, as we saw with his metaphor in *Grace Abounding* of the lost sinner as a child fallen into a 'Mill-pit'.[98]

Although Bunyan uses the locational similes of the lake, the prison and the pit, hell is a condition as well as, or rather than, a place, and one that the damned have about them, like Marlowe's Mephistopheles:

> Why this is hell, nor am I out of it:
> Thinkest thou that I who saw the face of God,
> And tasted the eternal joys of heaven,
> Am not tormented with ten thousand hells
> In being deprived of everlasting bliss!

In line with Bunyan's concern with consciousness, and in particular the anguish of conditions of loss, abandonment and guilt (as in *Grace Abounding*), there is misery at being who one was:

> A block, a stock, a stone, or clot,
> Is happier than I.

Remorse, though, results chiefly from what the sinner had earlier decided to do and to be, and nowhere is Bunyan's – non-predestinarian – sense of willed damnation clearer than in the lines:

> Ah, *Will*, why wast thou thus inclin'd
> Me ever to undo!

Despair is made total by knowledge, of the eternity of punishment:

> For ever, shineth in the fire,
> Ever, is on the chains.[99]

We have already seen something of Bunyan's literary technique in *One Thing is Needful*. The versification can be forced – 'man' rhymed with 'stand', 'alas' with 'cross', 'great' with 'cheat' (though that last pair may have formed a rhyme in Bunyan's English pronunciation). The stanza form, though, is much freer than in his novice piece of poetry, *Profitable Meditations*. He is now able to break free of the enclosed quatrains that had imprisoned him in the earlier work, in which sentences invariably finish at the end of stanzas and, generally, clauses at the end of lines. In *Profitable Meditations* this rigidity of the rhymed stanzas had made for a jingle effect. Instead, Bunyan now occasionally employs a freer form of stanza, in which we are less conscious of the tyranny of rhyme and metre and aware of more natural speech rhythms:

> ... behold
> The rayes and beams of glory, and
> Find there his name inrol'd
>
> Among those glittering Stars of light.

Another emergent literary technique is the use of minor variants in lines of verse:

> This shall we see, thus shall we be ...
> This we shall hear, this we shall see.

We have only to consider how effective this echo device was, when used, for example, by Spenser and Donne, to realize the extent to which Bunyan was now emerging as a conscious artist.[100]

Ebal and Gerizzim[101]

The poem which Bunyan published along with *One Thing is Needful* – *Ebal and Gerizzim* – was, perhaps surprisingly, his last work in verse for almost twenty years – though verse was included in *Peaceable Principles and True* (1674), the two parts of *The Pilgrim's Progress* (1678, 1684), *The Holy War* (1682) and (briefly) in *The Greatness of the Soul* (1683).

In Deuteronomy 27: 11–17, the mountains Ebal and Gerizzim symbolize, respectively, a curse and a blessing. Bunyan deals with Gerizzim, the blessing, much more extensively than with Ebal, awarding it 655 compared with 215 lines. He abandoned the quatrain form of *Profitable Meditations* and *One Thing is Needful*; the greater metrical freedom that he had gained in the latter, by running on sentences between lines and stanzas, was at his disposal in *Ebal and Gerizzim*, in which he adopted the form of the heroic couplet, with blocks of continuous verse broken up into paragraphs. The flow of sentences running through the rhyme scheme creates an impression of natural speech and also of rapid pace:

> An after-word still runneth in my mind,
> Which I shall here expose unto that wind,
> That may it blow into that very hand
> That needs it. Also that it may be scan'd
> With greatest soberness ...[102]

While one agrees with Graham Midgley that the style of the work is that of a sermon – though a 'familiar and confidential' one – it does not seem to be a congregational sermon, but one addressed, as it were, to a single person. This is indicated by the replacement of the 'sung' format of the ballad with the more natural 'rhyming prose' of heroic couplets, and by the employment throughout of the second-person singular to convey a feeling of intimacy, in the same one-to-one register as, say, in *The Imitation of Christ*. Therefore, the poem should be considered as an exercise in personal pastoral care, a homily addressed to the individual reader:

> But first I would advise thee to bethink
> Thy self ...[103]

Issued alongside *One Thing is Neeedful*, *Ebal and Gerrizim* continues, as an 'after-word', the former's treatment of the 'four last things'. In line with his homiletic, pastoral purpose, urging decision on his readers, Bunyan seems to continue with the withdrawal he made, in the practical counselling of *One Thing is Needful* and *Profitable Meditations*, away from the high doctrine of predestination he had set out in *The Law and Grace Unfolded* and which he was to develop further in *A Defence of the Doctrine of Justification, by Faith* and *A Confession of My Faith* (both 1672). His anxiety to underline the urgency of existential choice is now uppermost:

> Now that thou may'st awake, the danger flye,
> And so escape the death that others dye ...
> 'Tis for thy life, O do it not refuse.

The choice to be made is that of taking advantage of 'Gospel-priviledges', of following the saints, of desiring to prefer 'the blessing' to 'worldly pelf':

'What say'st thou? will't not yet unto him come?' Indeed, there is a claim, which seems extraordinary in the light of Bunyan's normative doctrine of humanity and the will, that the Spirit:

> ... sets the will at liberty to chuse
> Those things, that God hath promis'd to infuse
> Into the humble heart.

This suggestion of voluntary choice – the freed, if not the free, will – is sustained in a series of questions on what the individual ought to seek, all introduced with an interrogative or conditional subjunctive form of the verb 'to will' and implying options – 'Woudst', 'Woudest'.[104]

In this work, then, Bunyan's pastoral rhetoric, urging decisions on his reader, seems almost to get the better of his deterministic theology. It is true that he denies our ability to achieve holiness ourselves, but his indication that we may 'choose to live' 'holy lives' enables him to convey, with ever-increasing literary skill, the dramatic urgency of the decisions that the individual must make. One would not wish to exaggerate the tendency in Bunyan to play up free will or to suggest human righteousness, nor even to suggest an ambivalence of approach between Bunyan the theologian in *Law and Grace* and Bunyan the pastoralist in the poems. The second instalment of *Ebal and Gerrizim,* in particular, restates the soteriological orthodoxies of *Law and Grace*: obeying God's law is indispensable – and impossible, so that the only refuge for its fulfilment is: 'If unto Jesus Christ they ... fly.'[105]

With the group of works studied in this chapter, Bunyan announced his arrival as a religious author. His range was already considerable, and took in controversy, devotional writing, dogmatic theology and pastoral counselling. His intellectual powers were formidable, as was his capacity for exposition. Even so, some of his most effective writing was not in the field of ratiocinative theology so much as in experiential, emotive, and autobiographical discourse. He had discovered a range of voices, from the exclamatory and rhapsodic mode to solid analytical composition and from tensely written prose to lyrical verse. Next, he was to add commentaries on church life and worship to his repertoire, as well as further forays into controversy, along with ethics and allegory.

Notes

1. For the rise of Quakerism, see: Hugh Barbour, *The Quakers in Puritan England* (New Haven, CT, and London, 1964); W. C. Braithwaite, *The Beginnings of Quakerism* (London, 1912; reprinted York, 1981); Barry Reay, *The Quakers and the English Revolution* (London, 1985); T. L. Underwood (ed.), *Miscellaneous Works of John Bunyan*, vol. I (Oxford, 1980), pp. xvi–xx1. Alan Sell, *Church Planting: A Study of Westmorland Nonconformity* (Worthing, 1986).

2. Figures from Michael Watts, *The Dissenters: From the Reformation to the French Revolution* (Oxford, 1978), p. 509.

3. For the establishment of Quakerism in Bedfordshire, see Underwood (ed.), *Miscellaneous Works of John Bunyan*, vol. I, p. xxiv.

4. *Grace Abounding*, p. 39.

5. John Bunyan, *Some Gospel-Truths Opened*, in Underwood (ed.), *Miscellaneous Works of John Bunyan*, vol. I, pp. 7–113 and xxx–xxxi, esp. pp. xxxi–xxxii for analysis of the work's structure; also available in G. Offor (ed.), *The Works of John Bunyan* (3 vols; Glasgow, 1854), vol. II, pp. 129–75. For the context of the controversy, see T. L. Underwood, '"It Pleased Me Much to Contend": John Bunyan as Controversialist', *Church History* 57 (1988), pp. 456–69 and esp. pp. 458–9, and Ann Hughes, 'The Pulpit Guarded: Confrontations Between Orthodox and Radicals in Revolutionary England', in Anne Laurence, W. R. Owens and Stuart Sim (eds), *John Bunyan and His England 1628–1688* (London and Ronceverte, WV, 1990), pp. 31–2. For a summary of the debate and Bunyan's association of the Quakers with the Ranters, see B. R. White, '"The Fellowship of Believers": Bunyan and Puritanism', in N. H. Keeble (ed.), *John Bunyan: Conventicle and Parnassus* (Oxford, 1988), pp. 15–16.

6. *Gospel-Truths*, pp. 7 and xvii. Bunyan used the term 'notionist', which in Fox's vocabulary betokened a speculative dabbler in religious ideas, for one 'puffed up in his fleshly mind, and advanceth himself above others'. In common with contemporaries such as Baxter (see N. H. Keeble (ed.), *The Autobiography of Richard Baxter* (London and Melbourne, 1974), pp. 73–4), Bunyan linked Quakers and Ranters (see above, ch. 1, n. 71), the former being viewed as a kind of 'respectable' version of the latter.

7. *Gospel-Truths*, pp. 61, 64.

8. *Ibid.*, pp. 17, 63, 101–11, 94–6 and *passim*; cf. Underwood's discussion of Bunyan's use of repetition, in *ibid.*, p. xxxvii.

9. *Gospel-Truths*, pp. 90–9.

10. *Ibid.*, pp. 18, 45–7.

11. *Gospel-Truths*, pp. 31ff.; for George Herbert's image of a lease in *Redemption*, see R. S. Thomas (ed.), *A Choice of George Herbert's Verse* (London, 1967), pp. 23–4; see also Francis Lyall, 'Of Metaphors and Analogies: Legal Language and Covenant Theology', *Scottish Journal of Theology* 32

(1979) pp. 1–17. Batson reminds us of John Donne's retailing metaphor, 'In Adam we were sold in grosse; in our selves we are sold by retail': E. Beatrice Batson, *John Bunyan: Allegory and Imagination*, (London and Canberra, 1984), p. 67; compare also Donne's:

> Father, part of his double interest
> Unto thy kingdome, thy Sonne gives to mee,
> His joynture in the knottie Trinitie
> Hee keepes, … and he
> Hath made two Wills, which with the Legacie
> Of his and thy kingdome, doe thy Sonnes invest.

John Donne, *Divine Poems*, XVI, in Sir Herbert Grierson (ed.), *The Poems of John Donne* (London, New York and Toronto, 1933), p. 300.

12. For Bunyan and covenant theology, see Richard L. Greaves (ed.), *Miscellaneous Works of John Bunyan*, vol. II (Oxford, 1976), pp. xxi–xxxii.

13. *Gospel-Truths*, p. 103; for Anselm, see R. W. Southern, *St. Anselm and his Biographer: A Study of Monastic Life and Thought 1059–c.1130* (Cambridge, 1966), ch. III.

14. Burton may be credited with launching the cliché that was to haunt Bunyan's career, the image of the yokel who 'hath neither the greatness nor the wisdom of the world to commend him' – with the usual obligatory citation of 1 Corinthians 1: 26–8: *The Epistle Writ by Mr. Burton, Minister at Bedford,* in *Gospel-Truths*, p. 11.

15. See *ibid.*, pp. 72–3.

16. e.g. *Gospel-Truths*, pp. 40, 70, 109.

17. For Bunyan's repudiation of the imitation of Christ, see also Isabel Rivers, 'Grace, Holiness and the Pursuit of Happiness: Bunyan and Restoration Latitudinarianism', in Keeble (ed.), *John Bunyan*, pp. 61–2.

18. Roger Pooley, though, shows that Bunyan 'does recognise that he needs a Christ within as well: 'Spiritual Experience and Spiritual Autobiography', *The Baptist Quarterly* 32 (1988), p. 394.

19. Underwood, '"It Pleased me Much to Contend"', pp. 458–9; *Gospel-Truths*, p. 59.

20. M. G. F. Bitterman, 'The Early Quaker Literature of Defense', *Church History* 42 (1973), p. 205.

21. Edward Burrough, *The True Faith of the Gospel of Peace Contended for, in the Spirit of Meekness* (London, 1656), in Ellis Hookes (ed.), *The Memorable WORKS of a Son of THUNDER and Consolation: Edward Burroughs* (London, 1672).

22. John Brown, *John Bunyan, His Life, Times and Work* (2nd edn; London, 1886), pp. 111–15; there were verbal clashes between Bunyan and the Quakers at the Bedford market cross; Burrough recalled a speech by Bunyan at Pavenham, Bedfordshire, in April 1656, further public speaking by

Bunyan and Burton in St Paul's, Bedford, in May 1656, and statements by Bunyan and his fellow church members John Fenn and John Child in November. For Burrough, see Elizabeth Brockbank, *Edward Burrough. A Wrestler for Truth* (London, 1949) and Richard L. Greaves and Robert Zaller (eds), *Biographical Dictionary of British Radicals in the Seventeenth Century* (3 vols; Brighton, 1982–4) vol. I, p. 108.

23. Burrough, *The True Faith*, pp. 136, 140 (*recte* 137), 147, 151–2.

24. Burrough portrayed the Quakers as a 'company of poor people', oppressed by a professional clergy of 'Scribes and Pharisees', 'murthering Priests' (*ibid.*, p.139) – stealing from Bunyan and his fellows their clothing as God's chosen ones from among the poor and simple.

25. *Ibid.*, pp. 138, 141. For the Nayler episode, see Braithwaite, *Beginnings of Quakerism*, pp. 244–73; Geoffrey Nuttall, 'James Nayler: A Fresh Approach', *Friends Historical Journal*, supplement 26 (1954); William G. Bittle, *James Nayler 1618–1660: The Quaker Indicted by Parliament* (Richmond, IN, 1986); and Maryann S. Feola, 'Fox's Relationship with Nayler', in Michael A. Mullett (ed.), *New Light on George Fox (1624 to 1691): A Collection of Essays* (York, 1993), pp. 101–9.

26. Burrough, *The True Faith*, pp. 137 (*recte* 140), 138, 141–2, 149, 150–1. The parallels between Burrough's faith-with-works soteriology and Tridentine definitions may help explain hostile comparisons with the first Quakers and Catholics: see J. Kent, 'The "Papist" Charge Against the Interregnum Quakers', *Journal of Religious History* 12 (1983), pp. 180–90.

27. Burrough, *The True Faith*, p. 149.

28. *Ibid.*, p. 143.

29. *A Vindication of the Book Called Some Gospel-Truths Opened*, in Underwood (ed.), *Miscellaneous Works of John Bunyan*, vol. I, pp.121–219 and xxxii–xxxv where there is an analysis of the works's structure); also in Offor (ed.), *Works of John Bunyan*, vol. II, pp. 176–214.

30. *A Vindication*, pp. 132 ff. In defending Burton from the charge of preaching 'for hire', Bunyan in effect ducked the issue, pointing at some unidentified clergy as 'dumb dogs' (p. 205), the traditional Puritan slur against non-preaching ministers, based on Isaiah 56: 10. He felt much more confident in defending his own, unpaid ministry and went on to launch a classic radical Puritan attack against the social as well as the religious abuses of those who pursued '*great Benefices, and Parsonages … [who] so run, for these tithe-cocks and handfuls of Barley, as if it were their proper Trade, and calling*' (*ibid.*, p. 127).

31. *Ibid.*, pp. 140, 169.

32. Keeble (ed.), *Autobiography of Richard Baxter*, p. 73; *A Vindication*, p. 139. A significant contrast between Baxter and Bunyan as writers is that, while Baxter gives a straightforward account – 'the Quakers, who were but the Ranters turned from horrid profaneness and blasphemy to a life of extreme austerity' – Bunyan said much the same, but with a vividness of

image that exactly captured what many contemporaries thought: 'Only the *Ranters* have made [their opinions] thred-bare at an Ale-House, and the Quakers have set a new glosse upon them again, by an outward legall holinesse.'

33. *A Vindication*, pp. 217, 215.

34. Edward Burrough, *Truth (the Strongest of all) Witnessed Forth in the Spirit of Truth against all DECEIT* (London, 1657), in Hookes (ed.), *The Memorable WORKS*, pp. 275–309.

35. *Ibid.*, pp. 279, 281–2, 290, 294–5, 304–5.

36. Underwood, '"It Pleased Me Much to Contend"', pp. 459–63.

37. Hookes (ed.), *The Memorable WORKS*, pp. 290, 310–24.

38. *The Doctrine of the Law and Grace Unfolded*, in Greaves (ed.), *Miscellaneous Works of John Bunyan*, vol. II, pp. 11–226 and xv–xxvii; also in Offor (ed.), *Works of John Bunyan*, vol. I, pp. 493–575.

39. *Law and Grace Unfolded*, pp. 12, 13, 14–16; Underwood, '"It Pleased Me Much to Contend"', pp. 465–6; for Bunyan and Scripture, see Christopher Hill, *The English Bible and the Seventeenth-Century Revolution* (London, 1993), pp. 27, 33, 121–2, 206, 230, 235, 372, 390, 406.

40. See *Law and Grace Unfolded*, pp. 17–19, 22–3, 25–6, 27–8, 29, and xxi–xxxii.

41. *Law and Grace Unfolded*, pp. 31, 35; also see *ibid.*, pp. xix–xx, for John Dod's and Richard Cleaver's hugely popular *A Plain and Familiar Exposition of the Ten Commandments*, which went through nineteen editions by 1635; see also Charles H. George and Katherine George, *The Protestant Mind of the English Reformation* (Princeton, NJ, 1961), pp. 106, 123, 130, 137, 151, 159, 247, 292–3, 422–3.

42. *Law and Grace Unfolded*, p. 36; for Perkins's open letter to *All Ignorant People that Desire to be Instructed*, see H. C. Porter (ed.), *Puritanism in Tudor England* (London, 1970), pp. 275–8; see also Eamon Duffy, 'The Godly and the Multitude in Stuart England', *The Seventeenth Century* 1 (1986), p. 32.

43. *Law and Grace Unfolded*, pp. 36–9.

44. *Ibid.*, pp. 39, 40, 48, 51: my emphasis.

45. *Ibid.*, pp. 52, 54, 55, 58, 59, 61.

46. *Ibid.*, p. 66.

47. *Ibid.*, pp. 77–8, 80; I owe the reference to Charles Wesley to the kindness of the Revd Eric Lacey, Rector of Heysham, Lancashire. For Bunyan's religious individualism, see Roger Pooley, '*Grace Abounding* and the New Sense of Self', in Laurence *et al.* (eds), *John Bunyan*, pp. 105–14.

48. See *Law and Grace Unfolded*, pp. 76–81, xxvii.

49. *Ibid.*, pp. 88–91 and xxv.

50. *Ibid.*, pp. 89–90, 101.

51. *Ibid.*, pp. 95–6, 98–100. Compare the negotiations between the Father and the Son in Book XI of *Paradise Regained*, in which Milton develops, from

1 John 2: 12, the theme of Christ's sacrificial advocacy which Bunyan was to explore fully in his 1688 work *The Advocateship of Jesus Christ*:

> [the Son] ... let me
> Interpret for him [mankind], me his advocate
> And propitiation; all his works on me
> Good or not good ingraft, my merit those
> Shall perfect, and for these my death shall pay.
> Accept me, and in me from these receive
> The smell of peace toward mankind. Let him live
> Before thee reconciled, ...
> To whom the Father, without cloud, serene:
> All thy request for man, accepted Son,
> Obtain; all thy request was my decree.

52. *Law and Grace Unfolded*, pp. 104, 107, 109, 108; also see Tessa Watt, *Cheap Print and Popular Piety 1550–1640* (Cambridge, 1991), pp. 173-6.

53. *Law and Grace Unfolded*, pp. 109, 112. For depictions of the mental and emotional, as well as the physical, anguish of the Passion in medieval English literature, see examples in Carleton Brown (ed.), *Religious Lyrics of the XIVth Century* (Oxford, 1924) – for instance, the deeply poignant *Christ's Prayer in Gethsemane* (p. 82, no. 62) or *Homo Vide quid pro Te Patior* (p. 93, no. 77), from the school of Richard Rolle, and relating Christ's exacerbated sufferings directly to the individual's failure of response:

> Of all the payne that I suffer sare,
> with-in my hert it greuves me mare
> The vnkyndenes that I fynd in the,
> that for thi lufe thus hynged on tre.

See also the remarkable essay by Kathleen Powers Erickson, 'Pilgrims and Strangers: The Role of *The Pilgrim's Progress* and *The Imitation of Christ* in Shaping the Piety of Vincent van Gogh', *Bunyan Studies* 4 (1991), esp. pp. 20–4.

54. See *Law and Grace Unfolded*, pp. 136–43.

55. See *ibid.*, pp. 143–6.

56. *Ibid.*, pp. 146, 147.

57. *Ibid.*, p. 157. For Burrough in Bedfordshire, see Brockbank, *Edward Burrough*, pp. 106-7.

58. *Law and Grace Unfolded*, p. 184.

59. *Ibid.*, pp. 169, 199, 206, 202, 223, 226. For the idea of the sinlessness of the elect, and the tension between objective external election and personal holiness, see J. C. Brauer, 'Puritan Mysticism and the Development of Libertinism', *Church History* 19 (1950), pp. 153–79.

60. John Bunyan, *Profitable Meditations, Fitted to Man's Different Condition. In a Conference between Christ and a Sinner*, in Graham Midgley (ed.), *Miscellaneous Works of John Bunyan*, vol. VI (Oxford, 1980), pp. 4–35 and xv–xlviii.

61. For the ballad, see Peter Burke, 'Popular Culture in Seventeenth-Century London', in Barry Reay (ed.), *Popular Culture in Seventeenth-Century England* (London, 1985), p. 49; James Sharpe, 'The People and the Law', in *ibid.*, pp. 256–8; Watt, *Cheap Print*, pp. 13–14, 257, 262, 268, 270, 318; and, especially for 'godly' popular literature, Bernard Capp, 'Popular Literature', in Reay (ed.), *Popular Culture*, pp. 218–21, and Duffy, 'The Godly and the Multitude', pp. 41–9.

62. For Bunyan on the ballad, see Midgley (ed.), *Miscellaneous Works of John Bunyan*, vol. VI, pp. xxx and ff.

63. Duffy, 'The Godly and the Multitude', pp. 41–9; Watt, *Cheap Print*, pp. 81–90. For the 'songe of foure preistes', see Michael Mullett and Leo Warren, *Martyrs of the Diocese of Lancaster* (Preston, 1987), pp. 52–3.

64. *Profitable Meditations*, stanza III, p. 5.

65. See *ibid.*, p. 4: 'To the reader'.

66. *Ibid.*, pp. 4–35.

67. *Ibid.*, stanzas IV, XIII, XVIII, pp. 5–7.

68. See *ibid.*, stanzas XLIII–LXXII, pp. 11–16. In Book IX of *Paradise Lost*, Milton presents Satan as one who uses the classical arts of rhetoric:

> As when of old some orator renown'd
> In Athens or free Rome, where eloquence
> Flourish'd …

while in *Absalom and Achitophel* (l. 228), Dryden's Satan-like tempter works: 'With studied arts to please.' For Bunyan and Milton, see Hill, *The English Bible*, pp. 371–3.

69. *Profitable Meditations*, stanzas LXXIX, LXXIV, LXXXVIII, pp. 17–19.

70. *Ibid.*, stanzas CIV, CV, CVIII, CIX, CX, CXIX, pp. 22–4. For the character and power of death in medieval drama and in sermons, see Robert Potter, *The English Morality Play: Origins, History and Influence of a Dramatic Tradition* (London and Boston, MA, 1975), pp. 40–7, and G. R. Owst, *Preaching in Medieval England: An Introduction to Sermon Manuscripts of the Period c.1350–1450* (Cambridge, 1926), pp. 340–4. For the strong survival in seventeenth-century English popular writing and iconography of themes of the *danse macabre* and the *memento mori*, see Watt, *Cheap Print*, pp. 113, 163–4 and plate; Christopher Marlowe, *Doctor Faustus*, I, iii.

71. *Profitable Meditations*, stanza CXXIV, p. 25. For Bruegel's *Triumph of Death*, see *Pieter Bruegel The Elder* (text by Wolfgang Stechow, The Library of Great Painters; New York, 1969), pp. 76–7.

72. *Ibid.*, stanzas CXLIV, CLVII, pp. 29, 31.

73. *Ibid.*, stanzas CLXIV, CLXXVII, CLXXXII, pp. 32, 34, 35.

74. *I Will pray with the Spirit*, in Greaves (ed.), *Miscellaneous Works of John Bunyan*, vol. II, pp. 229–86 and xxxviii–xliv; also in Offor (ed.), *Works of John Bunyan*, vol. I, pp. 623–40.

75. *Law and Grace Unfolded*, p. 182; see also p. 211.

76. 'Relation of the Imprisonment', p. 129; *I Will Pray with the Spirit*, p. 236. For sixteenth- and seventeenth-century English Protestant and Puritan views of prayer, see Greaves (ed.), *Miscellaneous Works of John Bunyan*, vol. II, p. xliii; Horton Davies, *Worship and Theology in England* (5 vols; Princeton, NJ, 1961–75), vol. II: *From Andrewes to Baxter and Fox* (1975), pp. 187–94, 507–10; Geoffrey Nuttall, *The Holy Spirit in Puritan Faith and Experience* (Oxford, 1947), ch. IV; A. Elliott Peaston, *The Prayer Book Tradition in the Free Churches* (London, 1964), pp. 124–5.

77. For Bunyan's prison sermon-treatises, see Brown, *Bunyan*, p. 161. For seventeenth-century homiletics, see Davies, *Worship and Theology*, vol. II, pp. 161–77; *Law and Grace Unfolded*, pp. 177–84.

78. *I Will Pray with the Spirit*, pp. 235, 237, 239.

79. For Field's *A View*, see Porter, *Puritanism in Tudor England*, pp. 115–38 and esp. p. 123; for Baxter on the Prayer Book, see Keeble (ed.), *Autobiography of Richard Baxter*, pp. 163–4; and on prayer, see Greaves (ed.), *Miscellaneous Works of John Bunyan*, vol. II, p. xliii.

80. *I Will Pray with the Spirit*, pp. 242, 243.

81. *Ibid.*, pp. 244, 245, 246; see also Michael Mullett, '"Deprived of our Former Place": The Internal Politics of Bedford, 1660–1688', *Bedfordshire Historical Record Society* 59 (1980), pp. 2, 6, 7. Greaves shows that Bunyan approached, but 'stopped short' of, Seeker and Quaker 'silent waiting upon the Spirit alone': Greaves (ed.), *Miscellaneous Works of John Bunyan*, vol. II, p. xlii.

82. Cf. John Bossy, 'The Mass as a Social Institution', *Past and Present* 100 (1983), pp. 29–61.

83. *I Will Pray with the Spirit*, pp. 247–8; *Grace Abounding*, p. 116. For 'The Seconde Parte of a Register', see Porter, *Puritanism in Tudor England*, p. 224.

84. *I Will Pray with the Spirit,* pp. 256–7.

85. See *ibid.*, pp. 269–70. For Bunyan's acceptance of the English Bible as the Scripture – 'our English Bible is a true copy of the original' – see Gordon Campbell, 'Fishing in Other Men's Waters: Bunyan and the Theologians', in Keeble (ed.), *John Bunyan*, pp. 139–40; also Juliette Dusinberre, 'Bunyan and Virginia Woolf: A History and a Language of Their Own', *Bunyan Studies* 5 (1994), esp. pp. 22–6.

86. *I Will Pray with the Spirit*, pp. 276, 273, 283, 283, 284, 285; Mullett, '"Deprived of our Former Place"', p. 7. For the experiential, un-academic tone of the work and the link between its emphasis on immediacy and its

anticlericalism, see Greaves (ed.), *Miscellaneous Works of John Bunyan*, vol. II, p. xliv.

87. For Bunyan's *A Mapp* and its genre, including Perkins's version, see W. R. Owens (ed.), *Miscellaneous Works of John Bunyan*, vol. XII (Oxford, 1994), pp. 419–23 and xxv–xxvii.

88. *One Thing is Needful: Or, Serious Meditations Upon the Four Last Things, Death, Judgment, Heaven, Hell,* in Midgley (ed.), *Miscellaneous Works of John Bunyan*, vol. VI, pp. 63–102 and xlix–li (Midgley addresses several textual issues in *ibid.*, pp. 58–62); also in Offor (ed.), *Works of John Bunyan*, vol. III, pp. 726–37.

89. *One Thing is Needful*, stanza 1, p. 65.

90. For *Knight, King, Clerk Wend to Death*, see Brown (ed.), *Religious Lyrics*, pp. 249, 252, nos. 158, 159; *One Thing is Needful*, stanzas 11, 9, 16, 12, pp. 66–7; Huston Diehl, '"To Put Us In Remembrance": The Protestant Transformation of Images of Judgment', in David Bevington *et al.*, *Homo, Memento Finis: The Iconography of Just Judgment in Medieval Art and Drama* (Kalamazoo, MI, 1985), pp. 179–81; Watt, *Cheap Print*, pp. 110–15, 163–4. For Quarles's emblem of death's dart, see Rosemary Freeman, *English Emblem Books* (New York, 1961), frontispiece and pp. 122–3; for an earlier version of the dart, see Hieronymus Bosch's (*c.*1450–1516) *Death of the Miser*, in Bevington *et al.*, *Homo, Memento Finis,* plate 21.

91. *One Thing is Needful*, stanzas 35, 42, pp. 69–70. For Bunyan's repudiation of death-bed repentance (in *Mr. Badman*), see below, pp. 227–8.

92. *One Thing is Needful*, stanzas 10, 22, 50, pp. 73–8.

93. *Ibid.*, stanzas 18, 23, 9, pp. 73–5; see also notes, pp. 322–3. Pamela Sheingorn, in '"For God is Such a Doomsman": Origins and Development of the Theme of Last Judgment', in Bevington *et al.*, *Homo, Memento Finis*, pp. 24–5, traces the individualization of the Judgement back to the conversion of the Germanic tribes.

94. *One Thing is Needful*, stanza 34, p. 94; Diehl, '"To Put Us In Remembrance"', pp. 182, 185.

95. *Ibid.*, stanzas 8, 12, 20, 25, 31, 69, pp. 80–8.

96. *Ibid.*, stanzas 4, 9, p. 90; Diehl, '"To Put Us In Remembrance"', pp. 187–8.

97. *One Thing is Needful*, stanzas 10, 19, 24, pp. 91–2; see *Paradise Lost*, Book I.

98. See *One Thing is Needful*, stanzas 25–35, pp. 92–4; Psalms 28: 1; 30: 9; 88: 4; Isaiah 14: 15; 38: 17–18; *Grace Abounding*, p. 62.

99. Marlowe, *Doctor Faustus*, I, iii; *One Thing is Needful*, stanzas 80, 76, 89, pp. 99–101.

100. *One Thing is Needful*, stanzas 44–5, pp. 70–1; stanzas 62, 67, p. 87. Edmund Spenser, *Epithalamion*, in E. de Selincourt (ed.), *The Poetical Works of Edmund Spenser* (London, 1912), pp. 580–4; Dr Johnson believed that there was 'reason to think that [Bunyan] had read Spenser': James Boswell,

The Life of Samuel Johnson (ed. John Canning; London, 1991), p. 145. John Donne, *A Hymne to God the Father* and *Epithalamion made at Lincolnes Inne*, in Grierson (ed.), *Donne Poetical Works*, pp. 125–8, 337–8.

101. John Bunyan, *Ebal and Gerizzim; Or The Blessing and the Curse*, in Midgley (ed.), *Miscellaneous Works of John Bunyan*, vol. VI, pp. 103–28 and li–liii; also in Offor (ed.), *Works of John Bunyan*, vol. III, pp. 737–45.

102. *Ebal and Gerizzim*, p. 105, ll. 4–8.

103. *Ibid.*, p. 105, ll. 22–3.

104. *Ibid.*, pp. 105–14, ll. 32–3, 36, 178, 358–60.

105. *Ibid.*, p. 123, l. 680.

FOUR
Bunyan's Mature
Writings on Faith and
Churchmanship

Vital to any proper understanding of Bunyan is a group of works of the early 1670s in which he set out the basics of his churchmanship and his theology. Writings of this period, to be examined in this chapter, such as *A Confession of my Faith, and A Reason of my Practice in Worship* (1672), *Differences in Judgment About Water-Baptism, No Bar to Communion* (1673) and *Peaceable Principles and True* (1674),[1] can be contrasted with the edifying prison writings and spiritual autobiography of the 1660s. Now at liberty, Bunyan focused on the practical work of helping to determine the ordering of his church and its relationship with other forms of church membership. In his ecclesiological writings his primary aim was to avoid strict baptismal criteria for membership of the church: 'though I dare not Communicate with the open Prophane, yet I can with those visible Saints that differ about *WATER-BAPTISM*'.[2]

At the same time, in Bunyan's eyes the church was not dogmatically exclusive but ought, rather, to recruit the godly without too much insistence on credal uniformity. The way Bunyan uses the term 'visible Saints' puts us in mind of G. F. Nuttall's identification of 'fellowship' – church membership without excessive scrutinizing of members' beliefs (as distinct from their conduct) as a primary characteristic of the Independent churches.[3] As a pastor, Bunyan was certainly concerned with moral discipline and with an upright life as a criterion for sainthood, but he was relatively indifferent to precise doctrinal or sacramental distinguishing marks. In *A Confession of my Faith* Bunyan set out a basic agenda of Reformed dogmatics – God's majesty and omnipotence, the orthodox doctrine of the Trinity, the scriptural presentation of the Incarnation as an historical event. In unfolding his doctrine of the work and person of Christ in the classic Pauline-Lutheran version, Bunyan insisted that the righteousness of Christ crucified was imputed to the sinful man or woman only as an outer clothing, an offer to be received only by a faith implanted by God in the elect, with the sinner, though, remaining essentially that, or rather, in Lutheran and Calvinist terms, *simul justus et peccator*, a 'justified sinner' who has no merit from the works of the law.[4]

Bunyan adopts a 'supra-lapsarian' exposition of election, God's choice being determined before the Creation and the Fall, though centring utterly on Christ, without whom there was neither election, grace nor salvation.[5] Election is irresistible. It is noteworthy that in this, admittedly brief, treatment of election, there is no examination of the reprobation of the unregenerate. Bunyan deals with the 'calling' as the means whereby their election is directed at individuals. The major virtues – faith, with love and hope – are considered partly in the context of the pastoral needs of the church, for example the need, with love, for 'overlooking the infirmities of the brethren'. Bunyan's treatment of Scripture is unswervingly literalist: 'That all the holy scriptures are the words of God' – comprising a record of the Creation and a guide to good conduct. Finally, he tacks on a brief appendix, '*Of Magistracy*', reciting the advantages of having 'a well qualified Magistrate', as well as the patience necessary when this was not the case. This work was published within the period immediately following the Declaration of Indulgence, and appreciation of the ruler as '*the minister of God to thee for good*', as well as Bunyan's insistence on the obligation to '*be subject; not onely for wrath, but also for conscience sake*' may reflect his growing esteem for kingship.[6]

A *Confession of my Faith* reveals Bunyan once more as a powerful commentator, producing a lapidary summary of Reformation theology. Having thus established his doctrines, he proceeds to unfold the nature and life of the church.

The debate over baptism

Bunyan's *A Reason of my Practice in Worship*[7] is concerned with the value and the limits of ecclesiastical separation. In it he was attempting to prevent separation from an unholy church from turning into endless schism, to avoid which he urged that the Christian *did* separate from the Established Church but did not separate from other saints over questions of secondary beliefs or sacramental ordinances. Bunyan's test for church membership was qualitative, depending on the profession of 'faith and holiness'. However, this insistence on criteria to be assessed on the basis of a person's profession presented him with a problem of discernment concerning (a)

the inscrutability of the identity of the elect – a cherished Calvinist principle – and (b) the possibility of plausible hypocrites entering the church
by putting on a convincing show of the necessary qualities. Bunyan could
not be sure of the identity of the elect, but he could be positive that members of the Church of England were not of it, and he solved his second
difficulty by assuming that an ostensible 'visible Saint' actually was one,
and not a hypocrite. This was a provisional solution, which, at a time when
separate church membership carried enough disadvantages to deter the
fraudulent, offered the possibility of building a church with a satisfactory,
if not perfect, membership. Bunyan gave the act of separation an impressive
set of scriptural warrants. His terminology conveys horror at the danger
of defilement through commingling: his revulsion at 'Mixed communion',
at people 'commixing themselves' and at the 'mingled people' remind us
of Calvin's horror, described by William Bouwsma, in the face of 'mixture'. Bunyan's references to clear distinctions between the godly and the
ungodly in the Old Testament allowed him to code his attacks on the Established Church. However, this treatise was not primarily concerned with
the Church of England, but rather aimed at widening the fellowship of the
gathered church.[8]

On this issue Bunyan set out his attitude to any rigorism over baptism
that threatened to divide and weaken the separate churches. That sacrament, he wrote, was worthy of 'reverent esteem' and (in what may have
been an implicit but unstated aside against the Quakers) was not to be
abandoned as a rite. Yet, important as baptism was, it was far from being
essential, and it was indeed possible to commit idolatry – 'even with Gods
own appointments' – by making too much of the sacrament, those 'shad-
dowish, or figurative ordinances'. Far from insisting on baptism as a prerequisite for church membership, Bunyan preferred to rely on the experiential
testimonies which the gathered churches used to examine applicants for
membership: 'a faithfull relation ... a discovery of their faith and holyness;
*and their declaration of willingness to subject themselves to the laws and
government of Christ in his Church*'. In such testimonies, the persons's
interior state, which to Bunyan's way of thinking was far more important
than any outside form, received expression.[9]

Contrasting baptism with circumcision, Bunyan saw the proper function
of the former not as inducting, but as instructing into church membership.
The vital precondition was living faith and righteousness, good conduct,
'moral duties Gospellized' – and the churches in their scrutiny of applicants should make 'more use of the ten commandments'. Such insistence on
'moral duties' (a) made the gathered church distinct from the world's profane people – made it exclusive of those – and (b) gave it a membership of

the re-born, with or without 'water baptism', making it inclusive of them.[10]

Given the primacy of moral criteria and living faith, Bunyan argued that 'Water-baptism' should be waived in the cases of those who possessed the heart of the matter but not the 'light' – that is to say a persuasion on their consciences to accept the ordinance: Bunyan would 'hold communion' with such scrupulous-minded visible saints. Though he did not use the term himself, he accepted the concept of *adiaphora*, 'things indifferent' – which he rendered as 'circumstances' – secondary usages, which the church, because Christ had set his followers free, was at liberty to take up or not. Amongst these, he included baptism itself, as an observance for whose sake it was not worth breaking the peace of the church. It was a sign that had great value for those who valued it, but, for those who in conscience could not, plentiful other signs were available. There was a further danger that those who insisted on baptism as a precondition of church membership – 'Vain man!' – would boast of it as a meritorious achievement. In an appeal for understanding and accommodation, Bunyan listed the common traits of all the godly – though he insisted that those who esteemed baptism must undergo it and that those who did not must not, since for them it would violate their consciences. As a pastor, Bunyan knew well the symptoms of discord in a congregation, the vividly des-cribed 'whisperings, back-bitings, slanders' for which he was inclined to blame the rigorists over the issue of baptism. His call, 'let us therefore leave off these contentions', reflects pastoral problems in post-Restoration Nonconformist communities, whose social introversion and intense doc-trinal interests increased the likelihood of controversy within them. He sets out instances from both the Old and New Testaments in which taboos were broken, and he establishes the primacy of the bond of love uniting Christians whose distinctions were annulled in Christ (cf. Colossians 3); the common characteristic of election takes precedence over the more superficial differences between baptized and un-baptized. Somewhat surprisingly, in these passages Bunyan does not explore the theme of Chris-tian freedom in any systematic Pauline or Lutheran way.[11]

Bunyan's dialectical skill is on display in a dialogue with an imaginary opponent of inter-communion between the baptized and the un-baptized, an exchange in which the reader is abruptly confronted, in the midst of a solemn theological discourse, with the realism of Bunyan's language: 'If this be all the respect thou hast for them and their Ministry, thou mayest have as much for the worst that pisseth against the Wall' – a drunkard. Underlying this dialogue may be the possibility of the kind of two-tier membership that characterized some forms of Independency around this time – a system in which certified church members worshipped alongside less committed or more occasional attenders. However, Bunyan, as spokes-man for a church that was ultimately exclusive in character, still ruled out an open relationship with Christian churches at large: 'Keep a strict separa-tion … from communion with the open prophane.' If there were visible saints in the wider world, they must come over wholeheartedly into the gathered communion.[12]

Despite the high value that he attached in this work to his church of saints, Bunyan's *A Reason of my Practice* cannot be described as a sectarian work or a 'Baptist' book. However, in a subsequent work – *Differences in Judgment About Water-Baptism, No Bar to Communion* – Bunyan, while maintaining the inclusive ethos of *A Reason of my Practice*, addressed issues of particular, and indeed urgent, interest to Baptist churches. This new treatise extended his defence of his own position into the more contro-versial arena of a debate with leading proponents of a strict line of exclusion from communion of those not christened by Baptist criteria. Bunyan's position on the sacrament – that believers' baptism was not an essential prerequisite for church membership – derived directly from Gifford, who solemnly charged his Bedford flock to avoid making any 'rent from the true Church' over the issue. Whereas Gifford deprecated controversy over baptism primarily on the more practical grounds of upholding peace in the church, William Dell, the Cambridge radical who was highly influen-tial in the religious life of Bedfordshire in the 1650s, taught a spiritualized baptismal theology, which contrasted the inner baptism of Christ with the outer baptism of water by John. It may be that Bunyan's attitude was influ-enced both by Gifford's stress on maintaining unity in the church and also by Dell's Quaker-like tendency to disparage sacramental baptism *per se*. It would certainly have been consistent with Bunyan's Calvinist stress on election to play down any Arminian-style view of the role of the sacra-ments in conferring grace. Yet Bunyan's efforts to hold the Bedford church to the traditional Dell–Gifford view were being challenged both by impor-tant elements within the Baptist churches and, seemingly, by individuals within the Bedford church itself. In the church at large, Bunyan's refusal, set out in *A Reason of my Practice*, to insist on believers' baptism as the indispensable mark of the visible saint was opposed by leading Baptists such as William Kiffin, a rich merchant, former MP and senior minister of the prestigious Devonshire Square Particular Baptist Church in London, and Henry Danvers, a prominent Baptist who had sat in the Barebones Parliament. Kiffin shared the authorship of *Some serious reflections* which attacked Bunyan as a '*Machivillian, a man devilish, proud, insolent, pre-sumptuous*'.[13]

Nothing was more likely to make Bunyan bridle than even implied slurs about his social background, and he charged Kiffin with disdaining his 'Person, because of my *low* descent among men'. Personalities apart, this debate of the early 1670s was vital to the future development of the churches in which Bunyan had found his spiritual home, since it concerned the question of the quality and extent of their membership. Bunyan, standing 'for Union, Concord, and Communion with Saints, as Saints', invoked one of the pioneers of the Baptist churches, Henry Jessey, in support of his case for a relatively open membership. Bunyan's sense of the supremacy of the spirit over forms can be seen as coming under attack from what Watts has portrayed as the literalness and legalism of Baptists over their sacrament: 'Baptism ... had always threatened to become the Baptists' fetish' – while Kiffin allegedly claimed to have performed a baptismal miracle. Bunyan's contributions to the debate – or, as Brown put it, 'war' – over baptism expressed his spiritualist ideals and his opposition both to formalism and to divisiveness. Yet those works may also be seen as the product of a distinct provincial viewpoint – the Dell–Gifford–Bunyan Bedfordshire tradition – and also to have been redolent of the more charismatic spirituality of the 1650s. The growing insistence within Baptist churches on believers' baptism was a natural response to a post-Restoration need for tighter organization and membership standards and a developing sectarian consciousness. Bunyan was becoming marginalized by such developments. Excusing himself from a Baptist debate over the issues in London, he seems to have been cut off from the Baptist mainstream by his very eirenicism over the sacrament: Whitley claimed that he had 'isolated himself from any group of permanence within reach'.[14]

It was not that Bunyan set out to antagonize 'fellow' Baptists, and in *Peaceable Principles and True* – a reply to the exclusive Baptists Thomas Paul and Henry Danvers – his relatively quiet tone counters Danvers's depiction of him as 'egregiously ignorant' and 'self-condemning'. Yet if Bunyan was becoming cut off from the Baptist centre, he was, at the same time, reaching out to a wider audience. Works such as the forthcoming *The Pilgrim's Progress* reached far beyond Baptist churches, and Bunyan's ecumenical churchmanship matched this wide appeal: 'I tell you, I would be, and hope I am, *a Christian*; and chuse, if God shall count me worthy, *to be called a Christian.*' In his exchanges with Fowler and his encounter with the close Baptists, he was continuing to contend with specialists. Following a published sermon – *The Barren Fig-Tree* – in 1673, he produced a technical typological work – *Light for Them that Sit in Darkness* – in 1675, and then in the same year, matching his increasingly broad outreach, there followed a work of elementary catechesis – *Instruction for the Ignorant.*[15]

Instruction for the Ignorant

In this work, which may represent some withdrawal on his part from the world of specialist theological debate, Bunyan adopts a didactic style and format: 'Prepared, and presented ... in a plain and easie Dialogue, fitted to the Capacity of the weakest.' Targeted at '*those unconverted ... who have been at any time under my Preaching, and yet remain in their sins*', it is aimed at a readership of catechumens and children, and adopts an elementary approach markedly different from that found in Bunyan's more advanced theological and controversial writings.[16]

Instruction for the Ignorant opens with the most basic points, starting with the number of gods. Using the format of interrogative catechesis, Bunyan tries to give the little speeches as much of a natural conversational form as possible: '*Shall I propound a few more questions? ... Before you conclude ... Have you ... another instance?*' – and so on. However, the conversational mode is unconvincing, partly because people do not normally converse along the lines of: '*Well, I am glad that you have shewed me that I must worship God by confession of sin*', and partly because the pretence of Bunyan's pupil-interlocutor's being 'ignorant' is undermined by his alert dialectics: '*Is not this* [God's severe judgement on sinners] *just as when my Father bids me be naught if I will, but if I be naught, he will beat me for it?*'[17]

It is true, as Offor wrote, that this work is catholic, in the sense that it is not marked by sectarian peculiarities. Nevertheless, it is very much Bunyan's work, and features his particular emphases, albeit derived from Reformation principles. These include his stress on human corruption ('in that day that we were born, we were polluted in our own Blood'), and on sin (twenty-five questions) and hell (eight questions). Bunyan was a particularly strong exponent of the dominant cultural values of his day which saw the child as a repository of original sin, its wayward nature to be corrected by close and disciplined nurture. He was pessimistic about the moral capacity of children, as typifying human nature in its sinful state: 'their inclinations naturally run to vanity'. *Instruction for the Ignorant* offers scant comfort to any young readers: 'Q. *Did ever God punish little Children for sin against him?* – A. Yes: when the Flood came, he drowned all the little Children.' Bunyan did not see the young person as a free spirit formed by a benign nature or fresh from God's presence and trailing clouds of glory, but rather as a child of wrath, an imperilled soul that had to be intimidated into docility – for its own good. Children were as liable to the punishments of hell as were adults. Indeed, Bunyan's pessimistic attitude towards children represented, in a heightened form, the negative attitude to humanity as a whole which he put forward in this work: 'a lothsome, polluted, wretched, miserable Sinner'. In Calvinist terms, would-be meritorious actions, performed without real, justifying faith by such a sinful wretch, were sins.[18]

However, alongside Bunyan's fidelity to Luther's assumptions concerning God's forensic dealings with mankind, there developed an awareness of the transformative as well as the salvific power of justifying faith. In mainstream Lutheran soteriology, justification was an objective, legal fact. Its beneficiaries remained justified sinners rather than became visible saints. Their acceptability *coram Deo* was imputed to, but not imparted upon them, and their progress towards holiness was not envisaged, since, turning his back on the whole late medieval and neo-Pelagian devotional tradition, Luther insisted that sinners were saved not by imitating Christ, but solely through the transfer to them of the legal 'benefit' of Christ crucified. In pure Lutheran terms, that forensic transaction outside the individual, rather than any spiritual growth within, was what mattered. However, alongside his acceptance of a divine judicial decision being implemented in a justifying operation from outside upon persons, Bunyan perceived a gradual and individual process of sanctification taking place within men and women: justifying faith possessed 'life' and 'proveth it self to be of the right kind by its Acts and Operations in the mind of a poor sinner'. The divine decree issued in favour of all who were to be justified could also set in motion in individuals a developmental process of attaining personal holiness and, indeed, Christ-likeness. Bunyan employs the verb 'to come', with all its connotations of continuous process – for example, 'Faith comest' – to express his appreciation of the gradually unfolding regeneration of individuals helped on their way with resources provided by the church – 'hearing … the Word of God', praying, discoursing, reading and meditating. Bunyan was no Pelagian or even Arminian, and Baxter faulted him for extreme Calvinist predestinarianism leading to antinomianism. He did not envisage redemptive self-help, since 'Justifying Righteousness is only to be found in the Lord Jesus Christ'. However, he did combine this Lutheran formulation on the indispensability of an external righteousness, imputed once and for all in the past-perfect tense, with a lively perception of individuals within the church making prayerful, self-denying, commandment-obeying progress in a continuous tense towards their goals. Although in 1672 Bunyan attacked Fowler for the 'Quaker and Romanist' proposition that Christ endowed man with a real and interior righteousness, in *Instruction for the Ignorant* he moves on from the simpler category of the justified sinner, and even approaches the position that evangelically-minded Catholics in the sixteenth century based on St Augustine, according to which the sinner, to whom the merits of Christ were imputed, acquired a capacity for merit. Bunyan's emergent saint is no mere sinner vested in the borrowed righteousness of Christ, but rather experiences 'a receiving of [Christ] with what is in him as the gift of God to thee a sinner': 'For right Faith quickneth to Spiritual Life, Purifies and Sanctifies the Heart; and worketh up the Man that hath it, into the Image of Jesus Christ.' Such progressive sanctification involved the need for the confession of sins, though this is not, of course, envisaged as sacramental confession, nor even as confession before a congregation, which some medieval heretics based on James 5: 16, but as an individual self-analysis before God, linked to Bunyan's view of valid prayer. Bunyan's insights into the possibility of personal holiness leads him into an ecstatic prose – 'Yes, Yes … O! No!' – culminating in a vision of the second coming, 'glorious and dreadful'.[19]

Prayer was a vital component of holiness, and Bunyan dealt with it in *Instruction for the Ignorant*, albeit briefly, no doubt because he had considered it at length in *I Will Pray with the Spirit* in 1662. Obedience to God's laws was a second essential feature of holiness, though Bunyan emphasizes here its function in conveying assurance of election: 'Q. *How shall I know that I am one of those, to whom God will give these things?* A. When thou followest hard after God in all his Ordinances.'[20] The third component of holiness was self-denial, by means of which the individual made step-by-step progress towards sanctification as he or she took 'up his cross daily'. Though it is expressly rejected – 'God doth not require Self-Denial as the means to obtain Salvation' – the conclusion that one's austerities in some way merited salvation is only narrowly avoided, using an ambivalent formula: 'Self-denial prepareth a man, though not for the pardon of his sins, yet for that *far more exceeding and eternal weight of Glory, that is laid up only for them that deny all that they have for the Lord Jesus.*' Bunyan is writing here about the achievement of personal sanctification, though, in his quest for balance and his care for Reformed doctrine, he intrudes a corrective against a human-centred optimism: 'every one by nature are accounted sinners'. Indeed, a mood of pessimism returns in a concluding meditation reminiscent of the gloomier aspects of the medieval *artes moriendi* tradition: 'Know 'tis a sad thing to lie a dying, and to be afraid to die; to lie a dying and not to know whither thou art a going; to lie a dying, and not to know whether good Angels or bad must conduct thee out of this miserable World.'[21]

Stylistically, although there are occasional flashes of conversational realism, the dialogue of *Instruction for the Ignorant* is too crowded with scriptural references to be anything but stilted. Bunyan does, though, show some of that ability, on which Hill comments, to make the transcendent immediate through analogies with a familiar English environment of his day: thus, the wicked are punished far away from this earth, just as malefactors were executed in those gallows to be found outside seventeenth-century county towns. A personal note is struck in Bunyan's identification of the grave sin of spreading 'lies and scandals' about godly preachers: he was clearly still smarting from the allegations made in the Beaumont case of the previous year. He also highlights the sin of witchcraft, which he had condemned in a lost work of 1659. There are further recollections of his own unconverted youth and of '*my play and sports*' which stand in a young person's way to salvation. There is also a moment of acute mystification: 'Q. *Is not God's deferring, a sign of his anger?* A. Sometimes it is not, and sometimes it is.'[22]

The Strait Gate

In 1676 Bunyan published *Saved by Grace* and *The Strait Gate*, the latter apparently having its genesis in a preaching encounter when, as Doe related, Bunyan was accused of wanting charity by emphasizing 'the fewness of those that should be saved'. Bunyan, in fact, strongly reasserted the small-ness of the number of the elect, but in doing so did not counsel despair, but rather reaffirmed a markedly 'Puritan' sense of tension, insecurity and effort. The work's keynote word, repeated no fewer than fifty-two times in just two pages of the Offor edition (sometimes twice or thrice to a line), is 'strive', a verb that conveys resolute action, and the antithesis equally of predestinarian despair at the inevitability of damnation and presumption at the certainty of salvation. Supplementing that verb are a set of images all connoting endeavour – images of battling, of running (as with Paul in 1 Corinthians 9: 24–5) and of wrestling (Ephesians 6: 12). Throughout, Bunyan's theme of a personal struggle to be saved – difficult to square with strict predestinarianism – is to the fore: 'direct us, not only to talk of, or to wish for, but to understand how we shall, & to seek that we may be effectualy saved'. These themes, of the gate, of struggle and of progress, anticipate *The Pilgrim's Progress*, soon to appear.[23]

The image of the strait gate is Christ's own, Bunyan imagining Him as a preacher casting around for references that would be grasped by His audience; in devising the figure of the narrow gate, Jesus 'had doubtless his eye upon some passage … of the old testament, with which the Jews were well acquainted'. In Bunyan's version, the gate was the church, 'to let in, or to keep out', a portal associated with scrutiny and possible rejection. Bunyan's view of the law is clearly set out here: its fulfilment did not confer justification, but justification could not be awarded without its 'leave'.[24] *The Strait Gate* contains much of Bunyan's characteristic outlook – his sense of estrangement between the world and the godly, depicting the saints and the world in a constant battle by each to overcome the other; his suspicion of the temptations of sexuality and domesticity: 'thy bed and table, thy wife and husband'; his feeling of kinship with the martyrs: 'They ... have devised all manner of cruel torments ... wilde beasts, banishments, hunger, and a thousand miseryes'; his linking of spiritual and moral striving with a work ethic: 'Thou maist help thy faith, and thy hope in the godly managment of thy calling.'[25]

In this work, tension and anxiety are exacerbated by the prospect that the seeming godly might be damned. 'Professors' were in particularly grave danger: '*depart from me* ... you, *you,* you that I mean!', Bunyan has Christ saying to the apparently virtuous, in a prose of rising urgency. Did the anxiety he thus fostered affect him too? He was aware that the distinction he enjoyed in the church was far from being a guarantee of safety: 'the preacher ... may ... be in danger of damning, notwithstanding all [his] attainments ... these words, *I say unto you,* are a Prophesie of the perdition of some that are famous in the congregation of Saints'. The reasons that such were prone to damnation were (a) that professors might be merely that, professing without practising righteousness; and (b) that they were liable to commit the terrible sin against the Holy Ghost, the unpardonable offence of backsliding on the part of those introduced to godliness. The conclusion anticipates themes in Bunyan's most sustained essay in practical ethics, *Mr. Badman*: 'the most of professors are for imbezzeling, mispending, and slothing away their time, their talents, their opportunities to do good in'. Their eventual realization of their exclusion from eternal life is conveyed through the use of a language of high drama and horror: 'never did malefactor so unwillingly turn off the ladder, when the rope was about his neck, as these will turn away, in that day, from the gates of heaven to hell ... Lord, Lord, the pit opens her mouth upon us'.[26] The conclusion that to identify oneself with the true elect one would need to act rather than profess would have been an inescapable one for many of Bunyan's readers. Although 'none is of power to keep himself', God 'worketh together with his children', and 'they that would then have that kingdom must now strive lawfully to enter'. Those who were pious only in a conventional way were to be discarded from the membership of the elect, who in turn would have to be defined as a miniscule element of the unremittingly holy: 'Professors shall make a great heap, among the many that shall fall short of heaven.' The effect of Bunyan's insistences on his pious readers may have been that of creating or intensifying heavy pressures towards perfectionism, similar to the drive for righteousness set up in such works as *The Whole Duty of Man*, attributed to Richard Allestree, William Law's *Practical Treaties on Christian Perfection* and *A Serious Call to a Devout and Holy Life*, and Jeremy Taylor's *Rules of Holy Living and Dying* – the kind of perfectionist literature which, as Watts writes, 'made impossible demands on the moral and spiritual resources of the ordinary believer'.[27]

The stress on personal perfection in Bunyan's formulation in *The Strait Gate* was made all the heavier through his systematic elimination of church membership from the means of redemption. Though, as he showed in *Instruction for the Ignorant*, the preaching and praying of the church were aids to the godly, membership in itself provided no guarantees: 'with reference to profession and church constitution, a people may be called the people of God; but ... they may be truly the generation of his wrath'. The grounds of Bunyan's relative indifference to church membership and to the church's ordinances, as evident in *A Reason of my Practice in Worship*, are clearly exposed. Opposed to any complacency arising from church membership as, in itself, a means of redemption is Bunyan's individualistic insistence on effort on the part of the lone contender – summed up in the character of Christian in the first part of *The Pilgrim's Progress* – and on his or her determined avoidance of the 'sloth and idleness of some professors'. This emphasis on vigour is maintained through the use of a prose style that conveys urgency with repeated impassioned appeals to 'professors': 'To be saved! what is it like being saved?... O this *Mount Sion*! O this *heavenly Jerusalem*!' An atmosphere of drama is also aroused through the citation of Gospel parables, all highlighting themes of choice and rejection – the sower, the tares, the wise and foolish virgins, and so on. Both Israel in the Old Testament and the early church in the New provided 'types and examples' of the ultimate unreliability of church membership *per se* as a passport to redemption. Everything depended on inner disposition, including a repentance that must be perfect, for '[t]here is a repentance that will not save, a repentance to be repented of'. It is as if Bunyan has lost Luther's trust in God's preparedness to save regardless of man's works, and that we are back again in a kind of pre-Reformation world of hyperanxious perfectionism, scrupulosity and self-laceration: Bunyan, for instance, lists eight grades of rejection of sin, but concludes that the repentant sinner might still, 'after all this ... perish, for want of saving repentance'. Thus, once more, in this work of homiletic exhortation, Bunyan's urge to encourage his auditors alters the balance of the Reformed doctrines that he set out in his more theoretical works.[28]

Notes

1. *A Confession of my Faith, and A Reason of my Practice in Worship*, in T. L. Underwood (ed.), *Miscellaneous Works of John Bunyan*, vol. IV (Oxford, 1989), pp. 131–87 and xxviii–xxx; *Differences in Judgment About Water-Baptism, No Bar to Communion*, in *ibid.*, pp. 193–264 and xxx–xxxiii; *Peaceable Principles and True*, in *ibid.*, pp. 269–290 and xxxiii–xxxvi. All three works also in G. Offor (ed.), *The Works of John Bunyan* (3 vols; Glasgow, 1854), vol. II, pp. 593–657.

2. *A Confession*, p. 132. In his Introduction Underwood shows that one of the work's purposes is to fulfill 'something of a pastoral responsibility in making Bunyan's faith and practice clear at the beginning of his pastorate in Bedford' (p. xxix); for a summary of the background to the debate over baptism, see B. R. White, 'Bunyan and Puritanism' in N. H. Keeble (ed.), *John Bunyan: Conventicle and Parnassus* (Oxford, 1988), pp. 17–18.

3. G. F. Nuttall, *Visible Saints: The Congregational Way 1640–1660* (Oxford, 1957), ch. 2. For the tradition through the centuries, see Alan P. F. Sell, *Saints: Visible, Orderley and Catholic* (Geneva, 1986).

4. *A Confession*, pp. 143–4.

5. See R. T. Kendall, *Calvin and English Calvinism to 1649* (1979), pp. 30, 56; John H. Leith, *Introduction to the Reformed Tradition: A Way of Being the Christian Community* (revised edn; Atlanta, GA, 1981), p. 117; Heinrich Heppe, *Reformed Dogmatics Set Out and Illustrated from the Sources* (trans. G. T. Thomson; London, 1950), ch. 8.

6. *A Confession*, pp. 151–3.

7. *A Reason of my Practice in Worship*, pp. 153–87.

8. John Calvin, *Institutes of the Christian Religion* (ed. John T. McNeil, trans. Ford Lewis Battles; 2 vols; Philadelphia, PA, 1975), vol. II, pp. 922–3; *A Reason*, pp. 157–8; William J. Bouwsma, *John Calvin: A Sixteenth Century Portrait* (New York and Oxford, 1988), pp. 34–6.

9. *A Reason*, pp. 160, 162, 164, 173.

10. *Ibid.*, p. 165.

11. *Ibid.*, pp. 170–3,176. For adiaphorism, see Martin Luther, *The Freedom of a Christian* (1520), in John Dillenberger (ed.), *Martin Luther: Selections from his Writings* (New York, 1961), pp. 72–3, 84–5, and Bernard K. Verkamp, *The Indifferent Mean: Adiaphorism in the English Reformation to 1554* (Athens, OH, and Detroit, MI, 1977).

12. *A Reason*, pp. 183, 185.

13. *Differences in Judgment About Water-Baptism, No Bar to Communion*, in Underwood (ed.), *Miscellaneous Works of John Bunyan*, vol. IV, pp. 190–264, see p. 193; for Dell's and Gifford's position on baptism, see John Brown, *John Bunyan: His Life, Times and Work* (2nd edn; London, 1886), pp. 235–6; for the background to the debate, see Underwood (ed.), *Miscellaneous Works of John Bunyan*, vol. IV, pp. xxx–xxxiii, and A. C. Underwood

and J. H. Rushbrooke, *A History of the English Baptists* (London, 1947), pp. 103–4. For Danvers and Kiffin, see Michael Watts, *The Dissenters: From the Reformation to the French Revolution* (Oxford, 1978) pp. 94n., 112, 127–8, 140, 144n., 163–4, 205, 212, 213, 257–8, 361–2, and B. R. White, *The English Baptists of the Seventeenth Century* (London, 1983), pp. 58, 70–2, 75–6, 78–81, 83–4, 90–1, 94, 97, 105, 112, 128–30, 133–4, 135, 137–8, and for Danvers, see Richard L. Greaves, *Saints and Rebels: Seven Nonconformists in Stuart England* (Macon, GA, 1985), ch. 6.

14. *Differences in Judgment*, pp. 193, 194, 195, 250, 252–64; Watts, *The Dissenters*, pp. 144n., 127, 205; W. T. Whitley, *A History of British Baptists* (London, 1923), p. 137. For Jessey and his views on baptism, see Richard L. Greaves and Robert Zaller (eds), *Biographical Dictionary of British Radicals in the Seventeenth Century* (3 vols; Brighton 1982–4), vol. II, pp. 140–1.

15. *Peaceable Principles and True*, in Underwood (ed.), *Miscellaneous Works of John Bunyan*, vol. IV, p. 270. For *The Barren Fig-Tree*, see Graham Midgley (ed.), *Miscellaneous Works of John Bunyan*, vol. V (Oxford, 1986), pp. 9–64 and xiii–li; also available in Offor (ed.), *Works of John Bunyan*, vol. III, pp. 561–85. For *Light for Them that Sit in Darkness* and *Instruction for the Ignorant*, see Richard L. Greaves (ed.), *Miscellaneous Works of John Bunyan*, vol. VIII (Oxford, 1979), pp. 53–160, 391–436 and xliii–l, xxx–xliii; also available in Offor (ed.), *Works of John Bunyan*, vol. I, pp. 391–436 and vol. II, pp. 675–90.

16. *Instruction*, pp. 4, 5, 7.

17. *Ibid.*, pp. 39, 43, 34, 17.

18. Offor (ed), *Works of John Bunyan*, vol. II, p. 675 ; *Instruction*, pp. 12–15, 17, 21; Calvin, *Institutes*, vol. I, p. 812.

19. *Instruction*, pp. 27, 29, 32–4; Alister E. McGrath, *Reformation Thought: An Introduction* (Oxford, 1988), pp. 83–4; Bernard M. G. Reardon, *Religious Thought in the Reformation* (London and New York, 1981), pp. 53–6; Dermot Fenlon, *Heresy and Obedience in Tridentine Italy: Cardinal Pole and the Counter-Reformation* (London, 1972); for Baxter's strictures, see Greaves (ed.), *Miscellaneous Works of John Bunyan*, vol. II, p. xxv.

20. *Instruction*, pp. 36–7.

21. *Ibid.*, pp. 42–4.

22. *Ibid.*, pp. 14, 16, 17, 18, 37; Christopher Hill, 'John Bunyan's Contemporary Reputation', in Anne Laurence, W. R. Owens and Stuart Sim (eds), *John Bunyan and his England 1628–1688* (London and Ronceverte, WV, 1990), p. 9.

23. For Bunyan's *Saved by Grace*, see Greaves (ed.), *Miscellaneous Works of John Bunyan*, vol. VIII, pp. 165–228 and l–liii; also available in Offor (ed.), *Works of John Bunyan*, vol. I, pp. 336–61; *The Strait Gate*, in Midgley (ed.), *Miscellaneous Works of John Bunyan*, vol. V, pp. 66–130; also available in Offor (ed.), *Works of John Bunyan*, vol. I, pp. 363–90 (for the

repetition of 'strive', see *ibid.*, pp. 369–70). For the doctrine, content, homiletic nature and prose of the group (with *The Barren Fig-Tree* and *The Heavenly Foot-man*) in which Midgley places *The Strait Gate*, see Midgley (ed.), *Miscellaneous Works of John Bunyan*, vol. V, pp. xiii–xlvi; *The Strait Gate*, pp. 72, 81, 84.

24.   *Ibid.*, pp. 76–9.
25.   *Ibid.*, pp. 83–5.
26.   *Ibid.*, pp. 91–4, 97–8 see also Christopher Hill, 'Bunyan, Professors and Sinners', *Bunyan Studies* 2,1 (1990), pp. 7–25.
27.   *The Strait Gate*, pp. 75–88, 110; Watts, *The Dissenters*, pp. 425–7, 432.
28.   *The Strait Gate*, pp. 69–130.

FIVE

The Pilgrim's Progress, Part I

Bunyan's fame rests chiefly – perhaps disproportionately – on the two parts of *The Pilgrim's Progress* (1678 and 1684). It is possible that without this best seller Bunyan would be known to historians as a figure of some importance in the development of post-Restoration Nonconformity – perhaps on a level with someone like William Kiffin.[1] It is all the more strange that he should owe his fame, far beyond the history of seventeenth-century radical Protestantism and into the realms of popular literature, to a work which is, on the face of it, hardly typical of his overall *oeuvre*, though, as Roger Sharrock points out, the rich metaphorical furnishings of *The Pilgrim's Progress* are anticipated in his earlier, non-fictional writings, while the great allegory contains scholastic method and homiletic arrangement of a kind to be found in Bunyan's more self-evidently doctrinal corpus.[2] Despite such similarities and continuities between his 'minor' works and his acknowledged masterpiece, Bunyan's literary output before 1678 characteristically comprised sermon treatises, polemical tracts, ecclesiological and sacramental dialectics, Reformed soteriology, and so on – most of it exactingly cerebral. *The Pilgrim's Progress*, in contrast, is in the form of popular art designed for entertainment, and has the merits – clarity, a strong narrative line, vigorous diction – as well as the demerits – naïvety, occasional technical awkwardness – of amateur popular literature. Whether or not it was aimed at children – as, expressly, was his *A Book for Boys and Girls* (1684) – it became a children's classic; even Huckleberry Finn 'read considerable in it now and then. The statements was interesting but tough.' In the Romantic era, the book's apparent suitability for and appeal to children allowed for its reclassification – in terms of approval, given the Romantics' general admiration for childhood – as a children's book. Southey's attitude was typical: 'there is a homely reality about [*The Pilgrim's Progress*]; a nursery tale is not more intelligible in it's [*sic*] manner of narration, to a child'. A doting father, George Crabbe recorded how his daughter 'Caroline, now six years old, reads incessantly and insatiably.

She has been travelling with John Bunyan's "Pilgrim", and enjoying a pleasure never, perhaps, to be repeated.'[3] *The Pilgrim's Progress* had become a genteel reading primer for post-infancy.

Whilst appreciating Sharrock's warning against over-medievalizing Bunyan, and his suggestion that the form of *The Pilgrim's Progress* is that of a universal genre – the story – we might add that the more specific category to which the work belongs is that of the medieval romance, a form made available to the youthful Bunyan by Richard Johnson's *Seven Champions of Christendom* (1607). This compilation of chivalric tales held him in thrall, just as knightly tales such as *Amadis de Gaules* fascinated the young Ignatius Loyola. Whereas, following his conversion, Loyola adapted the ideals of the romances – self-sacrifice, male comradeship, obedience, crusading ardour, knightly dedication – to form the ethos of his Society of Jesus, Bunyan, having as part of the price of his second birth thrown over the stuff of the romances, made use of their scenic apparatus to adorn, explain and allegorize a Reformed schema of salvation.[4]

Bunyan's story is not of the species of the parable, that is to say a narrative containing abiding truths presented through the medium of everyday or real life; rather, *The Pilgrim's Progress* is an allegory grounded in fantasy, those of the chivalresque at its most elaborate – complete with giants and enchanted palaces, castles and kings' champions and all the other paraphernalia and cast of the chivalric cycles.[5] This being the case – and because Bunyan is describing a world of the super-real – it would be to miss the point to praise the 'realism' of the 'close observation' of his projection of 'landscape'. Charles Firth, sentimentalizing Bunyan as the ideal type of the English countryman entirely at home in his rustic world and able to describe it artlessly and naturalistically, complimented the author on his mastery of 'the landscape of his native Midlands ... those landscapes from Bedfordshire'.[6] In fact, though, apart from one or two observations on roads and paths that do seem to have been based on real seventeenth-century English route patterns (a tinker was a man of the roads), the landscape in *The Pilgrim's Progress* was not a closely observed environment but a neutral nowhere, a colourless wash on which are painted polychrome and gilded literary images culled from the romances. James Turner comments on the sparseness of Bunyan's scenery and scenic description: 'Bunyan's [landscape] is minimal – a wilderness without, a prison within ... [His] descriptive style runs forward with its fingers in its ears ... The whole *Progress* takes place in a symbolic dream-land.' Turner also speculates that Bunyan's uncertainty and inconsistency about visualized landscape – his maplessness – arose because he was not (as Firth tried to show him to be) entirely at home in his English world or able to give a naturally sensitive depiction of it, but was a stranger – a pilgrim – excluded from a privileged establishment which owned England in the sense of being in possession (and, after 1660, being *back* in possession) of its soil : 'The units of topographical space (heights and depths, lands, fields, hills, houses and roads) are inseparable in Bunyan's imagination from the social means of their control. from lordship, tenure and sale, trespass, action and enclosure claims.'[7] Bunyan's pilgrim does not travel through a carefully described countryside, but makes a 'progress', a mental, moral and spiritual evolution. *The Pilgrim's Progress* provides a roughly spatial framework for what is, in effect, a diagram of the stages of salvation, of the kind drawn up by Perkins and constructed by Bunyan himself in *A Mapp Shewing the Order & Causes of Salvation and Damnation* (1663 or 1664).

If *The Pilgrim's Progress* is not, then, an itinerary, David Seed observes that it is largely a recording of discourse. Bunyan's abiding metaphor, that of pilgrimage, may have been suspect for its connotations of popery (though, as Brainerd Stranahan shows, it was anchored in the Epistle to the Hebrews, which would have given it a more acceptable metaphorical base[8]). Equally, if not more, reprehensible from the point of view of the Protestant literalist approach, was the allegorization of Scripture: Bunyan's 'extratextual' apologia for his allegorical method, a convention in the genre, was made all the more necessary by current misgivings about allegorizing the Bible's literal meaning. But if the metaphor of the pilgrimage and the method of allegory were, in their different ways, suspect, discourse was exalted in the gathered churches, and, as Seed comments, 'Dialogue accounts for most of *The Pilgrim's Progress* in terms of sheer bulk.'[9] Bunyan emphasized the companionable nature of this discourse, which we may compare with the converse of the church members which, in *Grace Abounding*, he recalled gave him so much heart-easing: 'Then I saw in my Dream, they went very lovingly on together; and had sweet discourse of all things that had happened to them in their Pilgrimage.'[10] Conversation in *The Pilgrim's Progress* mirrors the exchanges taking place in the gathered churches, in which participants disclosed their spiritual case-histories; the following excerpt, in which Christian evokes the alternation in his consciousness of crisis – 'perplexity' – and calm 'golden hours' is an example:

> Pru[dence] *Do you not find sometimes, as if those things were vanquished, which at other times are your perplexity?*
> Chr[istian] Yes, but that is but seldom; but they are to me Golden hours, in which such things happen to me.[11]

A longer dialogue also derives from the way in which the gathered churches elicited convincing accounts of their conversions from prospective members:

Chr. Then *Christian* began and said, *I will ask you a question. How came you to think at first of doing as you do now?*
Hope[*full*] Do you mean, How came I at first to look after the good of my Soul? [12]

Hopeful replies in an agonized narrative of his conversionary experience: we are once again in the world of *Grace Abounding*, a world of relentless self-analysis and self-disclosure, of unsparing recall of inner psychological states, and the release conferred by a scriptural passage vouchsafing redemption :

Chr. *And did you indeavour to mend?*
Hope. Yes, and fled from, not only my sins, but sinful Company too; and betook me to Religious Duties, as Praying, Reading, weeping for Sin ... *&c.*
Chr. *And did you think your self well then?*
Hope. Yes, for a while ...
Hope. ... One day I was very sad, I think sader then at any one time in my life ... But I replyed, Lord, I am a great, a very great sinner; and he answered, *My grace is sufficient for thee* ...
Hope. I know something of this my self; for before I knew my self it was so with me. [13]

Discourse, then, matters crucially in *The Pilgrim's Progress*: the book is a dialogue at least as much as it is a travelogue; indeed, at one point Christian has to issue a kind of reminder that what is being undertaken is a journey:

Hope. ... I would know where we are.
Chr. *We have not now about two Miles further to go thereon.*

He still insists, though, on the primacy of the discourse: '*But let us return to our matter.*' Yet for all the importance of discourse in *The Pilgrim's Progress*, we should also be aware of Bunyan's view of the limits on the utility of talk: a figure who represents discourse alone, without action or good disposition, Talkative, a character no doubt drawn from persons encountered in Bunyan's church – '*a shame to all Professors*' – is strongly censured. Talkative is a brilliant comic creation who can expatiate on: 'things heavenly, or things earthly; things Moral, or things Evangelical;

things Sacred, or things Prophane; things past, or things to come; things forraign, or things at home; things more Essential, or things Circumstantial: provided that all be done to our profit'. He believes: 'that *hearing* and *saying* will make a good Christian, and thus he deceiveth his own Soul ... *Paul* calleth some men, yea, and those great Talkers too, *sounding Brass, and Tinckling Cymbals*'. The centrality of deed and inner condition – 'Deed and Truth' – in *The Pilgrim's Progress* extends the theme of action in *The Strait Gate*. The work's central metaphor, that of the journey, is one of vigorous activity, while countering it is the notion of sleep as the epitome of inaction. Bunyan employs the scriptural images of sleep as representing indifference, and wakefulness as betokening vigilance, as in Matthew 26: 40–6, Mark 13: 33–7, 1 Thessalonians 5: 5–6, and Romans 13: 11. The purpose of this book (though it was written under the conventions of dream literature) was to activate its readers: '*Yea, it will make the sloathful, active be.*' Slumber is a mortal danger to the pilgrims:

Hope. ... let us lie down here and take one Nap.
Chr. *By no means ... lest sleping, we never awake more.*[14]

Sleep, involving the loss of vigilance and the loss of control, is one of the many terrors confronting Christian. In contrast, a figure whom he passes by unharmed, but whose introduction we might expect to bring out the best of Bunyan's horror writing – the pope – is treated briefly and dismissively. Bunyan's pope is a most unterrifying character, a once potent persecutor grown decrepit and derisory; though still alive – barely – he seems about to join ancient paganism as a relic of history:

I espied a little before me a Cave, where two Giants, *Pope* and *Pagan*, dwelt in old time, by whose Power and Tyranny the Men whose bones, blood, ashes, &c. lay there, were cruelly put to death ... [B]ut I have learnt since, that *Pagan* has been dead many a day; and as for the other, though he be yet alive, he is by reason of age, and also of the many shrewd brushes that he met with in his younger dayes, grown so crazy and stiff in his joynts, that he can now do little more then sit in his Caves mouth, grinning at Pilgrims as they go by, and biting his nails, because he cannot come at them.[15]

Apprehensiveness, then, with regard to the papacy, would be groundless: the old terrifying oppressor of the saints can now only utter empty threats and has become a laughing stock. How was it that Bunyan was, seemingly, thus able to dismiss the dread of popery that gripped his compatriots? One possible answer is that, when *The Pilgrim's Progress* came out in February 1678, he reflected a relative absence of paranoia in the period before the allegations made in the late summer by Israel Tonge and Titus Oates of a plot to assassinate Charles II so as to set up a Romanist regime. To set against that possibility is the fact that those editions that appeared after the alleged Popish Plot had been made public, although they did show extensive changes elsewhere in the text, left untouched Bunyan's depiction of the papacy as a harmless back number of history.[16]

Bunyan's portrayal of the papacy as a threat that was no longer to be taken seriously was the product not so much of observations on current events, as of an historical and eschatological overview which he reduced to a brief satirical incident in his allegory. Whatever minor changes took place in Bunyan's apocalyptic expectations, he retained his confidence in the demise of the papal Antichrist. In 1665 in *The Holy City* he had eagerly forecast the destruction of the 'shaking, tottering, staggering, kingdom of Rome'. In the early 1680s in *Of Antichrist, and His Ruine* he reflected on the history of the papacy, its defeats in the pre-Reformation period and the major blows it suffered, especially from the Tudor monarchs.[17] Thus, the apparently light-hearted and indeed comic dismissal of popery in *The Pilgrim's Progress* should be seen as a condensed and simplified version of a larger eschatological and historical vision, in which the blows suffered by the papacy in a series of encounters from the late medieval heresies to the Reformation and beyond are summarized as 'the many shrewd brushes that he [the pope] met with in his younger dayes'.

Just as *The Pilgrim's Progress* encapsulates in one brief incident Bunyan's apocalyptic expectations concerning the papacy, so the work also contains, again in brief and coded form, his attitudes to government, kingship and the social order. As an outcome of his anti-papal apocalyptic and his experience of persecution, Bunyan dealt with kingship sympathetically, whereas he castigated the legal system, the gentry, Parliament and great wealth. By the time he came to write *The Pilgrim's Progress*, experience taught him that his foes populated the legal, social and political establishment – apart from the king. As W. R. Owens writes: 'if what you were chiefly interested in was toleration, it made sense to look to the King, rather than Parliament, in Restoration England'. In *Of Antichrist, and His Ruine*, Bunyan distanced his figure of the king from the gentlemen who conspired to alienate his people from him, and in *The Holy City* he differentiated the kings, who took an active part in building the New Jerusalem, from their nobles, who ignored the task.[18] In *The Pilgrim's Progress*, likewise, Bunyan was positive about monarchy, but used figures from the social and political hierarchy below the king, and allusions to Acts of Parliament, as the basis for his moral denunciations. Christian serves a great king: '*Chr.* But I have let my self to another, even to the King of Princes ... I have given him my faith, and sworn my Allegiance to him.'[19] Images of earthly kingship, of allegiance, fealty and treason, could be legitimately used as metaphors for God's sovereignty.

In contrast, nobility provides Bunyan with a figurative base for the vices: 'the Lord *Old man*, the Lord *Carnal delight*, the Lord *Luxurious*, the Lord *Desire of Vain-glory*, my old Lord *Lechery*, Sir *Having Greedy*, with all the rest of our Nobility'. A marginal note makes it entirely clear that he intends a social comment: '*Sins are all Lords and Great ones*.' The temporizer By-ends is specifically of the gentry, albeit a parvenu: 'I am become a Gentleman of good Quality; yet my Great Grand-father was but a Waterman'; his wife was: 'my Lady *Fainings* Daughter, therefore she came of a very Honourable Family, and is arrived to such a pitch of Breeding, that she knows how to carry it to all, even to Prince and Peasant'. By-ends and his wife also stand for monied wealth, having links with the prosperous town of Fair-speech where he has 'very many Rich kindred'. The attack on wealth is particularly loud at the hill Lucre, where stands the tempter Demas '*Gentleman*-man like': 'that Treasure is a snare to those that seek it, for it hindreth them in their Pilgrimage'.[20]

Bunyan's repudiation of wealth was part of a wider rejection of the temporal world, represented by Vanity Fair and all its ephemeral temptations: '[A]s Houses, Lands, Trades, Places, Honours, Preferments, Titles, Countreys, Kingdoms, Lusts, Pleasures, and Delights of all sorts.' His alienation from 'the world, the flesh and the devil' took in indifference to its division into nation-states – 'Countreys, Kingdoms', the 'kingdoms of the world' (Matthew 4: 8): 'the *Britain* Row, the *French* Row, the *Italian* Row, the *Spanish* Row, the *German* Row' were merely the subdivisions of a great mart and its deceptive baubles. As for the world's institutions, Bunyan used his recollections of his court case to attack what he regarded as an unjust legal system. Brown suggested that Bunyan's model for the character of the hectoring judge in Faithful's trial in Vanity Fair was Kelyng. In fact, as we saw above in Chapter 2, Bunyan received a fair hearing at Kelyng's hands. The model for much of the dialogue is not Bunyan's court appearances, but his wife's attempt to intercede for him before the judges in 1661. Just as Hategood rails at Faithful in the Vanity Fair trial – '*Judg.* Sirrah, Sirrah, thou deservest to live no longer, but to be slain immediately upon the place' – so one of the judges hearing Elizabeth Bunyan loses all control of his passions: 'He preach the word of God! said *Twisdon* (and withal, she thought he would have struck her) ... God! said he, his doctrine is the doctrine of the Devil.' Bunyan borrowed phrases from his account of Elizabeth's appeal and worked them into the Vanity Fair trial:

[from Elizabeth Bunyan's appeal]:
My Lord, said Justice *Chester*, he is a pestilent fellow, there is not such a fellow in the country again.
[from Faithful's trial]:
Judge. .... this man ... is one of the vilest men in Countrey ...
Super[*stition*, a witness]. ... this I know, that he [Faithful] is a very pestilent fellow.[21]

He also drew on his recollections of the kind of allegations made against him and his like after the Restoration and especially after Venner's rising. In 1662 Bunyan was accused of political conspiracy in the capital: 'They charged me also, that I went thither to plot and raise division, and make insurrection.' Christian faces more general allegations of subversion: 'He neither regardeth Prince nor People, Law nor Custom; but doth all that he can to possess all men with certain of his disloyal notions.' Christian and Faithful also face their own variant of the accusation made against Nonconformists in post-Restoration England – that they had been guilty of inciting Civil War: 'Then were these two poor men brought before their Examiners again, and there charged as being guilty of the late Hubbub that had been in the *fair*.'[22]

If Bunyan used the court scenes in *The Pilgrim's Progress* to make veiled attacks on the legal machine under which he had suffered, he was equally scathing about the penal statutes of the Cavalier Parliament. Each of the decrees by which Pharaoh, Nebuchadnezzar and Darius enacted persecution becomes an 'Act'; Darius, constrained into a course of persecution by a powerful assembly (see Daniel 6), provides an apt analogy for Charles II's difficult relations with Parliament in this area; the way in which the repressive 'Acts' are listed and summarized gives them the appearance of a code of laws, exactly like the Clarendon Code.[23]

Following his farcical trial, Faithful is sentenced to a death of what Hammond calls 'baroquely complicated extravagance' – scourging, buffeting, lancing, stoning, stabbing and burning.[24] Elaborate it all may be, but its instalments bring together the sufferings of Christ (scourging, beating and lancing), of Stephen (stoning), of other early Christian martyrs (stabbing, etc.) and of the English martyrs in the pages of Foxe (burning). In Bunyan's mind all these sufferings formed the background to and made meaningful his own privations and those of thousands of his fellow-Nonconformists under the laws prevailing in post-Restoration England.

To take one example, as Hammond points out, the imprisonment of Faithful and Christian in an iron cage was actually undergone by the Dissenting minister John Child, who was known to Bunyan. However, the corollary to Penn's 'no cross, no crown' was that a cross merited a crown – and Faithful is indeed triumphantly vindicated:

> Now, I saw that there stood behind the multitude, a Chariot and a couple of Horses, waiting for *Faithful*, who (so soon as his adversaries had dispatched him) was taken up into it, and straightway was carried up through the Clouds, with sound of Trumpet, the nearest way to the Coelestial Gate.[25]

Hammond argues that this heavenly outcome defuses the social ire that we have seen expressed in *The Pilgrim's Progress* against the nobility and gentry; the Christian will receive a celestial crown, and although the moral faults of the rich and powerful are condemned, a this-worldly solution is not offered. Bunyan espouses a 'strictly conservative' political outlook and – no Leveller or Digger – expresses hopes which are 'centred on the next world, not on this'.[26]

This is a persuasive view in many ways: Bunyan undoubtedly played his part in the long-term overhaul of Nonconformist political attitudes, leading to the greater passivity that was evident most especially after 1689. However, the Bunyan who had written *A Few Sighs from Hell* two decades before the appearance of the first part of *The Pilgrim's Progress* was still capable of invoking revenge – in his mind no less real for being eschatological – against persecutors. The Last Judgement was to be a day of wrath and of apocalyptic retribution:

> When he shall come with sound of Trumpet in the Clouds, as upon the wings of the Wind, you [the saints] shall come with him; and when he shall sit upon the Throne of Judgement, you shall sit by him; yea, and when he shall pass Sentence upon all the workers of Iniquity ... you also shall have a voice in that Judgement, because they were his and your Enemies.[27]

Using satirical metaphor and eschatological prediction to condemn the social, political and legal system that had kept him prisoner for so many years, Bunyan could hardly fail to attack the Church of England. His hostility to the Anglican liturgy can be read into Faithful's charge that *'whatever is thrust into the worship of God, that is not agreeable to divine Revelation, cannot be done but by an humane Faith, which Faith will not profit to*

Eternal Life'.[28] The theme of salvation and faith that is here introduced indicates that, though Campbell may well be right to say that 'we should be ill-advised to search for Bunyan's theology in *The Pilgrim's Progress*', we should also pay heed to Sharrock's analysis of theological polemic in the character of Mr Worldly-Wiseman, a tempter into false assurance of righteousness through the works of the law and based on Edward Fowler: Fowler/Wiseman opposes justification by faith and tries to 'render the Cross odious' to Christian.[29]

Fowler's positions, as Bunyan perceived them, also come under attack in the opinions on justification of the character Ignorance:

> *Ignor[ance]*. I believe that ... I shall be justified before God from the curse, through his gracious acceptance of my obedience to his Law ... *Chr.* ... 2. *Thou* [Ignorance] *believest with a* False *Faith, because it taketh Justification from the personal righteousness of Christ, and applies it to thy own.*[30]

Yet, although Bunyan rejected a soteriology of self-assurance which he ascribed to Fowler, he himself, especially in his repudiation of the inactive and verbal religion of Talkative, seems again to move away from a Reformation doctrine of justification by faith alone, and to place confidence in the role, not of the individual's election or saving faith, but in his or her moral actions and works: 'The Soul of Religion is the practick part ... at the day of Doom, men shall be judged according to their fruits. It will not be said then, *Did you believe?* but, Were you *Doers,* or *Talkers* only? and accordingly shall they be judged.'[31] In what reads like a denial of justification by faith – 'It will not be said then, *Did you believe?*' – Bunyan cites in his support the Epistle of James, the scriptural *locus classicus* of works righteousness and rejected by Luther for that reason; having acknowledged James 1:27 on what constituted 'pure religion', or, as Bunyan put it, 'the Soul of Religion', he went on to cite the passage so often taken to be the antithesis of Protestant solafideanism: 'Even so, faith, if it hath not works, is dead, being alone' (James 2:17). Campbell maintains that, because *The Pilgrim's Progress* concerns man's struggle rather than God's plan, the work avoids Reformed soteriology:

> [T]he doctrine of election ... does not affect the Christian of *The Pilgrim's Progress*. Many of the doctrines to which Bunyan subscribed are mentioned incidentally in the course of the book, but none is essential to Christian's progress ... [I]n *The Pilgrim's Progress*, he eliminates the truths that are set in the mind of God, such as the doctrine of election.

However, whereas he seems to propose works-righteousness to Talkative
– the epitome of the complacent professor who disputed any necesity for
good works – when he rebuts Ignorance's confidence in the efficacy of
personal merit, Bunyan restates justification by faith, in Christ alone: '*true
Justifying Faith puts the soul (as sensible of its lost condition by the Law)
upon flying for refuge unto Christs righteousness*'. In this work, then, Bunyan
does not so much contradict his own acceptance of the Protestant doctrine
of justification by faith, as strive for a balance between the antinomian
error of faith (or talk) without good works and Pelagian over-confidence in
personal virtue. Bunyan also makes Ignorance deliver a warning against
the danger of antinomian immorality that might arise out of an excessive
trust in the redeeming work of Christ: 'What! would you have us trust to
what Christ in his own person has done without us? This conceit would
loosen the reines of our lust, and tollerate us to live as we list.'[32]

While he denigrated the works-righteousness represented by the distinctly non-Calvinist Mr Worldly-Wiseman, Bunyan can be seen to be
criticizing aspects of what we might recognize as Puritanism. The character
of Talkative is a brilliant parody of love of discourse for its own sake. But
Talkative's futility is all the more marked in that his conversation is, in
theological terms, correct from Bunyan's point of view: 'the necessity of the
New-birth, the insufficiency of our works, the need of Christs righteousness, *&c.*' In the margin Bunyan comments ironically on 'Talkatives
fine discourse'. Yet Talkative's fault is not simply garrulity; rather, it arises
from his over-emphasis on the very theology of salvation that lay at the
centre of Bunyan's outlook: 'all is of Grace, not of works: I could give you
an hundred Scriptures for the confirmation of this'. Bunyan redoubles his
sarcasm in his marginal comment on Talkative's over-assurance in faith
without works: '*O brave* Talkative.' This character's immorality, greed,
harshness and self-indulgence – 'as he *talketh now* with you, so will he *talk*
when he is on the *Ale-bench*' – represent the perils of an ultra-antinomian
formula of faith without works.[33]

Bunyan's discerning attitude to aspects of godly religion extended to
diffidence expressed in *The Pilgrim's Progress* over the ordinances of the
church. Campbell observes that the Palace Beautiful, standing for the
gathered churches, is 'just by the highway side', not on the route to salvation, and that Christian is not baptized on entering the church' – the latter
point being consistent with the view of baptism set out in *A Confession of
My Faith, and A Reason of my Practice in Worship*. On the other hand, *The
Pilgrim's Progress* celebrates some important features of the life of the
gathered churches. For example, as Campbell points out, Christian's reception at the Palace Beautiful is modelled on the admission procedures of

the Bedford congregation. Discourse is patterned on the godly converse of the separatist churches. The Puritan sabbatarianism that Bunyan was to unfold in *Questions about the Nature and Perpetuity of the Seventh-Day Sabbath* (1685) receives its recognition in the account of how Christian finds the key to his freedom – 'called Promise' – in the early hours of a Sunday morning.[34]

The Pilgrim's Progress, then, is a Puritan book, and concerned with the life of the gathered churches. That said, it was not guaranteed a favourable reception from all members of such churches. For one thing, its literary form was made up of comedy and fiction. Where Milton adopted the voice of epic to 'justify the ways to God to men' in *Paradise Lost*, Bunyan chose the much less elevated forms of satire, laughter and popular fiction for his setting of the drama of man's redemption, arousing a hostile reaction from the Baptist Thomas Sherman, who objected to the 'lightness and laughter' of the book. Bunyan's defence was that in his work gravity hid her visage behind a smile:

> Some things are of that Nature as to make
> Ones fancie Checkle while his Heart doth ake.[35]

We have already glimpsed comedy in the depiction of the absurdly loquacious Talkative. It is also present, in a black version, in the babble of the jury during Faithful's trial in Vanity Fair: '*Hang him, hang him,* said Mr. *Heady. A sorry Scrub,* said Mr. *High-mind. My heart riseth against him,* said Mr. *Enmity. He is a Rogue,* said Mr. *Lyar. Hanging is too good for him,* said Mr. *Cruelty.*' Bunyan's defence of his comic approach, as of his employment of motifs from the romances, rested also on the claim that such devices sugared the pill of doctrine:

> They [readers] *must be grop'd for, and be tickled too,*
> *Or they will not be catcht, what e're you do.*

Enjoyment – 'delight' – is also aroused through the tension of the narrative. Bunyan was an effective suspense writer, setting up cliffhanger scenes of extreme peril followed by sudden rescue: 'Yet the *Fiends* seemed to come nearer and nearer, but when they were come even almost at him, he cried out with a most vehement voice, *I will walk in the strength of the Lord God*; so they gave back, and came no further.' Another scene, Christian's rescue from drowning, takes some of its power from its echoes of Christ's saving of Peter.[36]

Although Bunyan found his narrative apparatus in rehashed tales whose origins lay in the 'popish' hagiographies of St George, St David, St Anthony and the rest, he did not feel that he had to spend much time defending his genre source. Nick Shrimpton observes that Richard Johnston's chivalric heroes in *The Seven Champions of Christendom* were as much assisted by destiny as Calvinist saints were by predestination.[37]

A remaining objection to his literary approach that Bunyan felt he had to counter was that he indulged in metaphor: 'Metaphors make us blind.' Bunyan dealt with the objection that metaphors mislead and deceive at considerable length in his prefatory 'Authors Apology'. Yet, though there was a long-standing Puritan preference for plain and literal discourse, few of the godly would have been able to resist Bunyan's defence that:

> *His* [God's] *Gospel-laws, in olden time* [were] *held forth*
> *By Types, Shadows and Metaphors.*

Perhaps, though, Bunyan's metaphorical approach was, or was becoming, objectionable, and, indeed, archaic, not so much from the point of view of Puritan literalism, but from the vantage point of a changing élite culture increasingly linked to scientific discovery and becoming suspicious of the mental world of metaphor. The increasing need in late Stuart England for an exact language to convey scientific meaning led to the de-poetization of speech and meaning, the conversion of poetry into verse, the erosion of imaginative meaning and the marginalization of metaphor. S. J. Newman summarizes Francis Bacon as maintaining that 'the popular mind is too unreliable, too anthropomorphic, too infected by faith and creativity to perceive things as they really are'; before he came along, Bacon believed, the human intellect was 'like an enchanted glass, full of superstition and imposture'. Natural philosophy had been impeded by 'the similitudes of human actions and arts' – a dismissive use of the word 'similitude', which was repeated by Glanvill, the writer on homiletics, in the year of the appearance of the first part of *The Pilgrim's Progress*, when Glanvill advised preachers to avoid 'the use of vulgar Proverbs and homely similitudes'.[38]

Yet Bunyan's classic is a 'similitude': *The Pilgrim's Progress From This World To That which is to come: Delivered under the Similitude of a Dream* – the term being assertively repeated in 'The Authors Apology'. Although Bunyan was an exact writer on theology, with complex numbered discourses appearing within *The Pilgrim's Progress*, he was not of a scientific frame of mind. It is the character of Shame, the supreme exponent of Restoration values, of 'the brave spirits of the times', who derides the godlys' 'want of understanding all natural Science'. In *The Pilgrim's Progress* Bunyan is the spokesman for a pre-scientific culture based on symbol, poetry, simile and allegory – 'similitude' – rather than the laboratory exactitude and literalness looked for in Baconian language.[39]

Looking at the details of Bunyan's metaphorical range in this work, we find that some similes revolve around money and trade: Little-faith is robbed by Guilt and others of the 'spending Money' which represents his spiritual resources; a man's sins are his standing debt in God's account – 'Gods Book'. Bunyan also draws upon Scripture for metaphor, building with lavish detail, for instance, on Peter's image of the dog returning to its vomit. There is imagery based on nature: 'Why [says Christian to Hopeful], I did but compare thee to some of the Birds that are of the brisker sort, who will run to and fro in untrodden paths with the shell upon their heads.'[40] Apart from individual figures, there is an underlying metaphor running through the work, which accompanies that of the voyager: the warrior. Shrimpton argues that, whereas the figure of the pilgrim is apt for the Christian's progression towards conversion, the metaphor of warfare is appropriate for the constant struggle that the individual has to wage following conversion. Bunyan is certainly concerned with conflict in *The Pilgrim's Progress*, and in the great battle scene between Christian and Apollyon he depicts the war that the Christian must wage, with the sword of the spirit, against the forces of evil; he takes a metaphor and uses it for an allegory. For this particular encounter, though, Bunyan did not draw on his own experience of warfare, but used the chivalric romances as his source. The 'military metaphor' of Bunyan's book was culled from other books. The archaic weapons and forms of hand-to-hand combat in the duel between Christian and Apollyon were in no way related to the warfare of gunnery, siege and massed infantry movement that Bunyan had known in the 1640s. The illustrations for the 1678 edition show Christian fighting alone and wearing full armour, carrying a spear, helmeted and plumed, parrying and thrusting with sword and shield. He is no seventeenth-century trooper, but a solitary and knightly St George, 'clad with northern steel from top to toe', and facing Apollyon as the dragon, a figure based on the opponents who bar the way of the heroes in the medieval cycles. Figures like the King's Champion come straight out of chivalric lore. Thus, the battle metaphor in *The Pilgrim's Progress* stemmed not from personal observation, but from a literary tradition, one that emphasized two features of the hero – his solitude and his manliness.[41]

Though he is accompanied, Christian loses his friend, the martyred Faithful and, to underline his solitude, his relationship with Hopeful is marked by tension and male aggression rather than by friendship:

Hope. *Why art thou so tart my Brother? ...*
Chr. ... Here therefore, my Brother, is thy mistake.
Hope. *I acknowledge it; but yet your severe reflection had almost made me angry.*

Christian battles alone, the solitary Puritan contender merged with the loneliness of the knight errant. This means that relationships are a hindrance to him, as with Bacon's 'He who hath wife and children hath given hostages to fortune; for they are impediments to great enterprises.' Family is a weight impeding Bunyan's pilgrim's progress. In the opening narrative of the book, and recalling Bunyan's account of his melancholy self-absorption and psychological isolation from his family in *Grace Abounding*, Christian is shown as being concerned for his wife's and children's fate, but as being misunderstood by them: 'they also thought to drive away his distemper by harsh and surly carriages to him'. The prerequisite of Christian's embarking on his redemptive pilgrimage is his abandonment of his family: 'but his Wife and Children perceiving it [his departure], began to cry after him to return: but the Man put his fingers in his Ears, and ran on crying, Life, Life, Eternal Life'. Christian and his family, for all his professed love of them, are essentially estranged: '*Chr*. Why, my Wife was afraid of losing this World; and my Children were given to the foolish delights of youth.' This lack of understanding on his family's part shows them to be '*implacable to good*', so much so that Christian is cleared of any responsibility for their fate. 'Wives, Husbands, Children' are also part of the alluring impedimenta of Vanity Fair.[42]

As free of family ties as any knightly hero, Christian is at the centre of a pervasive concern with masculinity: Mr Worldly-Wise warns him of the dangers of spiritual cogitations which '*unman men*'; in words borrowed from Latimer's rallying call to Ridley as recorded by Foxe, Faithful is bidden to 'play the man'; in a warning against recklessness, Christian counsels Hopeful not to 'be tickled at the thoughts of our own manhood'; 'yet I cannot boast of my manhood', says Christian, taking stock of how little of his survival he owes to himself; an allegation that Christian has to deal with is that 'a tender conscience was an unmanly thing'; the pilgrims were to '*Be vigilant, and quit themselves like Men*'. Though the second part of *The Pilgrim's Progress* was to contain more in the way of feminine themes, it, too, was much taken up with images of a lone male struggle.[43]

The language of *The Pilgrim's Progress*, terse and exclamatory, conveys a sense of action and tension:

But Oh how nimbly now did he go up the rest of the Hill! ... *Ah thou sinful sleep! how for thy sake am I like to be benighted in my Journey! ...*

Then said *Christian* to himself again, These Beasts range in the night for their prey, and if they should meet with me in the dark, how should I shift them? how I should escape being by them torn in pieces?

The force of such passages is intensified by the use of a strong Anglo-Saxon diction; only eight out of seventy-one words just reproduced are of Romance origin and sixty-one of them are monosyllables. Dialogue is vivid and realistic:

Chr. *And what did you do then?*
Hope. Do! I could not tell what to do ...
Ignor. *What! You are a man for revelations!*

The Pilgrim's Progress is replete with scriptural citations and marginalia, but, through giving them his own diction and rhythms, Bunyan lends freshness and realism to familiar scenes and characters: 'Witness *Peter*, of whom I made mention before. He would swagger, Ay he would: He would, as his vain mind prompted him to say, do better, and stand more for his Master, then all men.'[44] Speaking here is a Protestant's scepticism about the claims of a saint, popery's special saint, but Peter's boastfulness – his 'swagger' – is conveyed all the more sharply in the dismissive conversational aside 'Ay he would'.

For so long consigned to the nursery and dismissed as a simple book for simple people, *The Pilgrim's Progress* is, in fact, a literary work of considerable artistry and sophistication. Those qualities are also on display in Bunyan's moralistic novel, *Mr. Badman*.

Notes

1. Compare Sir Charles Firth: 'To contemporaries outside his own sect the author of *The Pilgrim's Progress* was nothing but a dissenting preacher with some little reputation among Nonconformists' – cited in Roger Sharrock (ed.), *The Pilgrim's Progress: A Casebook* (London and Basingstoke, 1976), p. 81.
2. Roger Sharrock, 'Life and Story in *The Pilgrim's Progress*', in Vincent Newey (ed.), *The Pilgrim's Progress: Critical and Historical Views* (Liverpool, 1980), pp. 51–4. Dayton Haskin in 'The Burden of Interpretation in *The Pilgrim's Progress*', *Studies in Philology* 79 (1982), pp. 256–78, shows how the book placed a 'benign interpretation' on scriptural evidence for one's election.
3. Mark Twain quoted in *The Independent on Sunday*, *The Sunday Review*, 8

August 1993, p. 11. For Southey and Crabb, see Sharrock (ed.), *The Pilgrim's Progress*, p. 57. Bunyan's (apparent) plebeian naturalness, which had set him as a discount with the Augustans, gave him a new currency with the Romantics: see N. H. Keeble, '"Of Him Thousands Do Daily Sing and Talk": Bunyan and his Reputation', in Keeble (ed.), *John Bunyan: Conventicle and Parnassus* (Oxford, 1988), pp. 246–7, 252–6. For a plot summary of *The Pilgrim's Progress*, see Roger Sharrock, *John Bunyan* (London, 1954; reissued 1968), pp. 74–87.

4. For Loyola's early reading, see William V. Bangert, SJ, *A History of the Society of Jesus* (2nd edn; St Louis, MO, 1986), p. 4.

5. For allegory and parable, see Valentine Cunningham, 'Glosing and Glozing: Bunyan and Allegory', in Keeble (ed.), *John Bunyan*, esp. pp. 237ff., and Thomas H. Luxon, *Literal Figures: Puritan Allegory and the Reformed Crisis in Representation* (Chicago and London, 1995), ch 6; for intention, truth, fiction, allegory and metaphor in *The Pilgrim's Progress*, see Barbara A. Johnson, '"Falling into Allegory": The "Apology" to *The Pilgrim's Progress* and Bunyan's Scriptural Methodology', in Robert G. Collmer (ed.), *Bunyan in Our Time* (Kent, OH, and London, 1989), pp. 113–37.

6. Firth, quoted in Sharrock, *John Bunyan*, pp. 91–2; Lindsay ('Bunyan had a deep feeling for Nature') used considerable ingenuity in locating the scenes of *The Pilgrim's Progress* in the English countryside: 'The Slough of Despond lies north of Dunstable ... The Delectable Mountains are in the Chilterns': Jack Lindsay, *John Bunyan: Maker of Myths* (London, 1937; reprinted New York, 1969), pp. 170–3.

7. James Turner, 'Bunyan's Sense of Place', in Newey (ed.), *The Pilgrim's Progress*, pp. 92, 94, 97; see also Christopher Hill, *The English Bible and the Seventeenth-Century Revolution* (London, 1993), p. 131.

8. Brainerd Stranahan, 'Bunyan and the Epistle to the Hebrews: His Source for the Idea of Pilgrimage in *The Pilgrim's Progress*', *Studies in Philology* 79 (1982), pp. 279–96.

9. David Seed, 'Dialogue and Debate in *The Pilgrim's Progress*', in Newey (ed.), *The Pilgrim's Progress*, p. 69; E. Beatrice Batson, *John Bunyan: Allegory and Imagination* (London and Canberra, 1984), pp. 29–30.

10. James Blanton Wharey (ed.), *The Pilgrim's Progress from this World to That which is to Come* (revised by Roger Sharrock; Oxford, 1960), p. 66; for the dating of the composition of the first part of *The Pilgrim's Progress*, see *ibid.*, pp. xxix–xxxv.

11. *Ibid.*, p. 50; for the narratives of conversion, see Roger Pooley, 'Spiritual Experience and Spiritual Autobiography', *The Baptist Quarterly* 32 (1988), p. 396.

12. *The Pilgrim's Progress*, p. 137.

13. *Ibid.*, pp. 139, 142–3, 151.

14. *Ibid.*, pp. 151, 84, 77, 79–80, 6, 136. Kaufmann, though, writes that Bunyan 'hints that the Christian life is as much a matter of rest as it is of movement':

U. Milo Kaufmann, 'The Pilgrim's Progress and the Pilgrim's Regress: John Bunyan and C. S. Lewis on the Shape of the Christian Quest', in Collmer (ed.), *Bunyan in Our Time*, p. 189.

15. *The Pilgrim's Progress*, p. 65.

16. John Brown, *John Bunyan: His Life, Times and Work* (2nd edn; London, 1886), pp. 264–5; W. R. Owens, '"Antichrist Must Be Pulled Down": Bunyan and the Millennium', in Anne Laurence, W. R. Owens and Stuart Sim (eds), *John Bunyan and His England, 1628–1688* (London and Ronceverte, WV, 1990), pp. 81–2; I. M. Green writes that 'Bunyan certainly shared the anti-Catholic prejudices of his day, but if his work contained fewer attacks on Catholic doctrine than that of two or three generations earlier, this was in line with the partial decline of the negative [anti-Catholic] side of English Protestantism': 'Bunyan in Context', in M. Van Os and G. J. Schutte (eds), *Bunyan in England and Abroad* (Amsterdam, 1990), pp. 1–11; see also *The Pilgrim's Progress*, 'Introduction'.

17. *The Holy City*, in J. Sears McGee (ed.), *Miscellaneous Works of John Bunyan*, vol. III (Oxford, 1987), p. 72; *Of Antichrist, and His Ruine*, pp. 431–504.

18. Owens, '"Antichrist Must Be Pulled Down"', pp. 82, 92; Hill adds: 'For Bunyan persecutors were the Church of England and the Anglican gentry, against whom Charles and James seemed possible allies': Hill, *The English Bible*, p. 321.

19. *The Pilgrim's Progress*, p. 57.

20. *Ibid.*, pp. 94, 99, 106, 107; it is possible that the figure of Demas, 'the son of Abraham', having Judas for a father, contains a vestigial anti-Semitism. For social commentary, see Brean S. Hammond, '*The Pilgrim's Progress*: Satire and Social Comment', in Newey (ed.), *The Pilgrim's Progress*, p. 123; Brainerd Stranahan, 'Bunyan's Satire and its Biblical Source', in Collmer (ed.) *Bunyan in Our Time*, pp. 50–1; and, for discussion of Cantarow's view of the vices as 'members of the upper classes', see David Herreshof, 'Marxist Perspectives on Bunyan', in *ibid.*, p. 179.

21. *The Pilgrim's Progress*, pp. 88, 89, 95, 94; *A Discourse between my Wife and the Judges*, in *Grace Abounding*, pp. 127–8.

22. *Some Carriages of the Adversaries of God's Truth with me*, in *Grace Abounding*, p. 130; *The Pilgrim's Progress*, pp. 93, 91.

23. See *Ibid.*, p. 96.

24. Hammond, 'Satire and Social Comment', p. 121; *The Pilgrim's Progress*, p. 97.

25. *The Pilgrim's Progress*, p. 97. Hammond, 'Satire and Social Comment', p. 119; Pooley also relates Faithful's form of execution to those of three Marian martyrs recorded by Foxe: see Roger Pooley, 'Plain and Simple: Bunyan and Style', in Keeble (ed.), *John Bunyan*, p. 106; see also Barrie White, 'John Bunyan and the Context of Persecution', in Laurence *et al.*, *John Bunyan*, pp. 56–7, and Richard L. Greaves, 'Amid the Holy War: Bunyan and the Ethic of Suffering', in *ibid.*, pp. 63–75 and esp. pp. 70–5.

26. Hammond, 'Satire and Social Comment', pp. 126–7, 130.

27. *The Pilgrim's Progress*, p. 160.

28. *Ibid.*, p. 95.

29. Gordon Campbell, 'The Theology of *The Pilgrim's Progress*', in Newey (ed.), *The Pilgrim's Progress*, p. 261; see also Campbell, 'Fishing in Other Men's Waters: Bunyan and the Theologians', in Keeble (ed.), *John Bunyan*, esp. pp. 149–51; also Isabel Rivers, 'Grace, Holiness and the Pursuit of Happiness', in *ibid.*, pp. 63–7; *The Pilgrim's Progress*, pp. 17–24: Fowler's patronizing attitude to Bunyan (see Brown, *Bunyan*, p. 234) may have provided the basis for similar attitudes on the part of Mr Worldly-Wiseman: '*How now, good fellow … hear me, I am older than thou!*' (*The Pilgrim's Progress*, pp. 17–18).

30. *Ibid.*, p. 147.

31. *Ibid.*, pp. 79–80. Gordon Campbell picks up the 'discrepancy [which] arises between the theological position which [Bunyan] had inherited from the Bedford congregation and his practical private beliefs. Although he insisted in theory that the human will could play no part in salvation, in practice he never eased to exhort his readers to repent of their sins': Campbell, 'Fishing in Other Men's Waters', p. 149.

32. Campbell, 'The Theology of *The Pilgrim's Progress*', pp. 257, 261; *The Pilgrim's Progress*, p. 148. For the work's Christocentricity, see J. H. Alexander, 'Christ in *The Pilgrim's Progress*', *Bunyan Studies* 1, 2 (1989), pp. 22–9; see also Geoffrey Nuttall, 'The Heart of *The Pilgrim's Progress*', *American Baptist Quarterly* 7 (1988), pp. 472–83.

33. *Ibid.*, pp. 76, 77, 78.

34. Campbell, 'The Theology of *The Pilgrim's Progress*', pp. 251–2; *The Pilgrim's Progress*, p. 118.

35. Hammond, 'Satire and Social Comment', p. 118. Compare the (fictionalized) attack on the place of humour in Christian divinity in Umberto Eco, *The Name of the Rose* (trans. William Weaver; London 1984), pp. 467–79. The second part of *The Pilgrim's Progress*, p. 170.

36. *The Pilgrim's Progress*, pp. 97, 3, 63, 157–8; Matthew 14: 23–32.

37. Nick Shrimpton, 'Bunyan's Military Metaphor', in Newey (ed.), *The Pilgrim's Progress*, pp. 205–24.

38. *The Pilgrim's Progress*, p. 4. Bacon quoted in S. J. Newman, 'Bunyan's Solidness', in Newey (ed.), *The Pilgrim's Progress*, pp. 233–4, 249n. 20. Johnson, 'Falling into Allegory', pp. 133–6.

39. See, for example, the complex numbered discourse in *The Pilgrim's Progress*, pp. 153–4; Shame's attack on the godlys' ignorance of science, in *ibid.*, p. 72.

40. *Ibid.*, pp. 125–6, 140, 152, 129; 1 Peter 2: 22.

41. Shrimpton, 'Bunyan's Military Metaphor', pp. 207, 218; *The Pilgrim's Progress*, pp. 56–60; *The Pilgrim's Progress a facsimile reproduction* (Old Woking, Surrey, 1978), pp. 100, 107. For some of the connotations of

'north' and 'northern' in Bunyan, see Hill, *The English Bible*, p. 124.

42. *The Pilgrim's Progress*, pp. 128–9, 9, 10, 51, 88; Bacon, 'Of Marriage and Single Life', in Sir Francis Bacon, *The Essayes or Counsels, Civil and Morall* (ed. Michael Kiernan; Oxford, 1985), p. 24.

43. *The Pilgrim's Progress*, pp. 18, 131, 132, 72, 74.

44. *The Pilgrim's Progress*, pp. 45, 140, 148, 131.

SIX

Mr. Badman and
The Holy War

The Life and Death of Mr. Badman

In 1679 Bunyan published another expanded sermon, *A Treatise of the Fear of God,* developing the exploration of the covenants of works and grace which he had set out in *The Doctrine of the Law and Grace.* Then, in 1680 came *The Life and Death of Mr. Badman.*[1] The work is the obverse of *The Pilgrim's Progress* in that it recounts the descent of an individual to damnation, rather than his ascent to salvation. Bunyan seems to have envisaged it as a counterpart, if not a corrective, to *The Pilgrim's Progress*: James Forrest and Roger Sharrock have argued that it offered a serious, moralizing homily to those critics who had faulted the humour and metaphor of *The Pilgrim's Progress.*[2] The book is a narrative, and, though it has been widely acclaimed as a pioneer of the novel form, it is, rather, a proto-novel, in that, although it possesses the novel's element of narration, it lacks another key genre requirement, that of character analysis or development; theological predetermination prevents character exploration. The principal *dramatis personae*, Mr Badman himself and his first and second wives, are neither developed not explored: they are emblems of simple evil or simple goodness. Badman is trapped in his evil nature by his reprobation from birth; he can no more escape his badness than could the figures of the vices in a medieval morality play.

The work is addressed to the disciplinary and pastoral concerns of the gathered churches. It is conducted in the form of a dialogue by a small chorus of 'two old Puritans',[3] Wiseman and Attentive, the first of whom is unmistakably Bunyan himself, recounting incidents from his pastoral experience and dealing with the issues of church discipline that he regularly confronted – mixed marriages, drunkenness, avarice, extravagant dressing and so forth. Badman is 'conceived ... partly as a projection of the weaknesses to which the saints themselves are liable'.[4] It that sense, the book's scope is limited and introverted: it is aimed at the churches of saints. In another sense, though, it is concerned with the moral state of England at large. Richard Greaves is right to say that the Nonconformist's introspection, or moral 'autoinquisition', was 'more important than any obligation to know the state of the nation', but, as he also shows, such knowledge of and concern with wider issues beyond the individual and the church were by no means ruled out: 'Am I a mourner for the sins of the land?' was included in Joseph Alleine's list of twenty-nine interrogatories for the godly – a neat combination of introspection with public concern.[5] *Mr. Badman* is an outcome of that continuing Nonconformist anxiety about the nation's morals that would later be reflected in Dissenter involvement in the Societies for the Reformation of Manners at the end of the seventeenth century and in productions such as Philip Doddridge's hymn 'Alas for Britain and her sons!'[6] As with Doddridge's 'backsliding Israel', Blake's 'Auguries of Innocence', Wordsworth's 'London, 1802' and Kipling's 'Recessional', the conviction could be summed up in the phrase '*o tempora, o mores*': a regret for the moral decline of English society, measured by the standards of higher rectitude at some point in the past.[7] In *Mr. Badman* Bunyan is insistently concerned with the moral state of England, beyond the confines of the separated churches: 'England *shakes and totters already*', he writes; wickedness was '*like a flood to drown our English world ... Wolves in Sheeps Cloathing swarm in* England *this day*.' The age was '*licentious*', awash with 'Badness'. Sin was swallowing up the nation, 'sinking it', bringing its people to a 'temporal, spiritual and eternal ruin'. Unidentified '*men of Gods wrath*' – possibly an allusion to Catholic insurgents and/or invaders in this, the height of the Popish Plot and Exclusion crisis, – were '*about to deal with us*'.[8]

Bunyan's fears for the moral health of the nation had several implications. One was political: there was a lack of moral example, indeed, the setting of a particularly bad example, by those who should have provided a lead. Bunyan gave point to this charge in dealing with 'uncleanness' depicting the way that the 'great ones' made this 'one of the most reigning sins in our day';[9] if the possibility of a pun in the otherwise unusual word 'reigning' is allowed for, this could be read as a reference to Charles II's womanizing.

A further implication of Bunyan's condemnation of a national moral malaise was that he would focus on those faults which most gravely weakened the collective standing of England as a moral commonwealth. Foremost among those offences was Sabbath-breaking, to which Bunyan devoted considerable attention, since the strict, enforced, public observance of the Sabbath, in which the English were distinguished among Protestant nations,[10] was, for the godly, the badge of a covenant of the entire realm with God, as it had been with the Israel of old. Bunyan's interest in the moral condition of England also induced him to intersperse his narrative of the downfall of his main character with instructive news stories from around the country – from courtrooms, taverns, houses, gallows and mines. Further, since Bunyan was delineating a nation in serious moral disrepair, he had to indicate a point in time in the past when matters had been better ordered. His observation that punishment for bastardy 'in Olivers dayes ... was then somewhat severe'[11] suggests that the moral golden age he had in mind was the 1650s. In contrast with that era of godly rule, Bunyan harshly judged the moral collapse of Restoration England. Yet, though appalled by what he saw around him, Bunyan had by no means abandoned concern for English society or become exclusively concerned with the internal affairs of his church. Rather, he retained a sense of moral citizenship and of concern for the state of the nation. As with the Nonconformist minister Oliver Heywood, who carefully recorded divine judgments on offenders,[12] Bunyan sought to show God continually intervening to prevent the moral breakdown of English society; to do this, he chose scriptural texts such as Ezekiel, which revealed God's retributive actions towards Israel at large.[13]

Mr. Badman is made up of a mainline narrative, interspersed with reflections on conduct and punctuated by subsidiary incidents intended to sustain the force of the main narration. That main narration is inexorable rather than tense. Where there is no choice, there can be no drama, and Badman's end is entirely predictable from his beginning. This is because he is who and what he is – Mr Badman: man and bad, and bad because man, in his natural or unregenerate state. In *Instruction for the Ignorant*, Bunyan had set out his doctrine of evil in the child as the archetype of man's sinful nature: '[*W*]*e came into the World polluted* ... We are the fruit of an unclean thing, are defiled in our very conception, and are by nature the Children of wrath.'[14] In *Mr. Badman,* children are again shown as being corrupt in their natural state. They: '*come polluted with sin into the World* ... *Indwelling sin* ... Man in his birth is compared to an ass (an unclean Beast) ... even in Childhood, even in little children, *Pride* will first of all shew it self.'[15] Nature and the ineradicability of original sin – given that Christ's role in removing it (as distinct from expiating only 'actual' sins) is discounted[16] – are crucial. Nurture counts for less; sin may be learned by example, '*but Example is not the root*' – nature is. Conversely, none of the earnest endeavours of Badman's 'godly' parents, none of their application of the 'rod of correction', could rid him of his characteristic sins. As an apprentice, '[h]e had a good master, he wanted not good Books, nor good Instruction, nor good Sermons, nor good Examples, no nor good fellow-Servants neither, but all would not doe' to amend him. We might venture to ask what, from Bunyan's point of view, was the utility of all these pious provisions, just as we might enquire what possible further contribution Bunyan's evil companions could make to his total irredeemability. For Badman cannot rid himself of his evil nature: he entered 'polluted with sin into the World', and when he came, as inevitably he did, to steal, he did it as a result of 'the delusion of his own corrupt heart'.[17]

If, though, his evil nature were not enough to seal his fate, God is determined to destroy Badman: *quem deus vult perdere, prius creat*. It is all worked out in advance. God abandons Badman: he is 'left of God … *thou shalt be turned over to the ungodly … till I shall visit thee with Death and Judgment*'. When he joined a group of evil companions, '[i]t was the Judgement of God that he did, that is, *he came acquainted with them, through the anger of God* … He chose his Delusions and Deluders for him, … that he might be destroyed.' Is it possible, then, to feel any compassion for one who might be seen as the helpless victim of a cruel and vengeful God? That would certainly not have been consistent with Bunyan's views or purpose. It is true that the biography of Badman contains some stray expressions of what might be taken for pity; for example, at one of his periodic crises, Attentive exclaims: '*Alas poor* Badman!' and Wiseman adds: 'poor wretch, as he is, he is gone to his place'. However, the author was not setting out to stir up pity for a flawed and tragic hero in this book, which relentlessly actualizes the decree of reprobation. There is, it should be said, an occasional suggestion of volition in Badman's evil courses: he 'chose death, rather than life', and his wickedness lay in part in intention: 'He that would be bad is bad.' However, Badman's predisposition to choose evil arose from his evil disposition and 'they be not bad deeds that make a bad man, but he is already a bad man that doth bad deeds'. God was in total control, of character, of individuals' damnation and salvation, and of all circumstances, including economic ones; for, when men failed in business, 'the immediate hand and Judgment of God' could be detected, in punishment for some sin or as a test 'to trye their Graces'. God's absolute mastery of events precluded any possibility of accident: a drunken mishap afflicting Badman with a broken leg is 'A Judgment of God upon him'. Three stories taken from the work by Samuel Clarke, to which Bunyan gives the title *Looking-glass for Sinners*, including a Faustian narrative of one who sold his soul and a horror story featuring the devil, confirmed that God masterminded all eventualities. Like the Quakers, whose minutes recorded the misfortunes of their persecutors as divine judgements, Bunyan describes an omnipotent deity doling out temporal as well as eternal and infernal punishments.[18]

Badman's vicious life, then, is the outcome of his vicious character as a reprobate in the more technical sense. Since he is what he is, his life, with its absence of choice and freedom, could hardly provide an object lesson for others to decide on a particular course of life. A predetermined biography leading to death and damnation, *Mr. Badman* cannot work as an exemplary tale. Attentive's concluding wish is for Wiseman's '*Prayers that God will give me much grace, that I may neither live nor die as did Mr.* Badman'.[19] However, acquiring such grace was not something one could oneself do, either through the sacraments of a church, or through personal merit: one either was or was not saved, and there was nothing to be done about it, at least in terms of avoiding damnation, though the atmosphere of tension in *The Pilgrim's Progress* indicates that Bunyan envisaged more room for personal involvement in the salvation of the elect. Yet, while *Mr. Badman* cannot function satisfactorily as a cautionary story, the biography does allow Bunyan to deliver a series of miniature homilies featuring issues of concern in the gathered churches: Sabbath observance, sex, economic conduct, dress and fashion, and marriage and endogamy.[20] The advice to readers to avoid various forms of misconduct acts independently of the narration of Badman's predestined downfall and sometimes leaves it for extended periods.

Bunyan's treatment of Sabbath observance is relatively brief and does not stray from the main stem of the narrative for very long. Nevertheless, strict observance of Sunday – the Nonconformists' 'sole red-letter day' – was crucial in the identification of visible saints and in distinguishing them from sinners: '*he that cannot abide to keep one day holy to God, to be sure he hath given a sufficient proof that he is an unsanctified man*'. Such a one had Bunyan himself been before his conversion – 'one that took much delight in all manner of vice, and especially that was the Day [Sunday] that I did solace my self therewith'.[21] Neglect of Sunday's obligations is sharply observed: young Badman would 'lurk in by-holes among his Companions, untill holy Duties were over'. Sabbath-breaking was a familiar problem with the gathered churches: in 1676, for instance, a member of the Bedford congregation 'made acknowledgement of summe miscarrages the Church had charged him with as namely, breaking the Saboth'. The Nonconformist literature recounting punitive providences directed at sinners was particularly severe on Sabbath violation, for this was indeed the day that the Lord had made, 'an Emblem of the heavenly Sabbath above'.[22]

Following Sabbath-breaking – '*in all manner of idleness*' – Badman's next sin was swearing. This does not seem to have been a particularly serious problem in Bunyan's church and was an infraction that would come within Roger Sharrock's category of offences not so much typically committed by

professors, as identifying their enemies and opposites: it had characterized Bunyan himself in his unconverted state, when a 'loose and ungodly'
woman had told him that he 'was the ungodliest fellow for swearing that
ever she heard in all her life'. The fact that swearing was a sin of the unconverted and the ungodly made it one of those defects in English society that
it was part of Bunyan's purpose to castigate in *Mr. Badman*.[23] Oaths were
employed (as Bunyan had used them in his youth) to 'make my words have
authority', to authenticate statements and to *'put authority or, terrour into
his words, to stuff them full of the sin of Swearing'*; swearing also conferred
an aura of maleness – to 'shew themselves the more valiant men' – and of
gentility. It was, according to Bunyan, widely thought that to 'swear is
Gentleman-like'. As with other aspects of the swing of the pendulum of
moral fashion after 1660, such as theatre-going and casual sex, swearing
was modish in Bunyan's society – Charles II was a connoisseur and the
habit was adopted by those men of fashion, the *'Damme* Blades' vividly
caught by Bunyan like characters in a Restoration comedy. It was indeed
'one of the common sins of our age', and to be condemned as part of
Bunyan's proclaimed intention in *Mr. Badman* of denouncing all *'that
wickedness* [which] *like a flood is like to drown our English world'*.[24] Yet, as
well as being a trendy habit, cursing and swearing (Bunyan drew an elaborate distinction between them) could also be seen as archaisms left over
from a bygone age of popery, though still prevailing in Protestant England in the form of oaths sworn 'by Idols, as by the *Mass,* by our *Lady,* by
Saints'.[25]

Such a pedigree for swearing would have been sufficient to induce Bunyan to condemn it. But why, especially when cursing was not an acute
problem in the gathered churches, did he denounce it as vehemently as he
did and at such length? Part of the answer lies in the fact that he was a man
of words and discourse, a preacher and an author. We have already seen,
in *Grace Abounding*, how much impact words had on him: the voice from
heaven which stopped his games; the rebuke that put an end to his own
cursing; the talk of the pious women of Bedford which so 'affected' him;
the scriptural passages that had such an alarming impact on him, making
him 'sick', 'faint and fear'. Bunyan's detestation of swearing and cursing,
though, had deeper significance than simply his preoccupation, as a writer
and preacher, with words. For him and for much of the culture around
him, words still had an autonomous efficacy. Part of Bunyan subscribed to
a Protestant post-sacramental and post-miraculous world-view, but this
Puritan devoted to words and the Word also expected locutions to have
material effects. This is evident in his condemnation of the casual oath
wishing 'the Pox, or Plague upon' people; today we might regard such a

malediction as no more than bad taste within a society only recently visited by a lethal outbreak of plague. Bunyan, though, believed that swearers would 'see accomplished upon them' such curses as the fashionable '*God-damme me*'. Two horrific *exempla*, which he recounts to strengthen his case against cursing, reveal his expectation that verbal utterances would have practical consequences. The first is told with every circumstance of time and place and concerns a woman surface-worker at a mine in Derbyshire who, denying a theft by expressing a wish to be swallowed up if she were guilty, met, according to Bunyan, just that fate, having, in effect, cursed herself. The second story involves the mentally handicapped son of an alehouse-keeper, who amused his patrons by getting the boy to curse him with such phrases as 'devil take you'; in Bunyan's account, the devil did just that, entering the man's torso in a particularly painful possession.[26]

The realistic detail provided in these stories – the busy Derbyshire mine, the rough alehouse, probably somewhere in the south Midlands – underscores their authenticity as incidents. Yet it is not the veracity of the narrations that is at issue, but their causal interpretation, and Bunyan's is unmistakably supernaturalist. The modern reader, with a post-magical mind-set, is inclined to construct natural explanations for what happened in the two incidents: in the first, the reportage reads like a sudden, but all too likely, subsidence at a pit, in the second like a cancer diagnosis. But Bunyan does not entertain such morally neutral, naturalistic or materialistic explanations; the disasters in question took place because of the utterance of words, functioning autonomously like malign charms. In this book, Bunyan also confirmed his belief in witchcraft, which he condemned in a lost work of 1659. He would have been fully in sympathy with a finding in a witch trial held at Lancaster earlier in the century, in which what would seem to us today patently to have been a naturally induced stroke was explained to the court as the result of a witch's curse.[27] However, in the two scenes recounted by Bunyan the intentions to cause the consequences were absent: the words uttered possessed a power in their own right, that of magic in an absolute sense, independent even of human intention.

Following his treatment of swearing, Bunyan continues through his canon of sins, both those incident to the churches of saints and those more likely to be prevalent in the wider world. His treatment of Badman's drunkenness is perfunctory (though this *was* a problem confronting the gathered churches). Few details illustrate this passage – Badman frequents '*Taverns* and *Tippling-houses*', stealing from his master to buy drink – and few supportive anecdotes are provided.[28] It is, though, in his concern with another current ill, one that loomed large in the disciplinary proceedings of the

separate churches – 'Uncleanness' – that Bunyan exerts himself most strenuously. In his evocation of sexual misconduct, Bunyan writes erotically
and is even sympathetic to Badman's vulnerability to sexual temptation.
The powerful erotic writing is derived from Scripture, Bunyan admitting
the 'enchanting and bewitching pleasures' of sex, and imagining Badman's
temptress inviting him to sin with verbal seductions both erotic and exotic:
'*I have decked my bed with coverings of Tapestry, with carved works, with
fine Linnen of Ægypt: I have perfumed my bed with Myrrhe, Aloes, and
Cinnamon; come let us take our fill of love untill the Morning; let us solace
our selves with loves.*'²⁹

Bunyan's awareness of the power of sex, along with his fear of sexually assertive women, make him see Badman as, in part, a victim of female
seduction:

> [*I*]*t is a deadly thing to young men, when such beastly queans, shall, with
> words and carriages that are openly tempting, discover themselves unto
> them; It is hard for such to escape their Snare* … [T]hey are … very
> tempting … And, indeed, the very eyes, hands, words and ways of such,
> are all snares and bands to youthful, lustful fellows.*³⁰

However, by pointing out men's responsibility for women's seduction,
Bunyan corrects any impression that women as temptresses are to blame
for men's lapses. Moralistic misogyny is present, but is balanced by awareness of the responsibility of both genders for sexual concupiscence: 'for
though I doubt not but *that* Sex [the female] is bad enough this way, yet I
verily believe that many of them are made Whores at first by the flatteries
of *Badmans* fellows'. Men's sexual hold over women, viewed as deriving
from their economic and social power, is exposed as an evil within Bunyan's
own society; it is structured into a system of kept women – 'misses' in
Restoration parlance. In one of Bunyan's stories, a seducer tells his 'Miss'
that if she becomes pregnant she can say that she has conceived by the
Holy Spirit. Wiseman, perhaps speaking for Bunyan in a recollection of an
incident in which he was pastorally involved, and over which he may have
felt guilty for his failure to act, comments: 'he [the seducer] was a great
man, and I was poor and young so I let it alone'.³¹ Far, then, from presenting women in the colours of predatory Jezebels, Bunyan shows them as
being trapped in sexually disadvantaged roles by economic inequality and
dependence. In a society without effective contraception, it was women
who faced the stigma, the poverty and, often, the horror of unwanted and
unmarried motherhood. Women's helplessness in the face of male exploitation is revealed in a story, which has an unmistakable ring of horrifying

veracity, of a 'brave young Gallant' who threw his mistress's new-born child into the fire.[32]

If illicit sex thus led to tragedy, the prevalence of syphilis offered Bunyan occasion for reflection on the link between sin and its temporal punishment; witness his capacity to evoke horror in his depiction of venereal disease: '*the Foul Disease,* now called by us the *Pox* ... so nauseous and stinking, so infectious to the whole body ... *I knew a man once that rotted away with it; and another that had his Nose eaten off, and his Mouth almost quite sewed up thereby.*' Though Bunyan claimed to find a reference to syphilis in the Old Testament, he was aware of it as an evil within his own society – '*the Foul Disease,* now called by us the *Pox*' – and one that could be identified as a natural result of a natural cause: 'It is a Disease, that where it is, it commonly declares, that the cause thereof is uncleanness ... We see that this disease is entailed ... to this most beastly sin, nor is there any disease so entailed to any other sin, as this to this.'[33]

Alongside and, perhaps, in conflict with his acceptance of the operative function of words, Bunyan, in his epidemiological diagnosis, adopts a simple formula of natural causation, according to which promiscuous sex results in venereal disease, to which it is 'entailed' directly, without going through an intermediate stage of divine punitive intervention. Bunyan is here moving away from an interpretation of divine judgement on sins, towards a rational analysis of natural cause and effect – rather like the seventeenth-century Barcelona tanner Miquel Parets, who, in his journal of a plague year, revealed an acceptance of a non-supernatural (though anthropocentric) explanation for catastrophe – man's imprudence – and along with it a consequent practical, prudent, non-supernatural, non-'magical' approach to problem-solving.[34] Seventeenth-century Europeans' unfolding awareness of natural cause and effect increasingly – even with Bunyan – excluded God and sin from the causative equation, but also increasingly put men and women, especially through the adoption of prudent precautions, in control of harm and its avoidance: if interpersonal contagion rather than sin encouraged plague, quarantine, rather than *quarant' ore,* was the solution. Promiscuity led to disease, not circuitously, via God's punishment, but as a scientifically observable unmediated consequence; in exposing the 'health risks' of promiscuity, as of drunkenness, Bunyan made *Mr. Badman* a manual not so much for eluding hellfire – which, as we saw, Badman could not escape – as for the avoidance of risky behaviour and the prudent preservation of health – and of wealth, pointing out that: 'The evil effects thereof [promiscuity] in this world ... This sin is destructive to the Body.' Lust, like drink, wasted treasure: 'and men ... will not stick, so they may accomplish their desire, to lay *their*

Signet, their Bracelets, and their Stuff to pledge, rather than miss of the fulfilling of their lusts'. The subordinate anecdotes and reflections on them make *Mr. Badman* a handbook for Nonconformists getting on with their lives, avoiding imprudence and risk as much as shunning sin, 'the old Puritan heroism ... giving way to the new Nonconformist caution'.[35]

Two images recurring throughout the book are used to highlight the themes of imprudence, risk, danger and their correctives: the horse and the gallows. As the narrative of his dealings with Agnes Beaumont showed, Bunyan, like Fox and Wesley, was a man on horseback; he was a preacher and administrator used to the saddle and covering an extensive area, taking in Cambridgeshire, Suffolk, Essex, Hertfordshire and London. An habitual rider, then, Bunyan scatters images associated with the horse throughout this book: Badman's flattering friends batten off him 'like Horse-leaches'; in his decline, Badman 'went now like a tyred Jade, the Devil had rid him almost off his leggs'; in his calculating hypocrisy, he was 'as a stalking-Horse'. The horse, with its combination of speed and unpredictability, provided him with a metaphor of danger to point up the need for caution in everyday business affairs. Thus, a young man who had married deceitfully was riding, when 'his horse threw him to the ground, where he was found dead at break of day'. Other men are thrown fatally by their mounts, either in drink – 'from the *pot* to the *grave*' – or in uttering blasphemy. Later, a hint that, for a while, Badman was a mounted highwayman sharpens the impression of the dangerous nature of his life, for highwaymen, though figures of glamour in popular culture, faced a high risk of finishing up in the gallows.[36]

The frequent use of hanging, especially for theft, in early modern England brought it within the range of possibility for many, in particular poorer, English people. The terror of the gallows fills the pages of *Mr. Badman* as a running warning against leaving the path of virtue: there is a vivid comparison of one damned and complacent with a prisoner condemned to be executed and seeming, by having the irons struck from his legs, to be about to be released; Bunyan also recalls the thief *'upon the Ladder, with the Rope about his Neck ...* (when ready to be turned off by the Hangman)'; in Essex, *'a Doctor of Physick ... and his Whore'*, having committed serial infanticide, *'were hanged for it, in or near to* Colchester'; in a particularly realistic narrative, an habitual thief, 'old *Tod'*, bursts into Hertford assizes 'in a green suit, with his Leathern Girdle in his hand, his Bosom open, and all on a dung sweat', to confess, and is hanged with his wife – a cautionary tale 'pat to our purpose'; in Wellingborough a woman robs her master and, having confessed to Wiseman, is afraid to make restitution lest, in doing so, she be discovered and hang for the offence; in Bedford two church members lapse, so that God 'gave them up to the company of three or four men, that in less than three years time, brought them roundly to the Gallows, where they were hanged like Dogs'.[37]

These capital punishments and the crimes that led to them took place in ordinary marketing and manufacturing towns around the Midlands and the South-East – such as Colchester, Hertford, Wellingborough and Bedford. They were quiet, hard-working places, where the godly were relatively thick on the ground and where there abounded the sort of literate artisans and their families at whom works such as *Mr. Badman* were aimed. Bunyan's theatre of God's judgement is small-town provincial England, embracing his own direct experience. The actuality of the stories was important to Bunyan's didactic purpose. He accepted as a fact of life the casual frequency of capital punishment for larceny, lacking Fox's more socially radical critique of executions for petty theft.[38] His purpose was not to end capital punishment, but to keep his readers, so to speak, from the gallows. The commonness of hangings, plus the fact that, in terms of social class, they were likely to happen to people like his imagined readers, may have convinced Bunyan of the need for caution, prudence, self-control and self-vigilance on the part of those to whom he was preaching this extended sermon – a fondness for the alehouse, for instance, would lead assuredly to the gallows. The need for total probity, especially over money and property, whose theft, Bunyan's record showed, led to hangings, induced him to produce a code of economic ethics for the saints – holding up the dissolute Badman as its antithesis – a code that would shelter them from risky crime, including fraud, and protect their commercial and industrial interests.[39]

The foundations of good, cautious business practice were to be laid during an artisan's or trader's apprenticeship. In Stuart England, Nonconformists, typically coming from the social strata in which apprenticeship, was the principal avenue to a livelihood, took this institution of medieval craft origin, injected it with their own values, and adapted it to strengthen bonds within their various denominations.[40] For Bunyan, apprenticeship was suffused with ideals of moral and religious nurture: the good master acted as much in the role of a godly superintendent as in that of a professional trainer. Such a master's home was a church in miniature, a place of '*praying ... reading of Scriptures,* and *hearing,* and *repeating* of Sermons'.[41] Thus trained in sober and religious habits, the godly youth (though not Badman) was equipped to avoid the self-indulgence, extravagance and incaution that led to debt and the debtors' prison, for – in the eyes of Quakers as well as in Bunyan's church – debt deliberately or carelessly acquired was the greatest of economic offences, leaving creditors in need and exposing oneself and one's family to risk and poverty.[42] Unlike Badman, but like that *petit bourgeois* archetype, the Georgian Quaker William Stout of Lancaster,[43] the Nonconformist in trade must avoid the time-wasting, money-wasting gregarious blandishments of the alehouse, with its flattering spongers driving their victim – 'Jack-pay-for-all' – steadily into poverty; Bunyan may not have been an *habitué* of the 'alehouse culture', but he knew how to capture the atmosphere of the place.[44] As well as abstaining from the pleasure principle, unlike Badman, who 'was naturally given to Idleness', the Nonconformist in trade must work diligently in his calling.[45]

The trouble with the calling, and with staying for life in 'the place and Calling into which he was put by his Parents' – a kind of vocational predestination – was that it might result in poverty, even though the trader '*wrought hard, and fared meanly, been civilly apparelled*'. Perhaps God was punishing such a one 'with leanness, and hunger, and meanness, and want' for failure to 'improve' on an initial 'good dispensation' to him. The trader so punished should accept his poverty, for a 'poor condition has preventing mercy attending of it' – preventing, that is to say, the sins of the rich.[46]

Bunyan was operating within assumptions about work and wealth that Calvin would have endorsed: the ideal of modest sufficiency, suspicion of riches, acceptance of or even reverence for poverty. Bunyan, like Calvin, had in mind a world of small-town traders and artisans whose prosperity or poverty depended on their own efforts and frugality – and on God's dispensation towards each of them. In contrast, Badman aims for spectacular riches by following the markets. A speculator, he watches tax rates and recessions – 'the Badness of the times' – and takes advantage of the opportunities of a proto-capitalist economy, especially 'the new Engine of *Breaking*', which was the systematic exploitation of bankruptcy. Bunyan knew how such businesses operated – perhaps as a craftsman he had been cheated – and showed how Badman could get his creditors to accept repayment terms of 25 per cent. His schemes were successful, at least in the short term, making him wealthier 'by several thousands of pounds'.[47]

What lessons were to be learned by Bunyan's readers from his contrasting portrayal of an honest and, possibly, poor trader, and of a dishonest and wealthy player of markets? Sharrock was surely right to say that in *Mr. Badman* Bunyan 'gives us the first literary example of the late Puritan principle that personal dissoluteness is bad for business'.[48] In the longer term, Badman and his second wife become 'as poor as *Howlets*'. Whether or not his wealth was acquired legally, it was got dishonestly, and dishonest wealth perished: 'They get nothing that cozen and cheat.'[49]

Badman's fall from sensational wealth – at the height of his fortunes he was at least a millionaire in modern values – to destitution contained object lessons in prudence. Overnight fortunes were likely to be picked up as a result of chance, rather than as a result of God blessing His favoured ones with modest affluence. The Quaker William Stout delighted in observing the dizzy ascents and precipitous collapses of merchants who overreached themselves. The solution lay in prudence over the long term, underpinned by the expertise of senior members of the church. The Quaker meetings put such wisdom at the disposal of Friends, and Bunyan provides the same sort of guidance in *Mr. Badman* – 'Good advice', 'Good counsel again'.[50] The advice was not designed for buccaneer capitalism, or intended to make sudden fortunes, like those of the commodity traders whose windfall profits 'usually quickly moulter', but it was aimed at minimizing the dangers of risk: 'beware of launching further into the world, than in an honest way … for the further in, the greater fall … And it should put them upon a diligent looking to their steps, that in their going they should hear the Ice crack, they may timely goe back again.'[51]

Bunyan combines the advice available in Nonconformist churches with echoes of economic thinking going back to the Middle Ages, along with the related influences of a 'simple village economy in which the customer's needs came first' and of a closely regulated borough market. Such influences can be detected in Bunyan's treatment of prices, weights, measures and quality, in all of which he had the consumer first in mind. His approach is more reminiscent of Scholasticism than of *laissez-faire* liberalism: 'every man that makes a prey of his advantage upon his neighbours necessities, to force from him more than in reason and conscience, according to the present prizes of things such comodity is worth: may very well be called an Extortioner'. Included amongst those censured are wholesalers who buy cheap and sell dear; money-lenders (the term used, 'Usurers', is both moralistic and backward-looking); pawnbrokers, who are – using another obsolescent pre-individualistic term – the '*pest and Vermin of the Common wealth*'; and the entrepreneur who will 'sell for as much as by *hook* or *crook* he can get for his comodity'. We even have the impression that with Bunyan, as with theologians before the late middle ages, it is commerce itself that is morally suspect: 'There may be and is sin in trading'.[52]

Bunyan, then, seems to espouse a traditional code of economic conduct in which sellers look after the interests of buyers, and in which shortages and buyers' needs and appetites are not exploited and goods are not advertised ('commended'): 'The complete acceptance of a money economy, found a generation later in the novels of Defoe, is truer to the actual development of Dissent, and utterly alien to Bunyan's thought.'[53] In Sharrock's formulation, the crucial word is 'complete', for he argues that the economic casuistry in *Mr. Badman* is 'transitional' between regulated and free-market economics. Despite his insistence that trade be governed by the older ethical and social dictates, Bunyan knows that, in an age of ever-increasing self-interest, his attempt to dictate to the market would be resented: 'Perhaps some will find fault for my medling *thus* with other folks matters.' While Bunyan's acceptance of a market ruled only by its own laws and rhythms may indeed be far from 'complete', it *is* partial, putting him somewhere between regulation and liberalism, and, in one important respect, closer to the latter. This is the case over prices, where Bunyan has to admit that, though the just price might be a desirable notion, God Himself did not set prices, '*but all things that we buy and sell do ebbe and flow, as to price, like the Tide*'. Though Bunyan offers guidance on how to act fairly in the face of price instability, his advice is clichéd or, as Sharrock says, 'vague'. The choice of a tidal image is significant: tides are not controlled by precepts, and only a Canute would try to alter their courses. In a vital area of capitalist economics – the pricing of commodities – Bunyan moved towards a concept of the sovereignty of market forces, in which the acceptable price is the current price, the market price, 'the present price of things'. That said, late medieval Scholastics also approached the somewhat circular perception that the just price might be the price set by competitive traders that purchasers were prepared to pay.[54]

Bunyan's discourse on economics in *Mr. Badman* is lengthy and frequently shuts out Badman completely. Yet Bunyan is an economist despite himself, for his moral goals go far beyond markets. It is his villain who is *homo œconomicus*. Sensual, grasping, egoistic, clever, materialistic, Mr Badman is 'Restoration man' to a tee – like Pepys at his worst – obsessed with 'Trades, Houses, Lands, great Men, great Titles, great places'; as Stuart Sim puts it: 'in his many vices [Badman] is designed to symbolise the Restoration society Bunyan so despised'.[55]

In his views and speech, Badman encapsulates the values and attitudes current in fashionable society in Restoration England. His is the kind of sardonic language used against Nonconformists by judges such as Jeffreys: 'this is your precise Crew'. Espousing a modish scepticism, Badman believes in 'Fortune, ill Luck, Chance', rather than in Providence, and holds that Scripture is the source of all the 'dissensions and discords that are in the Land'. However, though he professes to believe that conventicles conceal 'uncleanness', with his godly parents and apprenticeship in a religious home, Badman is an apostate from the church of saints, like members of Bunyan's congregation who deserted and, indeed, turned against it after the Restoration. Badman did not only abandon the church, but went from apostate to traitor, and enlisted as an informer, like one of those who profited from the second Conventicle Act. There was widespread repudiation of persecution, especially in places like Bedford, where, as we saw, an attempt to enforce the second Conventicle Act in the year of its passage, 1670, brought the town to a standstill. Bunyan must have had such events in mind when he recounted how Badman had to restrain his informing activities because he was 'a Tradesman' and 'must live by his neighbours'. Sharrock commented that 'sympathy for the persecuted was general at [a] middle class level'.[56] In such circumstances, the role of informers in enforcing the hated statute and, in effect, compelling magistrates to enforce it (since justices faced heavy fines for refusing to act on information of conventicles) was indispensable, and they were all the more detested by the Nonconformist community for that role. Richard Greaves vividly describes the Dissenters' attacks on informers. In terms of morale, though, reprisals on these foes seen to be taken by God were more satisfying to the Nonconformists than their own acts of self-defence. Bunyan's tales of the misfortunes of informers – for example, one who was bitten by a dog, causing gangrene, so that 'His flesh rotted from off him before he went out of the world' – closely parallel similar accounts compiled by the Quakers. 'There can be no pleasure in the *telling* of such stories', Bunyan piously observed, but he had to admit that 'to hear of them may do us a pleasure', since they confirmed that God both judged and avenged the enemies of His people.[57]

Bunyan's estrangement from the tone of Restoration society extended to its styles of dress. Though he was forced to admit the allure of the 'bewitching and tempting' sartorial sensuality of an England released from decades of restraint, he condemned, in terms that sound churlish, or, as Forrest and Sharrock say, 'brutal', the 'naked shoulders, and Paps hanging out like a Cows bag'. He was concerned, though perhaps not too ardently, to prevent his fellow-professors from drifting into stylish fashions, '*light and wanton Apparrel ... Gold, and Pearls, and costly array*'. However, unlike the Quakers, who for long preserved an archaic stereotype of 'Puritan' dress, the Baptists and Independents acquired no sectarian uniform, beyond general strictures on simplicity, and these, clearly, were being disregarded as a consequence of the increasing affluence of some members; even '*good Ministers*' encouraged them, with the excuse that 'their *Parents*, their *Husbands*, and their *breeding* calls for it'. Bunyan was not alone among Nonconformists in calling for a burning of the vanities, but he also seems to have been aware that on issues such as cosmetics and jewellery he was fighting a losing battle and would be ignored as a 'dull sounding Ramshorn', while his church members went 'deckt and bedaubed with their Fangles and Toyes', and 'painted persons' attended worship. Some of the influences of Restoration fashion were invading the gathered churches and Bunyan seems to have been half-resigned to the fact; there is perhaps rueful humour in Wiseman's recollection of a woman member's reply to her 'reproof' for wearing 'fond and gaudy garment', that '*The Tailor would make it so.*'[58]

Bunyan also deprecated current trends in the area of marriage, deploring freedom of choice as a stalwart partiarchalist: 'It is too much the custom of young people now ... to make their own Choyce.' He is especially concerned with the pastoral issue of mixed marriages: 'a deadly thing indeed, and therefore, by the Word of God, his people are forbid to be joyned in marriage with them [outsiders]'. Badman's first wife is an undeveloped character, with few traits beyond her piety, but, if she has a fault, it is her 'unadvisedness' in relying on 'her own poor, raw, womanish Judgment', in not taking the counsel of the church and 'a Godly Minister or two' before marrying Badman. To prevent such imprudence, Bunyan proposed a system of congregational consultation, somewhat along the lines of the Quaker arrangements for approving of members' marriages, though with control exercised not by both male and female Friends, but by 'Godly and Judicious, and unbiassed men'.[59]

Mismatched through her imprudence, heartbroken by her husband's sins, Badman's wife approaches her great scene, her death, which is reminiscent of the medieval *artes moriendi*, in that she 'dyed bravely', having forgiven Badman and made an edifying speech. In its pathos, Badman's wife's dying speech – 'I am thy dying wife ... thou wilt never see me more with comfort ... And with that she wept, the Children (also) wept ... Children, said she, I am going from you' – looks forward to the eighteenth- and nineteenth-century novel, whereas a pious fantasy about a '*godly old Puritan*' being accompanied to heaven by '*the melodious Notes of Angels*' has the feel of a medieval *exemplum*. However, the story of the angelic transport of one of the elect underlines the same message as is contained in the small theatre of Bunyan's wife's death: the assurance of their salvation.[60]

In contrast, Badman was to go to his death not with due assurance, but 'wholly at quiet', in a deluding state of presumption. The fatal insouciance of his *modus moriendi* was part of God's design to trap him, to seal his damnation through his lack of recognition of his plight: 'God gave him up *now* to a reprobate mind, to hardness and stupidity of Spirit ... the saddest Judgement that can overtake a man.' Thus, the deity deprived him of even that 'sence and sight of his sin ... [whereby] he might repent and be saved'. The double bind was that, even had Badman had some awareness of his sin, it would still have been insufficient, falling short of the exacting requirements of perfect contrition, which involved not just crying out to God, but required the penitent to 'cry to God for mercy', and not only to cry, but to do the right sort of crying – 'strong crying, hearty crying'. The terrible anguish of Faustus's: 'O, I'll leap up to my God: who pulls me down?' might have been met in the case of Badman with the reply that 'God pulls him down.'[61] Badman's death, and the elimination of any chance of his being saved by contrition, represent an application to one case of the doctrine of reprobation in its most relentless form. Since evil reprobates have no prospect of anything but damnation, any repentant strategies they adopt are inevitably rendered futile. Thus, Badman's brother had *seemed* to achieve a form of contrition: 'his Conscience began to be awakened, and he began to roar out of his ill-spent Life'. However, whereas Badman went to his death in a state of heedless tranquillity, his brother's problem was the opposite – despair, evident in his (entirely appropriate) distrust of God's mercy. Despair or presumption: for those foreordained to eternal death it hardly mattered, though what in a good person might have appeared to be presumption was in fact assurance (as with Bunyan's wife), while a good person's anxiety was an entirely proper 'consternation of spirit', or 'agony of spirit'. On the other hand, 'if a man that has all his dayes lived in notorious sin, dyeth quietly ... that is an uncontrollable proof of his damnation' – and, we might add, if a sinner died in terror, that too was 'uncontrollable proof of his damnation': predestined sinners were not sup-posed to win.[62]

Badman and his ilk were caught in a terrible trap: his first glimpse of awareness of his sins had no fruits, for 'he only had guilt for his sinful actions', not for his sinful state, so that his guilt was inadequate; and, at the last, God deprived him even of that indispensable (though insufficient) sense of his sin. His case and that of his brother showed that both an excess and a shortage of confidence merely confirmed the damnation of the sinner. Sinful man was blocked in, his exits sealed off by God's tactic of closing off options. Because the *deus ex machina* was in control of the plot from before the beginning of the action, the deaths of sinners could not be true dramas, certainly not in the way that the medieval 'hour of our death' contained conflict of high suspense and uncertain conclusion. With the omnipotent Augustinian-Calvinian God involved, there were no dramatic surprises in those predestinate last hours, which only confirmed sovereign and eternal decrees. It will come as no surprise that, as we saw in our discussion of *One Thing is Needful*, Bunyan repudiated the tradition of final repentance: 'I must confess I am no admirer of sick-bed repentance'. The deathbed admittedly furnished some material for reflection, but none for any air of uncertainty. Bunyan had at his conceptual disposal none of the sacramen-tal machinery, the conviction of free will and choice, the acceptance of accumulated personal merit, that had in the middle ages made possible the depiction of the *hora mortis* as a time of the tensest imaginable battle for a soul. In Bunyan's predestinarian view, as the hour of a sinner's death approached, God, as it were, agreed to put up no struggle and, giving the devil his due, surrendered the sinner to Satan – an almost Manichean idea of the devil's sphere: 'let the Devil enjoy them peaceably, let him carry them out of the world unconverted quietly'. It was, though, by God's sovereign will that the devil claimed his victims. Angry and vengeful – 'God will be even with wicked men' – God moves in to close all Badman's escape routes: 'he had a mind to damn [Badman] for his sins, and therefore would not let him see nor have a heart to repent for them, lest he should convert, and his damnation, which God had appointed, should be frustrate'. However, for the trap to work best – it is Bunyan who uses the phrase 'Snares and Traps to wicked men' – the fate of the damned must be kept from them until the last possible moment, at which point the full horror of what awaits them can at last be revealed: 'Oh! when they see they must shoot the Gulf and Throat of Hell!'[63]

Bunyan's literary technique in *Mr. Badman* is strong rather than subtle. Aiming to draw the most realistic picture of his central character – 'Here ... *thou hast him lively set forth as in* Cutts' – he chooses direct and forceful language, emphasizing smell, as in the account of how, after his death, Badman '*is not buried as yet, nor doth he stink*'. The sustained note of horror, which is the single most prominent feature of the narration, is maintained through the use of such language: the ageing Badman declined, 'consumptive ... surfeited ... [gouty] ... with a tang of the Pox in his bowels'; he died in an odour of unsanctity, with 'a spice of the foul disease upon him'. There is also pictorial vividness: the young Badman 'would stand gloating, and hanging down his head in a sullen, pouching manner'.[64]

Sometimes the narrative draws back from its own horror: during one particularly chilling story – of an adulterous woman who sees the devil at her deathbed – Attentive squeamishly exclaims: '*These are sad storyes, tell no more of them now*'. Exclamatory language is a notable feature of the book's style. Attentive asks if Wiseman has more to say about Badman, and receives the answer: 'More! we have yet scarce throughly begun'. When Attentive asks about Badman's need to go bankrupt, Wiseman's exclamatory response is almost violent: '*Need!* What do you mean by *need?*' Acting as a chorus, Attentive cries out, '*Oh! Sirs! what a wicked man was this!*' and denounces Badman with 'A professor! and practice such *villainies* as these!' A particularly powerful series of exclamatory perorations brings the book to a close.[65]

The work's metaphorical structure also tends to the horrific and the immediate: Badman 'swarmed with sins, even as a Begger does with Vermin'; an old drunkard 'will sleep till he dies, though he sleeps on the top of a Mast'. More contrived images – a cockatrice's den, a boar hunt, the 'horns of the golden Altar', all of which are found less often in the Bedfordshire countryside than verminous beggars and slumbering drunkards – are taken, unacknowledged, from such Old Testament sources as Isaiah, Psalms and Exodus.[66]

The English used in *Mr. Badman* is vernacular and idiomatic. Corrupt professors are 'slithy, rob-Shop, pick-pocket men'. Those who would 'boggle' at sin, Badman would term 'Fools and Noddies', 'frighted with the talk of unseen Bug-bears'. When he wanted to endear himself to his wife, he would address her, in enduring Midland parlance, as 'his *duck*'. If Badman was inclined to charge his wicked second wife with her infidelities, she would 'lay in his dish' his own indiscretions; when it came to their worldly goods, in her extravagance she could 'whirl them about as well as he'; they became 'as poor as *Howlets*', having 'brought their *Noble* [ten shillings] to *Ninepence*'.[67]

The dialogue form is, on the whole, successfully sustained. Throughout, Wiseman prompts and encourages Attentive, and vice versa. Sharrock pointed out a passage in which Bunyan loses control of his dialogue form: '*Atten. I take the liberty to speak thus of Mr. Badman, upon a confidence of what you, Sir, have said of him, is true.*' Later, Bunyan gets round a certain repetitiveness on his own part by devising an absent-minded and inattentive Attentive: 'I told you before, but it seems you forgot.'[68] There are points at which the dialogue falls flat: a lyrical celebration of Sunday – 'an Emblem of the heavenly Sabbath above' – evokes the woefully inadequate response: '*There may be something in what you say*'. There is also some implausibility in the plot, as when young Badman's wicked companions try to dissuade him from covetousness, or when he decides to attend godly sermons 'for novelties sake'. Such minor faults apart, in *Mr. Badman* Bunyan achieves considerable success in combining a horror story with an essay in Reformed soteriology.[69]

The Holy War

In 1682 Bunyan published *The Greatness of the Soul*, a reflection on death and the afterlife originally preached as a sermon at Pinners' Hall. Then, in 1682, came *The Holy War*, an allegorical basis for which was the political battle in Restoration England for the control of the nation's cities and boroughs and especially for their key role as parliamentary constituencies.[70] With the destruction of the first Whig party in and after 1681, this long-running struggle was renewed, with the crown and its Tory allies gaining ascendancy in urban government. Mansoul in *The Holy War* is modelled on a chartered borough for whose mastery rival forces contend politically and militarily. The book's language is of corporation personnel, charters and civic documents. An issue that confronts us is the extent to which *The Holy War* is, as some writers have supposed, a political satire on a vital ingredient of the Tory Reaction, the assumption of control over municipal government by the monarchy and the Tories. We need to establish the degree of alignment between the allegorical content of the book and what was happening politically to English towns in the earlier 1680s. To do this, we shall, first, summarize briefly the narrative of *The Holy War* and then review the crown and Tory 'borough policy' of the Tory Reaction. We may then be able to judge the extent of the allegorical dependence of this work on a phase of political history.

In *The Holy War*'s narrative Satan – Diabolus – and the rebel angels plan to outwit the victorious God – Shaddai – by conquering His new and glorious creation, Mansoul. Diabolus seduces its people, gains entry into and takes over the town and its government, deposing and replacing the recorder, Mr Conscience, and installing a new mayor. Shaddai, however, learns of the fall of Mansoul and agrees to a plan formed by His son, Emmanuel, to liberate the place. An earlier attack splits Mansoul into parties, but following the rejection of Diabolus's peace proposals, Emmanuel mounts a successful recapture. The town is then freely pardoned, the corporation is reconstructed, Diabolus's partisans are punished and a chief secretary is left by Emmanuel to guide the community. Even so, the victory is incomplete. Diabolonians continue to agitate, and after Emmanuel's departure they initiate a fresh campaign of doubt and persecution; a second liberation by Emmanuel ushers in His promise to return once more: 'hold fast till I come'.[71]

Bunyan's foundation for his allegory of the soul is a broad sweep of sacred history surveying the Fall and the Atonement, the decline of Christianity and the persecution of the godly, probably the Reformation and, expectantly, the final coming of Christ.[72] This grand Miltonesque drama is mirrored in struggles taking place within the individual soul, with the alternating victories of temptation and grace, as in *Grace Abounding*. What relationship, then, might this epic have had with the more transitory and political struggle for the English municipalities in the 1680s? Having summarized the bare plot of *The Holy War*, we turn to describe, again in outline, the implementation of governmental and Tory policies on the English towns in the Tory Reaction, so as to establish if, or to what extent, Mansoul, as well as standing for the church and the soul of man, represented an English town – Bedford, perhaps, Whig- and Nonconformist-inclined – under attack from hostile political forces.

In 1681 a London and Middlesex grand jury, empanelled by Whig sherrifs, refused to proceed with the prosecution, set in motion by the crown, of the Whig leader, the Earl of Shaftesbury. The state and its allies in the city replied with a series of manoeuvres that led to Tory dominance in London's hitherto Whig-controlled government, and with a trial in the courts of the charter of self-government of the metropolis, resulting in its forfeiture to the crown in 1683. The constitutional and political collapse of the capital – Europe's greatest city and the nursing mother of Whiggery – ensured that other, lesser boroughs could hardly withstand an offensive aimed at administrative and parliamentary control and centralization directed from Whitehall by officers of the crown, and sustained in the provinces by Tory gentry, urban corporation personnel and Anglican clergy. Using the recall of old charters and the issue of replacements which provided for new crown controls over corporation members, the campaign embraced: (a) a purge of Whigs; (b) their substitution by Tories; (c) a drive towards the electoral control of the parliamentary boroughs, which returned the overwhelming majority of MPs; and (d) a practical and theoretical exercise in absolutism, of which centralization of power is always an essential feature.[73]

It is possible to read *The Holy War* as a satirical parable based on the borough campaign. Himself the inhabitant of an ancient chartered borough, Bunyan knew urban institutions well and was a monitor of current political events; he was, to say the least, no Tory.[74] With a municipal corporation playing the part in this work of man's soul captured by Satan, we see the unfolding of metaphors and the deployment of vocabulary borrowed from the Tory-absolutist methods used for subordinating English town government in the 1680s. Thus, for example, in the 'new-modelling' of Mansoul, and reflecting the large-scale changes in the personnel of English corporations during those years, Diabolus puts out the existing mayor ('Lord *Understanding*') and recorder ('Mr. *Conscience*'), replacing them a new mayor ('Lord *Lustings*') and a new recorder ('*Forget-good*'), along with a new panel of aldermen who were all given the names of vices, from 'Mr. *Incredulity*' to 'Mr. *Atheism*'.[75] At this level *The Holy War* takes on the appearance of a critical commentary on a plan to dominate the English towns, and through them the House of Commons, adopted by the central government and its Tory partners in the 1680s. Other parallels strengthen the impression of a satire on current events: 'a new Oath, and horrible covenant' of loyalty to Diabolus begins to look like the oaths of allegiance and supremacy and the renunciation of the Presbyterian Covenant inserted into the 1661 Corporations Act, which excluded Nonconformists from borough corporations and whose renewed implementation in the early

1680 assisted the purge of Whigs from urban government. Emmanuel, on taking Mansoul, has the members of Diabolus's corporation arrested and reinstates his own mayor, renewing the town's charter, with extra privileges; Mr. Prywell, who uncovers a plot to subvert Mansoul's new allegiance to Emmanuel, has been tentatively identified by both Sharrock and Greaves with Sir Edmund Berry Godfrey, who took the testimony of Titus Oates's Popish Plot in 1678; Greaves hints that the '*Lecture-bell*', which warns the Mansoulians of a Diabolonian coup, is 'perhaps a reference to Nathaniel Vincent's morning-lectures against Popery in Southwark'; while Sharrock suggests that the character of Mr Filth, who introduces 'Odious Atheistical Pamphlets and filthy Ballads & Romances full of baldry' into the Mansoul is a 'hit' at the Tory journalist Roger L'Estrange. I have elsewhere ventured to see in Mansoul's honest recorder, Mr Conscience, a covert allusion to Bedford's pro-Nonconformist deputy-recorder, Robert Audley; the petition that the Mansoulians address to Emmanuel when under threat from Diabolus may have echoes of the mania for party-political petitioning to the crown, which began with the attempt to pressurize Charles II to allow a Whig-dominated Parliament to sit in 1680.[76]

Such a search for hidden, and not so hidden, allusions to political developments can indeed deepen our appreciation of *The Holy War* – provided, though, that we see the work as much more than a satirical political commentary, 'a puritan *Absalom and Achitophel*', little more than a reflection on current events. While it is true that the work focuses 'on both the immediate historical context and the cosmic scale', in this, his most 'deeply meditated' work to date, Bunyan was working on a vast panoramic canvas, 'an epic of the religious history of mankind'; Sharrock rightly suggested resemblances with, or even influences from, *Paradise Lost*. This is a matter of emphasis, but perhaps we should not over-stress *The Holy War*'s character as a satire on an aspect of the Tory Reaction. The book is much more than a coded attack on governmental policies of centralization and Tory control pursued during the early 1680s. For one thing, the methods of control were not in themselves decried: Emmanuel himself is a 'regulator', a political fixer who engineers a massive overhaul of local government upon his capture of Mansoul. Possibly, also, attempts to locate the book too much in the politics of its author's own day may skew our understanding of its overall historical reach. To give an example, it may well be the case that the characters of the 'Bloodmen' – 'a people that have their name derived from the *malignity* of their nature' – are borrowed from the 'Tory persecutors of Nonconformists under Charles II'. However, as the names of their captains – Cain, Nimrod, Ishmael, Esau, Saul, Absalom, Judas and, above all, Pope – tell us, their roles are played out in the work's longer-range and, indeed, apocalyptic, programme, perhaps including the persecution of the saints by Rome before the Reformation; certainly, this schema goes far beyond the immediate context of post-Restoration party politics. It may also be true that *The Holy War* 'gives a remarkably accurate forecast of the gradual downfall of the Bedford corporation'; but if so, it would have to be a very long-range forecast, since, in 1681, when Bunyan wrote *The Holy War*, the 'borough policy' was nearer to its infancy that to its conclusion, and Bedford's new Tory charter would not be issued until 1684.[77]

Arguably, then, the politics of the 1680s provided some, but not too much, of the material for *The Holy War*. The central metaphor of the work, as its title tells us, is not politics, but war; that is to say, it is part of a long Christian tradition, going back to Paul and running, for instance, through Erasmus and his *Enchiridion Militis Christiani*, Loyola and his pervasive military metaphor, General Booth and his Salvation Army, and Baring-Gould with his 'Onward, Christian soldiers'; *The Holy War* is Bunyan's contribution to the tradition of analogy between the Christian life and armed struggle, with the sense of conflict intensified, in Bunyan's case, by a Puritan's awareness of uncompromising polarizations.[78] In his age of protracted religious warfare, both on the Continent in the form of the Thirty Years War, and at home in the shape of the Civil Wars, the idea of militancy for religious belief was more than metaphorical. Bunyan seems to allude to his own involvement in the latter conflict: '*For my part, I (my self) was in the Town.*'[79]

Yet, as with the borrowings in *The Pilgrim's Progress* from the chivalric corpus, the military manoeuvres and technology that Bunyan evokes in *The Holy War* are archaic, and transferred from one literary genre, the romance, to another, the allegory. Few stones and even fewer slings were, at least officially, deployed in the sort of engagement in which Bunyan and numbers of his, now ageing, readers had fought: sappers and canoneers did more to reduce seventeenth-century garrisons and castles than any battering rams out of the tales of derring-do. Likewise, the part played by heraldic banners in *The Holy War* – 'Mr. *Thunder* ... bare the black Colours, and his Scutcheon was the three burning Thunder-Bolts' – bears out the essential unreality of Bunyan's military metaphor, for, once Charles I had raised his gorgeous standard at Nottingham in 1642, in a gesture of conscious nostalgia for a feudal world under attack, armorial flags did not loom large in a conflict that was, on the whole, waged with grim and monochrome doggedness. The splendid colour and glamour that Bunyan could muster in his description of battle – 'O how the Trumpets sounded; their Armor glittered, and how the Colours waved in the wind. The Princes

Armor was all of Gold' – take us, and took Bunyan's readers, a long way from the grey slog of seventeenth-century warfare as it was actually conducted. But the poetic unreality of Bunyan's battle reportage, based on the reading rather than the direct experience of his youth and his choice of an archaic and romanticized military scenery, allowed him to produce an unalloyed literary metaphor of the contest for the soul, without the reader's being sidetracked into seeing his battle scenes as alluding to more recent conflicts.[80]

For all that, *The Holy War* does contain some allusions to less ancient forms of warfare, including references to gunnery. In addition, the religious results of military victories in the Civil Wars are reflected in *The Holy War* in the account of how Emmanuel sets up a preaching ministry in captured Mansoul, made up of four officers, to preach sound doctrine to the corporation in regular lectures – a vivid vignette of plain russet-coated captains, Bible in one hand, sabre in the other, and of the way that parliamentarian victories ushered in godly preaching in English towns. The passage may also suggest that, in Bunyan's historical overview, he accorded a special place to the English Civil War.[81]

Yet, *The Holy War* is not really about the English Civil War – or about the politics of the Tory Reaction – any more than *The Pilgrim's Progress* is about a real journey. Our full understanding of this complex book depends upon our own understanding of metaphor and of Bunyan's use of it. That, in turn, depends on our awareness of which factor is dominant in the duality present in any metaphor, which half is 'serving' and which half is 'being served' – the subject and the predicate of metaphor, so to speak. When we say: 'Shall I compare thee to a summer's day?', we mean to compare the loved one to a lovely day, and not a May day to the loved one; in the dance of metaphor we need to ask which partner is 'leading'. In *The Holy War* the idea of a pardon issued by Emmanuel to the Mansoulians works well because it is based on close observation of the way the English royal prerogative of mercy functioned in the seventeenth century, especially in Bunyan's lifetime, in favour of the Dissenters, emancipated by an extra-legal prerogative of mercy in 1672–3; Bunyan himself hoped to be the recipient of a free pardon in 1661, when, 'at the coronation of kings, there is usually a releasement of divers prisoners'. Whether some Nonconformists were, because of their theological propensity to emphasize unmerited grace and free pardon from God, predisposed intellectually to accept arbitrary pardons from kings, as many did in 1672–3 and 1687–8, is a moot point. The one I wish to make here is that the model of a royal pardon in *The Holy War* is introduced not by way of political commentary on kingship, but so as to lend metaphorical depth and clarity to the idea of God's free forgiveness. To take one further example of the direction in which the metaphors run in *The Holy War*, Bunyan's treatment of a corporate office which was central to the government's policy towards the towns in the 1680s – that of recorder – was not intended to comment on the processes by which recorders were appointed in boroughs, but rather to draw on the paraphernalia of local government to produce a likeness of the function of conscience within man's soul. Thus, *The Holy War* forms, essentially, a Puritan religious metaphor for the struggle for the possession of the individual human soul. It only occasionally and obliquely borrows from, and lends to, an account of current political developments.

Notes

1. James F. Forrest and Roger Sharrock (eds), *The Life and Death of Mr. Badman Presented to the World in a Familiar Dialogue Between Mr. Wiseman, and Mr. Attentive* (Oxford, 1988); also in G. Offor (ed.), *The Works of John Bunyan* (3 vols; Glasgow, 1854), vol. III, pp. 590–665; for a summary of the plot, see Roger Sharrock, *John Bunyan* (London, 1954; reissued 1968), ch. V. For *A Treatise of the Fear of God*, see Richard L. Greaves (ed.), *Miscellaneous Works of John Bunyan*, vol. IX (Oxford, 1981), pp. 5–132 and xxv–xxxiv; also in Offor (ed.), *Works of John Bunyan*, vol. I, pp. 437–91.

2. 'As I was considering with my self what I had written concerning the Progress of the Pilgrim from this World to Glory … It came again into my mind to write, as then, of him that was going to Heaven, so now, of the Life and Death of the Ungodly, and of their travel from this world to Hell': *Mr. Badman*, p. 1; *ibid.*, pp. xii–xiii.

3. Sharrock, *John Bunyan*, p. 106.

4. *Ibid.*, p. 110.

5. Richard L. Greaves, 'To Be Found Faithful: the Nonconformist Tradition in England, 1660–1700', in Greaves, *John Bunyan and English Nonconformity* (London and Rio Grande, OH, 1992), pp. 22–3.

6. The hymn was written for a fast-day, an occasion of collective recollection:

> Alas for Britain and her sons!
> What hath she not to fear?
> The sins that ruined Salem once
> O how triumphant here!

From *Scriptural Hymns by the Rev. Philip Doddridge, D. D* (ed. John Doddridge Humphreys; London, 1839), pp. 152–3: I am indebted for this reference to my friend George Bell.

7. *Ibid.*, p. 102; compare Blake's:

> The Whore & Gambler, by the State
> Licens'd, build that Nation's Fate.
> The Harlot's cry from Street to Street
> Shall weave old England's winding Sheet.
> The Winner's Shout, the Loser's Curse,
> Dance before dead England's Hearse.

from 'Auguries of Innocence' in John Wain (ed.), *The Oxford Library of English Poetry* (3 vols; London, 1987), vol. II, p. 225; and Worsworth's:

> Milton! thou shouldst be living at this hour:
> England hath need of thee; she is a fen
> Of stagnant waters; altar, sword, and pen,
> Fireside, the heroic wealth of hall and bower,
> Have forfeited their ancient English dower
> Of inward happiness.

from 'London, 1802', in *ibid.*, p. 274; and Kipling's:

> Judge of the nations, spare us yet,
> Lest we forget – lest we forget!

from 'Recessional 1897', in *ibid.*, vol. III, pp. 277–8.

8. *Mr. Badman*, pp. 2, 7, 10, 13; Richard L. Greaves, 'John Bunyan and the Changing Face of Popery, 1665–1684', in Greaves, *John Bunyan and English Nonconformity*, pp. 133–4.

9. *Mr. Badman*, p. 49.

10. Keith L. Sprunger, 'English and Dutch Sabbatarianism and the Development of Puritan Social Theology, 1600–1660', *Church History* 51 (1982), pp. 24–38.

11. *Mr. Badman*, p. 54.

12. J. Horsfall Turner (ed.), *The Rev. Oliver Heywood, B.A., 1630–1702; His Autobiography, Diaries, Anecdote and Event Books* (4 vols; Bingley, Yorkshire, 1882–5), vol. I, pp. 355–6; vol. III, p. 195; see also Sprunger, 'English and Dutch Sabbatarianism', p. 24.

13. *Mr. Badman*, p. 7.

14. *Instruction for the Ignorant*, p. 12.

15. *Mr. Badman*, pp. 17, 118.

16. *Ibid.*, p. 17.

17. *Ibid.*, pp. 17, 19, 40, 22.

18. *Ibid.*, pp. 57, 43, 60, 64, 86, 92, 99, 134; for the Quaker variant of 'judgements' against their oppressors, see William Sewel, *The History of the Rise,*

Increase, and Progress of the Christian People called Quakers (2 vols; 5th edn; London, 1811), vol. I, pp. 578-81 and Michael Mullett, *Sources for the History of English Nonconformity 1660-1830* (London, 1991), p. 100; see also U. Milo Kaufmann, 'Spiritual Discerning: Bunyan and the Mysteries of the Divine Will', in N. H. Keeble (ed.), *John Bunyan: Conventicle and Parnassus* (Oxford, 1988), pp. 182-4; for Samuel Clarke's *A Mirror or Looking-Glass both for Saints, and Sinners*, see Lynn Veach Sadler, *John Bunyan* (Boston, MA, 1979), pp. 68, 73, 145, n. 4.

19. *Mr. Badman*, p. 169.

20. For such issues in the disciplinary oversight of the Bedford church, see *Mr. Badman*, pp. xiii–xiv.

21. Michael Watts, *The Dissenters: From the Reformation to the French Revolution* (Oxford, 1978), p. 313 (quoting A. G. Matthews); *Mr. Badman*, pp. 24-6; *Grace Abounding*, pp. 9-10; John Brown, *John Bunyan: His Life, Times and Work* (2nd edn; London, 1886), p. 312.

22. *Mr. Badman*, pp. 24-5 ; Sharrock, *John Bunyan*, p. 100; *Grace Abounding*, p. 11.

23. *Ibid.*; *Mr. Badman*, pp. 26, 27-37, 5-9. For condemnations of swearing in Dent's *The Plaine Mans Path-Way to Heaven*, see *Mr. Badman*, p. xvi.

24. *Mr. Badman*, pp. 27, 29, 30, 7.

25. *Grace Abounding*, pp. 10-11, 14-15, 17-25; *Mr. Badman*, p. 29.

26. *Mr. Badman*, pp. 30, 31, 35, 32-7. For Bunyan's sense of the power of words, see also Maxine Hancock, 'Bunyan as Reader: The Record of *Grace Abounding*', *Bunyan Studies* 5 (1994), esp. pp. 76-80.

27. James Crossley (ed.), *Pott's Discovery of Witches in the County of Lancaster, 1613* (*Chetham Society*, 1st series, vol. VI; 1845), S2. For belief in natural and supernatural cause and effect, see *Mr. Badman*, pp. xx–xxi.

28. For drunkenness among members of Nonconformist churches, see Mullett, *Sources*, pp. 27, 37, 54; and for 'uncleanness', see *ibid.*, pp. 28, 86; *Mr. Badman*, pp. 45-7.

29. *Ibid.*, pp. 48-50.

30. *Ibid.*, pp. 49-50.

31. *Ibid.*, pp. 54-5.

32. *Ibid.*, pp. 52-3.

33. *Ibid.*, p. 51; Bunyan's source, Job 31: 3, refers only to a 'strange punishment'.

34. James Amelhang (ed. and trans.), *A Journal of the Plague Year: The Diary of the Barcelona Tanner Miquel Parets 1651* (Oxford and New York, 1991); see also *Mr. Badman*, pp. xix–xxvi.

35. *Mr. Badman*, p. 50; Sharrock, *John Bunyan*, p. 111.

36. For Bunyan's itinerancy, see Richard L. Greaves, 'John Bunyan and Nonconformity in the Midlands and East Anglia', in Greaves, *John Bunyan and English Nonconformity*, p. 99; *Mr. Badman*, pp. 64, 65, 68, 69, 132, 87; for highwaymen, see Peter Burke, *Popular Culture in Early Modern Europe*

(Aldershot, Hants, 1994), pp. 165–6, and Frank McLynn, *Crime and Punishment in Eighteenth-Century England* (London and New York, 1989), p. 77; for the representation of exemplary moral drama in literature, see Lincoln B. Faller, *Turned to Account: The Form and Function of Criminal Biography in Late Seventeenth- and Early Eighteenth-Century England* (Cambridge, Melbourne and New York, 1987), ch. 1. The highwayman interval in *Mr. Badman* brings the book close to the picaresque tradition to which some commentators have aligned it: see *Mr. Badman*, p. xxvi.

37.   *Mr. Badman*, pp. 165, 22, 53, 23, 38, 48, 44.

38.   John L. Nickalls (ed.), *The Journal of George Fox* (Cambridge, 1952), pp. 65–6.

39.   For the economic thought in *Mr. Badman*, see Jack Lindsay, *John Bunyan: Maker of Myths* (London, 1937; reprinted New York, 1969), ch. 23 and p. 211 (*Mr. Badman* is 'the great bourgeois novel'); E. Beatrice Batson, *John Bunyan: Allegory and Imagination* (London and Canberra, 1984), ch. 4 – 'Central to Bunyan's position is his belief that making money without working for it militates against the building of a strong Christian character' (p. 64); and Christopher Hill, *The English Bible and the Seventeenth-Century Revolution* (London, 1993), p. 158 – 'Bunyan [wrote] *Mr. Badman* to teach the godly how to behave in [the] perplexing world of the capitalist market'; see also *Mr. Badman*, pp. xxx–xli.

40.   For the Quaker apprenticeship system, see Michael A. Mullett, *Radical Religious Movements in Early Modern Europe* (London, 1980), pp. 130–1.

41.   *Mr. Badman*, p. 60.

42.   Reiterated Quaker advice 'that the payment of just debts be not delayed by any professing truth' (1692) and solicitude that Friends discharge 'their contracts and just debts in due time, so as to ... avoid open scandal and reproach on the Society' (1732) typify much Nonconformist thinking on the subject: *Extracts from the Minutes and Epistles of the Yearly Meeting of the Religious Society of Friends* (London, 1861), pp. 93, 101. In 1677 Bunyan's church 'withdrew Communyan' from a member 'for contracting many debts which he nether was able nether did he so honestlye and Christianly take care to pay his creditors in due time as he oght': quoted in *Mr. Badman*, pp. xiii–xiv.

43.   J. D. Marshall (ed.), *The Autobiography of William Stout of Lancaster, 1665–1752* (*Chetham Society*, 3rd series, vol. VI; 1967), p. 21.

44.   *Mr. Badman*, p. 64; for the social life of the alehouse, see Paul Clark, 'The Alehouse and the Alternative Society', in D. Pennington and K. Thomas (eds), *Puritans and Revolutionaries: Essays in Seventeenth-Century History Presented to Christopher Hill* (Oxford, 1978), pp. 47–72.

45.   *Mr. Badman*, p. 65.

46.   *Ibid.*, pp. 93, 94.

47.   A. Biéler, *La Pensée économique et sociale de Calvin* (Paris, 1961), pp. 310–11, 317; *Mr Badman*, pp. 88–9.

48. Sharrock, *John Bunyan*, p. 110.

49. *Mr. Badman*, pp. 88–91, 148, 106 (margin); 'howlets' are young owls.

50. Marshall (ed.), *Autobiography of William Stout*, pp. 144–6, 156, 200–10; *Mr Badman*, pp. 92–3.

51. *Ibid.,* pp. 109, 99; in the late seventeenth and early eighteenth centuries Quaker Yearly Meetings warned 'that none trade beyond their ability nor stretch beyond their compass', that none 'launch forth into trading and worldly business beyond what they can manage honourably and with reputation', that none 'overcharge themselves with too much trading and commerce, beyond their capacities to discharge with a good conscience towards all men;', and 'that friends be very careful to avoid all pursuit after the things of this world, by such ways and means as depend too much on hazardous enterprises': *Rules of Discipline of the Religious Society of Friends with Advices of their Yearly Meeting* (3rd edn; London, 1834), pp. 268–9.

52. Sharrock, *John Bunyan*, p. 111; *Mr. Badman*, pp. 108, 110, 113 (margin); R. H. Tawney, *Religion and the Rise of Capitalism: A Historical Study* (London, 1926), pp. 34–7.

53. *Mr. Badman*, pp. 111–15 ; Sharrock, *John Bunyan*, p. 112. Where Bunyan subordinated economic drives to ethical imperatives, Defoe tended to evaluate moral issues in terms of their economic repercussions; thus a merchant's unfaithfulness in a love affair was deplored for the harm it did to his business 'credit': Daniel Defoe, *The Complete English Tradesman* (New York, 1970), pp. 157–8; see also Richard Schlatter, *The Social Ideas of Religious Leaders 1660–1688* (London, 1940), pp. 214–16.

54. Sharrock, *John Bunyan*, pp. 110, 111; *Mr. Badman*, pp. 110, 115; Tawney, *Religion and the Rise of Capitalism,* pp. 40–1, 295–6.

55. *Mr. Badman*, p. 153; Stuart Sim, '"Safe for Those for Whom it is to be Safe": Salvation and Damnation in Bunyan's Fiction', in Anne Laurence, W. R. Owens and Stuart Sim (eds.), *John Bunyan and His England 1628–1688* (London and Ronceverte, WV, 1990), p. 154; also Sim, 'Isolating the Reprobate: Paradox as a Strategy for Social Critique in *The Life and Death of Mr. Badman*', *Bunyan Studies* 1, 2 (1989), esp. pp. 30–1, 40.

56. *Mr. Badman*, pp. 128, 127, 79: compare Jeffreys' hectoring of Baxter – 'this is your presbyterian cant': N. H. Keeble (ed.), *The Autobiography of Richard Baxter* (London and Melbourne, 1974), p. 262; Brown, *Bunyan*, pp. 206, 218–20; Sharrock, *John Bunyan*, p. 110.

57. For the second Conventicle Act, see J. P. Kenyon (ed.), *The Stuart Constitution: Documents and Commentary* (Cambridge, 1966), pp. 383–6; Greaves, 'To Be Found Faithful', pp. 15–16; *Mr. Badman*, pp 82–3; for Fox's account of 'several strange and sudden judgements … upon conspirators against me', see Nickalls (ed.), *The Journal of George Fox*, p. 180.

58. *Mr. Badman*, pp. 122–5 and xviii.

59. *Mr. Badman*, pp. 67, 72, 73; Batson, *John Bunyan*, p. 62; for ideas of marriage in *Mr. Badman*, see Schlatter, *Social Ideas of Religious Leaders*, p. 17;

on male hegemony in Baptist churches, see J. F. McGregor, 'The Baptists: Fount of all Heresy', in J. F. McGregor and B. Reay (eds), *Radical Religion in the English Revolution* (Oxford, 1984), p. 47; for the Quaker system of control of weddings, see Michael Mullett, '"The Assembly of the People of God": The Social Organisation of Lancashire Friends', in Mullett (ed.), *Early Lancaster Friends* (Centre for North-West Regional Studies, Occasional Paper, No. 5; Lancaster, 1978), pp. 13–15.

60. *Mr. Badman*, pp. 141–2, 143, 144; for the medieval conventions of 'dying well', see Philippe Ariès, *At the Hour of Our Death* (trans. Helen Weaver; Harmondsworth, 1981), pp. 14–18, 106–10.

61. *Mr. Badman*, pp. 157, 150, 153, 154; Christopher Marlowe, *Doctor Faustus*, V, ii.

62. *Mr. Badman*, pp. 160, 161; for *Mr. Badman*'s place in the tradition of the 'four last things', see *Mr. Badman*, pp. xxix–xxx.

63. *Mr. Badman*, pp. 138, 162, 163, 164, 169; Ariès, *The Hour of Our Death*, pp. 123, 607; Lynn Veach Sadler suggests that Bunyan was setting out to correct the tendency of 'some of the brethren [who] had gone so far as to use deathbed actions as indications of election or reprobation and ... both writers and readers needed to be reminded that God's ways are inscrutable': *John Bunyan*, p. 72.

64. *Mr. Badman*, pp. 3, 2, 148, 21; for the use of smell in *Mr. Badman*, see Veach Sadler, *John Bunyan*, p. 144, n 2.

65. *Mr. Badman*, pp. 53, 83, 89, 90, 98 ; for exclamatory dialogue, see Batson, *John Bunyan*, p. 58.

66. *Mr. Badman*, pp. 24, 46, 5, 141.

67. *Ibid.*, pp. 97, 84, 136, 145, 148.

68. *Ibid.*, pp. 147, 26, 48; Roger Sharrock, *John Bunyan*, p. 113.

69. *Mr. Badman*, pp. 25–6, 127; the book's place in literary history, and especially in the evolution of the novel, has received comment: Richard Church saw 'a picture of a worldly financial rogue, ... drawn with a subtle detail worthy of the great novelists of the eighteenth and nineteenth centuries': *The Growth of the English Novel* (London, 1951; reprinted 1968), pp. 35–6; James Sutherland appreciated 'a brilliant transfer of English middle-class life in the seventeenth century ... in hard, bright colours. The dialogue has ... a coarse vitality that it would be hard to parallel elsewhere': *English Literature in the Late Seventeenth Century* (Oxford, 1969), pp. 333–5.

70. James Forrest and Roger Sharrock (eds), *The Holy War made by Shaddai upon Diabolus* (Oxford, 1980), with 'Introduction', pp. ix–xxxix: also in Offor (ed.), *Works of John Bunyan*, vol. III, pp. 253–373; for *The Greatness of the Soul, And unspeakableness of the Loss thereof*, see Richard L. Greaves (ed.), *Miscellaneous Works of John Bunyan*, vol. IX (Oxford, 1981), pp. 137–245 and xxxiv–xxxix; also in Offor (ed.), *Works of John Bunyan*, vol. I, pp. 104–50.

71. For a plot summary, see Sharrock, *John Bunyan*, pp. 121–3.

72. For the historical span of *The Holy War*, see p. xxviii; on the epic quality of the book, Bowman quotes Tillyard: 'No other work has so good a claim to be called England's Puritan epic': *John Bunyan*, p. 85; John R. Knott, in '"Thou Must Live Upon My Word": Bunyan and the Bible', in Keeble (ed.) *John Bunyan*, pp. 168–70, firmly anchors the work in Scripture.

73. For a summary of the political developments of the period, with particular reference to Bedford and Bedfordshire, see *The Holy War*, pp. xxi–xxiv.

74. Richard L. Greaves, 'The Spirit and the Sword: Bunyan and the Stuart State', in Greaves, *John Bunyan and English Nonconformity*, pp. 101–26.

75. *The Holy War*, pp. 18, 25, 26.

76. *Ibid.*, pp. 31, 181; Richard L. Greaves, 'Bunyan and the Changing Face of Popery', in Greaves, *John Bunyan and English Nonconformity*, p. 135; Sharrock, *John Bunyan*, p. 126; Mullett, '"Deprived of our Former Place": The Internal Politics of Bedford, 1660–1688', *Bedfordshire Historical Record Society* 59 (1989), pp. 13–14. Hill tentatively suggests that the limping Lord Willbewell in *The Holy War* may be the disabled Shaftesbury, and his clerk, Mr Mind, Shaftsbury's secretary John Locke. Hill adds that *The Holy War* 'is an allegory about the soul of man and about the history of mankind. It is also about the purges and counter-purges which took place in a corporation like Bedford between 1650 and 1682' : Christopher Hill, 'John Bunyan's Contemporary Reputation', in Laurence *et al.* (eds.), *John Bunyan*, pp. 11–12. Although Greaves is convinced of the primacy of soteriological issues in *The Holy War*, he recognizes that the work is also concerned to a considerable extent with current political commentary: 'While the most basic meaning must be soteriological ... the political allusions and the militant imagery combine in an unmistakable indictment of Charles II's government during the bitter conclusion of the exclusion crisis. Diabolus, after all, tyrannises Mansoul as its king, remodelling the corporation, making havoc of the statutes of Shaddai, and spoiling the law books ... The bedrock supporters of Diabolus, the notorious Bloodmen, symbolised the more militant Tories' : Richard L. Greaves, 'Amid the Holy War: Bunyan and the Ethic of Suffering', in Laurence *et al.* (eds), *John Bunyan*, pp. 67–8. Sharrock and Forrest further explore the parallels between the political events of the late 1670s–early 1680s and incidents in *The Holy War* and deal with the variant chronology between the dates of the book's authorship and the implementation of the Tory Reaction in Bedford: see *The Holy War*, pp. xiv–xxv. For the Bedford recorder Robert Audley, see Lindsay, *John Bunyan*, pp. 214–16 ; Lindsay had no doubts about the political identifications in *The Holy War*: 'Diabolus is seen to be Charles II' (*ibid.*, p. 216).

77. *The Holy War*, p. 228; Mullett, '"Deprived of our Former Place"', pp. 36, 22–3; Greaves, 'Bunyan and the Changing Face of Popery', p. 135; Sharrock, *John Bunyan*, pp. 118, 121, 122, 125, 127. Forrest and Sharrock argue that Bunyan was able to sketch out the likely fate of Bedford on the

basis of the capitulation of such places as neighbouring Northampton in the early stages of the Tory Reaction: see *The Holy War*, pp. xxiv–xxv; they go on to explore the apocalyptic dimensions of the work in *ibid.*, pp. xxv–xxix. See also Donald Mackenzie, 'Rhetoric versus Apocalypse': The Oratory of *The Holy War*', *Bunyan Studies* 2,1 (1990), pp. 33–43.

78.   Ephesians 6: 10–17. Batson provides a survey of works employing the metaphor of Christian warfare, from the fifth century and the Middle Ages through the sixteenth and seventeenth centuries: *John Bunyan*, p. 72; Veach Sadler, in *John Bunyan*, p. 81, considers seventeenth-century works with *The Holy War*'s theme – in 1639 Thomas Fuller published *The Historie of the Holy Warre*.

79.   *The Holy War*, p. 2; Hill, *The English Bible*, p. 81.

80.   *The Holy War*, pp. 36, 69; the complexity of the heraldic devices is well explored by Batson in *John Bunyan*, p. 81.

81.   *The Holy War*, pp. 139–46.

SEVEN

The Pilgrim's Progress, Part II

The second part of *The Pilgrim's Progress* forms not so much a sequel as a re-working of Part I.[1] Once again, Bunyan opens with the convention of a dream, in which a narrator, Mr Sagasity, begins to recount the progress of Christian's widow to heaven; this redundant device of an intermediary narrator is soon dropped. Christiana receives a letter of invitation from a king, and, with her four sons, is joined by a younger woman, Mercie; attempts by Mrs Timorous to dissuade Christiana from her pilgrimage fail. As they approach the gate, Christiana and Mercie are menaced by '*ill-favoured ones*' and are saved by the Reliever. A visit to the House of the Interpreter involves instruction, a meal and a bath. Leaving the Interpreter's house, the party, in the custody of their guide, Great-heart, proceed to the Hill Difficulty, passing Simple, Sloth and Presumption, all of whom have been executed. Lions outside the Palace Beautiful are abetted by a giant, Grim, who is slain by Great-heart. The pilgrim group stays a month at the Palace, where they are looked after by Providence and Charity, who instruct Christiana's sons. Mercie is 'offered love' by Mr Brisk, who 'pretended to religion'; Mathew, one of Christiana's sons, develops acute stomach cramps from having eaten forbidden fruit, and is cured by pills made from the flesh and blood of Christ. The pilgrims pass, with relative ease, through the Valley of Humiliation, and the Valley of the Shadow of Death, where Great-heart provides stalwart guardianship. A new giant, Maul, is decapitated by Great-heart and the group is gradually joined by Honest, Valiant-for-truth, Feeble-mind, Fearing and Ready-to-halt. The pilgrims stay at the house of Gaius, again for about a month; there is hospitality and further instruction, in the form of a quiz. Mathew marries Mercie and another son marries Gaius's daughter Phebe; an excursion is mounted to kill the giant Slay-good. Mr. Mnason is the pilgrims' host in the town of Vanity Fair. Great-heart leads a raid to take Doubting Castle and make an end of Giant Despair. In a magnificent climax, the pilgrims cross the River of Death, one by one, to pass into the Promised land.[2]

Given the centrality of female characters in the second part of *The Pilgrim's Progress* – 'A FEMALE PILGRIM'S PROGRESS' – discussion has turned on the book's underlying attitude to women. In contrast to *The Holy War*, in which the whole vast action and long list of characters are male-dominated (apart from the fleeting Lady Fear-nothing), or *Mr. Badman*, in which woman is shown as temptress, evil schemer or passive and colourless saint, women in *The Pilgrim's Progress*, Part II, have active and positive roles. That is why the work has so often been acclaimed as a book in favour of women, especially in their religious capacity. Victorian commentators were particularly enthusiastic about the book's importance in this respect. Offor cited a view that '[t]he Second Part is peculiarly adapted to direct and encourage female Christians'. Brown wrote of the way the book balanced 'the record of the religious life in man by the story of that same life as it shows itself in woman', and went on to endorse a suggestion that the two women characters reflected Bunyan's two wives.[3]

More recent commentators have also explored the possibilities for greater recognition of women in Part II of *The Pilgrim's Progress*. Lynn Veach Sadler sees Bunyan as compensating for an earlier refusal to countenance separate women's church meetings and 'to offset the grim picture of Christian's family in Part I'. Roger Sharrock describes the 'feminine and practical' atmosphere of Part II, relating it to the key role of women in the revival of the Bedford church in this period. The lone struggle having been accomplished by Christian in Part I, women need no longer be considered as impedimenta. Female friendship, love and empathy replace a rigid soteriological schema as a guide to redemption, especially in the case of Mercie. Keeble is also aware of the strong role given to women in Part II, citing the 'strength of character' that Brown saw as a reflection in Christiana of Bunyan's brave second wife Elizabeth: 'the crucial decisions in Part II', Keeble writes, 'are made by women separate from men: Christiana is a widow and Mercie, unmarried, is not in her father's care ... Is patriarchy, perhaps, one of the giants to be slain on the way to the Celestial City?' Keeble goes on to explore the love and friendship of the two leading women as the basis for their adventure. Mrs Timorous's voicing of patriarchalist cautions is firmly rejected as 'fleshly': 'Pilgrimage', writes Keeble, 'expects – and demands – no less from a woman than a man.' There is a real adventure in Part II – the adventure of women taking on a brave enterprise without displaying 'feminine' timidity. Further, Gaius's encomium of women rebuts that 'misogyny that would brand all women with the culpability of Eve. An androgynous ideal of sanctity' is on offer in this work.[4]

It is indeed the case that the second part of *The Pilgrim's Progress* can present women as strenuous and effective people in control of their destinies. As a character, Christiana is all the stronger in that she is not a self-evidently predestined saint. Initially a lax Christian who had 'hardened both mine own heart and yours' (her children's) against Christian, and who had '*abhorred that Life*' (of a pilgrim), she seems to will herself into a conversion and – Bunyan here apparently setting aside Reformation soteriology – to become the mistress of her fate by choosing to accept her invitation: 'I have now a price put into mine hand to get gain, and I should be a Fool of the greatest size, if I should have no heart to strike in with the opportunity.' Christiana and Mercie deliberately set out – 'design' – 'to attain … excellent Glories'. So dynamic is Christiana that she makes an effective intercession on Mercie's behalf, so that the latter's invitation comes, not directly from the king, but through Christiana. Christiana's former imperviousness to grace – as she tells her sons, 'I have sinned away your Father … I am that Woman that was so hard-hearted' – highlights the power of her change of heart: 'but now I also am come [Christian's way], for I am convinced that no way is right but this'. The employment of the parable of the vineyard further emphasizes the operation of the will in a change of life: 'He answered and said, I will not: but afterwards he repented, and went.'[5] If Christiana is a figure with a self-determining will, she is also one with sufficient doctrinal knowledge, intelligence and teaching skill to bring up her sons to the remarkable level of theological sophistication that they reveal in the course of a catechetical interrogation by Prudence, who tells Christiana: 'You are to be commended for thus bringing up your Children.'[6]

While, as an individual, Christiana possesses strong and effective traits, including a forceful will-power, women at large receive favourable coverage in this work. The virtues Prudence, Piety and Charity are female characters; Gaius delivers an eulogy of women, who are 'highly favoured, and … are sharers with us in the Grace of Life'.[7] Yet, for all that, we need to be aware – as Keeble certainly is – of the limits to Bunyan's liberalism over gender. As Sharrock put it, 'Bunyan's characterisation is guided by conventional seventeenth-century notions of women as the weaker vessel.' Indeed, it would be surprising to find that in this work Bunyan was able suddenly to abandon the patriarchalist views that had guided his thinking throughout his ministry – despite the authority he accorded to the inspired women of Bedford in *Grace Abounding*. We might recall that in that work, and while recognizing his wife's efforts on his behalf, he tended to view her role as that of a messenger who was presenting a petition that he had composed. The case of Agnes Beaumont illustrates the 'roughness' that Bunyan could show towards women, no doubt an outcome of his anxiety to dissociate himself from scandal: '[I]t is a rare thing to see me carry

it pleasant towards a Woman; the common Salutation of a woman I abhor
… Their Company alone, I cannot away with. I seldom so much as touch
a Womans Hand.'[8]

Bunyan voiced male authoritarianism in his pastoral tract, *Christian
Behaviour*, published in the same year as the Beaumont incident. In that
work, the cold, smug, silent and distant tyranny that Bunyan recommends
to the husband of an 'unbelieving' or 'carnal' wife amounts to a kind of
married divorce, imposed on the marriage by the all-powerful husband:
'When thou speakest, speak to purpose: 'tis no matter for many words,
provided they be pertinent. *Job* in a few words answers his wife, and takes
her off from her foolish talking … Let it all be done without rancor, or the
least appearance of anger.' Then, on the eve of the publication of the second
part of *The Pilgrim's Progress*, Bunyan's *A Case of Conscience Resolved*
(1683) set the scene for the anti-feminism to be found not far beneath
the surface of the 1684 work.[9] This booklet should be seen, along with the
writings on baptism in 1672–4 and *Questions about the Nature and Perpetuity of the Seventh-Day Sabbath* (1685), as part of Bunyan's continuing
contribution, as a leading preacher and church administrator, to debates
about the organized life of the gathered churches. He provided his own
account of how, through the emergence of separate meetings in Bedford and
the encouragement of 'Mr. K.', the issue had arisen: '*Wether, where a Church
of Christ is Situate, it is the Duty of Women of that Congregation, Ordi-
narily, and by Appointment, to Separate themselves from their Bretheren.*'[10]

In rejecting that overture, Bunyan produced a theoretical view of women
in the church, which he developed allegorically in the second part of *The
Pilgrim's Progress*. Both the ecclesiological and the allegorical works praised
women's piety: '*many of your Sex eminent for piety … [T]he love of Women
in Spirituals … oft times out-goes that of Men*'. However, in Bunyan's view,
women's devotional prowess and purely spiritual equality did not qualify
them – quite the reverse – for equal status, and even less for leadership, in
the church. He saw women in terms of the more emotionally based char-
isms, and for that reason, and in patriarchalist terms of control by superior
– male – 'power', rejected their capacity to minister:

To appoint Meetings for divine Worship … *Is an Act of Power:* which
Power, resideth in the Elders in particular, or in the Church in General.
But never in the Women as considered by themselves … Are they to be
the audible mouth there, before all, *to God?* No verily … The Holy
Ghost doth particularly insist upon the inability of Women … They are
forbidden to teach, yea to speak in the Church of God … they are weak,
and not permitted to perform Publick Worship to God.

A *locus classicus* of Judaeo-Christian patriarchalism, Genesis 2, is repeatedly cited to establish women's weakness, especially their proneness to the seductive – male – temptations that had led them in the first place to be beguiled into holding separate meetings: *'Yet I dare not make your selves the Authors of your own miscarriage in this. I do therefore rather impute it to your Leaders; who ... have put you upon a work* so much *too heavy for you.'* [11]

The current of misogyny running through *A Case of Conscience*, and especially the work's insistence on women's weakness, are reincorporated in the second part of *The Pilgrim's Progress*, including a close textual parallel: Bunyan, in *A Case of Conscience*, and his mouthpiece Gaius, in *The Pilgrim's Progress*, both preface the denigration of women's religious role with a conventional and patronizing compliment: what Bunyan says – *"Tis far from me to despise you, or to do anything in your reproach'* – Gaius repeats, with 'I will now speak on the behalf of Women, to take away their Reproach'. In both works there is an appreciation of the place of women in sacred history, especially in their enthusiastic response to Christ, yet, even then, their role is described in the past tense. It was true that women had parity of grace with men – 'are highly favoured, and ... sharers with us in the Grace of Life'. However, the bestowal of grace in the spiritual sphere did not qualify women for any part in the practical affairs of the church. Women remained the weaker vessels and even their strengths represented, as it were, the obverse of their weakness. Despite his acknowledgment of the *'valour and fortitude of minde'* of some female early martyrs, the terms that Bunyan uses of women in both *A Case of Conscience Resolved* and *The Pilgrim's Progress*, Part II, suggest emotional rather than intellectual capacities: women showed spontaneous loyalty towards Christ and wept for him; their virtues were love and piety, a word which has connotations of the emotive religiosity of *pietas* and of the female anguish of the *pietà*. [12]

Bunyan's stress on women's affective capacities – an appreciation which had led him to value the charismatic spirituality of the godly women of Bedford – provided him in this work with an *entrée* into ecstatic modes. In discourse with Great-heart, Christiana breaks into a rhapsody reminding us, perhaps, of Teresa of Ávila: *'methinks it makes my Heart bleed to think that he should bleed for me. Oh! thou loving one, Oh! thou Blessed one. Thou deservest to have me ... Thou deservest to have me all.'* However, it is significant that these almost erotically charged ecstasies follow Great-heart's impressively cerebral discourse on such exacting matters as the 'Natures and Office' of Christ: 'He has two Natures in one Person, plain to be *distinguished, impossible* to be *divided*' – women have hearts and raptures, men have minds and syllogisms. It is all the more typical of Bunyan's view of male intellect and female emotion that the sequel to Christiana's flight is a bumpy landing piloted by Great-heart and offering a reminder of – what were for Bunyan characteristically female – pious emotions; woman was essentially mutable: 'You speak now in the warmth of your Affections, will it, think you, be always thus with you?'[13] Pressing home the patriarchal relationship with an address to 'my Daughters', Great-heart illustrates his remarks by re-telling a nursery story recounted earlier because (the Interpreter had said), 'you are Women, and [such things] are easie for you'. Great-heart has now become the women's male '*Guide, and Conductor*', patiently answering their childlike questions: 'Mercie ... *What are those three men? and for what are they hanged here?*' In contrast to such wide-eyed simplicity, Christiana's sons display an extraordinary intellectual acumen. Where Christiana and Mercie recount dreams, Christiana's son James delivers an articulate ratiocination: 'Prue. *And how doth God the Holy Ghost save thee? Jam.* By his *Illumination,* by his *Renovation,* and by his *Preservation.*' No less implausibly, the second youngest boy explains God's purpose in saving men, another discourses learnedly of God's pre-Creation being, and two of the brothers conduct a dialogue full of wisdom far beyond their years: '*Jam.* No fears, no Grace'. But, though children, these are males and, although Prudence commends Christiana 'for thus bringing up your Children', the truth is that 'The Boys take all after their Father, and covet to tread in his Steps.'[14]

It becomes, then, apparent that the second part of *The Pilgrim's Progress* is about male achievement, operating under the shadow of Christian's manliness in Part I. It is true that Part II is a gentler book than its predecessor – 'more soothing and comforting'. There is in it a hint of refinement: '*There is a desire in Women, to go neat and fine.*' Tender endearments are offered instead of the rough banter of Part I: – 'my Darlings ... sweetheart'. Pleasing domestic details and dainty, if not entirely digestible, meals (for example, one of wine, milk, butter, honey, apples and nuts) recur: 'Now Supper was ready, the Table spread, and all things set on the Board.' Music is heard – 'Excellent Virginals' and 'Musick in the House, Musick in the Heart, and Musick also in Heaven'. Christiana herself sings and plays, minstrels play, accompanying a singer with 'a very fine voice', and a shepherd sings a scriptural song. With its evocation of the deep sisterly love between Christiana and Mercie – 'we will have all things in common betwixt thee and me ... loving *Mercie*' – the work has a loving kindness of tone that is lacking in the stern male militancy of Part I. Yet that masculine pugnacity is also present in Part II, where it serves to highlight the weakness of the female characters who, emotionally adept and intellectually limited, physically feeble and temperamentally timorous, need all the support of male characters, above all the knightly Great-heart, to complete their pilgrimage. In the romances from which the narration was derived a basic plot requirement was the rescue of helpless damsels by stalwart macho knights, but Bunyan adapts that form of story-telling to support a view of the life of the church in which the strong – dominant males – lend their indispensable aid to the winning of spiritual goals by less effective personalities, above all women.[15] We need, then, to appreciate the full extent of the weakness of the females in the narrative action, as well as in the discourses and the character delineations of *The Pilgrim's Progress* – the weakness that Bunyan, in *A Case of Conscience Resolved*, set out as the key disqualifier of women's playing any active role in the affairs of the church.

The first crisis (after Mercie has, somewhat unnecessarily, fainted) that reveals the weakness and vulnerability of the women in the story, and, by extension, of women in human life and the church, is an attempted rape of Mercie and Christiana by 'two very *ill-favoured ones*', at which point the women are rescued by the Reliever. The commentary on this incident exposes the danger in which women without male protection stand, so much so that they are depicted as at fault in going forth without a male guardian: '*being ye knew that ye were but weak Women, that you petitioned not the Lord there for a Conductor: Then might you have avoided these Troubles, and Dangers.*' So culpable was this neglect of theirs that it required a '*Confession of your folly*'; Mercie obliges: '*by this neglect, we have an occasion ministred unto us to behold our own imperfections*'. Keeble comments that the incident and the subsequent dissection of it suggest 'not so much that Christiana and Mercie were vulnerable to attack as that they were in some way responsible, if not guilty, for the attack'.[16]

Bunyan continues to sound that note of feminine weakness in the face of action and peril, the women themselves being fully aware of their feebleness. Mercie takes comfort from the hanging of Simple, Sloth and Presumption, for otherwise '*who knows else what they might a done to such poor Women as we are?*' Threats to the pilgrims from the giant Grim, whose 'Voice frighted the Women', and his lion allies, at whom 'the Women trembled as they passed', bring out the timorousness of the women and the increasing indispensability of Great-heart. Christiana thanks him in the tremulous tones of the rescued maidens in the romances – 'you have fought so stoutly for us' – and Mercie adds, 'How can such poor Women as we, hold out in a way so full of Troubles as this way is, without a Friend, and Defender?' Mathew tells Christiana, 'Mother fear nothing, as long as Mr. *Great-heart* is to go with us, and to be our Conductor.'[17]

In the Valley of the Shadow of Death the 'Women ... looked pale and wan', and when the giant Maul struck at Great-heart, 'the Women, and Children cried out' and 'did nothing but sigh and cry all the time that the Battle did last.' – though when Great-heart decapitated Maul, 'Then the Women and Children rejoyced.' The balancing within a prose couplet sums up Bunyan's whole attitude to male strength and female frailty: the pilgrims' friends bring them equipment that is 'fit for the weak, and the strong, for the Women, and the men'. Then led, of course, by Great-heart, the band proceeds, even though 'the Women and the Children being weakly, they were forced to go as they could bear'. When Great-heart and his team prepare to attack Giant Despair, they place 'the Women in the Road', the protection even of the weaklings – but *male* weaklings – Feeble-mind and Ready-to-halt being better than leaving them to their own devices. Now married to Mathew, and pregnant, 'being a young, and breeding Woman', Mercie has a pre-natal craving – for a mirror (though this apparently irrational female longing is in fact commendable, since the surprising glass shows the two faces of Jesus, prince and victim). When the party enters into difficult terrain, responsibility for their safety devolves entirely on the men Valiant and Great-heart; it was 'sorry going for the best of them all, but how much worse for the Women and Children, who both of *Feet* and of *Heart* were but tender'. Given her panic attacks, it is hardly the case that, as Monsignor Knox put it, 'Christian goes on a pilgrimage, Christiana on a walking tour'. Even so, her safety is ultimately guaranteed, by her male protectors. And she and Mercie are identified in terms of their masters: 'Gaius ... *Whose Wife is this aged Matron? and whose Daughter is this young Damsel?*'[18]

In contrast, those who show bravery, fortitude or intelligence are addressed or referred to in masculine terms: in the Valley of Humiliation, Christian, it is recalled, 'did here play the Man' – as had the early martyr Polycarp, and as does Great-heart throughout. However, while manliness is akin to godliness, seductive feminity is the most dangerous temptation, presented in the form of a brilliant creation, Madam Bubble. A 'bold and impudent Slut', who has the temerity to 'talk with any Man', she offers 'her *Body,* her *Purse,* and her *Bed*'; she is Bunyan's monster of female sexual aggression, and a vivid antidote to Christiana's passive and colourless virtue.[19]

The vapidity and vulnerability of Christiana, though, are deliberately intended, the tears she sheds and the delicate sensibility she represents summing up 'the weakness of women in a man's world'. Keeble sees a strain of 'sexist prejudice' in the language and scenes of Part II and shows how Christiana's story is subjugated to that of Christian: '"To be a Pilgrim"' is, Keeble concludes, 'to be a man.'[20] We need only add that the delivery of that message – that women, unaided and unsupervised by men, could exercise no autonomous religious role – had occupied Bunyan in the period immediately prior to the appearance of the second part of *The Pilgrim's Progress*, issuing in the publication of its more theoretical blueprint, *A Case of Conscience Resolved.*

It is possible, however, that Bunyan's deployment of powerless characters – the women, and also Fearing and Feeble-mind – and his programme for conducting them to their redemption arise not just out of gender issues in his church, but from an appreciation of the role of the church itself as an agency for the salvation of all its true members, both feeble and formidable. In Part II, Bunyan needs to delineate weak members of the church so that he can show it in its entirety as a collective reservoir of saving grace. A lessened stress on election and a heightened emphasis on the contribution of the church give us a 'Calvinism with a human face', as I. M. Green aptly terms it, in his discussion of the balance between evangelistic preaching and a determinist doctrine of salvation in Bunyan. Here, too, is the 'gentler mood', the focus on 'mercy rather than justice' that Stuart Sim sees in Part II.[21] A retrospective of Christian's career emphasizes his individual struggle: 'Poor *Christian*, it was a wonder that he here escaped [from the Valley of the Shadow of Death]; but he ... had a good heart of his own, or else he could never a-done it.'[22] It is also true that emphasis on personal effort, which must be unrelenting and sleepless, also characterizes Part II, forming an outlook in which repose is tantamount to peril. The epitome of restless individual endeavour – discourser, teacher, traveller, leader, morale-booster, giant-slayer – is Great-heart, but the point is now that his unceasing efforts are not directed at his own rescue, as were Christian's, but at that of the pilgrims: he is the church, supplying the needs of the weak with his strength.[23]

He is also a minister of the church – and may represent Bunyan – one who can help others because he has 'gone often through this Valley' of the Shadow of Death. Those of his 'calling' are 'intrusted' with the care of the weaker brethren. Two of these can be placed within a literary tradition, including Shakespeare's Malvolio, Jonson's Zeal-of-the-Land Busy, Butler's Hudibras and Dryden's Shimei: all satires on Puritan types, the difference being that Bunyan's satiric portraits are actually drawn by a Puritan. First, there is the depressive, indecisive, over-scrupulous and over-sensitive Mr Fearing, the Puritan 'tender conscience' captured in a perfect vignette:

[H]e was a Man that had the Root of the Matter in him, but he was one of the most troublesome Pilgrims that ever I met with in all my days ... He had, I think, the *Slow of Dispond* in his Mind ... he was a man of a choice Spirit, only he was always kept very low, and that made his Life

so burthensom to himself, and so troublesom to others ... that he often
would deny himself of that which was lawful, because he would not
offend ... Mr. *Fearing* was one that play'd upon ... the *Sackbut,* whose
Notes are more doleful than the Notes of other Musick are.

This portrait, though exasperated and gently mocking, is essentially sympathetic, with an appreciation of the proper place for Mr Fearing's anxious
melancholy, under pastoral care. A more overtly comical satiric projection
– indeed, a superb creation, whose comic success derives from his complacent self-knowledge, Malvolio without the malice – is Mr Fearing's
friend, Mr Feeble-mind:

> *I am ... a man of a weak and feeble Mind, and shall be offended and*
> *made weak at that which others can bear. I shall like no Laughing, I shall*
> *like no gay Attire, I shall like no unprofitable Questions. Nay, I am so weak*
> *a Man, as to be offended with that which others have a liberty to do.*[24]

Roger Sharrock suggested that Feeble-mind, with his rigorism over dress,
has 'something of the early Quaker in his composition'. But the weaknesses to which Fearing and Feeble-mind were prone – excessive anxiety
and extreme scrupulosity – were, like the dangerously ingenious antinomian
theories of Mr Self-will, exaggerated forms of the beliefs, practices and even
the virtues of the godly. Yet, wrote Sharrock, 'None of these hard cases is
rejected from Greatheart's gathered church' – far from it, for their redemption seems guaranteed and, at the climax of the book, the weaker characters,
beginning with Christiana, are the first to be summoned across the river to
the Celestial City.[25]

There is a most promising message contained here. Alongside the salvationary role of the believing community, represented by Great-heart, the
just are saved by faith: 'that how full of the Venome of Sin soever you be,
yet you may, by the hand of Faith lay hold of, and dwell in the best Room
that belongs to the Kings House above'. The contribution of the 'hand of
Faith' confirms the elements of Lutheran soteriology, which, as Green
shows, Bunyan imported from his study of the *Commentary on Galatians,*
modifying the rigours of his Calvinism. In answer to the question, '*Who
are they that must be saved?*', Christiana's son Joseph proposes, not election, but justification by faith: 'Those that accept of his Salvation'. The
character targeted for some of the most savage criticism in the book is he
who doubts his salvation, Fearing, with his paralysing dread of '*Sin, Death
and Hell*', and his 'Doubts about his Interest in that Celestial Country.'
Justifying faith, in the widest sense – *fiducia*, trust, confidence, faith-with-

hope – offers him a remedy. This saving faith was effective within the church as a community of faith, expressing its collective desire to be saved and the communicability of that wish from one to another (as with the transfer of hope from Christiana to Mercie). The 'humanised Calvinism' of Part II lays stress on the disposition and responses of the community of believers who are justified by their faith, rather than on the automatic operation of the eternal decrees on atomized individuals. The salvific combination of justifying faith with the help given by the church makes redemption remarkably easy for the weak, including, in Bunyan's projection, women, and certainly for Christiana, in contrast with Christian's hard lone sojourn. The virtue of prudence is, as ever, essential – in the Valley of Humiliation 'they were very careful, so they got down pretty well' – but the lions and Giant Grim are speedily dispatched and the pilgrims proceed on their journey, from one safe-house to another, from repast to choice repast, until they reach their goal. There is even a place for good works (though a citation from Paul would cover Bunyan from any allegations of soteriological revisionism); Mercie speaks: 'I do these things … *That I may be Rich in good Works, laying up in store a good Foundation against the time to come, that I may lay hold on Eternal Life.*' Yet, whatever the efficacy of works, the support of the church is essential. In restoring the balance from individual to community, Bunyan may indeed have been responding to a critic who charged that in Part I he 'had unduly neglected the communal life of the church'. Thus, he now highlights 'the outward, social problems of the holy community, and [turns] away from the dominating figure of the Christian hero'. In Bunyan's vision in Part II, the church is at the centre of a salvationary triptych, flanked by justifying faith and works, and diluting Calvinistic formulae. There is a consequent commendation of churchly provisions, including sacraments, as supports for those – such as Mercie – who are not initially, or patently, of the elect, but proceeding to grace and redemption in, or even by means of, the facilities of the church. We need to be aware of Bunyan's appreciation of the whole range of the church's 'services' and also of his vision of its place in the whole drama of redemption, in sacred history.[26]

An awareness of the importance of the church for those of uncertain election becomes apparent in Mercie's plea for admission at the Wicket-Gate: 'I am come, for *that,* unto which I was never invited.' Her subsequent examination by the Interpreter can be compared with the entry procedures of the Independent churches. Worship and sacraments begin to assume prominence; at the Interpreter's house there is a homily (in the form of proverbial aphorisms), a service, with music ('There was also one that did Sing.'), and a eucharist: 'Now Supper was ready.' Perhaps it is indicative of

Bunyan's view of the relative importance of baptism that it is after they have joined in the fellowship of the church that the pilgrims take a bath, though this total immersion leaves them 'sweet, and clean ... also much enlivened and strengthened in their Joynts'. A confirmatory *'Seal'* of church membership 'greatly added to their Beauty', and they were clad in white raiment. The provisions made at the house of Gaius, a Genevan-style inn which represents the church – having 'Preaching, Books, and Ordinances' – are a figure for 'the Feast that our Lord will make for us'. Sharrock described Part II as 'a proud piece of open communion propaganda', and, we would add, one in which the congregational and collective provisions of the church, centring on its sacraments, receive more prominence than the decrees of election and reprobation that loomed so large in *Mr. Badman*. If this is Bunyan's almost-Arminian churchmanship, it is also in line with his ongoing quest for balance between a guarded acceptance of freedom, works and sacrament, and the stricter predestinarian Calvinism of writings such as *A Discourse upon the Pharisee and the Publicane*, which we shall examine in the next chapter.[27]

The role of the church as an agency for redemption is underscored by Bunyan's sense of its importance within history. The Bedford church was itself established on New Testament foundations – a 'visible Church Communion according to the Testament of Christ ... a fellowship according to the order of the Gospell' – and in Part II of *The Pilgrim's Progress* Bunyan brought out this feeling of kinship between the church of saints of his own day and that of the New Testament: his pilgrims make a long and fruitful stay in the house of the 'very honourable Disciple', Gaius, Paul's companion (Acts 20: 4), where there is discourse of early martyrs from Stephen to Polycarp (though not of medieval or Marian martyrs, since at this point Bunyan wants to knit the allegorized church of saints directly to the apostolic church). Subsequently, they visit the house of 'Mr. *Mnason,* a *Cyprusian* by Nation, an old Disciple', his anglicization as 'Mr.' Mnason (Acts 21: 16), a 'Landlord', giving him the appearance of an English contemporary of Bunyan's. The continuing history of the church is reviewed and its dawning triumph can now be shown as being assisted by the witness of the pre-Reformation and Reformation martyrs; the harshest persecution ended with the sufferings of Faithful, presented as the type of the later martyrs, since when the people of Vanity Fair – the world at large – were:

> much more moderate now then formerly ... I think the Blood of *Faith-*
> *ful* lieth with load upon them till now; for since they burned him, they
> have been ashamed to burn any more: In *those* days we were afraid to

walk the Streets, but *now* we can show our Heads. *Then* the Name of a Professor was odious, *now*, specially in some parts of our Town ... Religion is counted Honourable.[28]

The reference to the Marian persecution and its termination – 'since they burned him, they have been ashamed to burn any more' – suggests that Bunyan wanted his readers to have England in mind when they read of 'some parts of our Town', where godliness had come to be held in esteem (though we should be aware of the ambiguities of that phrase 'counted Honourable', having, perhaps, some of the ambivalent connotations of our 'considered respectable'). His historical overview bespeaks Bunyan's confidence that in large parts of post-Reformation Christendom, more locally in England, and, more microscopically still, in Bedford, where persecution of Nonconformists had proved notably difficult to enforce, and where Bunyan himself remained at liberty throughout the Tory Reaction, godliness prospered and persecution was in retreat. There was, however, a shadow, and, as his work of the same year, *Seasonable Counsel*, showed, Bunyan was fully cognisant of persecution: in Part II '*Grim* or *Bloodyman*', who 'had taken it upon him to back the Lions' against the pilgrims, resembles the violent Tories – the 'Bloodmen' of *The Holy War*. Yet even taking into account temporary recurrences of persecution, the longer-term prospect for the church of saints and the Reformation was promising. A '*Monster* out of the Woods' come to 'carry away their Children' is taken from one of the 'old fables' of Bunyan's youthful reading. The tale in question, that of the national patron saint, George, and the dragon, popularized in Johnson's *Seven Champions of Christendom*, was an integral part of seventeenth-century English vernacular culture. Bunyan, though, was able to inject the boyish fantasies of 'George' with a sterner meaning, out of Revelation 17: 3: 'So he [the angel] carried me away in the spirit into the wilderness; and I saw the woman seated upon a scarlet coloured beast, full of names of blasphemy, having seven heads and ten horns.' The beast on whom Antichrist rode – the beast into whom Antichrist could transform himself, that 'propounded Conditions to men' – was popery. In the posthumously published, but nearly contemporaneous, *Of Antichrist, and His Ruine* Bunyan described the inevitable fall of Antichrist. It was true that, unlike the once formidable but now dilapidated Giant Pope of Part I of *The Pilgrim's Progress*, a creature that Bunyan, in the relative optimism of the period before 1678, could consign to the back pages of history, popery, as events in England and France in the late 1670s and early 1680s had shown, was still capable of mischief. Like the dragon of the George stories, who made fitful, if still alarming, forays from his lair, the beast of Revelation still had 'his certain Seasons to come out in, and to make his Attempts upon the Children of the People of the Town'. His longer-term prospects, however, were poor, despite his occasional fits of aggression – death agonies of the beast; under assault from the 'valiant Worthies' – probably an allusion to the 'Protestant Kings' who would bring down Antichrist: 'in process of time, he became not only wounded, but lame; also he has not made that havock of the Towns mens Children, as formerly he has done. And it is verily believed by some, that this Beast will die of his Wounds.'[29]

The high drama of the downfall of Antichrist is in no way lessened by its alignment with what had by now become a children's story and the stuff of surviving fairground playlets; indeed, the old romance was given a new lease of life by Bunyan's adaptation of it to an apocalyptic programme. The integration of the two narrations – the fireside tale of adventure and the millenarian cataclysm – allowed Bunyan to simplify drastically, while clinging on to the essentials of, the complex chiliastic vision he set out in *Of Antichrist*. The brilliant fusion, ultimately reducing the dread of popery to a figment from a folk tale, also confirms the extent to which Bunyan was at home, both in the story culture of his boyhood and in the culture of complex eschatological exegesis of his adulthood.[30]

While incidents such as the repulse of Antichrist link the church of saints to the most momentous events of history, space is also given to its more routine concerns. The abortive courting of Mercie by Mr Brisk, who 'pretended to Religion; but ... stuck very close to the World', provided an object lesson, such as Bunyan had delivered at greater length in *Mr. Badman*, on the undesirability of matches between the religiously miscegenated. Marriages between Mathew and Mercie and between James and Gaius's daughter provide, in contrast, ideals of marriages between the saints. Part II concludes with the apotheosis of the redeemed pilgrims, but, though the book closes there, it does not end, for there is a story beyond it, of the marriages ensuring 'the Increase of the Church in that Place where they were for a time'. The phrase 'for a time' reminds us of the apocalyptic expectation that was never very far from Bunyan's consciousness; even so, he envisaged the godly church as a normalized institution within what was, for the time being, a continuing world.[31]

Bunyan's literary technique is at its peak in the second part of *The Pilgrim's Progress*, even though the work lives under the shadow of Part I, and regular flashbacks suggest nostalgia for the action-packed saga of Christian. There is still a feeling of the amateur writer in this book. The few descriptions of natural beauty provide only the vaguest impression of general pleasantness, rather than any real evocation; on the other hand, there is an awareness, as part of the book's escape from an overwhelming

concern with sin and decay in everything one sees, of the capacity of the
Creation to provide religious instruction: 'Observe ... what the Heavens
and the Earth do teach you.' It is Bunyan's excessively literal vision that
leads him into such bathos as: 'Then they had her to a place, and shewed
her *Jacob*'s *Ladder*. Now at that time there were some Angels ascending
upon it.' Alongside a generally high quality of verse, and the much-loved
lines beginning, '*Who would true Valour see*', there is strained syntax and
appalling rhyme:

> [*they*] ... *will Grace*
> *Thee, and thy fellows with such chear and fair,*
> *As shew will, they of* Pilgrims *lovers are.*

The couplet celebrating the international success of Part I: '*In* France *and*
Flanders *where men kill each other/My* Pilgrim *is esteem'd a Friend, a
Brother*', is desperately weak.[32]

To set against such relatively minor defects, a major strength of Part II
is the force and variety of its prose. This can include elevated homiletic
language: '[T]he Righteousness that standeth in the Union of these two
Natures to his Office, giveth Authority to that Righteousness to do the
work for which it is ordained.' This reflection on Christ is followed by a
conceit, worthy of Donne, to the effect that, since His righteousness is
surplus to the needs of His two natures, He can give away the remainder
like a spare coat to a beggar; this rich allusion suggests both the two coats
of Luke 3: 11 and the Lutheran view of the justified sinner being clothed
in a coat of the righteousness of Christ. There is dexterity of fancy, too, in
the remark that the bill for the pilgrims' stay in the house of Gaius will be
paid by the Good Samaritan.[33]

Alongside such noble language as that in Great-heart's discourse, there
is – it is the glory of the book – a wonderful strength, flexibility, directness
and colloquial pungency of speech, with Bunyan's ability to capture character in dialogue now reaching its apogee. Mr Brisk's exclamation at
Mercie's constant work for charity – 'What always at it?' – captures in
those few words the brisk, brusque and unfeeling worldling. An outburst
by Mr Fearing, physically brave ('he could have bit a Firebrand, had it
stood in his way') and spiritually troubled, encapsulates, in a childish cry
his groundless anxieties: 'O, the *Hobgoblins* will have me.'[34]

There is a playwright's skill in the handling of dialogue. Repetition of
key phrases knits together the exchanges in such passage as: 'Then said
Mr. *Great-heart*, what things? What things, quoth the Gyant, you know
what things.' Great-heart has a particularly effective line in 'manly' speech;

at time it is aggressive – 'These are but Generals, said Mr. *Great-heart,* come to particulars, man'; at others back-slappingly matey: '*I know that thou art a Cock of the right kind*'; and at others again colloquially imperious, in the style of an avuncular sergeant-major: 'What Sir, you begin to be drouzy, come rub up.' Other characters have a handle on sharp and realistic speech. Mnason leaves his native Cyprus to tell the pilgrims, in salty provincial English: 'I promise you … you have gone a good stitch, you may well be a-weary.' As in Part I, exclamatory prose brings the speech alive: 'Think, said old *Honest,* what should I think?' We can almost hear Stand-fast's reaction to an apt description of Madam Bubble: 'Right, you hit it, she is just such an one.' Indeed, this tale of, on the whole, ordinary people – Henri Talon's 'middle-class novel' – puts over its points most effectively in expressively vernacular language. The pilgrims are in 'a pelting heat', and one of the children is 'almost beat out of heart'. The pilgrims do not converse – they 'chatted'; Mercie's unwanted suitor was '*a clog to my Soul*'; the pilgrims go out 'one sunshine morning', and when one of them is sad, 'the water stood in his Eyes'. Mathew '*did plash and did eat*' green plums, and as a result was 'pulled as 'twere both ends together'. There is a wealth and a strength of undiluted Anglo-Saxon prose: 'they made a pretty good shift to wagg along. The Way also was here very wearysom, thorow Dirt and Slabbiness … Here … was *grunting,* and *puffing,* and *sighing.*'[35]

Bunyan's metaphorical system was equally home-grown and, at least on the face of it, simple. Death-bed repentance, which Bunyan had decried in *Mr. Badman,* is now likened to one running a whole week's marathon in the last hour of Saturday night. There is startling crudity in the comparison of the wicked claiming virtue to a dog who '*should say, I have, … the* Qualities *of the* Child, *because I lick up its stinking Excrements*'. Christiana and her sons:

> … *like the Wain,*
> *Keep by the Pole, and do by Compass stere,*
> *From Sin to Grace …*

– the 'Wain' being the seven stars in the constellation Ursus Major, in popular mythology 'King Charles's chariot'. Similes of a robin and a spider, a chicken and her chicks, look forward to the emblems of *A Book for Boys and Girls* (1686), and, though scholastically allegorized, convey an atmosphere of domestic simplicity. It is only when we encounter Bunyan's working out of the metaphor of Mathew's plum-induced gripe that we realize how complex his 'domestic' imagery can be. Mathew is dosed by his anxious mother, every detail of the treatment being recorded. This is a medicine, based punningly on the popular patent cure of the time, Mathew's powders, but at every point the allegorical correspondence is brought out. There are twelve boxes of the medicine, like the twelve Apostles, and the treatment tastes bitter, like the word of God to a 'carnal' heart. Most audaciously of all, after Mathew has been treated with ineffective cures made up of the sacrifices of the Old Testament, the successful treatment is revealed to be prepared '*ex Carne & Sanguine Christi*' (putting on his best Bedfordshire Protestant homespun, Bunyan explains, '*The Lattine I borrow*'). There is a boldness in the image of Christ's blood as a cure for stomach cramps, a deployment of the mundane to illustrate the sublime worthy of the metaphorical adventures of a Donne or a Herbert, or, as Sharrock put it, 'The attempt to link Mathew's bowel troubles with the Fall of Man has a medieval wholeness of approach.'[36]

Perhaps there is a 'medieval' note – possibly from undercurrents in popular culture – in other features of the second part of *The Pilgrim's Progress*. How else are we to explain the insertion of motifs from medieval popular religion such as the pelican in her piety, her self-immolation for her young being an emblem in the bestiaries of Christ's dying for mankind – or how explain an image of divine love as 'an arrow with a point sharpened by love, let easily into the heart' – the vision of St Teresa made familiar to us by Bernini? Or how might we account for the way that Bunyan's pilgrims, like their medieval forebears, gawp at tourist-class curiosities, such as the equipment for Abraham's interrupted sacrifice?[37]

There is comedy in this work, with Feeble mind and Ready-to-halt making a comic duo, not without cruelty in the depiction. There is also strangeness, and a dream or nightmare quality, as with the sequence of the man '*that tumbled the Hills about with Words*', or the man 'cloathed all in White; and two men ... continually casting Dirt upon him ... [which] would in a little time fall off again'. A feeling of the surreal comes with the miraculous tailor who cuts cloth for the poor and always has the same amount of fabric left, and from the bizarre '*Fool*, and one *Want-wit*, washing of an *Ethiopian* with intention to make him white, but the more they washed him, the blacker he was'; we might imagine this done by Bruegel, as a pictorial proverb on the theme of folly. The dream-like mood is present also in the horrific 'Hole in the Hill ... the *By-way* to Hell', and in the magic looking-glass – Scripture – showing the different aspects of Christ, a haunting and weird fancy.[38]

Often relegated to the status of a mere epilogue to Part I, the second part of *The Pilgrim's Progress* may be considered, in literary terms, as Bunyan's masterpiece.

Notes

1. James Blanton Wharey (ed.), *The Pilgrim's Progress from this World to That which is to Come. The Second Part* (revised by Roger Sharrock; Oxford, 1960), pp. 165–311: also in G. Offor (ed.), *The Works of John Bunyan* (3 vols; Glasgow, 1854), vol. III, pp. 168–224.

2. For a plot summary, see Roger Sharrock, *John Bunyan* (London, 1954; reissued 1968), ch. 8.

3. *The Pilgrim's Progress*, p. 171, notes 1, 2; *The Holy War*, p. 150; *Mr. Badman*, pp. 65–7, 140–4, 145–8; John Brown, *John Bunyan: His Life, Times and Work* (2nd edn; London 1886), pp. 275–6.

4. Lynn Veach Sadler, *John Bunyan* (Boston, MA, 1979), p.109; Sharrock, *John Bunyan*, p. 140; N. H. Keeble, ' "Here is her Glory, even to be under Him": The Feminine in the Thought and Work of John Bunyan', in Anne Laurence, W. R. Owens and Stuart Sim (eds), *John Bunyan and his England 1628–1688* (London and Ronceverte, WV, 1990), pp. 135–8; for recent work on gender and religion in early modern England, see *ibid.*, p. 134, n. 10.

5. *The Pilgrim's Progress*, pp. 181, 189, 183, 188, 178, 198; Matthew 21: 29.

6. *The Pilgrim's Progress*, p. 224.

7. *Ibid.*, p. 261: Bunyan takes 'highly favoured' from the Authorized Version's form of the angel's salutation to Mary in Luke 1: 28.

8. Roger Sharrock, 'Women and Children' in Sharrock (ed.), *The Pilgrim's Progress: A Casebook* (London and Basingstoke, 1976), p. 178; *A brief Account of the Author's Call to the Work of the Ministry*, in *Grace Abounding*, p. 94.

9. *Christian Behaviour*, in J. Seary McGee (ed.), *Miscellaneous Works of John Bunyan*, vol. III (Oxford, 1987), pp. 27–8; *A Case of Conscience Resolved*, in T. L. Underwood (ed.), *Miscellaneous Works of John Bunyan*, vol. IV (Oxford, 1989), pp. 295–330 and the valuable background 'Introduction', pp. xxxvii–xliv: also in Offor (ed.), *Works of John Bunyan*, vol. II, pp. 658–74.

10. *A Case of Conscience Resolved*, p. 293; for the background to the dispute over women's meetings, including the possible identity of 'Mr. K.', see also Richard L. Greaves, *John Bunyan and English Nonconformity* (London and Rio Grande, OH, 1992), p. 67.

11. *A Case of Conscience Resolved*, pp. 295–6, 303, 306, 295 : Bunyan went on to satirize fashionable London Nonconformists for abandoning their male religious leadership in favour of high living, claimed the Protestant high ground against both the alleged gender equality of the Quakers and the Ranters and the 'nunnish' ways of Rome, and exploited Scripture in his favour ('the Holy Ghost doth insist') in the manner that, as McGregor shows, so alienated women seeking a proper place in the gathered churches: J. F. McGregor, 'The Baptists: Fount of all Heresy', in J. F. McGregor and B. Reay (eds), *Radical Religion in the English Revolution* (Oxford, 1984), p. 47.

12. *The Pilgrim's Progress*, p. 261; *A Case of Conscience Resolved,* pp. 294–5.

13. *The Pilgrim's Progress,* pp. 212, 210; *The Life of St. Teresa by Herself* (trans. J. M. Cohen; Harmondsworth, 1958), pp. 155–6: Gordon S. Wakefield fascinatingly compares Bunyan with St John of the Cross: '"To be a Pilgrim": Bunyan and the Christian Life', in N. H. Keeble (ed.), *John Bunyan: Conventicle and Parnassus* (Oxford, 1988), pp. 117–18.

14. *The Pilgrim's Progress,* pp. 202, 213, 224, 254, 259.

15. Offor (ed.), *Works of John Bunyan,* vol. III, p. 171; *The Pilgrim's Progress,* pp. 203, 202, 204, 222, 185, 186; for music, see Arleane Ralph, '"They Do Such Musick Make": *The Pilgrim's Progress* and Textually Inspired Music', *Bunyan Studies* 5 (1994), pp. 58–67.

16. *The Pilgrim's Progress,* pp.194, 196, 197; Keeble, '"Here is her Glory"', p. 142.

17. *The Pilgrims Progress,* pp. 214, 219, 220, 234

18. *Ibid.,* pp. 241, 245, 279, 281, 287, 296, 259; the authority of seventeenth-century fathers over their daughters is well captured in the scene in which Mnason 'stamped with his Foot, and his Daughter Grace came up' (*ibid.,* p. 274); Knox, quoted in Sharrock, 'Women and Children', p. 175; Underwood refers felicitously to Christiana's 'conducted tour of the historic sites of her husband's more adventurous pilgrimage before her': *A Case of Conscience Resolved,* p. xliv.

19. *The Pilgrim's Progress,* pp. 240, 302, 300; Keeble sees Madam Bubble as a powerful image of temptation: 'What the saint is above all required to resist is a promiscuous woman': '"Here is her Glory"', p. 139.

20. Sharrock, 'Women and Children', pp. 180–1; Keeble, '"Here is her Glory"', pp. 138–9, 141, 142–4: Greaves adds that the book 'does not indicate that Bunyan retreated from the traditional role of male superiority, and should not be interpreted as an attempt by Bunyan to place women on a plane equal to that of men': *John Bunyan and English Nonconformity,* p. 67.

21. I. M. Green, 'Bunyan in Context', in M. van Os and G. J. Schutte (eds), *Bunyan in England and Abroad* (Amsterdam, 1990), pp. 13–14; Stuart Sim, '"Safe for Those for Whom it is to be Safe": Salvation and Damnation in Bunyan's Fiction', in Laurence *et al.* (eds), *John Bunyan,* pp. 158–9.

22. *The Pilgrim's Progress,* p. 244.

23. For examples of Great-heart's campaigns, see *ibid.,* pp. 242–3, 289–97; see also Firth on his character, cited by Sharrock in *The Pilgrim's Progress: A Casebook,* pp. 99–100.

24. *The Pilgrim's Progress,* pp. 243, 249, 253, 270.

25. *Ibid.,* pp. 255–7; Sharrock, 'Women and Children', p. 184; Margaret Fell lodged a strong protest against Quaker meticulousness over dress: William C. Braithwaite, *The Second Period of Quakerism* (London, 1919), p. 518.

26. *The Pilgrim's Progress,* pp. 201, 225, 254, 236, 227; Green, 'Bunyan in Context', p. 13; Sharrock, 'Women and Children', pp. 185, 174–5; U. Milo Kaufmann, in 'Spiritual Discerning: Bunyan and the Mysteries of the Divine

Will', in Keeble (ed.), *John Bunyan*, pp. 178–80, emphasizes the reassurance to be found in Part II and the comfort it offers in place of the anxiety stirred up in Part I.

27.   *The Pilgrim's Progress*, pp. 190, 204, 207–8, 262; Sharrock 'Women and Children', p. 184; Sharrock drew attention (*ibid.*, p. 178) to the importance of the 'fine music' in Part II. For proverbs, see George W. Walton, 'Bunyan's Proverbial Language', in Robert G. Collmer (ed.), *Bunyan in Our Time* (Kent, OH, and London, 1989), esp. pp. 14–15. In 'Bunyan and the Holy Community', *Studies in Philology* 80 (1983), pp. 200–25, John R. Knott deals with concern with the church, in this work and elsewhere (including *Grace Abounding*), in Bunyan.

28.   Bedford Church Book, quoted in Brown, *Bunyan*, p. 81; *The Pilgrim's Progress*, pp. 258, 273, 274, 275; see also Thomas S. Freeman, 'A Library in Three Volumes: Foxe's "Book of Martyrs" in the Writings of John Bunyan', *Bunyan Studies* 5 (1994), pp. 47–57.

29.   *The Pilgrim's Progress*, pp. 218, 277–8; for *Seasonable Counsel* and *Of Antichrist, and His Ruine*, see below, ch. 8; it is significant that Great-heart and other representatives of the church only 'be-labored' the monster and 'made him make a Retreat' – the task of bringing down Antichrist belonged solely to kings: see W. R. Owens, '"Antichrist Must Be Pulled Down": Bunyan and The Millennium', in Laurence *et al.* (eds), *John Bunyan*, p. 89; the role of the church in weakening Antichrist lends support to Offor's suggestion (*Works of John Bunyan*, vol. II, p. 227, n. 4) that the 'valiant worthies' stand for the preachers of a series of anti-popish sermons in the 1670s.

30.   C. S. Lewis, 'The Vision of John Bunyan', in Sharrock (ed.), *The Pilgrim's Progress: A Casebook*, p. 196; Tessa Watt, in *Cheap Print and Popular Piety, 1550–1640* (Cambridge, 1991), pp. 22, 318, provides glimpses of the popular commemorations of St George.

31.   *The Pilgrim's Progress*, pp. 226, 311; Pooley links the conclusion of Part II to the *Book of Martyrs*: Roger Pooley, 'Plain and Simple: Bunyan and Style', in Keeble (ed.) *John Bunyan*, pp. 106–7.

32.   *The Pilgrim's Progress*, pp. 226, 233, 295, 168, 169; the verses (later becoming a school assembly standby hymn, set to music by Percy Dearmer), rhyme 'stories' with 'more is'.

33.   *Ibid.*, pp. 210–11.

34.   *Ibid.*, pp. 227, 254, 252.

35.   *Ibid.*, pp. 244, 247, 264, 273, 300, 301, 216, 227, 251, 229, 228, 296; Henri Talon, *John Bunyan* (London, 1964), p. 25.

36.   *The Pilgrim's Progress*, pp. 257, 284, 228–30; Sharrock, *John Bunyan*, p. 146.

37.   *The Pilgrim's Progress*, pp. 233–4. Bunyan had not acquired the scepticism of a contemporary, who discounted the 'devout fancies' of the medieval pelican story: *The Pilgrim's Progress*, notes, p. 346. The legend of the self-sacrificing pelican survived, though:

Lorsque le pélican, lassé d'un long voyage
Dans les brouillards du soir retourne à ses roseaux,
Ses petits affamés courent sur le rivage
En le voyant au loin s'abbatre sur les eaux,
…
Le sang coule à longs flots de sa poitrine ouverte.

Alfred de Musset, *La Nuit de mai*, in Douglas Parmée (ed.), *Twelve French Poets 1820–1900: An Anthology of 19th Century French Poetry* (London, 1966), p. 132.

38. *The Pilgrim's Progress*, pp. 285, 286, 287; the idea of washing Africans to make them white was proverbial of folly and futility – compare 'to cultivate sand, and wash Ethiopians', in John Galt, *Annals of the Parish* (1821; ed. James Kinsley, Oxford and New York, 1986), p. 107.

EIGHT
Bunyan's Last Writings

If Part II of *The Pilgrim's Progress* showed Bunyan at the height of his powers as an author, the last years of his life displayed an extraordinary quantity as well as quality of production: sixteen works came out in the 1680s, including some of his most important writings, such as *Mr. Badman* and *The Holy War*, and nearly half of his whole output, including fourteen posthumous works issued between 1689 and 1692, was delivered in the years 1684–92. In the year of his death he published no fewer than five items. Without his sudden death in August 1688, a continuing major contribution to the Nonconformist press could have been expected.[1]

In *A Holy Life*,[2] as in *Christian Behaviour* and *Mr. Badman*, Bunyan dealt with the duties of Christians in the family and society. There was also continuing concern with issues of current debate in his church, addressed in *Questions about the Nature and Perpetuity of the Seventh-Day Sabbath* (1685). In *A Book for Boys and Girls* (1686) Bunyan developed the emblem devices that he had adopted in the second part of *The Pilgrim's Progress*. A series of writings focused on the work and person of Christ. Despite the high drama of English politics during much of this period, references to matters of state are few and largely oblique.

Seasonable Counsel

This is the case with *Seasonable Counsel*, which appeared in 1684, at the height of the Tory Reaction.[3] Persecution of Dissenters, which had been flowing strongly since the onset of the Reaction in 1681, now reached a flood. Brown provided details both of the local scene, where, in Bedford, meetings of Bunyan's church virtually ceased between August 1684 and the end of 1686, and of the nationwide picture: massive fines on Nonconformists, indignities done to their ministers and dragonnades against meetings.[4] Bunyan's response to this repression was remarkably acquiescent. Indeed, Richard Greaves suggests there was a 'striking change' in his

political outlook during this part of the 1680s. There was critical, if alle-
gorical, commentary in *The Holy War*, with its 'reminder' of Charles II as
Diabolus and its caricatures of Tories as Atheism and False Peace. However,
even in *The Holy War* Bunyan did not include a 'call to arms'. In what
Greaves calls the 'critical supplement' to *The Holy War* – *Seasonable
Counsel* – the political message is even more passive:

> [H]e made it clear that in times of persecution the saints could do no
> more than patiently suffer and pray to God for deliverance from evil
> rulers. In this tract Bunyan expressed one of his profoundest insights:
> the necessity for Christians to suffer *actively* for righteousness by *will-
> ingly* embracing affliction.[5]

Greaves sees the same doctrines of non-resistance and, indeed, loyalism
being set out in the posthumous *Of Antichrist, and His Ruine* as in *Seasonable Counsel*, and links the tone of the latter to the serenity evident at
the close of the second part of *The Pilgrim's Progress*.[6]

Seasonable Counsel is a tract for a time of heavy suffering for Nonconformists, as Bunyan made plain in his preamble addressed to the 'Christian
Reader': '*Beloved, I thought it convenient, since many at this day are
exposed to sufferings, to give my advice touching* that *to thee.*' His description of persecution reads like a catalogue of the sufferings of so many
Dissenters in that period: 'They have had no House, no Land, no Money,
no Goods, no Life, no Liberty, left them to care for … Goods have been
confiscated, liberty has been in Irons.' Such a frank description might well
have attracted the attention of the authorities, at a time when Baxter was
dealt with savagely for some modest reflections on episcopacy. Yet a closer
reading of *Seasonable Counsel* shows the work's essential political innocu-
ousness and, indeed, its strong royalist commitment. In the aftermath of
the Rye House Plot, so disastrous for Nonconformists and Whigs, Bunyan
repudiated resistance to authority, 'with a word to those professors … that
are of an unquiet, and troublesome spirit … To wish the destruction of
your enemies doth not become you … If you believe that the God whom
you serve, is Supream Governour … pray keep fingers off, and refrain from
doing evil.'[7] Yet, not only was violent resistance ruled out as a solution to
the problems faced by the Nonconformists, but also the political methods
of the vote and the mass petition in which, as Whig supporters, they had
put their faith during the Exclusion Crisis were now repudiated: 'To
overcome evil with good, *is an hard task*. To rail it down, to cry it down,
to pray Kings, and Parliaments, and men in authority to put it down, this
is easier than to use my endeavour to overcome it with good.'

Bunyan's new model of the Nonconformist was de-politicized, markedly so in contrast with the frenetic electoral and propagandist activity of so many Dissenters in the years 1679–81. He was proposing political absti-nence to his fellow Nonconformists and a retreat into religion, private life and trade: 'Christians ... have other things to do than ... to meddle in other mens matters. Let us mind our own business, and leave the Mag-istrate to his work, Office and Calling ... A Christian ... has enough to do at home in his Heart, in his House, in his Shop, and the like.'[8] However, alongside that mood of disengagement Bunyan displayed a more positive royalism, and, indeed, a remarkable adhesion to divine-right principles that fall little below that of the University of Oxford's political manifesto of 1683.[9] Rulers existed not only as a constraint on evil but as a force for good. Subjection to the proper authorities was no mere matter of coer-cion, but was also demanded by conscience: '[T]he Magistrate is God's ordinance, and is ordered of God as such ... he is the Minister to thee for good, and ... it is thy duty to fear him, and pray for him, to give thanks to God for him, and to be subject to him ... *and that not only for wrath, but for conscience sake.*' The laws were both necessary and salutary: 'Magis-trates ... have fortified themselves from being attacqed with turbulent and unruly Spirits by *many* and *wholsome* Laws.'[10] No censor could find any-thing unexceptionable in Bunyan's pronouncing the laws, under which the Dissenters suffered, '*wholsome*'.

Nevertheless, there was a distinction drawn in Bunyan's political thought between the prince, '*supreme* in authority', and the '*inferior*' magistrates who governed in his name, 'by the King called to that imploy'. The latter were to be borne with rather than honoured, 'appointed ... to be a perse-cutor, and a troubler of Gods Church!' – the 'enemy' likely to 'act beyond measure, cruelly'. Their hour must be brief: 'Never grudge them their pre-sent advantages.'[11]

This was not the case with the supreme magistrate. When Bunyan spoke of the king, he referred not to an 'enemy', but to a protector, and indeed a shield against Tory-Anglican persecution, for 'Kings ... seldom trouble churches of their own inclinations.' Probably alluding to Charles's 1672 Declaration of Indulgence, he recalled: 'I have oft-times stood amazed ... at ... the *favour* of the Prince towards us ... and do make it my Prayer to God for the King.' Though Bunyan may have wished to see Charles once more assert himself as a barrier against Tory-Anglican intolerance, in terms of practical politics, the king's public commitment to the Established Church as the covenant underpinning the Tory Reaction had rendered such a hope out of date. Even so, naïve or not, Bunyan's view of the king as paternal protector, echoing a long-standing myth at the heart of European popular political consciousness, induced him to concentrate his attack on persecution, not in the England of his day, ruled by Charles II, but in lands controlled by papists or governed by popish princes – '*Ireland* [in 1641], *Paris* [in 1572], *Piedmont* [in 1655] … *France, Spain, Germany, Italy*', the Papal States and England under Mary Tudor, the '*Maryan* days'.[12]

However, Mary was an aberration from the Protestant commitment of the Tudors, which Bunyan explored in *Of Antichrist, and His Ruine*. After her, dedication to the Reformation and to the the war against Antichrist was reaffirmed by Elizabeth I. How could that godly prince have been a persecutor of the saints? There was no mention in *Seasonable Counsel* of the Elizabethan anti-separatist statute of 1593, or of the persecution that flowed from it, and the only oppression of an English Protestant that Bunyan recorded as having taken place during Elizabeth's reign happened in Rome. Elizabeth was definitive in Bunyan's Foxean view of the role of England's 'Protestant Kings' in bringing down Antichrist. It was because Antichrist was 'still alive' that a particularly positive loyalty to England's crown was due from the saints. *Seasonable Counsel* forms a tract of intense royalism.[13]

A Caution to Stir up to Watch against Sin

Also in 1684 Bunyan published a broadsheet, *A Caution to Stir up to Watch against Sin*. This brief foray into verse recalls *One Thing is Needful* and *Ebal and Gerizzim* (both 1664) and looks forward to *A Book for Boys and Girls* (1686) and *A Discourse of the Building, Nature, Excellency and Government of the House of God* (1688). Priced at a penny, and in the format of a fairground ballad printed on one side of a sheet, *A Caution* represented an attempt on the part of Bunyan and his publisher Nathaniel Ponder to adapt to the demands of an increasingly commercialized popular culture. However, the lack of incident in *A Caution* must have handicapped it in competition with a sensationalist popular press obsessed with crime, sex and the fabulous.[14]

A Discourse upon the Pharisee and the Publicane

Bunyan returned to prose in this work, published in 1685. Though he over-analysed Jesus's simple story, loading it with a lengthy Pauline denigration of works righteousness, Bunyan revealed his gifts for setting a scene, for explaining a context and for giving scriptural narrations up-to-date meaning for his readers. For example, he likened Jesus's Pharisee to a competitor who 'did carry the Bell, and did wear the Garland, for Religion': that is, perhaps, a competitor who took away the prizes at village sports. The Publican of the Gospel story appears in the character of a tax-farmer, one of the contractors who creamed off so much of Charles II's revenue until the system was abolished, and also as one of the 'vile and base' informers under the Conventicle Act, the trade taken up by Mr Badman. There is a side-swipe at the erstwhile national enemy, the Dutch, for the Publican is also up-dated as an avaricious Hollander levying taxes on his fellow-countrymen, perhaps during the French occupation in 1672 – a slur on the Dutch that was later felt to be so damaging that it was prudently removed from editions from September 1688 onwards.[15]

Questions about the Nature and Perpetuity of the Seventh-Day Sabbath

In this work Bunyan turned his mind to an issue of Christian observance, addressing the question of whether Christians should keep Saturday or Sunday as their holy day. The immediate stimulus for going into print on this issue was the seventh-day practice of the London congregation of Francis Bampfield, who died in the year of the publication of *Questions*, so that Bunyan's contribution to the debate may possibly have represented an attempt to close the matter.[16] Yet the seventh-day question was of more than passing concern. It involved the link between the timing of the Sabbath and the apocalyptic; the relationship of Christianity to Judaism; and the manner of keeping the Lord's day, along with law versus Christian freedom.

W. T. Whitley showed how the active millenarianism of the Fifth Monarchists was transmuted into the quieter observance by the Seventh-day Baptists of the Saturday Sabbath. Seventh-day observance had the adventist significance of the connection between the last day – of the week – and the last days. In his posthumous and unfinished *An Exposition of the Ten First Chapters of Genesis* Bunyan acknowledged the chiliastic significance of the seventh day, its number being constantly reiterated in Revelation:

Which Sabbath, as I conceive, will be the Seventh thousand of Years, which are to follow immediately after the World hath stood Six thousand first ... so in Six thousand Years he will perfect his Works and Providences that concern this World: As also he will finish the toil and travel of his Saints.

In *Questions* – a practical work on the church's worship rather than an apocalyptic commentary – Bunyan did not directly address the Sabbatarian-adventist question. However, in his advocacy of what was, in effect, a weekly day of commemoration of Easter and Pentecost, he was, at least by implication, proposing the recollection of the events of the church's foundation in the past, rather than the anticipation of an eschatological climax in the future, and thereby diluting messianic expectations linked to the sabbatarian observances of the church.[17]

On the relationship of Christianity to Judaism, Bunyan made no mention of the new Jewish presence in England; he saw Judaism as having only a past (as Augustine had); he said nothing of its eschatological significance; and he radically distanced Christianity from it – as he had in *The Pharisee and the Publicane*, with its rejection of Pharisaic works righteousness. In this last respect, Bunyan showed his kinship with the theologically anti-Judaic Luther, who found in Judaism an epitome of the religion of works righteousness.[18]

Bunyan's reiterated, indeed, almost incantatory, insistence on the true Sabbath as the first day of the week implies a contrast between the newness of the day of the Resurrection and the deadness of the Jewish 'old Sabbath' of the end of the week. This was, in turn, linked to his representation of the Judaism of that 'old Sabbath' in the past tense, a religion of history only, without a present or a future. In *Some Gospel-Truths Opened* Bunyan's claim that 'the Jews did put him [Christ] to death' led him into a depiction of the Jews continuing, and being punished, through time: 'Now God … doth most miserably plague them to this very day, for their crucifying of him … the Jews from that day to this, have been without a king.' In *Questions,* in contrast, the emphasis is on Easter Sunday rather than on the Good Friday for whose guilt Jews were being punished through all time. Although Jews, it was admitted, retained some token presence within Christendom, the theme of continuing divine vengeance against them was deleted and, as for their religion, it was as dead as its Sabbath: its 'Sanction' was 'gone', the validity it had once enjoyed having vanished, around the time of the Atonement, with the destruction of the Temple.[19] Yet Judaism played a part in Bunyan's dialectic, in that he equated it with legalism: Baptist Saturday observers were 'Jewifi'd, Legaliz'd'. This had implications for Bunyan's view of the proper mode, as well as the timing, of observing the Lord's Day. *Grace Abounding* attests the importance for Bunyan of careful Sabbath observance, but he may not have been an extreme sabbatarian, and his argument that re-scheduling the Lord's day to its Jewish time in the week would also impose a Pharisaic ban on harmless and necessary activities, may suggest that his essential concern as a Sunday observer was to prevent the day's elision – as in the popular culture of his youth – from a holy day to a holiday.[20]

This may suggest adiaphorism, like that of Calvin, or Paul, whom Bunyan quoted as one who 'leaves the observation or non-observation of [days], as things *indifferent* to the *Mind* and Discretion of the Believers'. Yet, in Bunyan's view, Paul intended freedom not to observe the Jewish Sabbath rather than the option of not keeping the Christian Sunday. The first day of the week was 'The *Lords day*' which God Himself 'remembers' and therefore to be fixed firmly to Sunday, regardless of altering circumstances: 'Were I in *Turkie* ... I would keep the *first day* of the week *to God*.' Rejecting those radicals who saw every day as the Lord's, Bunyan made a special claim for Sunday's unique pre-eminence.[21]

A Book for Boys and Girls

The twin works, *A Discourse upon the Pharisee and the Publicane* and *Questions about the Nature and Perpetuity of the Seventh-day Sabbath*, both decrying forms of legalism associated in Bunyan's mind with the Jewish religion, do not, with their protracted exegesis, make for entertaining reading. Bunyan's only publication of the following year, the verse *A Book for Boys and Girls*, a series of emblems whose moral and religious meaning is explained, has been acclaimed for its capacity to delight.[22] Graham Midgley writes that the work 'shows Bunyan at his best and most adventurous as a poet, and expresses more completely the many sides of his personality'. These grandfatherly tales, in which Bunyan took on the persona of 'a sort of religious Aesop', began, from their 1707 edition onwards, to appear with illustrations, culminating in a handsome version of 1780 showing the characters in late eighteenth-century costume. The plates in the Offor edition feature pretty Victorian middle-class children and a highly respectable beggar. Sharrock suggested that Bunyan's use of emblems in this work for the expression of ideas dated him in a symbolically thinking world that preceded 'Cartesianism and the Royal Society'. As he had in the two parts of *The Pilgrim's Progress*, Bunyan was employing, for the purposes of religious instruction, an art form that had passed into the domain of vernacular and nursery culture.[23]

A comparison of two of Bunyan's excursions into poetry, separated by twenty-two years – *One Thing is Needful* (1665) and the work now under consideration – suggests changes in his circumstances and temperament over two decades. In 1665 he was poor, confined and anxious over his still undetermined future and the sorry state of his family. A sense of that downcast condition emerges from a reading of *One Thing is Needful*, its gloomy fixation on the 'last things' and its preoccupation with hell. The whole tone of *A Book for Boys and Girls* is entirely different, reflecting the mellowing that had taken place in Bunyan's personality over the two decades in question. To take one example of the lightening of his outlook, in *Grace Abounding* he recorded the mortal terror instilled in him by the church bells: 'Should the Bell fall with a swing, it might first hit the Wall, and then rebounding upon me, might kill me'. Now, in *A Book for Boys and Girls*, he was able to use the bells as a constructive didactic image:

> These Bells are like the Powers of my Soul …
> The Ropes by which my Bells are made to tole,
> Are Promises (I by experience find.)[24]

We seem now almost to be in Herbert's poetic world of metaphorical interchange between the church as a building and as a 'transcendant place'. Bunyan's whole outlook had shifted, making him more at peace with the world around him. His practical circumstances had altered out of all recognition; he was a widely acclaimed Dissenting leader and a hugely successful author. The prisoner of 1665 remained at liberty at the height of the Tory Reaction. Haunted by his image of Bunyan as a life-long martyr and fugitive, Charles Doe, in his attempt to explain his hero's freedom during the Tory repression, reads unconvincingly, especially when we bear in mind the vigilance of the authorities and Bunyan's high profile: '[H]is enemies in the severe persecution at the latter end of Charles the Second's reign … often searched and laid wait for him, and sometimes narrowly missed him.' Doe's bumblingly incompetent security services are belied by the reality of an efficient post-Rye House Plot dragnet and 'rounding up of everyone thought to have political or religious opinions resembling those of the alleged conspirators'. Bedfordshire's record of radical Whiggery and support for Monmouth made its magistrates especially edgy, issuing their order of 1684: 'That all such laws as had been provided for the reducing all Dissenters to a thorow Conformity shall be forthwith put into a speedy and vigorous execution.'[25] There was, then, a machinery for apprehending Bunyan, had he been viewed as a troublemaker, but, whereas in 1660 the social anger of *A Few Sighs from Hell* may have contributed to his imprisonment, the political loyalism that we have seen on display in *Seasonable Counsel* may have kept him at liberty during this later period. He was not Doe's man on the run, and his drawing up of his 'will' in 1685 is more likely to have been a prudent measure by a cautious man in his later years than a precaution against renewed imprisonment. The 'will' itself indicates comfortable circumstances; the appellation 'Brazier' must now be regarded as a formality for this author and minister. His large family of now adult children were settled (though his son Thomas may have been a black sheep and, brought up in godliness, a model for Mr Badman); his relations with his 'well-beloved wife' were evidently good. The fine Sadler portrait of 1685, in itself a sign of fame and substance, and the copies made from it, show a successful, middle-aged, middle-class Englishman – a calm, intelligent, full-fleshed, well-barbered, alert and handsome face, with ministerial gown, book in graceful hand, fine lace collar and an overall air of mild and un-Puritan vanity. This comfortable figure, now at the height of his powers and repute, is the author of *A Book for Boys and Girls*, just as *One Thing is Needful* came from the pen of a destitute and depressed prisoner. There is satire in *A Book for Boys and Girls*, as in the lines:

> *Our* Bearded *men, do act like* Beardless *Boys;*
> *Our Women please themselves with childish Toys.*

But it comes in the bluff tones of Great-heart and is emphatically not world-rejecting, as is the voice of *One Thing is Needful*; in *A Book for Boys and Girls*, Bunyan was once more laying aside his graver self to sugar the pill of his gospel.[26]

The title of this work varied between early editions, but a regular inclusion was the sub-heading 'Country Rhymes', indicating rustic simplicity. The term also draws our attention to the use, not so much of literary models from the emblem tradition, as of natural scenes as object lessons, the result of close observation of the English countryside – a lark and a fowler, a flint in a stream, a swallow, a bee, a cloudy morning, a sunrise and a sunset, a mole, a cuckoo, country boys at play, an apple tree in blossom and a rose bush, a cackling hen, and so on. The significance of this interpretive use of the ordinary and the natural, especially in contrast with the absence of visual depiction in *One Thing is Needful,* is that Bunyan had by now abandoned the world-rejection of the earlier poem and was prepared to utilize the Creation for didactic purposes; this pedagogic 'natural theology' – which Christiana commended in the second part of *The Pilgrim's Progress* – suggests an acceptance of the essential goodness of a natural world, which, not fatally flawed by the Fall and sin, could teach lessons about its Maker.[27]

The Advocateship of Jesus Christ

Bunyan returned to Calvinist soteriology and Christology in 1688, with *The Advocateship of Jesus Christ*.[28] Greaves traces this work on 'Christ's role as an attorney who pleads the cause of the elect before God the supreme judge' to the law studies that Bunyan took up as a result of his imprisonment: the book was addressed, as Greaves says, to 'the saints, especially the recent converts' and to the better-off urban Nonconformists able to grasp his complex legal analogies. Bunyan's argument that Christ was a barrister who took on difficult cases was made in response to a preacher of neo-Pelagian views, who urged his auditors to make their cases watertight before Christ would take them up. To Christ's roles of sacrifice priest and king, Bunyan (even though he warned that 'similitudes must not be strained too far'), added that of lawyer, not in a metaphorical, but in a literal sense: Christ was not *like* an attorney, he *was* an advocate – a special pleader, in the first place for the saints, but, by extension, in a seemingly Arminian vision of the possible scope of his original propitiatory work, 'for the Elect throughout the World, and they that will extend it further, let them'.[29]

Good News for the Vilest of Men

In a remarkably productive year, Bunyan dealt with Christ's redeeming work in *Good News for the Vilest of Men*.[30] In *The Advocateship of Jesus Christ* he bemoaned the '[d]ecays that are among us, as to the Power of Godliness: And what abundance of foul miscarriages the generality of Professors now stand guilty of'. In *Good News* he kept up the attack on the moral malaise of a nation that 'doth swarm with Vile Ones as ever it did since it was a Nation'. Since Bunyan opened the work with a condemnation, as at the beginning of *Mr. Badman*, of the moral state of his country and then switched to describe Jerusalem, given the widespread assumption that England – 'our *Sion*', as the dedication of the Authorized Version calls it – was the second Israel, it might be tempting to read into his survey of the country's parlous state a coded attack on the furtherance of Catholicism by James II, perhaps veiled as the Old Testament king, Manasseh:

> *Jerusalem* … was the place and seat of Gods Worship, but now decayed, degenerated, and apostatized. The Word, the Rule of Worship, was rejected of them, and in its place they had put and set up their own Traditions … *Jerusalem* was now therefore greatly backslidden, and become the place where Truth and true Religion was much defaced …
>
> I will come to *Manasseth* the King. So long as he was a ringleading Sinner, the great Idolater, and Chief for Devilism, the whole Land flowed with wickedness; *For he made them to sin* … and do worse than

the Heathen that dwelt round about them ... But when God converted
him, the whole Land was reformed. Down went the Groves, the Idols
... and up went true Religion.[31]

Yet, tempting as it might be to read into this a review of the onward march
of popery under James II – scriptural exegesis playing its customary role
of concealed political comment – there are arguments against such a
reading. The most obvious of these is the fact that by 1688 James II's policies of encouraging Catholicism were not having a great deal of success
and the king was not filling the land with his faith. Nor was he himself
a very plausible Manasseh, least of all because Manasseh saw the error of
his ways – something no-one could ever accuse James of doing, not even
when most under pressure to do it during the Exclusion Crisis – and re-
converted.[32]

A further reason for not interpreting *Good News* as a commentary on
developments such as the advancement of Catholicism by James is Bunyan's
introduction into the account of himself, in one of the autobiographical
glimpses that feature in these late works. The reminiscence recalls his
sinful, pre-converted state, when he 'infected all the Youth of the Town
where I was born, with all manner of youthful Vanities'. Conversely, his
conversion had a beneficial effect on the same local community: 'some of
them perceiving that God had mercy upon me, came crying to him for
mercy too'. Bunyan's injection of himself, his youthful moral failings –
which never, though, included being popishly affected – and the impact of
his conversion on Bedford into the narrative, confirms that this work is not
about the progress of popery in James II's England, but concerns the moral
lives of individuals and, beyond them, of the local communities – 'Place,
town or family' – that made up the nation.[33]

A Discourse of the Building Nature, Excellency and Government of the House of God

Bunyan returned to verse in this further work of 1688, a celebration of the
church and its key role in salvation: *Salus extra ecclesiam non est*:

> The man that *worthily* rejected is,
> And cast out of this House, his part in Bliss
> Is lost for ever, turns he not again,
> True Faith and Holiness to entertain.

The broad fellowship of the church must not be disrupted for the sake of intrusive dogmatism:

> For those that have *private* opinions too
> We must *make* room, or shall the Church undo.

Bunyan also used the opportunity of an analysis of the ministries in the church to re-assert the anti-feminism of *A Case of Conscience Resolved*:

> I read of *Widows* also that should be
> Imployed here for further decency;
> I dare not say they are in *Office*, tho
> A Service here they are appointed to;
> They must be very *Aged, Trusty, Meek*.[34]

Solomon's Temple Spiritualized

The church is also the subject of this lengthy typological study, in prose, written in the tradition of finding, in the Old Testament, figures for the New. The intensity with which the typology is pressed home – Christ crucified is the roast meat of the Temple sacrifices, 'drest up in *Chargers,* and set before the Congregations of the Saints' – may startle the reader; Bunyan's misogyny is again vented: 'The Church of Christ, alas, is of her self a very sickly *puely* thing, a Woman, a weaker Vessel ... when the custom of Women [menstruation] is upon her, or when she is sick of love.' Richard Greaves adds that this work – of 1688 – evinces continuing optimism about the religious role of kings.[35]

With an allegorical work, *The Water of Life*, reminding us of Christianity as *religio aquae,* Bunyan completed all the works published in his lifetime. An extensive repertoire of posthumous writings followed between 1689 and 1692 – the works in which, as Christopher Hill writes, he may have 'revealed more of his mind ... than in those which he published himself'.[36]

Of Justification by an Imputed Righteousness

This is a completed work, though it lacks Bunyan's customary preface. In it, he returned to the subject of his first writings, against Quakerism, in

1656–7, and of his rebuttal of Fowler in 1672: vicarious atonement. The tract, says Hill, is one of only three of the posthumous writings to which a political censor might not have taken exception, and, indeed, it is a straightforward restatement of Pauline-Lutheran soteriology, citing Galatians and Romans extensively. Any tendency on Bunyan's part – for instance in the second part of *The Pilgrim's Progress*, or in the 'almost Arminian power of decision' attributed to man which Greaves finds in *Good News for the Vilest of Men* – to write as if, in practice, the just were in part saved by their own will and efforts is corrected in this more theoretical, and entirely Protestant, work.[37]

The Desire of the Righteous Granted

Bunyan had delivered an earlier version of this work as a sermon to a London church in 1685 or 1686 – the address of which Doe recalled: 'Mr. Bunyan preached so New-Testament like that he made me admire, and weep for joy, and give him my affections'. The work celebrates church fellowship, which, 'rightly managed, is the glory of all the World. No place, no community, no fellowship [is] adorned and bespangled with those beauties as is a Church rightly kit together to their head, and lovingly serving one another.'[38]

The Acceptable Sacrifice

The third of what Hill views as politically innocuous last works, *The Acceptable Sacrifice*, was prepared for the press by Bunyan before his death and carries a preface by the London millenarian Independent minister, Bunyan's friend, George Cokayne. In this impassioned experiential work, there is a return to the anguished feelings of *Grace Abounding*:

> there is a Necessity of breaking the Heart, in Order to Salvation; … *now* the Heart lies open, *now* the *Word* will prick, cut and pierce it; and it being cut, prick'd, and pierced, it bleeds, it faints, it falls, and dies at the Foot of God, unless it is supported by the Grace and love of God in Jesus Christ.[39]

*   *   *

In these last works Bunyan was producing authentic Protestant theology and devout edification. In another group of posthumous writings, though, he has been seen as composing, and withholding from publication, works too dangerous to be released. Greaves's projection of him as not so much the politically and socially disengaged saint, solely 'devoted to the pursuit of piety and the conversion of souls', but as a man of his time deeply involved in its secular concerns urges us to look at the bulk of his posthumous works from the point of view of the social, political and controversial ecclesiastical material they contain, so as to ask if their being withheld from publication was, as Hill argues, likely to have been an act of prudential self-censorship.[40]

An Exposition on the Ten First Chapters of Genesis

A consideration of one of the works on Hill's list of self-censored publications, *An Exposition on the Ten First Chapters of Genesis*, and in particular a review of hypotheses as to why it remained unfinished, is revealing of differences of approach to Bunyan between nineteenth-century commentators, such as Cheever, who saw him as a 'universal' religious genius, and modern scholars concerned with the more immediate and political context of his writings. Offor, for whom the political background to Bunyan's works was of so little significance that he made no attempt to group them chronologically, saw the 'good Bunyan' of the Genesis commentary as an untutored mechanical – a model for the 'vast number of pious and enlightened mechanics who adorn this country' – and one whose lack of education highlighted the working on him of the Holy Spirit to produce a religious revelation removed from time and place, a graduate of the Spirit's 'university unshackled by human laws'. If anything was remarkable, it was that Bunyan had produced as much as he did of a scriptural exposition, traditionally the product not of charismatic inspiration, but of the highest academic prowess. Brown saw another side of that picture: the defects of Bunyan's education left him unfitted for the planned 'continuous Commentary on the Scriptures', which he over-ambitiously contemplated but which he had to abandon 'abruptly' before his death, and which was, as a result, a flawed, unfinished exegetical symphony.[41]

In this century considerable attention has been given to Bunyan as an opposition spokesman, whose works need to be considered closely in chronological context for the political messages, often covert, which they contain. Tindall saw *An Exposition* as an 'exercise in veiled sedition' and the other leading interpreter of the radical Bunyan, Hill, writes that *An Exposition* 'is certainly designed to convey points to which the censor might have objected if put directly'. Greaves adds that Bunyan's targets –

absolute monarchy, idolatry and persecution – date the composition of this work to the phase of the Tory Reaction that spilled over from the last period of Charles's reign to the first part of James's: 'The commentary may thus be unfinished not because of Bunyan's death (the typical explanation) but because changed political circumstances rendered his political attack imprudent.' Greaves adds that references in the work to the church's persecution date its composition outside the period between the first, April 1687, Declaration of Indulgence and Bunyan's death in August 1688 – whereas Owens thinks 'that Bunyan may have been working on [*An Exposition*] right up to the end of his life'.[42]

The problem is that there is little in the way of contemporary reference in *An Exposition* to allow us to date its commencement, progress and cessation. The quality of exposition in what we do have of the work allows us to discount, as a reason for its interruption, the inability of its author, as an uninstructed mechanical, to sustain it. However, there is internal textual evidence to allow us to hypothesize an authorial chronology and to venture a tentative guess as to why, and thus when, the commentary was abandoned. Allusions, at roughly three-quarters of the way through the text, to the plight of the 'Church of God in *England* ... upon the waves of Affliction, and Temptation' permit us confidently to date *An Exposition* to the period up to and including the Tory Reaction, as an approximate coeval of *Seasonable Counsel*. Then, within a few pages of the abrupt termination of *An Exposition*, having arrived at the tenth of Genesis's fifty chapters, Bunyan had turned his full attack on Rome as the author of false national churches, on '*Romish Babel*' and on '*Augustine* the Monk, come from *Rome* into *England*', to 'build his *Nineveh* here'.[43]

Clearly, such reflections would have given offence to 'Anglicans', their church being portrayed as a daughter of Rome, and might have exposed the author to fresh danger. However, he had not drawn back, in the perilous 1660s, in *I Will Pray with the Spirit*, from denigrating the Church of England as a sprig of Rome. The problem now was that, in his historical attack on the Established Church, he had broadened his vista to take in the Roman Church itself; he then broke off work on the treatise. By 1687 the anti-Catholic reflections that he had incorporated in his hermeneutics might have seemed inopportune from the pen of a leader of Dissent whose church was beginning to receive considerable benefits from a Catholic king. One would agree that prudential considerations counselled the abandonment of *An Exposition*, at about the – highly contentious – point where Bunyan suspended work (perhaps with later revisions in mind), but it is possible that they were not those of personal safety, but rather of refusing to hazard a tolerationist alliance being delicately constructed around the

throne. The goals of James's coalition of Catholics, Whigs and Nonconformists to achieve toleration required an extensive exercise of the royal
prerogative, so that, again, it would have been inapposite for Bunyan to
leave unrevised for publication within James's reign references to Nimrod
as the originator of 'Absolute Monarchy.'[44]

It may be that in 1687–8 Bunyan came to see such reflections and allusions as not only impolitic, but at the same time as detracting from his
central exegetical purpose in *An Exposition*, which was to ponder the sacred
history of Genesis, with a mass of essentially religious contemplations on
God, the Trinity, Creation, Adam and Eve, the Fall, Cain and Abel, Noah
and the Flood. It may, indeed, be the case that *An Exposition* can legitimately be read as containing typologies of Shaftesbury and his plans in
1682, or the Monmouth Rebellion in 1685, or the 'growing aristocratic
support for William of Orange' in 1688 – just as it may be possible to see
in Bunyan's hope of God's raising up 'a *Josias,* or a *Cyrus,*' to 'begin to
discover themselves to the Church, by way of Encouragement', an allusion to Nonconformist hopes entertained of James. In the end, though,
and whilst fully appreciating Greaves's insistence that we must be aware of
a Bunyan 'sensitive to political developments', we should also take account
of his overriding exegetical purpose in *An Exposition* – and of the possibility that he held it back from publication until such as time as he might
have time to reconsider minor passages of controversial content, which
could have proved unsuitable to the political strategies of 1687–8.[45]

Paul's Departure and Crown

Of this further posthumous work, Greaves comments that its respect for
law and dissuasives against rebellion counter Tindall's depiction of its
author as an 'inciter to sedition'. Its allusions to 'the murders and out-rage
that our Brethren suffer at the hands of wicked Men' indicate, as Owens
suggests, a composition during the Tory Reaction and a minor coda to
Seasonable Counsel, containing the same message of patient acceptance of
suffering.[46]

Israel's Hope Encouraged

Another work in the posthumous series, *Israel's Hope Encouraged*, contains some of Bunyan's most explicit references to the political events he
had witnessed:

[O]ur days indeed have been days of trouble, especially since the discovery of the Popish Plot, for then we began to fear cutting of Throats,
of being burned in our beds, and of seeing our Children dashed in
pieces before our Faces. But looking about us, we found we had a gracious King, brave Parliaments, a stout City, good Lord Maiors, honest
Sherifs, substantialLaws against them [the papists].

We have already looked at this work from the point of view of its partisan
commitment. Its Whig orientation is unmistakable, but it is also a remembered one, recalling events of nearly a decade before. The phrase 'a gracious
King' points also to Bunyan's overall royalism, to his acceptance of Charles's
Protestantism as being genuine, and even to his inclusion of him amongst
the 'Protestant Kings' who, as *Of antichrist, And His Ruine* showed, must
play their part in the destruction of the great enemy. Further, Bunyan's
direct citation from a sensationalist pamphlet issued by his publisher Ben-
jamin Harris, *An Appeal from the Country to the City* – 'cutting of Throats
... seeing our Children dashed in pieces before our Faces' – may, with its
hint of hysteria recollected in tranquillity, suggest that the worst fears
whipped up by extreme Whig propagandists to secure Exclusion had
proved to be groundless, or that God had saved his Englishmen from the
worst. Bunyan had not adopted the scepticism about the Popish Plot that
put its author in the pillory in 1684 – Oates's plot was for him the subject
of a 'discovery', not a fabrication – but in retrospect he had become in-
tensely dubious about the human and political means in which, he had
come to believe, people vainly put their trust: 'these we made the object of
our Hope, quite forgetting the direction in this exhortation, *Let Israel Hope
in the Lord*'. Bunyan's brief excursus on the Plot and Exclusion periods is
inserted to illustrate the need for Christians 'to make the Lord our Hope
only'. As we have seen, in his repudiation of petitioning and electioneering
in *Seasonable Counsel* Bunyan also expressed his disenchantment with
political agitation.[47]

The Saints' Privilege and Profit

The contents of this work, composed for the guidance of members of the
gathered churches in their everyday lives, provide no reason for any delay
in its publication, apart from its author's death, and its composition may
be assigned to late in James II's reign. The work is noteworthy for its lack
of anti-Catholic polemic, all the more so in that its theme of Christ's perfect

high priesthood, as set out in Hebrews, presented obvious opportunities for attacks on the Catholic ministry and the Mass. Bunyan had made such an attack explicit in *Of Antichrist, and His Ruine*, with his denunciation of the way Antichrist had 'intruded upon the Priestly Office of Christ, hath called himself *High-Priest* ... though God knows no High-Priest but one'. In keeping with this apparent restraint, there is only the mildest allusion to a Catholic rite, regarded by Protestants as idolatrous, and known in the Middle Ages as 'creeping to the Cross' on Good Friday – honoring the Crucifix, which, as Bunyan says inoffensively, 'some worship'. (He could not, though, hold back from a slight on 'Men' who 'make Altars, upon which, as they pretend they offer the Body of Christ'.)[48]

Christ a Compleat Saviour

Likewise, Bunyan establishes the all-sufficiency of Christ as intercessor in *Christ a Compleat Saviour*, but abstains from any polemics concerning Catholic intercession through the saints. There is no reason not to date the composition of this work to the period immediately preceding Bunyan's death, and his silence on the issue of Catholicism – whether induced by indifference, fear or more strategic considerations – is all the more remarkable when contrasted with the stream of attacks on Rome's doctrines and rituals by other eminent Nonconformist divines in the 1670s and 1680s.[49]

The Saints' Knowledge of Christ's Love

The direction of Bunyan's concerns in these late homiletic writings, focusing on the work of Christ, is illustrated in *The Saints' Knowledge of Christ's Love*, a profoundly scriptural composition with, Offor calculated, 440 biblical references.[50] There is an almost complete absence of political commentary and what there is is innocuous enough:

> Wherefore, who ever is set up on earth, they are set up by our Lord. *By me*', saith he, '*kings reign' and princes decree justice. By me princes rule* ... Nor are they when set up, left to do ... their own will and pleasure ... The bridle is in his own hand, and he giveth reins, or check, even as it pleaseth him. He has this power, for the well being of his people.

Bunyan presents here a classic Christian and scriptural doctrine of the divine right of kings – '*By me ... kings reign*' – and with it the corollary that rulers governing by the the authority of the source of justice must do so justly.[51]

A Discourse of the House of the Forest of Lebanon

This work may be linked with two others published in 1688, *A Discourse of the Building, Nature, Excellency and Government of the House of God* and *Solomon's Temple Spiritualized*, to form a three-part typological series on the church. Hill has found in *The House in the Forest of Lebanon* a warrant for resistance, in the words: 'And suppose they were the truly godly that made the first assault, can they be blamed?', though Greaves sees legitimation for only spiritual warfare and mental strife, quoting: 'the War is not carnal but spiritual ... made by way of *controversie, contention, disputation, argument, reasonings, &c*'. He adds that *The House of the Forest of Lebanon* repudiates the kind of militancy associated with the Fifth Monarchists: the godly were 'of a peaceable deportment'.[52]

Detachment from the world in favour of a purer spirituality, which is present throughout the late and posthumous writings, suffuses *The House of the Forest of Lebanon*, even in those passages which concern the political world beyond the church. Christ's 'Kingdom is not of this world, nor doth he covet temporal matters; Let but his wife his Church alone, to enjoy her purchased priviledges, and all shall be well.' Fifth-Monarchist militancy is firmly rejected in an apocalyptic programme, which places all its emphasis on Christ's actions – his 'managing': a 'quiescent millenarianism'. In contrast to the overt millenarian anti-popery of *The Holy City* and *Of Antichrist, and His Ruine*, Bunyan is now much more cautious in his anti-popish allusions. It is true that he reviews a longer-range Foxean account of the sufferings of the saints at the hands of the scarlet woman. However, he is now more concerned with a telescoped history of recent persecution, and with its cessation in a dawning toleration, of which, as Midgley writes, he was seeing 'the first glimpses' in 1687. His response is to emphasize the political quiescence of the church of saints: '[T]hey misapprehend concerning her, as if she was for destroying Kings, for subverting Kingdoms ... she moveth no Sedition, she abideth in her place, let her Temple-Worshippers but alone, and she will be as if she were not in the World.'[53] In Bunyan's version of the Quaker 'Lamb's war' – he spoke of 'the Lamb and the Army that follows him' – the saints withstood the aggressive forces of Antichrist in the defensive armour of suffering. But the state was not involved in this head-on collision between Christ and his forces, and Antichrist and his: 'Here is therefore no mans *person* in danger by *this* war … No man needs to be afraid to let Jesus Christ be chief in the world.'[54]

Between the writing of of *Antichrist, and His Ruine* and that of *The House of the Forest of Lebanon* Bunyan's thinking shifted in favour of a de-politicized apocalyptic, secularizing his political thought in such a way that the saints were to be taken up with the inner life of their churches (as recommended in *Seasonable Counsel*), rather than with public life, and with the spiritual crusade which concerned them, under Christ's sole leadership, uniquely. The state's role was now seen as a purely secular one – in fact the one set out in the Declarations of Indulgence of 1687 and 1688, of maintaining religious toleration, and 'let but Faith and Holiness walk the Streets without controule, and you [rulers] may be as happy as the world can make you': 'Render unto Caesar': 'I practise Religion in my Closet, in my Family, in the Congregation; but I defend this practice before the Magistrate, the King, and the Judge'. Bunyan's now greater detachment towards the state, implying a passive loyalty, without hoping from the state any more than it could award, and without envisaging for it any longer a role in a cosmic eschatological plan, might explain his reluctance to become actively involved in James II's plans to open up local government to non-Anglicans – as opposed to not discouraging others to become so involved. In this late work, so important for our understanding of Bunyan's final position on issues of church and state, there was still, it should be said, some residual acknowledgement of the possibility of royal involvement in the messianic drama that he continued to expect: 'even in Gospel times, Kings shall hate the Whore'. However, Bunyan's prevailing tendency in *The House of the Forest of Lebanon* was to delete kings from his eschatological agenda – at least in contrast with the leading role that he had given them in *Of Antichrist, and His Ruine*. It was not necessarily the case that James II could play no part in the downfall of the Antichrist: conflict between the papacy and Louis XIV had excited English Protestant hopes that even the latter would support the struggle. However James's at best ambiguous position induced Bunyan to efface from his millennarian programme any role for kings; Christ, leading the saints, was now seen as the sole initiator of the destruction of Antichrist. Yet kings, and even a popish king like James, could have a useful secondary function, so that Bunyan under James evolved a fresh theoretical view of the function of kingly government in maintaining an impartial framework in which individual subjects might worship as they wished: 'I practise Religion in my Closet'. Such an outlook would not have been incompatible either with a diffident acquiescence in, or a benevolent neutrality towards, James's policies of emancipating non-Anglicans – 'he certainly did not oppose some cooperation with the king' – when those policies were applied in Bedford in 1687–8.[55]

Of the Trinity and a Christian and *Of the Law and a Christian*

These two brief treatises in broadsheet format were also found amongst Bunyan's papers and were published by Doe after his death. They assert complete trust in Scripture as the source of Christian teaching and Bunyan's Reformation principle of Christian freedom. Preached within a fortnight of his death, Bunyan's *Last Sermon* reaffirms teaching on the new birth.[56]

*   *   *

The main thrust of the posthumous works is homiletic, doctrinal, pastoral, edifying – in all *religious*. As Greaves says: 'In 1688, when the minds of so many Englishmen were on the political failings of the monarch, Bunyan's message was of free grace for the vilest of sinners and divine intercession in the celestial court of the saints.' While their political content is, sometimes no doubt intentionally, often opaque, and needs an authorial chronology that must remain elusive to clarify its specifics, the proportionate volume of political to non-political material in the final works is so insignificant as to require a commentator, searching only for the nuggets of Bunyan's observations on matters of state, to disregard as so much spoil a mass of material that Bunyan himself regarded as his particular contribution as an author. Somewhere between the Brown–Offor projection of a Protestant man for all seasons – an essentially timeless voice delivering a spiritual message, largely independent of altering political circumstances – and the Tindall–Hill image of a 'turbulent, seditious and factious' plebeian, subversively addressing the political issues of his day, lies a truth about Bunyan. But, hard though this may be for twentieth-century *homo politicus* searching for the political element in all forms of discourse to digest, the authentic Bunyan may actually be closer to the Victorian version. True, his social critique could be corrosive, especially during his younger days, when *A Few Sighs from Hell* lashed out at a grossly unequal social order. But he was a man of the New Testament, which also combines social radicalism with political quiescence. 'Fear God, honour the king' is the abiding political message of Bunyan's final writings.[57]

Notes

1. Christopher Hill, 'John Bunyan's Contemporary Reputation', in Anne Laurence, W. R. Owens and Stuart Sim (eds), *John Bunyan and his England 1628-1688* (London and Ronceverte, WV, 1990), p. 10.

2. *A Holy Life,* in Richard L. Greaves (ed.), *Miscellaneous Works of John Bunyan,* vol. IX (Oxford, 1981), pp. 251-351: also in G. Offor (ed.), *The Works of John Bunyan* (3 vols; London, 1860), vol. II, pp. 507-47.

3. *Seasonable Counsel: Or Advice to Sufferers,* in Owen C. Watkins (ed.), *Miscellaneous Works of John Bunyan,* vol. X (Oxford, 1988), pp. 5-104 and esp. pp. xiii-xxx: also in G. Offor (ed.), *Works of John Bunyan,* vol. II, pp. 692-741.

4. John Brown, *John Bunyan: His Life, Times, and Work* (2nd edn; London, 1886), p. 343. For anti-Nonconformist repression in the Tory Reaction, see Watkins (ed.), *Miscellaneous Works of John Bunyan,* vol. X, pp. xiv-xv; Richard L. Greaves, *Secrets of the Kingdom: British Radicals from the Popish Plot to the Revolution of 1688-1689* (Stanford, CA, 1992), pp. 91-2; Michael Watts, *the Dissenters: From the Reformation to the French Revolution* (Oxford, 1978), pp. 254-7; B. R. White, *The English Baptists of the Seventeenth Century* (London, 1983), pp. 130-3; Michael A. Mullett, *James II and English Politics 1678-1688* (London and New York, 1994), p. 35.

5. Richard L. Greaves, 'Conscience, Liberty and the Spirit', in Greaves, *John Bunyan and English Nonconformity* (London and Rio Grande, OH, 1992), p. 68.

6. Richard L. Greaves, 'The Spirit and the Sword: Bunyan and the Stuart State', in *ibid.,* pp. 115-16.

7. *Seasonable Counsel,* pp. 5, 15, 99-100.

8. *Ibid.,* pp. 59, 33; N. H. Keeble (ed.), *The Autobiography of Richard Baxter,* (London and Melbourne, 1974), pp. 257-64; for censorship, see N. H. Keeble, *The Literary Culture of Nonconformity in Late Seventeenth-Century England* (Leicester, 1987), pp. 96-7, 98-101; for *Seasonable Counsel* in the context of the Rye House Plot, and Bunyan's repudiation of violence, see Greaves, 'Amid the Holy War: Bunyan and the Ethic of Suffering' in Laurence, *et al.* (eds), *John Bunyan,* pp. 63-75.

9. In J. P. Kenyon (ed.), *The Stuart Constitution: Documents and Commentary* (Cambridge, 1966), pp. 471-4.

10. *Seasonable Counsel,* pp. 39-40, 103; see also Douglas R. Lacey, *Dissent and Parliamentary Politics in England, 1661-1689: A Study in the Perpetuation and Tempering of Parliamentarianism* (New Brunswick, NJ, 1969), pp. 112-20, 135-5, 115-16; Lacey observes (*ibid.,* p. 110) that, after the Restoration, '[i]n general, Baptists were already of the same basic disposition as the Quakers, and when the King was restored each group affirmed its loyalty and declared that there should be no plots or insurrections against the government'. 'Inferior magistrates' were sometimes seen as acting as

checks on the undue exercise of royal power: Quentin Skinner, *The Foundations of Modern Political Thought* (2 vols; Cambridge, 1978), vol. II, pp. 230–5.

11.   *Seasonable Counsel*, pp 33, 35.

12.   *Seasonable Counsel*, pp. 35, 25, 48, 22.

13.   *Seasonable Counsel*, pp. 55, 40; for prophetic expectations about the English monarchy and the apocalypse, see William M. Lamont, *Godly Rule: Politics and Religion, 1603–1660* (London, 1969), pp. 23–4 and ch. 2.

14.   *A Caution to Stir up to Watch against Sin*, in Graham Midgley (ed.), *Miscellaneous Works of John Bunyan*, vol. VI (Oxford, 1980), pp. 177–82 and lv–lvi; also in Offor (ed.), *Works of John Bunyan*, vol. II, pp. 575–6; see also Margaret Spufford, *Small Books and Pleasant Histories: Popular Fiction and its Readership in Seventeenth-Century England* (Cambridge, 1985).

15.   *A Discourse upon the Pharisee and the Publicane*, in Watkins (ed.), *Miscellaneous Works of John Bunyan*, vol. X, pp. 111–235, esp. p. 117–19, and xxx–xxxviii; also in Offor (ed.), *Works of John Bunyan*, vol. II, pp. 217–77. For the customs farm, see C. D. Chandaman, *The English Public Revenue 1660–1688* (Oxford, 1975), pp. 28–9; references to the farm, replaced by direct collection in 1671, to the French in Holland (1672) and to the second Conventicle Act (1670) might date this work to around the time of the debate with Fowler, for whom the Pharisee, with his works righteousness, could be a type. Bunyan 'appears to have regarded the parable as the record of an incident that Jesus himself had witnessed and remembered': see Watkins (ed.), *Miscellaneous Works of John Bunyan*, vol. X, p. xxxii. For suggested reasons for the work's incomplete nature and for its place in Bunyan's evolving understanding of faith and justification – and the precedence of justification over faith – see *ibid.*, pp. xxxiii–xxxv.

16.   *Questions about the Nature and Perpetuity of the Seventh-Day Sabbath*, in T. L. Underwood (ed.), *Miscellaneous Works of John Bunyan*, vol. IV (Oxford, 1989), pp. 335–89 and xlv–lv (with references to further reading); also in Offor (ed.), *Works of John Bunyan*, vol. II, pp. 361–85; see also Greaves, *John Bunyan and English Nonconformity*, pp. 66–7; for Francis Bampfield, see Richard L. Greaves, *Saints and Rebels: Seven Nonconformists in Stuart England* (Macon, GA, 1985), ch. 7, and for comparisons between him and Bunyan, *ibid.*, pp. 183–4, 189, 209.

17.   W. T. Whitley, *A History of British Baptists* (London, 1923), pp. 85–6; see also David S. Katz, *Sabbath and Sectarianism in Seventeenth-Century England* (Leiden, New York, Copenhagen, Cologne, 1988), pp. 12–20, 24, 83–5, 144–5, and for Bunyan's contribution on the issue, *ibid.*, p. 115; *An Exposition of the Ten First Chapters of Genesis*, in W. R. Owens (ed.), *Miscellaneous Works of John Bunyan*, vol. XII (Oxford, 1994), p. 119; *Questions about the Seventh-Day Sabbath*, p. 369; for the Sabbath and the millennium, see Owens (ed.), *Miscellaneous Works of John Bunyan*, vol. XII,

p. xliii (for further reading, *ibid.*, n. 102), and Graham Midgley (ed.), *Miscellaneous Works of John Bunyan*, vol. VII (Oxford, 1989), pp. xxxv–xxxvii.

18. For Augustine and Judaism's termination with Christ, see Jeremy Cohen, *The Friars and the Jews: The Evolution of Medieval Anti-Judaism* (Ithaca, NY, 1982), pp. 19–22; for Bunyan and Judaism, see Underwood (ed.), *Miscellaneous Works of John Bunyan,*vol. IV, p. liv.

19. *Questions About the Seventh-Day Sabbath*, pp. 379–80; *Some Gospel-Truths Opened*, in Offor (ed.), *Works of John Bunyan*, vol. II, p. 145.

20. *Questions About the Seventh-Day Sabbath*, p. 388; an earlier seventeenth-century preacher condemned the Sabbath of the Jews 'which are too nice and too strikt in observing this day' – so much so that on it 'no body might in publicke scratch where it itched': in Katz, *Sabbath and Sectarianism*, p. 15.

21. *Questions About the Seventh-Day Sabbath*, pp. 353–4, 363, 376.

22. *A Book for Boys and Girls*, in Midgley (ed.), *Miscellaneous Works of John Bunyan*, vol. VI, pp. 190–269 and lvii–li; also in Offor (ed.), *Works of John Bunyan*, vol. III, pp. 747–62.

23. *A Book for Boys and Girls*, p. lvii; Brown, *Bunyan*, p. 356; Offor (ed.), *Works of John Bunyan*, vol. III, facing pp. 784, 758; Roger Sharrock, *John Bunyan* (London, 1954; reissued 1968), p. 99: for the emblem tradition, see *ibid.*, p. 100, and E. Beatrice Batson, *John Bunyan: Allegory and Imagination* (London and Canberra, 1984), ch. 6.

24. *Grace Abounding*, p. 13; *A Book for Boys and Girls*, p. 231.

25. 'The Windows' in R. S. Thomas, *A Choice of George Herbert's Verse* (London, 1967), p. 33; Charles Doe, 'The Struggler', in Offor (ed.), *Works of John Bunyan*, vol. III, p. 76; Brown, *Bunyan*, pp. 335, 350–1; Doe also exaggerated Bunyan's poverty, and perhaps Bunyan himself was hinting at his affluence in a couplet in *A Discourse of the Building, Nature, Excellency and Government of the House of God* (1688), quoted in Midgley (ed.), *Miscellaneous Works of John Bunyan*, vol. VI, p. lxii:

> My *House*, my *Wife*, my *Child*, they all grow old,
> Nor *am I e'er the younger for my Gold*.

Also see Midgley (ed.), *Miscellaneous Works of John Bunyan*, vol. VII, p. xxxvii. For the vigilance of the authorities following the Rye House Plot, see Greaves, *Secrets of the Kingdom*, pp. 189–91, 196–204; Bedfordshire also had a militant pro-Monmouth grouping: *ibid.*, pp. 284–5.

26. Brown, *Bunyan*, pp. 397–407: Bunyan may have moved into the ministry full-time at an early point, for two commentators described him as a tinker 'in the Morning of his dayes': Chandler and Wilson, quoted in T. L. Underwood and Roger Sharrock (eds), *Miscellaneous Works of John Bunyan*, vol. I (Oxford, 1980), p. xl; Offor (ed.), *Works of John Bunyan*, vol. I, frontispiece;

A Book for Boys and Girls, p. 190; for Bunyan' son, see Patricia Bell, 'Thomas Bunyan and *Mr. Badman*', *Bunyan Studies* 2,1 (1990), pp. 46–52.

27. For nature and the Fall, see T. F. Torrance, *Calvin's Doctrine of Man* (London, 1952), pp. 176, 179; Bunyan does not depart entirely from the tradition of seeing Creation as being flawed by sin, mankind having 'brought to bondage every thing created': compare Henry Vaughan's view of man as he who:

> Drew the curse upon the world and cracked
> The whole frame with his fall.

quoted in Batson, *John Bunyan*, p. 97; however, Bunyan's emphasis is on man's, not nature's, corruption, so that a creature such as a spider can provide instruction.

28. *The Advocateship of Jesus Christ*, in Richard L. Greaves (ed.), *Miscellaneous Works of John Bunyan*, vol. XI (Oxford, 1985), pp. 99–216 and xxxii–xliii, including the work's covenant theology, legal analogies and language, and Bunyan's earlier links with Fifth Monarchism: also in Offor (ed.), *Works of John Bunyan* (as *The Work of Jesus Christ as an Advocate*), vol. I, pp. 152–201.

29. Greaves, *John Bunyan and English Nonconformity*, pp. 103, 141; Keeble (*Literary Culture*, p. 143) discusses Bunyan's adaptation of his writing to the different strata of his readership; *The Advocateship of Jesus Christ*, pp. 99–100, 127, 144–5.

30. *Good News for the Vilest of Men*, in Greaves (ed.), *Miscellaneous Works of John Bunyan*, vol. XI, pp. 7–92 and xxi–xxxii; Greaves explores the work in the context of Bunyan's preaching on election and on such topics as the unpardonable sin and despair, and his pastoral care, taking account of the possible antinomian tendencies arising from stress on free grace; also in Offor (ed.), *Works of John Bunyan* (as *The Jerusalem Sinner Saved*), vol. I, pp. 68–103.

31. *The Advocateship of Jesus Christ*, pp. 99 and xliii; *Good News for the Vilest of Men*, pp. 7, 14, 36.

32. 1 Chronicles 33: 1–9.

33. *Good News for the Vilest of Men*, pp. 35–6; compare Bunyan's concern in *Mr. Badman* to censure the sins 'rife in a rural community or a market town': *Mr. Badman*, p. xvi.

34. *A Discourse of the Building, Nature, Excellency, and Government of the House of God*; in Midgley (ed.), *Miscellaneous Works of John Bunyan*, vol. VI, pp. 274–317; 313, 311, 291, lix–lxii; also in Offor (ed.), *Works of John Bunyan*, vol. II, pp. 578–90.

35. *Solomon's Temple Spiritualized*, in Midgley (ed.), *Miscellaneous Works of John Bunyan*, vol. VII, pp. 5–115; 80, 79; and, for the place of the work in Bunyan's writings and within the typological tradition, etc., pp. xv–xxvi;

also in Offor (ed.), *Works of John Bunyan*, vol. III, pp. 462–509; Greaves, *John Bunyan and English Nonconformity*, p. 118.

36. *The Water of Life*, in Midgley (ed.), *Miscellaneous Works of John Bunyan*, vol. VII, pp. 179–219 and, for interpretations of the 'water of life' in other places, typology and 'similitude', satire and parody, etc., pp. xliii–li; also in Offor (ed.), *Works of John Bunyan*, vol. III, pp. 538–59. Hill, quoted in Greaves, *John Bunyan and English Nonconformity*, p. 44. For the publication of the posthumous works, see Owens (ed.), *Miscellaneous Works of John Bunyan*, vol. XII, pp. xv–xvii.

37. *Of Justification by an Imputed Righteousness*, in *ibid.*, pp. 283–352 and xxv; also in Offor (ed.), *Works of John Bunyan*, vol. I, pp. 300–34; Hill, quoted in Greaves, *John Bunyan and English Nonconformity*, p. 44; Greaves (ed.), *Miscellaneous Works of John Bunyan*, vol. XI, p. xxi.

38. *The Desire of the Righteous Granted*, in W. R. Owens (ed.), *Miscellaneous Works of John Bunyan*, vol. XIII (Oxford, 1994), pp. 101–59; 130, xvi–xvii; also in Offor (ed.), *Works of John Bunyan*, vol. I, pp. 743–71. For the genesis of this work, see Greaves, *John Bunyan and English Nonconformity*, pp. 69–70; for Doe's encomium, see Brown, *Bunyan*, p. 385.

39. *The Acceptable Sacrifice*, in Owens (ed.), *Miscellaneous Works of John Bunyan*, vol. XII, pp. 13–82; 43–4, xvi, 3–5; for Cokayne, see Greaves, *John Bunyan and English Nonconformity*, pp. 64, 78, 96, 110–11, 117, 143–4, 148–9, 152–3, 156–9, 163, 169, 203, 209, 212.

40. *Ibid.*, pp. 169, 41–9.

41. *An Exposition of the Ten First Chapters of Genesis, and Part of the Eleventh.*, in Owens (ed.), *Miscellaneous Works of John Bunyan*, vol. XII, pp. 99–277, and for Bunyan and commentaries on Genesis, etc., pp. xxvii–xlvii; also in Offor (ed.), *Works of John Bunyan*, vol. II, pp. 414–502; George B. Cheever, *Lectures on The Pilgrim's Progress, and on the Life and Times of John Bunyan* (Glasgow and London, 1872), p. 133; 'Advertisement by the Editor', in Offor (ed.), *Works of John Bunyan*, vol. II, pp. 412–14; Brown, *Bunyan*, pp. 429–30: *The Exposition* broke off 'abruptly … and with this note, "*** This is all Mr. Bunyan hath writ of this *Exposition*, as we perceive by the blank paper following the manuscript"'.

42. Greaves, *John Bunyan and English Nonconformity*, p. 45; Owens (ed.), *Miscellaneous Works of John Bunyan*, vol. XII, p. xxv.

43. *An Exposition*, pp. 239, 270.

44. *Ibid.*, p. 267.

45. *Ibid.*, p. 227; Greaves, *John Bunyan and English Nonconformity*, p. 47; Owens (ed.), *Miscellaneous Works of John Bunyan*, vol. XII, p. xlvi.

46. *Paul's Departure and Crown*, in *ibid.*, pp. 357–97; 358, xv–xxiv; also in Offor (ed.), *Works of John Bunyan*, vol. I, pp. 722–42; Greaves, *John Bunyan and English Nonconformity*, pp. 123–4.

47. *Israel's Hope Encouraged*, in Owens (ed.), *Miscellaneous Works of John Bunyan*, vol. XIII, pp. 5–95; 21, xv, xvii; also in Offor (ed.), *Works of John*

Bunyan, vol. I, pp. 577–620. I agree with Roger Pooley ('Language and Loyalty: Plain Style at the Restoration', *Literature and History* 6 (1980), p. 15) that *An Appeal from the Country to the City* is 'so self-evidently a performance that one can see [the author] cranking the handle with his series of instructions to patriotic emotion': Bunyan would have been entirely in order to be ironic over its tone.

48. *The Saints' Privilege and Profit*, in Owens (ed.), *Miscellaneous Works of John Bunyan*, vol. XIII, pp. 165–252; 218, 220; also in Offor (ed.), *Works of John Bunyan*, vol. I, pp. 642–84; for a clue on the book's dating, see Midgley (ed.), *Miscellaneous Works of John Bunyan*, vol. VII, p. 193; *Of Antichrist, and His Ruine*, p. 492.

49. *Christ a Compleat Saviour*, in Owens (ed.), *Miscellaneous Works of John Bunyan*, vol. XII, pp. 257–333; also in Offor (ed.), *Works of John Bunyan*, vol. I, pp. 203–39. For a convincing explanation for Bunyan's silence on the religious issue of Catholicism, see Greaves, *John Bunyan and English Nonconformity*, pp. 130, 140.

50. *The Saints' Knowledge of Christ's Love*, in Owens (ed.), *Miscellaneous Works of John Bunyan*, vol. XII, pp. 339–415; also in Offor (ed.), *Works of John Bunyan*, vol. II, pp. 1–40, 1.

51. *The Saints' Knowledge*, p. 378.

52. *A Discourse of the House of the Forest of Lebanon* in Midgley (ed.), *Miscellaneous Works of John Bunyan*, vol. VII, and esp. 'Introduction: Historical Allegorizing and *The House of the Forest of Lebanon*', pp. xxxiii–xliii, including Bunyan's interpretive errors; also in Offor (ed.), *Works of John Bunyan*, vol. I, pp. 512–37; Greaves, *John Bunyan and English Nonconformity*, pp. 124–5.

53. *The House of the Forest of Lebanon*, pp. 153, 128, 129, xxxvi–xxxix; Greaves, *John Bunyan and English Nonconformity*, p. 152.

54. *The House of the Forest of Lebanon*, p. 153.

55. *Ibid.*, pp. 153, 155, 164; Owens (ed.), *Miscellaneous Works of John Bunyan*, vol. XIII, p. xxii; Greaves, *John Bunyan and English Nonconformity*, pp. 69, 152; Christopher Hill, *The English Bible and the Seventeenth Century Revolution* (London, 1993), p. 116, for Bunyan's possible type for James's 'alliance between dissenters and catholics against the Church of England'.

56. *Of the Trinity and a Christian* and *Of the Law and a Christian* and *Last Sermon*, in Owens (ed.), *Miscellaneous Works of John Bunyan*, vol. XII, pp. 403–5, 411–13, 87–94: also in Offor (ed.), *Works of John Bunyan*, vol. II, pp. 386–9 (with binding error), 755–8.

57. *The Advocateship of Jesus Christ*, p. xliii; for a skilled introduction to the alternative Bunyan, see Greaves, *John Bunyan and English Nonconformity*, pp. 42–4, 48, 102–3, 109–10.

Bibliography

BUNYAN'S WORKS

(1) G. Offor (ed.), *Works of John Bunyan*

I have made use of the 1854 3-volume edition, published by W.G. Blackie, Glasgow and reprinted by The Banner of Truth Trust, Edinburgh, and Carlisle, PA., 1991. Offor grouped the writings according to their thematic content, into three volumes: volumes 1 and 2 comprising the 'Experimental, Doctrinal and Practical' works, and volume 3 those of an 'Allegorical, Figurative and Symbolical' nature. The short titles of the works, in the form in which Offor rendered them, are given below according to his listing for each volume The dates I provide in parenthesis for publication are taken from the chronology in Anne Laurence, W.R. Owens and Stuart Sim (eds), *John Bunyan and His England 1628–1688* (London and Ronceverte, WV, 1990), pp. xix–xxii:

Volume 1

Grace Abounding to the Chief of Sinners (1666)
Bunyan's Prison Meditations (1663)
The Jerusalem Sinner Saved (*Good News for the Vilest of Men*, 1688)
The Greatness of the Soul (1682)
The Work of Jesus Christ as an Advocate (*The Advocateship of Jesus Christ*, 1688)
Christ a Complete Saviour (posthumous, 1692)
Come and Welcome to Jesus Christ (1678)
Of Justification by an Imputed Righteousness (posthumous, 1692)
Saved by Grace (1676)
The Strait Gate (1676)
Light for Them that Sit in Darkness (1675)

A Treatise of the Fear of God (1679)

The Doctrine of the Law and Grace Unfolded (1659)

Israel's Hope Encouraged (posthumous, 1692)

A Discourse Touching Prayer (*I Will Pray with the Spirit*, 1662)

The Saints' Privilege and Profit (posthumous, 1692)

The Acceptable Sacrifice (posthumous, 1689)

Paul's Departure and Crown (posthumous, 1692)

The Desire of the Righteous Granted (posthumous, 1692)

Volume 2

The Saints' Knowledge of Christ's Love (posthumous, 1692)

Of Antichrist and His Ruin (posthumous, 1692)

The Resurrection of the Dead, and Eternal Judgment (1665)

Some Gospel Truths Opened According to the Scriptures (1656)

A Vindication of Gospel Truths Opened According to the Scriptures (1657)

A Discourse upon the Pharisee and the Publican (1685)

A Defence of the Doctrine of Justification by Faith in Jesus Christ (1672)

Reprobation Asserted (spurious attribution, dated by Offor to *c.*1674)

Questions About the Nature and Perpetuity of the Seventh-day Sabbath (1685)

Of the Trinity and a Christian (posthumous, 1692)

Of the Law and a Christian (posthumous, 1692)

Scriptural Poems (spurious attribution, dated by Offor to 1701)

An Exposition on the First Ten Chapters of Genesis (posthumous, 1692)

A Holy Life the Beauty of Christianity (1683)

Christian Behaviour (1663)

A Caution to Stir up to Watch against Sin (1684)

A Discourse of the Building, Nature, Excellency, and Government of the House of God (1688)

A Confession of My Faith, and A Reason of My Practice (1672)

Differences in Judgment about Water Baptism No Bar to Communion (1673)

Peaceable Principles and True (1674, including a poem, *On the Love of Christ*)

A Case of Conscience Resolved (1683)

Instruction for the Ignorant (1675)

Seasonable Counsel (1684)

An Exhortation to Peace and Unity (dated 1688; not seriously attributed to Bunyan by Offor)

Bunyan's Last Sermon (posthumous, 1689)

Volume 3

The Pilgrim's Progress from this World to that which is to Come (first part, 1678; second part, 1684)

The Holy War Made by Shaddai upon Diabolus, for the Regaining of the Metropolis of the World (1682)

The Heavenly Footman (*c.*1671, posthumous, 1698)

The Holy City, or the New Jerusalem (1665)

Solomon's Temple Spiritualized (1688)

A Discourse of the House of the Forest of Lebanon (posthumous, 1692)

The Water of Life (1688)

The Barren Fig-Tree (1673)

Life and Death of Mr. Badman (1680)

A Few Sighs from Hell (1658)

One Thing is Needful (1665)

Ebal and Gerizim (1665)

A Book for Boys and Girls (1686)

(2) The Oxford Miscellaneous Works

The Oxford (Clarendon) edition of Bunyan's writings, undertaken by a team of scholars, under the overall editorial direction of Roger Sharrock, has now been completed and can be regarded as definitive. For purposes of this bibliography, which lists works by shorter forms of their titles, the editions of *Grace Abounding* and of the two parts of *The Pilgrim's Progress* which appeared before the *Miscellaneous Works* began appearing, are included:

> *The Pilgrim's Progress from this World to That which is to Come*, parts I and II, ed. James Blanton Wharey, 2nd edn revised by Roger Sharrock (Oxford, 1960)

> *Grace Abounding to the Chief of Sinners*, ed. Roger Sharrock (Oxford, 1962) includes 'A Relation of the Imprisonment of Mr. John Bunyan ...'; *A Discourse between my Wife and the Judges ... touching my Deliverance at the Assizes*; *The Narrative of the Persecution of Agnes Beaumont in the Year 1674*; *Continuation of Mr. Bunyan's Life*; and extracts from *The Bedford Church Book*

Two Bunyan classics were edited concurrently with the 13-volume series, but not as part of it:

The Holy War made by Shaddai upon Diabolus for the Regaining the Metropolis of the World, eds Roger Sharrock and James F. Forrest (1980)

The Life and Death of Mr. Badman, Presented to the World in a Familiar Dialogue Between Mr. Wiseman, and Mr. Attentive, eds James F. Forrest and Roger Sharrock (1988)

The Miscellaneous Works of John Bunyan, 13 volumes, general editor Roger Sharrock (Oxford, 1976–94):

Volume I, ed. T. L. Underwood (1980): *A Few Sighs from Hell; Some Gospel-Truths Opened according to the Scriptures; A Vindication of the Book Called Some Gospel-Truths Opened*

Volume II, ed. Richard L. Greaves (1976): *I Will Pray with the Spirit; The Doctrine of the Law and Grace Unfolded*

Volume III, ed. J. Sears McGee (1987): *The Holy City: Or, The New Jerusalem; Christian Behaviour; Being The Fruits of true Christianity; The Resurrection of the Dead*

Volume IV, ed. T. L. Underwood (1989): *A Defence of the Doctrine of Justification, by Faith; A Confession of my Faith, and A Reason of my Practice; Differences in Judgment About Water-Baptism, No Bar to Communion; Peaceable Principles and True; A Case of Conscience Resolved; Questions about the Nature and Perpetuity of the Seventh-Day Sabbath*

Volume V, ed. Graham Midgley (1986): *The Heavenly Foot-man; The Barren Fig-Tree; Profitable Meditations Fitted to Man's Different Conditions* (1661); *The Strait Gate*

Volume VI, ed. Graham Midgley (1980): *(The Poems): Prison Meditations Directed to the Heart of Suffering Saints and Reigning Sinners; One Thing is Needful: Or, Serious Meditations Upon the Four Last Things; Ebal and Gerizzim; Or The Blessing and the Curse; A Caution to Stir up to Watch against Sin; A Book for Boys and Girls; A Discourse of the Building, Nature, Excellency and Government of the House of God*

Volume VII, ed. Graham Midgley (1989): *Solomon's Temple Spiritualized; The Water of Life; A Discourse of the House of the Forest of Lebanon*

Volume VIII, ed. Richard L. Greaves (1979): *Light for Them That Sit in Darkness; Instruction for the Ignorant; Saved by Grace; Come, & Welcome, to Jesus Christ.*

Volume IX, ed. Richard L. Greaves (1981): *A Treatise of the Fear of God; The Greatness of the Soul, And unspeakableness of the Loss thereof; A Holy Life, The Beauty of Christianity*

Volume X, ed. Owen C. Watkins (1988): *Seasonable Counsel: Or, Advice to Sufferers; A Discourse upon the Pharisee and the Publicane*

Volume XI, ed. Richard L. Greaves (1985): *The Advocateship of Jesus Christ; Good News for the Vilest of Men (The Jerusalem Sinner Saved)*

Volume XII, ed. W.R. Owens (1994): *A Mapp ... of Salvation & Damnation* (1663 or 1664); *Of Justification by an Imputed Righteousness. The Acceptable Sacrifice, Or the Excellency of a Broken Heart; An Exposition of the Ten First Chapters of Genesis; Paul's Departure and Crown; Christ a Compleat Saviour; The Saints' Knowledge of Christ's Love; Of the Trinity and a Christian; Of the Law and a Christian; Last Sermon*

Volume XIII, ed. W. R. Owens (1994): *Israel's Hope Encouraged; Of Antichrist, and His Ruine; The Desire of the Righteous Granted; The Saints' Privilege and Profit*

OTHER SOURCES (*Primary Sources)

*Account of our Religion, Doctrine and Faith Given by Peter Rideman of the Brothers whom Men Call Hutterites (Rifton, NY; 2nd English edn, 1970)

*A Journal of the Plague Year: The Diary of the Barcelona Tanner Miquel Parets 1651 (ed. and trans. James Amelhang; Oxford and New York, 1991)

Alexander, J. H., 'Christ in *The Pilgrim's Progress*', *Bunyan Studies* 1, 2 (1989)

Ariès, Philippe, *At the Hour of Our Death* (trans. Helen Weaver; Harmondsworth, 1981)

**Bacon, Sir Francis, *The Essayes or Counsels, Civil and Morall* (ed. Michael Kiernan; Oxford, 1985)

Baldini, Umberto, *L'opera completa di Michelangelo scultore* (Milan, 1973)

Ball, Brian W., *A Great Expectation: Eschatological Thought in English Protestantism to 1660* (Leiden, 1975)

Bangert, William V., SJ, *A History of the Society of Jesus* (2nd edn; St Louis, MO, 1986)

Barbour, Hugh, 'The "Openings" of Fox and Bunyan', in Mullett, Michael (ed.), *New Light on George Fox*

Barbour, Hugh, *The Quakers in Puritan England* (New Haven, CT, and London, 1964)

*Barbour, Hugh and Frost, J. William, *The Quakers* (New York, Westport, CT, and London, 1988)

*Barrow: *Elizabethan Nonconformist Texts,* (8 vols; London, 1951–70); vol. III: *The Writings of Henry Barrow 1587–1590* (ed. Leland H. Carlson, 1962)

Bate, Frank, *The Declaration of Indulgence 1672: A Study in the Rise of Organised Dissent* (Liverpool, 1908)

Batson, E. Beatrice, *John Bunyan: Allegory and Imagination* (London and Canberra, 1984)

*Baxter: *The Autobiography of Richard Baxter* (abridged J. M. Lloyd Thomas; ed. and intro. N. H. Keeble; London and Melbourne, 1974)

Beddard, Robert, 'The Restoration Church', in Jones, J.R. (ed.), *The Restored Monarchy*

Bell, Patricia, 'Thomas Bunyan and *Mr. Badman*', *Bunyan Studies* 2,1 (1990)

Bevington, David *et al.*, *Homo, Memento Finis: The Iconography of Just Judgment in Medieval Art and Drama* (Kalamazoo, MI, 1985)

Biéler, A., *La Pensée économique et sociale de Calvin* (Paris, 1961)

Bitterman, M. G. F., 'The Early Quaker Literature of Defense', *Church History* 42 (1973)

Bittle, William G., *James Nayler 1618–1660: The Quaker Indicted by Parliament* (Richmond, IN, 1986)

Bosher, Robert S., *The Making of the Restoration Settlement: The Influence of the Laudians* (revised edn; Westminster, 1957)

Bossy, John, 'One More Allegory', *Bunyan Studies* 2,1 (1990)

Bossy, John, 'The Mass as a Social Institution', *Past and Present* 100 (1983)

Bouwsma, William J., *John Calvin: A Sixteenth Century Portrait* (New York and Oxford, 1988)

Brady, David 'The Number of the Beast in Seventeenth-Century England', *The Evangelical Quarterly* 45 (1973)

Braithwaite, Alfred W., '"Errors in the Indictment" and Pardons: The

Case of Theophilus Green', *Journal of the Friends Historical Society* 49 (1959–61)

Braithwaite, W. C., *The Beginnings of Quakerism* (London, 1912; reprinted York, 1981)

Braithwaite, William C., *The Second Period of Quakerism* (London, 1919)

Brauer, J. C., 'Puritan Mysticism and the Development of Libertinism', *Church History* 19 (1950)

Brockbank, Elizabeth, *Edward Burrough. A Wrestler for Truth* (London, 1949)

*Brown, Carleton (ed.), *Religious Lyrics of the XIVth Century* (Oxford, 1924)

Brown, John, *John Bunyan: His Life, Times and Work* (2nd edn; London, 1886)

*Bryant, Arthur (ed.), *The Letters, Speeches and Declarations of King Charles II* (London, 1935)

Buranelli, Vincent, *The King and the Quaker: A Study of William Penn and James II* (Philadelphia, PA, 1962)

Burke, Peter, *Popular Culture in Early Modern Europe* (Aldershot, Hants, 1994)

Burke, Peter, 'Popular Culture in Seventeenth-Century London', in Reay, Barry (ed.), *Popular Culture in Seventeenth-Century England*

*Burnet, Gilbert, *History of His Own Time* (abridged Thomas Stackhouse; London and Melbourne, 1986)

Burrage, Champlin, 'Fifth Monarchy Insurrection', *English Historical Review* 26 (1910)

*Burrough, Edward, *The True Faith of the Gospel of Peace Contended for, in the Spirit of Meekness* (London, 1656), in Ellis Hookes (ed.), *The Memorable WORKS of a Son of THUNDER and Consolation: Edward Burroughs* (London, 1672)

*Burrough, Edward, *Truth (the Strongest of all)Witnessed forth in the Spirit of Truth against all DECEIT* (London, 1657), in Hookes (ed.), *Works*

*Burton, Robert, *The Anatomy of Melancholy* (eds Floyd Dell and Paul Jordan-Smith; New York, 1948)

Caldwell, Patricia, *Puritan Conversion Literature: The Beginning of American Expression* (Cambridge, 1993)

*Calvin, John, 'The Author's Preface to the Commentary on the Book of Psalms', in John Dillenberger (ed.), *John Calvin: Selections from his Writings* (Missoula, MT, 1975)

*Calvin, John, *Institutes of the Christian Religion* (ed. John T. McNeil; trans. Ford Lewis Battles; 2 vols; Philadelphia, PA, 1975)

Camden, Vera J., 'Blasphemy and the Problem of the Self in *Grace Abounding*', *Bunyan Studies* 1,2 (1989)

Campbell, Gordon, 'Fishing in Other Men's Waters: Bunyan and the Theologians', in Keeble, N. H. (ed.), *John Bunyan: Conventicle and Parnassus*

Campbell, Gordon, 'The Theology of *The Pilgrim's Progress*', in Newey, Vincent (ed.), *The Pilgrim's Progress: Critical and Historical Views*

Capp, Bernard, 'Popular Literature', in Reay, Barry (ed.), *Popular Culture in Seventeenth-Century England*

Capp, Bernard, *The Fifth Monarchy Men: A Study in Seventeenth-Century English Millenarianism* (London, 1972)

Capp, B. S., 'The Millennium and Eschatology in England', *Past and Present* 57 (1972)

Carlton, Peter J., 'Bunyan's Language, Convention, Authority', *English Literary History* 51 (1984)

Chambers, P. Franklin, *Juliana of Norwich: An Introductory Appreciation and an Interpretative Anthology* (London, 1955)

Chandaman, C. D., *The English Public Revenue 1660–1688* (Oxford, 1975)

Cheever, George B., *Lectures on The Pilgrim's Progress, and on the Life and Times of John Bunyan* (Glasgow and London, 1872)

Christianson, Paul, 'From Expectation to Militance: Reformers and Babylon in the First Two Years of the Long Parliament', *Journal of Ecclesiastical History* 24 (1973)

Claiborne, Robert, *English: Its Life and Times* (London, 1994)

Clark, Paul, 'The Alehouse and the Alternative Society', in Pennington, D. and Thomas, K. (eds), *Puritans and Revolutionaries: Essays in Seventeenth-Century History Presented to Christopher Hill*

Clark, Peter, 'The Ownership of Books in England, 1560–1640: The Examples of Some Kentish Townsfolk', in Stone, Lawrence (ed.), *Schooling and Society: Studies in the History of Education*

Cohen, Jeremy, *The Friars and the Jews: The Evolution of Medieval Anti-Judaism* (Ithaca, NY, 1982)

Collinson, Patrick, *The Birthpangs of Protestant England: Religious and Cultural Change in the Sixteenth and Seventeenth Centuries* (Houndsmills, 1988)

Collinson, Patrick, *The Elizabethan Puritan Movement* (London, 1967)

Collmer, Robert G. (ed.), *Bunyan in Our Time* (Kent, OH, and London, 1989)

Cragg, Gerald R., *Puritanism in the Period of the Great Persecution* (Cambridge, 1957)

Cressy, David, 'Levels of Illiteracy in England 1530–1730', *Historical Journal* 20 (1977)

Cressy, David, 'Literacy in Seventeenth-Century England: More Evidence', *Journal of Interdisciplinary History* 8 (1977)

Cross, Claire, ' "He-goats before the Flocks": A Note on the Part Played by Women in the Founding of Some Civil War Churches', in Cuming, G. J. and Baker, D. (eds), *Studies in Church History,* vol. 8

Cuming, G. J. and Baker, D. (eds), *Studies in Church History,*vol. 8 (Cambridge, 1972)

Cunningham, Valentine, 'Glosing and Glozing: Bunyan and Allegory', in Keeble, N. H. (ed.), *John Bunyan: Conventicle and Parnassus*

*Cusanus: see Jasper Hopkins, *Nicholas of Cusa on Learned Ignorance: A Translation and an Appraisal of de Docta Ignorantia* (2nd edn; Minneapolis, MN, 1985)

Davies, Horton, *Worship and Theology in England* (5 vols; Princeton, NJ, 1961–75): vol. II: *From Andrewes to Baxter and Fox* (1975)

Davis, J. C., *Fear, Myth and History: The Ranters and the Historians* (Cambridge, 1986)

*Defoe, Daniel, *The Complete English Tradesman* (New York, 1970)

Delaney, Paul, *British Autobiography in the Seventeenth Century* (London, 1969)

deMause, Lloyd (ed.), *The History of Childhood* (London, 1976)

Diehl, Huston, ' "To Put Us in Remembrance": The Protestant Transformation of Images of Judgment', in Bevington, David *et al.*, *Homo, Memento Finis: The Iconography of Just Judgment in Medieval Art and Drama*

*Doddridge: *Scriptural Hymns by the Rev. Philip Doddridge, D.D.* (ed. John Doddridge Humphreys; London, 1839)

*Donne: *The Poems of John Donne* (ed. Sir Herbert Grierson; London, New York and Toronto, 1933)

*Dryden, John, *Absalom and Achitophel* (eds. James and Helen Kinsley; London, 1961)

Duffy, Eamon, 'The Godly and the Multitude in Stuart England', *The Seventeenth Century* 1 (1986)

Dusinberre, Juliette, 'Bunyan and Virginia Woolf: A History and a Language of Their Own', *Bunyan Studies* 5 (1994)

Eco, Umberto, *The Name of the Rose* (trans. William Weaver; London, 1984)

*Edwards, Thomas, *Gangraena: or A Catalogue and Discovery of many of the Errours, Heresies, Blasphemies and pernicious Practices of the Sectarians of this time* (London, 1646; reprinted Exeter, 1977)

Erickson, Kathleen Powers, 'Pilgrims and Strangers: The Role of *The*

Pilgrim's Progress and *The Imitation of Christ* in Shaping the Piety of Vincent van Gogh', *Bunyan Studies* 4 (1991)

Erikson, Erik H., *Young Man Luther: A Study of Psychoanalysis and History* (London, 1959)

*Evelyn: *The Diary of John Evelyn* (ed. E. S. de Beer; London, New York and Toronto, 1959)

Extracts from the Minutes and Epistles of the Yearly Meeting of the Religious Society of Friends (London, 1861)

Faller, Lincoln, B., *Turned to Account: The Form and Function of Criminal Biography in Late Seventeenth- and Early Eighteenth-Century England* (Cambridge, Melbourne and New York, 1987)

Fast Sermons to Parliament (27 vols; London, 1970–1), vol. 4

Fenlon, Dermot, *Heresy and Obedience in Tridentine Italy: Cardinal Pole and the Counter-Reformation* (London, 1972)

Feola, Maryann S., 'Fox's Relationship with Nayler', in Mullett, Michael A. (ed.), *New Light on George Fox (1624–1691): A Collection of Essays*

*Fox: *The Journal of George Fox* (ed. John L. Nickalls; Cambridge, 1952)

Freeman, Rosemary, *English Emblem Books* (New York, 1961)

Freeman, Thomas S., 'A Library in Three Volumes: Foxe's "Book of Martyrs" in the Writings of John Bunyan', *Bunyan Studies*, 5 (1994)

Friedenthal, Richard, *Luther* (trans. John Nowell; London 1967)

Friedman, Jerome, *Blasphemy, Immorality, Anarchy: The Ranters and the English Revolution* (Athens, OH, and London, 1986)

Furlong, Monica, *Puritan's Progress: A Study of John Bunyan* (London, Sydney, Auckland and Toronto, 1975)

*Gardiner, S.R. (ed.), *The Constitutional Documents of the Puritan Revolution 1625–1660* (3rd revised edn; Oxford, 1958)

George, Charles H. and Katherine, *The Protestant Mind of the English Reformation* (Princeton, NJ, 1961)

Greaves, Richard L., 'Amid the Holy War: Bunyan and the Ethic of Suffering', in Laurence, Anne *et al.*(eds), *John Bunyan and His England 1628–1688*

Greaves, Richard L., 'A Tinker's Dissent, a Pilgrim's Conscience', *Church History* 5 (1987)

Greaves, Richard L., *Deliver Us from Evil: The Radical Underground in Britain 1660–1663* (New York and Oxford, 1986)

Greaves, Richard L., *John Bunyan and English Nonconformity* (London and Rio Grande, OH, 1992)

Greaves, Richard L., 'John Bunyan: The Present State of Historical Scholarship', in van Os, M., and Schutte, G.J. (eds), *Bunyan in England and Abroad*

Greaves, Richard L., *Saints and Rebels: Seven Nonconformists in Stuart England* (Macon, GA, 1985)

Greaves, Richard L., *Secrets of the Kingdom: British Radicals from the Popish Plot to the Revolution of 1688–1689* (Stanford, CA, 1992)

Greaves, Richard L., 'The Organizational Response of Nonconformity to Repression and Indulgence: The Case of Bedfordshire', *Church History* 44 (1975)

Greaves, Richard L., 'The Origins of English Sabbatarian Thought', *Sixteenth Century Journal* 12 (1981)

Greaves, Richard L., *The Puritan Revolution and Educational Thought: Background for Reform* (New Brunswick, NJ,1969)

Greaves, Richard L. and Zaller, Robert (eds), *Biographical Dictionary of British Radicals in the Seventeenth Century* (3 vols; Brighton, 1982–4)

Green, I. M,' Bunyan in Context', in van Os, M., and Schutte, G. J. (eds), *Bunyan in England and Abroad*

Green, I. M., *The Re-establishment of the Church of England* (Oxford, 1978)

Gregg, Pauline, *Free-born John: A Biography of John Lilburne* (London, 1961)

Haley, K. H. D., *The First Earl of Shaftesbury* (Oxford, 1968)

Haller, William, *Foxe's Book of Martyrs and the Elect Nation* (London, 1963)

Hammond, Brean S., '*The Pilgrim's Progress*: Satire and Social Comment', in Newey, Vincent (ed.), *The Pilgrim's Progress: Critical and Historical Views*

Harris, Tim, *London Crowds in the Reign of Charles II: Propaganda and politics from the Restoration until the Exclusion Crisis* (Cambridge, 1987)

Haskin, Dayton, 'The Burden of Interpretation in *The Pilgrim's Progress*', *Studies in Philology* 79 (1982)

Hawkins, Anne, 'The Double Conversion in Bunyan's *Grace Abounding*', *Philological Quarterly* 61 (1982)

Henning, Basil Duke, *The House of Commons 1660–1690* (3 vols; London,1983)

Heppe, Heinrich, *Reformed Dogmatics Set Out and Illustrated from the Sources* (trans. G. T. Thomson; London, 1950)

Herbert: A Choice of George Herbert's Verse (ed. and intro. R.S. Thomas; London, 1967)

Herreshof, David, 'Marxist Perspectives on Bunyan', in Collmer, Robert G. (ed.), *Bunyan in Our Time*

Heywood: The Rev. Oliver Heywood, B.A., 1630–1702; His Autobiography, Diaries, Anecdote and Event Books (ed. J. Horsfall Turner; 4 vols; Bingley and Brighouse, Yorkshire, 1882–5)

Hill, Christopher, *Antichrist in Seventeenth-Century England* (Oxford: 1971)

Hill, Christopher, *A Turbulent, Seditious and Factious People: John Bunyan and his Church* (Oxford, 1988)

Hill, Christopher, 'Bunyan, Professors and Sinners', *Bunyan Studies* 2,1 (1990)

Hill, Christopher, *Change and Continuity in Seventeenth-Century England* (London, 1974)

Hill, Christopher, 'John Bunyan's Contemporary Reputation', in Laurence, Anne *et al.* (eds), *John Bunyan and His England*

Hill, Christopher, *Society and Puritanism in Pre-Revoluionary England* (London, 1964)

Hill, Christopher, *The English Bible and the Seventeenth-Century Revolution* (London, 1993)

Hill, Christopher, *The Experience of Defeat: Milton and Some Contemporaries* (London, 1987)

Hill, Christopher, *The World Turned Upside Down: Radical Ideas in the English Revolution* (London, 1972)

Holdsworth, William Searle, *A History of English Law* (17 vols; London, 1922–66), vol. VI.

Houlbrooke, R., *The English Family 1450–1700* (London, 1984)

Hughes, Ann, 'The Pulpit Guarded: Confrontations between Orthodox and Radicals in Revolutionary England', in Laurence, Anne *et al.* (eds.), *John Bunyan and His England*

Hussey, Maurice, 'John Bunyan and Arthur Dent', *Theology* 52 (1949)

Hutton, R., *The Rise and Fall of Merry England: The English Ritual Year 1400–1700* (London, 1994)

Illick, Joseph E., 'Child-rearing in Seventeenth-Century England and America', in deMause. L. (ed.), *The History of Childhood*

James, William, *The Varieties of Religious Experience: A Study in Human Nature* (38th Impression; London, New York and Toronto, 1935)

Johnson, Barbara A., 'Falling into Allegory: The "Apology" to *The Pilgrim's Progress* and Bunyan's Scriptural Methodology', in Collmer, Robert G. (ed.), *Bunyan in Our Time*

Jones, J. R. (ed.), *The Restored Monarchy 1660–1688* (London, 1979)

Jones, J. R., *The Revolution of 1688 in England* (London, 1972)

Katz, David S., *Sabbath and Sectarianism in Seventeenth-Century England* (Leiden, New York, Copenhagen, Cologne, 1988)

Kaufman, U. Milo, 'Spiritual Discerning: Bunyan and the Mysteries of the Divine Will', in Keeble, N. H. (ed.), *John Bunyan: Conventicle and Parnassus*

Kaufman, U. Milo, 'The Pilgrim's Progress and the Pilgrim's Regress: John Bunyan and C. S. Lewis on the Shape of the Christian Quest', in Collmer, Robert G. (ed.), *Bunyan in Our Time*

Keeble, N. H., '"Here is her Glory, even to be under Him": The Feminine in the Thought and Work of John Bunyan', in Laurence, Anne, *et al.* (eds), *John Bunyan and His England*

Keeble, N. H. (ed.), *John Bunyan: Conventicle and Parnassus* (Oxford, 1988)

Keeble, N. H., *The Literary Culture of Nonconformity in Late Seventeenth-Century England* (Leicester, 1987)

Kendal, R. T., *Calvin and English Calvinism to 1649* (Oxford, Oxford University Press, 1979)

Kent, J., 'The "Papist" Charge against the Interregnum Quakers', *Journal of Religious History* 12 (1983)

Kenyon, J. P., *The Popish Plot* (London, 1972)

Kenyon, J. P., *The Stuart Constitution: Documents and Commentary* (Cambridge, 1966)

Knott, John R., 'Bunyan and the Holy Community', *Studies in Philology* 80 (1983)

Knott, John R., jun., *The Sword and the Spirit: Puritan Responses to the Bible* (Chicago and London: Chicago University Press, 1971)

Knott, John R., '"Thou Must Live Upon My Word": Bunyan and the Bible', in Keeble, N.H. (ed.), *John Bunyan: Conventicle and Parnassus*

Köstler, Julius, *Life of Luther* (London, 1883)

Kuby, Lolette, 'The World is Half the Devil's: Cold–Warmth Imagery in *Paradise Lost*', *English Literary History* 41 (1974)

Lacey, Douglas R., *Dissent and Parliamentary Politics in England 1661–1689: A Study in the Perpetuation and Tempering of Parliamentarianism* (New Brunswick, NJ, 1969)

Lamont, William M., *Godly Rule: Politics and Religion, 1603–1660* (London, 1969)

Lamont, William, *Richard Baxter and the Millennium: Protestant Imperialism and the English Revolution* (London, 1979)

Lamont, William, 'Richard Baxter, the Apocalypse and the Mad Major', *Past and Present* 57 (1972)

Laurence, Anne, Owens, W.R., and Sim, Stuart (eds), *John Bunyan and His England 1628–1688* (London and Ronceverte, WV, 1990)

Leith, John H., *Introduction to the Reformed Tradition: A Way of Being the Christian Community* (revised edn; Atlanta, GA, 1981)

Lindsay, Jack, *John Bunyan: Maker of Myths* (London, 1937; reprinted New York, 1969)

*Luther: *A Commentary on St. Paul's Epistle to the Galatians based on Lectures Delivered by Martin Luther* (revised translation based on the English version of 1587, with intro. by Philip S. Watson; 2nd impression; London, 1956)

*Luther, Martin, *The Freedom of a Christian*, in John Dillenberger (ed.), *Martin Luther: Selections from his Writings* (New York, 1961)

Luther's Works (55 vols; eds Jaroslav Pelikan and Helmut T. Lehmann; St. Louis, MO, and Philadelphia, PA, 1960–86), vol. 54: *Table Talk* (ed. and trans. Theodore G. Tappert; Philadelphia, PA, 1967)

Luxon, Thomas H., *Literal Figures: Puritan Allegory and the Reformed Crisis in Representation* (Chicago and London, 1995)

Lyall, F., 'Of Metaphors and Analogies: Legal Language and Covenant Theology', *Scottish Journal of Theology* 32 (1979)

Macfarlane, A., *Marriage and Love in England: Modes of Reproduction 1300–1840* (Oxford, 1985)

McGee, J. Sears, *The Godly Man in Stuart England: Anglicans, Puritans and the Two Tables, 1620–1670* (New Haven, CT, and London, 1976)

McGrath, Alister E., *Reformation Thought: An Introduction* (Oxford, 1988)

McGregor, J. F. and Reay, B. (eds), *Radical Religion in the English Revolution* (Oxford, 1984)

McLynn, Frank, *Crime and Punishment in Eighteenth-Century England* (London and New York, 1989)

Miller, John, *Popery and Politics in England 1660–1688* (Cambridge, 1973)

Moorman, John, *A History of the Franciscan Order* (Oxford, 1968)

Morgan, John, *Godly Learning: Puritan Attitudes towards Reason, Learning and Education* (Cambridge, 1986)

Morton, A.L., *The World of the Ranters: Religious Radicalism in the English Revolution* (London, 1970)

Mullett, Michael A., '"Deprived of our Former Place": The Internal Politics of Bedford, 1660–1688', *Bedfordshire Historical Record Society* 59 (1980)

Mullett, Michael A. (ed.), *Early Lancaster Friends* (Centre for North-West Regional Studies, Occasional Paper No. 5; Lancaster, 1978)

Mullett, Michael A., *James II and English Politics 1678–1688* (London and New York, 1994)

Mullett, Michael A. (ed.), *New Light on George Fox (1624–1691): A Collection of Essays* (York, 1993)

Mullett, Michael A., *Radical Religious Movements in Early Modern Europe* (London, 1980)

Mullett, Michael A., *Sources for the History of English Nonconformity 1660–1830* (London, 1991)

Mullett, Michael and Warren, Leo, *Martyrs of the Diocese of Lancaster* (Preston, 1987)

Neale, J. E., *Elizabeth and her Parliaments* (London, 1957)

Newey, Vincent (ed.), *The Pilgrim's Progress: Critical and Historical Views* (Liverpool, 1980)

Newey, Vincent, '"With the Eyes of My Understanding": Bunyan's Experience and Acts of Interpretation', in Keeble, N. H. (ed.), *John Bunyan: Conventicle and Parnassus*

Newey, Vincent, 'Wordsworth, Bunyan and the Puritan Mind', *English Literary History* 41 (1974)

Newman, S. J., 'Bunyan's Solidness', in Newey, Vincent (ed.), *The Pilgrim's Progress: Critical and Historical Views*

Nuttall, G. F., *The Holy Spirit in Puritan Faith and Experience* (Oxford, 1947)

Nuttall, G. F., *Visible Saints: The Congregational Way 1640–1660* (Oxford, 1957)

Nuttall, Geoffrey, 'James Nayler: A Fresh Approach', *Friends Historical Journal*, Supplement 26 (1954)

Nuttall, Geoffrey, 'The Heart of *The Pilgrim's Progress*', *American Baptist Quarterly* 7 (1988)

Owens, W. R. '"Antichrist Must be Pulled Down": Bunyan and the Millennium', in Laurence, Anne *et al.*(eds), *John Bunyan and His England*

Owens, W. R., 'The Reception of *The Pilgrim's Progress* in England', in van Os, M. and Schutte, G.J. (eds), *Bunyan in England and Abroad*

Owst, G. R., *Literature and the Pulpit in Medieval England: A Neglected Chapter in the History of English Letters & of the English People* (2nd revised edn; Oxford, 1961)

Owst, G. R., *Preaching in Medieval England: An Introduction to Sermon Manuscripts of the Period c.1350–1450* (Cambridge, 1926)

Parker, T. H. L., *John Calvin* (London, 1975)

*Parmée, Douglas (ed.), *Twelve French Poets 1820–1900: An Anthology of 19th Century French Poetry* (London, 1966)

Peaston, A. Elliott, *The Prayer Book Tradition in the Free Churches* (London, 1964)

Pennington, D. and Thomas, K., *Puritans and Revolutionaries: Essays Presented to Christopher Hill* (Oxford, 1978)

*Pepys: *The Shorter Pepys* (selected and ed. Robert Latham; Harmondsworth, 1987)

Perkins, William 1558–1602: English Puritanist: His Pioneer Works on Casuistry, 'A Discourse of Conscience' and 'The Whole Treatise on Cases of Conscience' (ed. and intro. Thomas F. Merrill; Nieuwkoop, 1966)

Pettit, Norman, *Grace and Conversion in Puritan Spiritual Life* (New Haven, CT, 1966)

Pooley, Roger, '*Grace Abounding* and the New Sense of Self', in Laurence, Anne *et al.* (eds), *John Bunyan and His England*

Pooley, Roger, 'Language and Loyalty: Plain Style at the Restoration', *Literature and History* 6 (1980)

Pooley, Roger, 'Plain and Simple: Bunyan and Style', in Keeble, N.H. (ed.), *John Bunyan: Conventicle and Parnassus*

Pooley, Roger, 'Spiritual Experience and Spiritual Autobiography', *The Baptist Quarterly* 32 (1988)

Porter, H. C., *Puritanism in Tudor England* (London and Basingstoke, Macmillan, 1970)

Potter, Robert, *The English Morality Play: Origins, History and Influence of a Dramatic Tradition* (London and Boston, MA, 1975)

*Potts's Discovery of Witches in the County of Lancaster, 1613 (intro. James Crossley, *Chetham Society*, 1st series, vol. 6 (1845)

Ralph, Arleane, '"They Do Such Musick Make": *The Pilgrim's Progress* and Textually Inspired Music', *Bunyan Studies* 5 (1994)

Reardon, Bernard M. G., *Religious Thought in the Reformation* (London and New York, 1981)

Reay, Barry (ed.), *Popular Culture in Seventeenth-Century England* (London, 1985)

Reay, Barry, *The Quakers and the English Revolution* (Hounslow, 1985)

Rivers, Isabel, 'Grace, Holiness and the Pursuit of Happiness: Bunyan and Latitudinarianism', in Keeble, N.H. (ed.), *John Bunyan: Conventicle and Parnassus*

Ross, Aileen M., 'Paradise Regained: The Development of John Bunyan's Millenarianism,' in van Os, M. and Schutte, G. J.(eds), *Bunyan in England and Abroad*

*Rules of Discipline of the Religious Society of Friends with Advices ... of their Yearly Meeting (3rd edn; London, 1834)

Sadler, Lynn Veach, *John Bunyan* (Boston, MA, 1979)

Schlatter, Richard, *The Social Ideas of Religious Leaders 1660–1688* (London, 1940)

Schüking, Levin L., *The Puritan Family: A Social Study from the Literary Sources* (trans. Brian Battershaw; London, 1969)

Seed, David, 'Dialogue and Debate in *The Pilgrim's Progress*', in Newey, Vincent (ed.), *The Pilgrim's Progress: Critical and Historical Views*

Sewel, William, *The History of the Rise, Increase, and Progress of the Christian People called Quakers* (2 vols; 5th edn; London, 1811)

Shammas, C., 'The Domestic Environment in Early Modern England and

America', *Journal of Social History* 14 (1980)

Sharpe, James, 'The People and the Law', in Reay, Barry (ed.), *Popular Culture in Seventeenth-Century England*

Sharrock, Roger, 'Bunyan Studies Today: An Evaluation', in van Os, M. and Schutte, G. J., (eds), *Bunyan in England and Abroad*

Sharrock, Roger, *John Bunyan* (London, 1954; reissued 1968)

Sharrock, Roger, 'Life and Story in *The Pilgrims Progress*', in Newey, Vincent (ed.), *The Pilgrim's Progress: Critical and Historical Views*

Sharrock, Roger, 'Temptation and Understanding in *Grace Abounding*', *Bunyan Studies* 1 (1988)

Sharrock, Roger, 'The Origins of A Relation of the Imprisonment of Mr. John Bunyan', *Review of English Studies* 10 (1959)

Sharrock, Roger (ed.), *The Pilgrim's Progress: A Casebook* (London and Basingstoke, 1976)

Sharrock, Roger, '"When at the First I Took my Pen in Hand": Bunyan and the Book', in Keeble, N.H. (ed.), *John Bunyan: Conventicle and Parnassus*

Sheingorn, Pamela, '"For God is Such a Doomsman": Origins and Development of the Theme of Last Judgment', in Bevington, David *et al.*, *Homo, Memento Finis: The Iconography of Just Judgment in Medieval Art and Drama*

Shrimpton, Nick, 'Bunyan's Military Metaphor', in Newey, Vincent (ed.), *The Pilgrim's Progress: Critical and Historical Views*

Sim, Stuart, '"Safe for Those for Whom it is to be Safe": Salvation and Damnation in Bunyan's Fiction', in Laurence, Anne, *et al.* (eds), *John Bunyan and His England*

Skinner, Quentin, *The Foundations of Modern Political Thought* (2 vols; Cambridge, 1978)

Slack, Paul, *Poverty and Policy in Tudor and Stuart England* (London and New York, 1988)

Smith, Nigel, *Perfection Proclaimed: Language and Literature in English Radical Religion 1640–1660* (Oxford, 1989)

Solt, Leo F., 'Anti-Intellectualism in the Puritan Revolution', *Church History* 24 (1956)

Southern, R. W., *St. Anselm and His Biographer: A Study of Monastic Life and Thought 1059–c.1130* (Cambridge, 1966)

Spenser: The Poetical Works of Edmund Spenser (ed. E. de Selincourt; London, 1912)

Sprunger, Keith, L., 'English and Dutch Sabbatarianism and the Development of Puritan Social Theology, 1600–1660', *Church History* 51 (1982)

Spufford, Margaret, *Small Books and Pleasant Histories: Popular Fiction and its Readership in Seventeenth-Century England* (Cambridge, 1985)

Spufford, Margaret, 'The Schooling of the Peasantry in Cambridgeshire 1575–1700', in Thirsk, Joan (ed.), *Land, Church and People: Essays Presented to Professor H. P. R. Finberg*

*St Teresa of Àvila: *The Life of St. Teresa by Herself* (trans. J.M. Cohen; Harmondsworth, 1958)

Stachniewski, John, *The Persecuting Imagination: English Puritanism and the Literature of Despair* (Oxford, 1991)

*Statutes: *The Statutes at Large* (ed. Danby Pickering; 23 vols; London, 1762–6), vol. VI: *From the First year of Q. Mary, to the Thirty-fifth Year of Q. Elizabeth, inclusive*

Stechow, Wolfgang, *Pieter Bruegel The Elder* (New York, 1969)

Stockdale, Eric, 'Sir John Kelyng, Chief Justice of the King's Bench 1665–1671', *Bedfordshire Historical Record Society* 59 (1980)

Stone, Lawrence (ed.), *Schooling and Society: Studies in the History of Education* (Baltimore, MD, and London, 1976)

Stone, Lawrence, 'The Educational Revolution in England, 1540–1640', *Past and Present* 38 (1964)

Stone, Lawrence, *The Family, Sex and Marriage in England 1500–1800* (London, 1977)

Stranahan, Brainerd, 'Bunyan and the Epistle to the Hebrews: His Source for the Idea of Pilgrimage in *The Pilgrim's Progress*', *Studies in Philology* 79 (1982)

Stranahan, Brainerd, 'Bunyan's Satire and its Biblical Source', in Collmer, Robert G. (ed.), *Bunyan in Our Time*

Stranahan, Brainerd, 'Bunyan's Special Talent: Biblical Texts as "Events" in *Grace Abounding* and *The Pilgrim's Progress*', *English Literary Renaissance* 11 (1981)

Talon, Henri, *John Bunyan* (London, 1964)

Tawney, R. H., *Religion and the Rise of Capitalism: A Historical Study* (London, 1926)

The Autobiography of William Stout of Lancaster, 1665–1752 (ed. J. D. Marshall; *Chetham Society*, 3rd series, vol. 6 (1967)

The Oxford Library of English Poetry (ed. John Wain; 3 vols; London, 1987)

The Victoria History of the County of Bedford (3 vols; London, 1972)

Thikstun, Margaret Olofson, 'The Preface to Bunyan's *Grace Abounding* as Pauline Epistle', *Notes and Queries* 230 (1985)

Thirsk, Joan (ed.), *Land, Church and People: Essays Presented to Professor H.P.R. Finberg* (Reading, 1970)

Thomas, Keith, *Religion and the Decline of Magic: Studies in Popular Beliefs in Sixteenth- and Seventeenth-Century England* (London, 1971)

Thomas, Keith, 'Women and the Civil War Sects', *Past and Present* 13 (1958)

Tindall, William York, *John Bunyan: Mechanick Preacher* (New York, 1964)

Toon, Peter, *God's Statesman: The Life and Work of John Owen, Pastor, Educator, Theologian* (Exeter, 1971)

Torrance, T. F., *Calvin's Doctrine of Man* (London, 1952)

Turner, James, 'Bunyan's Sense of Place', in Newey, Vincent (ed.), *The Pilgrim's Progress: Critical and Historical Views*

Tyacke, Nicholas, *Anti-Calvinists: The Rise of English Arminianism c.1590–1640* (Oxford, 1987)

Underwood, A. C. and Rushbrooke, J.H., *A History of the English Baptists* (London, 1947)

Underwood, T. L., '"It Pleased Me Much To Contend": John Bunyan as Controversialist', *Church History* 57 (1988)

van Os, M. and Schutte, G.J. (eds), *Bunyan in England and Abroad* (Amsterdam, 1990)

Verkamp, Bernard K., *The Indifferent Mean: Adiaphorism in the English Reformation to 1554* (Athens, OH, and Detroit, MI, 1977)

Waddell, Helen, *The Desert Fathers* (London, 1936; reprinted 1977)

Wakefield, Gordon, '"To be a Pilgrim": Bunyan and the Christian Life', in Keeble, N. H. (ed), *John Bunyan: Conventicle and Parnassus*

Wallace, Ronald, S., *Calvin's Doctrine of the Christian Life* (Edinburgh and London, 1959)

Walton, George W., 'Bunyan's Proverbial Language', in Collmer, Robert G. (ed.), *Bunyan in Our Time*

Watkins, Owen C., *The Puritan Experience* (London, 1972)

Watson, Foster, *The English Grammar Schools to 1660: Their Curriculum and Practice* (Cambridge, 1908)

Watson, M. R., 'The Drama of *Grace Abounding*', *English Studies* 46 (1965)

Watt, Tessa, *Cheap Print and Popular Piety 1550–1640* (Cambridge, 1991)

Watts, Michael, *The Dissenters: From the Reformation to the French Revolution* (Oxford, 1978)

Wesley: The Works of the Rev. John Wesley, A.M., Sometimes Fellow of Lincoln College, Oxford (14 vols; 4th edn; London, 1840–2), vol. I

White, B. R., *The English Baptists of the Seventeenth Century* (London, 1983)

White, B. R., '"The Fellowship of Believers": Bunyan and Puritanism', in Keeble, N. H. (ed.), *John Bunyan: Conventicle and Parnassus*

White, B. R., *The English Separatist Tradition: From the Marian Martyrs to the Pilgrim Fathers* (London, 1975)

White, Barrie, 'John Bunyan and the Context of Persecution', in Laurence, Anne *et al.* (eds), *John Bunyan and His England*

Whiteman, Anne (with Clapinson, Mary) (ed.), *The Compton Census of 1676: A Critical Edition* (London, 1986)

Whitley, W. T., *A History of British Baptists* (London, 1923)

*Winstanley, Gerrard, *The Law of Freedom in a Platform or, True Magistracy Restored* (ed. Robert W. Kenny; New York, 1973)

Wrightson, Keith, *English Society 1580–1680* (London, 1982)